Hon. Politician:
Mike Mansfield of Montana

Louis Baldwin

"This is a very extraordinary man, and the country and the world should know it."

—Senator Jacob Javits

MOUNTAIN PRESS PUBLISHING COMPANY
MISSOULA, MONTANA
1979

Library of Congress Cataloging in Publication Data

Baldwin, Louis.
    Hon. politician, Mike Mansfield of Montana.

    Bibliography: p.
    Includes index.
    1.   United States — Politics and government — 1945 —
— Addresses, essays, lectures.   2.   Mansfield, Michael
Joseph, 1903-   I.   Mansfield, Michael Joseph, 1903-
Hon. politician, Mike Mansfield of Montana. 1979.
II.   Title
E838.5.M365   1979   320.9'73'092   79-10993
ISBN 0-87842-106-8

To Maureen and Mike Mansfield
— and to Ginnie, with love.

Foreword

In a city surfeited with words, Mike Mansfield's succinctness was legendary. He was never hypnotized by the sound of his own voice, nor did he expect others to be. When he had something to say, however, he usually said it with an eloquence that reflected the dispassionate intelligence, sympathetic tolerance, and gentle sensitivity that characterized all his public life.

Hon. Politician, a kind of biographical anthology, offers a collection of selected speeches as examples of that eloquence, as they occurred chronologically during his Washington career. It is, in a sense, a response to a remark made by Senator Jacob Javits about Mansfield, on the floor of the Senate: "This is a very extraordinary man, and the country and the world should know it."

Contents

INTRODUCTION: HONOR ON THE HILL

A CAPITOL LIFE

THE SPEECHES

Introduction: Honor on the Hill

"It could probably be shown by facts and figures," Mark Twain once wrote, "that there is no distinctly American criminal class except Congress." Will Rogers was kinder, perhaps out of gratitude for all that comic material. The U.S. Congress he said, was "the best money can buy."

Although individual members of Congress may be popular back home, Congress as a whole has rarely scored much higher than organized crime in the public opinion polls, and at times it has plumbed depths inaccessible even to Richard Nixon. It is not an entirely idle comment that on Capitol Hill stand two houses of ill repute.

The ill repute, be it for political prostitution or for unbecoming buffoonery, surely is undeserved. We can hardly blame our elected representatives for holding a mirror up to human nature, for reflecting the faults and foibles as well as the virtues of American society. Congress has its share of charlatans and boobies, but not demonstrably out of proportion to the people's share. Like the society at large, it can act decisively, as in the reaction to Pearl Harbor; generously, as in the Marshall Plan; unjustly, as in its long neglect of the black community; uncertainly, as in the school busing controversy; deliberately, as in the Nixon debacle. It mirrors the popular political spectrum, from chauvinism to pacificism, from miserliness to prodigality, from tyranny to anarchy, from manic malice to foolish fondness — all with a great deal in between.

1

Thus Congress takes a lot of lumps on almost every major issue because, being unable to satisfy citizens at both ends of the specttrum, it generally opts for somewhere in the middle, where it hopes the consensus is. It cannot, for example, provide services without spending money, despite some irrepressible illusions to the contrary. So it spends some money to provide some services, tries to make sense out of the public opinion polls, and hopes uneasily for reelection.

Is it meaningful, therefore, to criticize Congress as unsatisfactory when it fails to conform to one's personal ideology? Or can it be legitimately, reasonably criticized only for being unrepresentative? Some of us can condemn it for not getting the country out of Vietnam fast enough, but only if we forget that it was partly representing millions of people (including three Presidents and several Secretaries of State and Defense) who didn't want to get out any faster, as well as millions of others who didn't want to get out at all (withdrawal is no substitute for victory). We can say that it failed to rein in the runaway inflation of 1974 and -75, but only if we forget that it was also representing millions of people (including two Presidents and assorted Secretaries of Treasury and Commerce) who cannot stomach wage and (especially) price controls. We can say that it was slow to fumigate the White House, but only if we forget that it was representing millions of people who still maintain that the Watergate affair was the biggest media frame-up since the Crucifixion.

Representative Representatives

Critics who accuse Congress of being unrepresentative usually rest their case on the seniority system and on the Senate filibuster. The case has plenty of merit and can be readily bolstered with historical, and indeed some historic, illustrations. It is, however, by no means impervious to response.

For one thing, concentrations of power in Congress usually reflect similar concentrations of power in the electorate, in which a solid, determined minority can assert its will over a less unified, less single-minded majority. Because of seniority, for instance, Southern conservatism is considered disproportionately powerful in committee operations. Yet is is also true that among the

2

electorate Southern conservatism has displayed for many decades a more passionate and more durable solidarity than probably any other single political force in the country. In this respect, the distribution of power in Congress cannot be legitimately labeled as entirely unrepresentative. Much the same can be said even of the filibuster in the Senate, at least since 1917, when the two-thirds cloture rule was introduced. Only a really dedicated minority can use the filibuster to practical advantage, as in the endless debates over civil rights bills and over such other issues as the supersonic transport. The filibuster, of course, can cut both ways.

Probably no one would argue that the House, for all its seniorities, is less representative of the people today than it was under the control of Speaker Joe Cannon seventy years ago, although it may be less "efficient." Power tends to concentrate among legislators, as it does among people generally. Surely a good (and Constitutional) case can be made that power wielded by many competing hands is in the long term more conducive, or at least less threatening, to representative government than power in one iron grip, even of a majority. Whatever the unattainable ideal, this would seem to be the practical alternative to tyranny that we must live with, however firmly we may hold to the ideal as goal and criterion.

The Rights of the Few

Even the ideals deserve some scrutiny. Traditionally the ideal grass on the other side of the fence is an inviting green only in contrast with the browner stubble on this side. Congress is indeed constitutionally unable to respond immediately and efficiently to the majority will of the moment, but this is largely because it is Constitutionally designed to allow minority views to surface and even to prevail, and thus to resist a dictatorship of a fleeting majority. Critics who flay Congress for being slow to enact legislation tailored to their own particular ideologies — even when they are right in their usually gratuitous assumption that they speak for the majority — are asking for trouble on a vote day after tomorrow. The use of the Senate filibuster by Northern liberals, for instance, is a tribute to its versatility, as well as to their flexibility. There is no view more precious than a minority view when it is mine own.

3

Finally, power concentrations in Congress, like those among the people, are not static. They change as views change and as criticisms take effect. The past few years, for example, have seen a steady erosion of Southern conservative power. In the fifties Lyndon Johnson introduced the precept that every Senator, including every freshman, should have at least one important committee membership, even if it meant removing some fixtures from the major committees. As the South has grown increasingly Republican, Democratic committee chairmanships have grown increasingly liberal in both houses, a process accelerated by the influx of young liberals in the 1974 election. And in 1975 the filibuster was further weakened in the Senate by reducing, in effect, the requirement for invoking cloture from 67 votes to 60.

Congress, in short, is what representative democracy is all about, at least in the real world. By and large, it reflects the virtues and the failings of the sum of its constituencies. By and large, it tries to give the people the kind of government they want, even if it succeeds only in giving them the kind of government they deserve. It is an integral part of a government which may not be the best possible but which, in the long run, surely is the safest.

The Man from Montana

Among the most ardent defenders and scathing critics of Congress over the past thirty years has been Senator Mike Mansfield of Montana. This was the case especially during his sixteen-year tenure as majority leader in the Senate, when he regularly mixed his ardent defense of that body as an institution with occasional scathing criticism of particular instances of deplorable action — or, more often, inaction. And his comments received attention, though never as much as they deserved, not merely because he was a legislator of vast and detailed experience but also because he had earned a reputation, probably more than any member of Congress in its almost two hundred years, for being a man of honesty and fair dealing.

Honesty and fair dealing are not, of course, what automatically come to most Americans' minds when they think of politicians. Despite the idle mobs who jostle eagerly for handshakes and autographs, despite the nervous toadies who treated Richard

Nixon as His Presidency, despite the loyal supporters of Congressman Wayne Hays' petty tyranny, professional politicians seem to rank in public esteem somewhere below professional drug pushers. We even have a cliche, "inveterate politician," to suggest how incurable a severe case of politics can be.

For this strong current of cynicism in a democracy we should doubtless thank our lucky stars and stripes. Yet it could grow into a flood that washes away all individual distinctions, all recognition of individual merit. Such a flood already may be eroding our basic confidence in representative democracy, and thereby hangs the tale of, say, Germany between the two World Wars. It may be therapeutic to shift our attention now and then to the men and women in public life whose political title of "Honorable" is something more than a ludicrous irony. Mike Mansfield, for example.

Indeed, especially Mike Mansfield, who built a reputation for honesty and straightforward behavior during his 34 highly political years on Capitol Hill. He made his share of mistakes, as he would be the first almost eagerly to admit. He did his share of maneuvering to assure that his state received at least an equitable allotment of Federal largesse. He often may have suffered fools too gladly, and he certainly was too easy-going for some of his more opinionated and impatient colleagues. (The past tense will be used here consistently because the reference is to Senator Mansfield, although Ambassador Mansfield is of course alive and well and living it up in Tokyo.) Yet he also was a politician of quick intelligence, studied thoughtfulness, unceremonious erudition, stubborn common sense, conscientious diligence, realistic patience, gentle compassion, unobtrusive modesty. succinct eloquence, wry wit, and unassailable integrity, all e> pressed in the rigorous fairness and sympathetic consideration that he displayed in his daily work with his colleagues on both sides of the aisle. That work of a political lifetime surely will stand long as a memorial to the good sense of the Montana electorate.

He was an exemplary democratic politician because he did not expect legislation, or the results of any other government activity, to conform rigidly with his own political convictions. He accepted government by the people, and he did not confuse himself with the people. He recognized that every representative legislature will inherently include a variety of people with a wide

5

variety of opinions, some of them diametrically opposed. He held firmly to the fundamental belief that every such legislature, and especially the U.S. Senate, is not a legislative vending machine but a deliberative body in which compromises among competing ideas must be achieved to formulate laws deserving of popular acceptance. As a mature politician, he respected his colleagues as legitimate representatives of their constituencies, and he respected their ideas as legitimate expressions of a body of opinion, however much he might disagree with them. As a political realist, he tolerated Washington lobbyists as sources of useful information to legislators, although his own individual policy was to have no truck with them whatsoever. He neither practiced conformity nor demanded it. In the vernacular of a generation later than his, he had it all together.

On most issues he was a liberal Democrat. As a liberal he remained loyal to an enduring conviction that government was for the people, especially for those currently labeled "the disadvantaged." As a Democrat he remained loyal to an enduring though not inflexible conviction that this was the party through which such government was most likely to be achieved and sustained. But he didn't consider these convictions as divinely inspired axioms which only idiots or fiends could deny. Whatever his private impressions, he treated his political adversaries as people of intelligence and good intentions. He got along to get along, and not simply to get ahead.

Despite this lack of ambition or because of it, he did get ahead, performing a remarkable feat for such a very self-effacing man: he was elected to the floor leadership more often than any other individual in Senate history — eight consecutive times, for a total of sixteen years, and every time unanimously. That busy, often difficult period tells us quite a bit about Mansfield, as well as something about leadership.

It tells us something essential about Mansfield because character is so often revealed most clearly in relationships with subordinates. (We are speaking of subordinates here, as Mansfield might hasten to point out, not inferiors.) Despite the plebe status of freshman Senators and his own eminence as a kind of club president, Mansfield was invariably considerate and helpful to the newcomers. The following pages contain many tributes from

Senators who found him kind and sympathetic during their early days of awkward diffidence, whatever their particular political persuasion. To Mansfield, they were human beings before they were politicians; and, as human beings, they deserved whatever he could do for them. The pecking order was irrelevant. After all, as he was fond of saying, every Senator is the equal of every other.

This was his philosophy as an individual and as a leader. His leadership thus was controversial. Because he treated his colleagues with genuine respect, far beyond the conventions like the abuse of the word "distinguished"; because he tolerated and even encouraged opinions contrary to his own; because he was considerate of minority views; because he treated the Senate as a forum for debate and compromise, not as an assembly line for the mass production of legislation; because he could live with delay, especially if it enhanced reflection — for such reasons the quality of his leadership was questioned again and again. He remained unflustered by the criticism, occasionally defending himself but more often simply puffing on his pipe and smiling his tight smile, inscrutable as the Buddha.

Most of the criticism arose out of the contrast between his methods and those employed by his rambunctious predecessor, Lyndon Johnson, to whom Mansfield disarmingly, if not convincingly, has paid repeated tribute as the greatest majority leader in Senate history. Johnson's lapel-crumpling solicitations became legendary, so much so that, in their concentrated form, they are remembered as "The Treatment" — for the most part, ruefully. The Texan was an effective leader in the sense that he was a brilliant and tireless manipulator with an overpowering gift for persuasion. Indeed, much of the legislation that he favored passed the Senate during his tenure, though not nearly so much as in his early Presidential years, when Mansfield was majority leader. His tactics, however, left a residue of bitterness which weakened him politically and which often surfaced in Senatorial tributes to Mansfield in later years.

Muttering over Mansfield's "weak" leadership often grew quite audible when the crunch was on during debates on controversial legislation. During the grueling Senate battle over the Civil Rights Act of 1964, for instance, his gentler methods were subjected to much invidious comparison with those used by Johnson in squeezing through a rather toothless civil rights bill in 1960. Considerable pressure was brought to bear on Mansfield to speed things up, but he adamantly refused. "You're not going to wear down the Southerners with such tactics," he argued. "If anyone gets worn down, it will be the bill's proponents."

The pressure continued, finally including demands that he order continuous 24-hour sessions. He declined to do so except as a last resort — among other things, he was seriously concerned about the health of certain Senators — and rather testily accepted the challenge to compare his methods with those of 1960: "We debated it shaven and unshaven. We debated it without ties, with hair awry, and even in bedroom slippers. In the end, we wound up with compromise legislation. And it was not the fresh and well rested opponents of the civil rights measure who were compelled to compromise. It was, rather, the exhausted, sleep-starved, quorum-confounded proponents who were only too happy to take it."

Mansfield's leadership techniques flowed from the promise that he was, at most, first among equals. He represented his own constituency effectively, and he respected every other Senator's claim to do the same. Lapels remained undisturbed. He indulged in neither cajolery nor harassment. He used his prerogative of scheduling bills for floor action with restraint and notable impartiality. He confined persuasion to the merits of each issue, always seeking the practical compromise. He expanded the art of appealing to the Senate's highest common denominator, rather than catering to its lowest.

Those who prefer taut ships run by Captain Queegs grow restive in the doldrums, but this never bothered Mansfield, who was as realistic about the limits of tyranny as he was about the limits of democracy. He couldn't use strong-arm methods, he often told interviewers, because it would be against his nature: "You have to be yourself." But even if he tried and were successful, he would add, the success would soon evaporate, for harsh methods are ultimately self-defeating. Senators are "a bunch of independent people. I appeal to their reason and I try to appeal to their logic. If they have doubts, I advise them to give me the benefit of the doubt. Sometimes it works and sometimes it doesn't." The idea of asking for the benefit of doubts is a very practical one, of course. As

Hubert Humphrey has said, Senators "can't vote maybe."

The Quiet Revolution

Mansfield's staunch commitment to democracy in Senate procedures showed itself early in his tenure in the majority leadership, which automatically made him chairman of the Democratic Steering Committee. In that committee a small clique of seniority pooh-bahs had long dominated the process of making assignments to the various permanent Senate committees. In a rare display of rank, Mansfield replaced that system with the secret ballot for all contested nominations.

That was by no means all. The majority leader, besides being chairman of the Steering Committee and the Democratic Policy Committee (which helps the leader set up legislative priorities and greatly influences national party policy during GOP Presidencies) is also chairman of the Democratic Conference (the "caucus"), which is made up of all Senate Democrats. Under Mansfield's predecessors, its only function was to elect party leaders; under Mansfield, it was given also two other vitally important functions. Instead of being merely informed of committee assignments made by the Steering Committee, the Conference was given the right to overrule them, including chairmanships. And instead of being merely informed of the legislative goals defined by the Policy Committee for a given session, the Conference was given the right to change them. Although the initiative for these procedural modifications, which disseminated power and seriously weakened the bulldog grip of the seniority system, had come chiefly from Oklahoma's Senator Fred Harris, it was Mansfield who somehow managed to introduce them without spectacular confrontations or eruptions. One reason for this may have been that the relative harmony prevailing under his leadership discouraged mere contentiousness, especially against changes obviously designed to promote greater democracy in Senate operations. Another reason doubtless was his low-key manner of presenting the modifications. Shortly after their introduction a senator commented to a *National Journal* reporter that Mansfield had an "uncanny ability to take really precedent-smashing moves without appearing in the least to threaten entrenched interests."

Another major Mansfield contribution to Senate democracy, and efficiency as well, was his introduction of the "track system" to counteract the effect of the "unanimous consent" of all present which is technically required to conduct any business on the Senate floor. The system separated the morning and afternoon sessions, permitting the more routine bills to be passed in the morning session and leaving the more debatable business to be worked on, or over, in the afternoon session. Thus an extended debate, such as a filibuster, which could otherwise hold up all other Senate business, was now prevented from doing so, yet without denying long-winded opponents of a bill their chance to prolong its consideration. This was a typical Mansfield compromise, giving everyone something but no one everything.

At the urging of some liberal colleagues from both sides of the aisle, Mansfield introduced some other changes, though with misgivings serious enough for him to seek reassurance from Minority Leader Hugh Scott. A change related to the track system was the more detailed reorganization of the daily schedule so that short speeches would be made first and then routine business conducted, leaving the rest of the day for more time-consuming debates. The absenteeism problem also was addressed, by a reorganization of the legislative year which recessed the Senate during the last five days of each month and thus made truancies easier to schedule, as well as to live with. Finally, in major debates each side was limited to fifteen minutes for summaries, and blinking lights were installed to give warning of the final five minutes of roll calls, to permit announcing the vote in a reasonable time, regardless of latecomers. These changes, however, required daily unanimous consent.

Still another Mansfield innovation was the practice of inviting recognized authorities to Policy Committee luncheons, to brief the senators on both (or all) sides of complex issues. Although the educational value of these luncheons could not be readily measured, the mere revelation of complexity must have been therapeutic at times. A little learning is surely not so dangerous a thing as a lot of ignorance.

Mansfield's success as an innovator, or indeed as majority leader generally, would not have been possible without a superior staff. Headed by Capitol veteran Francis Valeo, secretary of the

Senate, it performed a myriad of tasks, both major and minor. Among its major functions was conducting research for recommending legislative priorities and proposing committee assignments (about 90% of which were routinely approved by the Steering Committee and the Conference). Under what Valeo called "gentlemanly" direction, it reflected the Senator's capacity to handle the daily grind as well as his conciliatory approach on controversial issues. It also reflected his innate thrift and dislike of unwieldy bureaucracies: since it consisted of only five people (one quarter the size of the Republican policy staff), it regularly operated on half of the funds allotted in the Senate budget. Its members were few, but they were intelligently selected professionals, eager to help their boss keep the Senate on course and in motion. As with other nonelected associates of Congress, their work was recognized largely in praise unsung.

"Call the Votes!"

One way in which Mansfield showed his respect for his colleagues was to give them responsibility. Although he often prodded laggard committee chairmen with memos and phone calls to extract bills from the committees' darker recesses, he regularly delegated his authority to manage bills on the floor, for example, feeling that someone like a committee chairman, or at least a committee spokesman familiar with the hearings on the bill and interested in its passage, could do a better job. To show that it was a genuine delegation of authority, he would relinquish the majority leader's desk up front and watch the proceedings, without kibitzing, from a desk at the back. Senate memories have it that Lyndon Johnson left that front desk only to go to the bathroom or the hospital, and never relinquished it to anyone until he became Vice President — and then reluctantly. Occasionally in his backseat retreat, when the proceedings grew especially glacial, Mansfield could be heard quietly muttering, "Call the votes, dammit!" But he'd let the floor manager have his day. Such modesty and self-effacement are not qualities that we usually associate with leadership. Yet, in a U.S. News and World Report poll of "distinguished persons" in the spring of 1976, Mansfield was voted one of the dozen most influential people in the country.

Mansfield's attributes thus made for enduring, not spectacular, leadership. Probably the most important was his trustworthiness, which is a quality more often encountered in government than headlines and editorials suggest. He could be relied on to keep his word and his counsel. He habitually played fair, and his colleagues responded in kind. As one of those colleagues once said in effect, you wouldn't even try to slip something over on Mike Mansfield because he was smart enough to probably catch you at it and gentle enough to make you feel lower than Judas Iscariot's sneakier second cousin.

If Congress were populated mostly by the disreputable characters that keep cropping up in the opinion polls, surely principled people like Mansfield would be relegated to the dunces' corner upon recognition and never be heard from again. Mansfield's long-term effectiveness, his almost universal popularity, and the affectionate esteem in which he was so widely held are tributes to the basic integrity and sensibility of at least most of his fellow politicians. On balance, maybe politicians aren't so different from the rest of us. Possibly they're even better.

As for the "principles" of effective leadership, American industry has had them under scrutiny for decades, in its efforts to train supervisors and managers, without reaching any firm conclusion on the relative productivity of tyranny versus freedom. If treating people decently is so difficult to evaluate as a means to an end, it might be well to consider such treatment — as Mike Mansfield obviously did — as an end in itself.

A Capitol Life

He was born on March 16, 1903, near the Hell's Kitchen section of Manhattan. Shortly thereafter he was christened Michael Joseph, although from then on he was to be known almost always as Mike, even in the most formal contexts. His parents were Irish immigrants. His father, a hotel porter, supported the family, though in something less than luxury. The first great change in his life came in 1910, when, because of his mother's death, he and his two younger sisters were sent to live with relatives who ran a grocery store in Great Falls, Montana.

He did not fall in love with the state immediately. He ran away from home three times. The first two leave-takings ended with a night in jail prior to a reluctant homecoming. The third was more successful but had to be delayed. He endured the unsolicited rigors of formal education until early in 1918, about a year after the United States declared war on Germany. Leaving the eighth grade to its own devices, he then embarked on a quest for broader horizons by leaving home again and this time joining the Navy, shortly before his fifteenth birthday. (The services tended to accept age declarations at face value.) Over the next four years he saw service with the Navy, Army and Marine Corps in locations ranging from the Atlantic Ocean (convoy duty) to the Far East (where, he found, he "loved the sights, sounds, smells, and the people of China"). This geographical variety in his plebeian military career (in the peace-shrunken services, his most exalted rank was private first class) offers sharp contrast with his political career, during which he spent 34 years working in the same building.

13

After his honorable discharge from the Marines in 1922, he returned to Montana and found work in the Butte copper mines as a mucker and then as a mining engineer. For the next several years his travel was mostly vertical, between the surface and the mines half a mile beneath it. A very bright young man, he found the work intellectually undemanding, and so, on one of his sojourns above ground in 1928, he impulsively enrolled at the Montana School of Mines.

The move was not entirely his own idea. He had met a pretty high school teacher named Maureen Hayes who, impressed with his intelligence but not with his job, urged him to pull himself out of the mines by completing his education. For him this meant quitting work and embarking on a crash program to finish grammar and then high school credits; for her it meant providing academic, financial and moral support. She helped him unflaggingly with his studies, cashed in her insurance to meet the tuition fees, and furnished inspiration during the inevitable periods of discouragement. Obviously, she had more than a passing interest in the young man.

Within a year he was enrolled at the state university in Missoula. The grind wasn't easy for someone with his academic background, but his intelligence and intestinal fortitude served him well. Six feet tall and rangy, he even found time to play end on the football team.

In 1933, at the advanced age of thirty, he was graduated. Before the graduation ceremony, he married the devoted woman who had almost literally made a new man of him. For Maureen and Mike Mansfield it was to be an enduring love match.

The following year he earned a master's degree in political science, and then for nearly a decade he taught history at Montana State University, now the University of Montana, with emphasis on the Far East and Latin America. (He remained nominally on the faculty throughout his 34-year leave of absence.) In 1940 — at about the time that their only child, Anne, was born — he and Maureen decided that he should enter the Democratic primary race for Congressman from the First District. This proved to be his first and last election loss.

Life Begins at Forty

Undaunted by the defeat, in 1942 he tried again. The incumbent was Jeanette Rankin, the first woman to be elected to the House of Representatives. A lifelong pacifist, she had been elected to her first term in 1916. This gave her an irresistible opportunity to vote against the U.S. declaration of war against Germany. She was not reelected in 1918. Her next election to the House, ironically, was in 1940, and a year later she was the only member of Congress to vote against declaring war on Japan. In January 1943 Mansfield replaced her in Congress. His career there was to prove much less quixotic than hers and much more durable.

He arrived for his first day in the House in the role of hayseed from Montana, wearing a rumpled tweed suit, a bow tie, and combat boots. It was wartime, of course, but Mansfield was never much given to symbolism. Clotheshorsemanship had not been an issue in his campaign. Although he did soon give up the combat boots for the comforts of oxfords, and later the bow tie for the sophistication of the four-in-hand, he remained unconventional enough to show up occasionally, long afterward, on the Senate floor in such casual regalia as a sports jacket and yellow socks. Whatever his faults, stuffy formality was not among them.

Regardless of raiment, his expertise on the Far East earned him an immediate assignment to the Foreign Affairs Committee, a flattering appointment for a callow freshman. Over the next year or so his work on the committee caught the sharp eye of President Franklin Roosevelt, who sent him on a secret war mission to gather information about China that would be helpful in determining postwar American policy. On his return he recommended support for Chiang Kai-shek as the only man who could unify China, whatever his shortcomings. It was an opinion destined to change with circumstances.

Theodore White tells a story of Mansfield's account to Roosevelt of his conversation with Major General Patrick Hurley, a pompously beribboned, insufferably garrulous yahoo whom the failing Roosevelt had sent to China to negotiate with the Communists. Mansfield, with the dispassionate crispness that was to be one of his hallmarks, reported drily, "I saw Major General Pat Hurley and we had a long talk. He talked for two hours and

15

forty-seven minutes, and I talked for thirteen minutes."

In October 1951 President Harry Truman made him a delegate to the sixth session of the United Nations, in Paris, where he had the dubious pleasure of debating with Soviet Foreign Minister Andrei Vishinsky. The debates were stimulating but the results were inconclusive.

He had held his own, however. By now he had been the object of enough prestigious publicity to aspire to the dignity of the upper house. In 1952 Montana's Democrats nominated him to run for the Senate against the Republican incumbent, a right-wing patriot named Zales Ecton. (Montana tends to be politically polarized, electing both immovable conservatives and irresistible liberals. Many western states share this characteristic; Arizona's Goldwaters and Udalls come to mind.) A parrot disciple of Joe McCarthy, Ecton charged Mansfield with being a dupe and coddler of Communists, and the great charlatan himself visited the state to underline the charges. Mansfield emerged from the nasty battle with a very narrow victory.

He was never again to skirt defeat so closely. As a Representative he had always been solicitous of his constituency, and he maintained his solicitude as a Senator. VIP's would often be kept waiting in his outer office while he visited genially with ordinary Montanans in his inner office. Each winter he sent Christmas cards, a colleague once reported, to practically everyone in Montana, with the possible exception of some recalcitrant elk and mountain sheep. The cards, of course, were signed "Mike," a name that many Montanans came to check on ballots almost by conditioned reflex. "If I forget Montana," Mansfield the realist often said, "they'll forget me. I know how I got here." In his second campaign for the Senate in 1958, he won every county and garnered 72% of the vote.

For all his assiduous devotion to his constituents, he did not consider himself their lackey. He voted his conscience, whatever the static from Montana. In 1968 he supported gun-control legislation despite some 25,000 protest howls from home. It was, he felt, in the national interest. It would not greatly affect the western states but was needed in the crowded east as part of the effort to hold down violent crime. The legislation passed, life remained tolerable in Montana, the howls subsided, and two years later he

16

was elected to his fourth Senate term by more than 60% of the vote. Some years later, he voted against installation of the antiballistic missile system, even though Montana was slated for one of the lucrative sites. As he once remarked to a lady interrogator at a Washington dinner party, he considered himself a Senator, not a voting machine. Concerning some issue or other, she had asked him, "What are your people back in Montana telling you to do?" "Madam," he replied, a bit stiffly, "my people don't tell me what to do. They sent me here. I do the voting."

In a Texan Shadow

As a freshman Senator in January 1953, he was delighted to find himself a beneficiary of Majority Leader Lyndon Johnson's new policy of giving new members at least one desirable committee assignment. In his case, not surprisingly, it was membership on the Foreign Relations Committee. This plum earned Johnson almost as much gratitude from Mansfield as he expected. In addition, Mansfield admired Johnson for his political and social principles as well as for his parliamentary competence. As a result, when Johnson asked him in 1957 to take the job of assistant floor leader, or whip, he overcame a severe case of reluctance to work so directly under the notoriously demanding Johnson, and agreed. The job turned out to be mostly routine, primarily because Johnson and his chief staff assistant, Bobby Baker, preferred to handle the more colorful and demanding, as well as the less savory, aspects of the Johnson leadership.

The job as whip lasted only four years. In January 1961 Johnson was elevated, or demoted, to the Vice Presidency. As whip, Mansfield was at least a leading candidate for the majority leadership. His chief rival was the ebullient Senator Hubert Humphrey, then the prolix prophet of the liberals, who was about as popular with Southern conservatives as a boll weevil. President Kennedy and Johnson, eager for some measure of harmony among Senate Democrats, urged Mansfield to seek the leadership in the interest of Senate unity. Mansfield, who for his part did not relish any prospect of 14-hour days and sleepless nights, demurred vigorously, even arguing that it would be politically unwise for the first Catholic President to have a Catholic working with him as Senate majority leader. But Kennedy could be very persuasive, and so Mansfield was urgently nominated for the post and then elected for the first of his eight consecutive times.

His first weeks in the job were difficult ones, largely because Johnson's legendary grip on perks and power proved very hard to loosen. Mansfield, never one to compete for status symbols, erred gravely on the side of tolerance. The new Vice President continued to occupy the "Taj Mahal," a pretentious suite of offices that he had acquired as majority leader, while Mansfield uncomplainingly operated out of relatively monastic accommodations. More significantly, Johnson kept right on participating strenuously in the Senate's legislative and policy conferences. Mansfield not only tolerated those Executive intrusions but even suggested that Johnson also preside over the party caucuses. His motion passed, 46 to 17, but over such a storm of minority protest that even Johnson caught on that his inhibiting presence was not in unanimous demand. Gradually the Vice President withdrew into the Vice Presidency, and Mansfield became majority leader in fact as well as in name.

The New Leader

As his old mentor faded from the Senate scene, Mansfield began infusing the leadership functions with his own principles and personality. His nomination of Hubert Humphrey as majority whip was typical: it included a ring of gentle defiance for Executive ears, a gesture of reconciliation with his foremost competitor for the leadership, and a recognition that Humphrey could make up for his own inability to provide fireworks on demand. Before long, the new majority leader's preference for reasonably regular working hours resulted in a daily schedule that allowed Senators, including Senator Mansfield, ordinarily to get home in time for dinner with their families. And his preference for democracy resulted in delegations of both responsibility and authority, so that the fifteen committee chairmen, for example, largely took over the floor management of bills recommended by their committees. "It's simply logical," Mansfield commented, since these are generally the people "who know most about those particular bills." In giving individual Senators opportunities to conduct themselves responsibly in the public interest, he consciously risked having his own will often thwarted. But he labored under no delusions of personal infallibility, and he deeply believed that the Senate should be treated as an assembly of thinking adults, not as a cattle drive.

Mansfield's workdays, unlike Johnson's, generally followed a set routine. An early riser, he regularly arrived at the Capitol before seven in his telephone-equipped chauffeured limousine, an official perquisite that he appreciated as a time-saver. After breakfast with his good friends, George Aiken, Republican Senator from Vermont, and his wife — Lola Aiken also worked at the Capitol, as her husband's unpaid office manager — he would spend most of the morning on routine matters in his office, preparing speeches, dictating correspondence, working with his staff on pending legislation, Senate scheduling, and a myriad of details that went along with the job. Then, shortly before the start of the day's session, he would show up at his desk on the Senate floor for his regular, if brief, press conference.

One mark of Mansfield's brisk honesty was his celebrated terseness in answering reporters' questions in these daily sessions, as well as on television interview shows like Meet the Press. Almost as laconic as another prominent Montanan, Gary Cooper, he was known among Washington journalists as the fastest gun in the Senate. Only a politician with nothing important to hide can indulge in replies like "Yep" and "Nope," but these were Mansfield's favorites. More incredibly, he would not hesitate to confess ignorance; his interviews were sprinkled quite liberally with responses like "Don't know" and "Can't say." As a result, in his occasional Sunday-morning TV interviews he regularly answered three times as many questions as the average interviewee. He knew better than most public personages when — and how — to keep his mouth shut.

Although he disliked publicity and had no press secretary, he liked most of the Congressional correspondents. It was for this reason, as well as out of a sense of public duty, that he held his informal daily press conferences. The reporters, for whom cynicism was and is a union card, nonetheless accepted him not only as a fast gun but also as a straight shooter. (All of his comments on public business, for instance, were "on the record.") Amid all the hot air, they found Mansfield interviews very refreshing.

After his morning news conference, since he usually skipped lunch, he would be ready (normally at noon) to open the day's proceedings on the floor with his customary request to the presiding officer, "Mr. President, I ask unanimous consent that the reading of the *Journal* of the proceedings of [the preceding session] be dispensed with."

The "morning" session as a rule ended about two o'clock, yielding immediately to the "afternoon" session, which was occupied with less routine business. Mansfield customarily stayed on the floor through much or most of both sessions, retreating to his office to meet with colleagues or visitors as occasion demanded. In his absence the majority whip — first Hubert Humphrey, then an unhelpful Russell Long, then a somewhat preoccupied Edward Kennedy, and finally a very helpful Robert Byrd — would take over. At day's end he would hasten home for a quiet dinner with Maureen.

Most evenings, that's where he stayed. The Mansfields kept to a restrained social schedule, their evenings out usually ending about ten, a sensible hour for a compulsive early riser.

During the sixties the contrast between Johnson's and Mansfield's leadership techniques evoked plenty of invidious comparisons, usually in newspaper editorials and media commentaries, but at times even on the Senate floor. (Ironically, Oregon's uncontrollable maverick, Wayne Morse, offered some of the shrillest laments over the "lack" of leadership.) In reply, Mansfield tried to distinguish between shadow and substance, acknowledging that he was "neither a circus ringmaster, the master of ceremonies at a Senate nightclub, nor a wheeler and dealer. . . ." Amid the criticism and the pressure, he maintained his integrity: he did not propose "as majority leader to be anything other than myself." He urged his detractors to look at the legislative record. "The results require no apology whatsoever."

During the three years of the Kennedy Administration the results included ratification of the nuclear test ban treaty and passage of legislation dealing with education, depressed areas, reciprocal trade, the minimum wage, the national highway system, housing, water pollution, unemployment compensation, health care, agriculture, aircraft piracy, public works, Federal agency reorganizations, Social Security, tariffs, communication satellites, NASA projects, soil and wildlife conservation, the Peace Corps, mental illness, the draft, equal pay for women, and medical training, among other things. There also was an unprecedented tax cut which increased Federal revenues by stimulating the economy and thus reduced the budget deficit. In addition, the Senate passed major bills for area redevelopment and mass transit, only to have both bills die in the House. The admitted failure to do everything that everyone wanted, in Mansfield's opinion, did not call for an explanation, much less an apology.

Whatever "weakness" there may have been in Mansfield's leadership, it arose not out of any personal weakness but rather out of personal stubbornness. On January 1, 1967, in reply to a question about how he "ran" the Senate Democratic Conference, he told the *New York Times*, "Most recently, I believe, I have been accused of acting as though I were president of a high school sorority. I do not think I regard the Democratic Conference as a sorority. Nor do I regard it, may I say, as a boy scout troop led by a scoutmaster. The leadership, as I view it, is an instrument of the Conference and the Senate as a whole, not the other way around. And so long as I remain leader I shall not be blustered, badgered or bluffed into reversing that order." To paraphrase Barry Goldwater, surely intransigence in the defense of democracy is no vice.

Although Mansfield abandoned the practice of meticulous pre-vote nose counting perfected by Bobby Baker, which had kept many Senatorial noses chronically and irritably out of joint, he kept a clinical eye on the Senate's temperature and usually could tell when a fever was coming on. In 1962 Kennedy urged him to bring two major bills to a vote, one on urban affairs and the other on Medicare. Mansfield protested that such action would prove premature, that there simply weren't enough votes for passage. Kennedy insisted, Mansfield complied, and both bills were defeated. Characteristically, Mansfield publicly accepted the blame "for exercising bad judgment." His role as shock-absorber between impatient executive and deliberative legislature was another aspect of his job that once led him to remark, "Being a Senator is the best job in the world, but the leadership is a headache." Minority Leader Everett Dirksen agreed, though of course in more florid terms. Senators, he said, were just naturally

21

unmanageable. "O great God, what an amazing and dissonant hundred personalities they are! What an amazing thing it is somehow to harmonize them. What a job it is!"

A Minor Majority

The filibuster made the job no easier. Early in 1964 Mansfield introduced the most important and far-reaching piece of civil rights legislation to come before Congress in a hundred years. Far stronger than the gutted bills passed in 1957 and 1960 during Johnson's leadership, it proscribed racism not only in education, employment, welfare and voting rights, but also in public accommodations like motels and restaurants. Further, unlike its paler predecessors, it provided for enforcement. And so, after it had passed the House by a vote of better than two to one, the Senate's Southern Democratic bloc greeted its approach with the foam-flecked rhetoric of the conditioned reflex. It was "hideous," cried Georgia's Senator Dick Russell, it would introduce the country to "an instrument of unparalleled tyranny and persecution," eventually resulting in galloping socialism and in the "mongrelization of our people." (He did not include the word "further.")

Mansfield took a less apocalyptic view. Aware of the irrelevant but irrepressible banality that "you can't legislate morality," he opened the debate by suggesting that, in the absence of a moral consensus within a society, legislation might well make all the difference. "There is an ebb and flow in human affairs which at rare moments brings the complex of human events into a delicate balance," he argued. "At those moments, the acts of government indeed may influence, for better or worse, the course of history. This is such a moment in the life of the nation. This is the moment for the Senate."

The ensuing filibuster lasted three months. It was a paradigm of the awkward situation that Mansfield faced throughout his long term of leadership. The Senate in 1964 was a "Democratic Senate" in the sense that the 67 nominal Democrats outnumbered the 33 Republicans. But among the Democratic members there lurked about 20 Southern recalcitrants whose loyalty on most important issues was not so much to the Democratic party as to the "conservative coalition" with the Republicans, who were only too happy

22

to join with their strange bedfellows in this unholy matrimony. Thus Mansfield's theoretical liberal majority of 67 was a practical minority of 47, give or take a few mavericks. For simple majority votes he could and usually did muster enough Southern or "moderate" Republican support for the magic number, but he needed a two-thirds majority of those voting in order to override a Presidential veto or to end a filibuster by invoking cloture. And of course the last vote needed was always the hardest to find.

The Mansfield miracle is that he was often able to gather the necessary majorities without losing his integrity or the good will and good opinion of his fellow Senators. As the stalemate over the Civil Rights Bill of 1964 wore on, he managed with a little persuasive compromise to collect enough Republican oil to lubricate the jammed machinery and to produce what was, for all its modifications, a piece of very radical legislation. He accepted the three months of numbing filibuster as the price of recognizing minority views, much to President Johnson's chagrin, but eventually he was able to go to Senator Russell and announce that he finally had the votes for cloture. It was an unprecedented announcement. Over the years eleven attempts had been made to end Senate filibusters of civil rights bills, and this twelfth attempt was the first to be successful. The bill passed the Senate 73 to 27. That success had required the help of many Senators, especially Humphrey and Dirksen, but it unmistakably bore the Mansfield stamp. Given the bitter hostilities involved, it was a triumph for a leadership based, as Mansfield has described it, on "logic, persuasion, accommodation, and understanding."

Sparks in the Chamber

Mansfield's ability to hold his temper in check came, he once said, from a boyhood experience in which an ill-considered remark earned him a painful drubbing from a much larger but thinner-skinned acquaintance. This does not mean, of course, that he kept his temper in absolute check for 34 consecutive years. But any loss of temper was briefly and promptly regretted. One day in December 1967, for instance, exasperated by a contentious remark of Ohio's rambunctious Frank Lausche, Mansfield replied curtly, "I think the Senator from Ohio is off his rocker." Next morning the

23

Congressional Record, which is subject to editing by the day's speakers before publication, reported his response as "I think the Senator from Ohio is off base in making a statement to that effect."

Nor did Mansfield get along equally well with every Senator. His second majority whip, Senator Russell Long of Louisiana, who reportedly had asserted that his real interest in the whip job was using it to feather Louisiana's nest, was no great favorite. One morning, also in December 1967, Long and a few confederates arrived on the floor early and, while the chamber was still almost empty, sneaked through a controversial bill restricting the welfare benefits allotted to families with dependent children. Maryland's freshman Senator Joseph Tydings, whom Mansfield had assigned to the floor to guard against any such sneak tactics, failed to recognize the bill because Long had identified it only by calendar number. When the hastily summoned Mansfield arrived on the floor, he freely admitted that Long's ploy had been "fully within the rules and regulations of the Senate" but forcefully condemned "the way it was done." He then managed to have the vote rescinded and consideration of the bill postponed. At the next election of a majority whip, in January 1969, Long was replaced by Senator Edward Kennedy. Since then Louisiana's gift to the oil industry has confined his pranks chiefly to his role as chairman of the Senate Finance Committee.

Gadfly

On domestic legislation Jack Kennedy, Johnson and Mansfield were virtually of one mind, and in this area loyal support from the Senator was almost automatic. This wasn't always true, however, in matters of foreign policy, in which Mansfield was most knowledgeable and interested. He was not so much an isolationist as a noninterventionist, distinguishing between U.S. participation in world affairs and U.S. domination or interference in other nations' business. The distinction was largely lost on the Kennedy-Johnson-Rusk and Nixon-Kissinger teams. Thus Mansfield, speaking as a Senator rather than as the majority leader, occasionally raised blood pressures in the White House and the State Department with unsolicited doses of maverick opinion. In 1961, for instance, he advocated turning West Berlin into a free and neutral city. This caused a number of West German officials to break out in hives, requiring prodigious applications of balm by overwrought U.S. diplomats trying to explain that he did not speak for the Kennedy Administration. In 1964 he reviewed his already dovish position on Vietnam and publicly called for an effort to neutralize both North and South Vietnam, a suggestion that shook the Johnson hawks down to their most sensitive pinfeathers and caused a heavy aspirin run on Saigon drugstores. And throughout the sixties and seventies he regularly raised Executive hackles with demands for major reductions in American troops stationed overseas, especially in Europe. Compliant and cooperative he almost always was. But not subservient. He did not impose dictation on any Senator, and as a Senator he did not accept it.

He had little trouble in this respect with President Kennedy, with whom, he has said, he had "a very, very close, very warm relationship." Four pictures of Jack Kennedy and a drawing of Jackie hung in his Capitol office. His Montana headquarters included a much enlarged, framed photograph with an inscription by Jack Kennedy. In the photo, the Congressional leaders are shown gathered outside the Oval Office with Kennedy after a meeting in 1962. Most are gazing rather fixedly at the camera, with Lyndon Johnson looking preoccupied and Hubert Humphrey looking somewhat anxious. The slightly blurred figure of Mansfield can be seen, with back to camera, marching out of the picture. And the inscription reads, "To Mike, who knows when to stay and when to go."

Kennedy, though never too diffident to specify just what in his judgment the Senate should do, generally had too much respect for Mansfield to lean on him very hard. Things were somewhat different with President Johnson, whose leadership was suffocatingly possessive and who did not suffer opposition gladly. (No pictures on the wall.) At meetings of the President with his Cabinet and the Joint Chiefs of Staff, which Mansfield often attended, the Senator sometimes found himself to be the only naysayer. Johnson "took it," Mansfield has remarked, "but I don't think he liked it."

25

Whose Leader?

During his Vice Presidency Johnson had learned that Mansfield the majority leader was a man of much greater independence than Mansfield the assistant leader. Although he often tried to avoid making demands that might aggravate the Senator's streak of Irish stubbornness, throughout his Presidency he seemed to think of him as his lieutenant, morally committed to uncritical obedience. Mansfield wasn't having any of *that* kind of relationship. His first serious confrontation with the President came at the beginning of Johnson's second year in office, in January 1965. The previous year of unprecedented legislation that Johnson, with Mansfield's help, had pushed through Congress in the name of the Great Society evidently had so turned Johnson's head that he forgot how sensitive Senators can be about pork-barrel cutbacks in their own states. (Much of the pork in those ill-famed barrels, of course, is lean and socially nourishing.) Looking for money to pay for his Great Society, as well as his plans for Vietnam, he cast an accountant's eye at the Veterans Administration and found some of what he was looking for. On January 12, without notice to Congress, the White House announced that eleven hospitals for veterans, four homes for old soldiers, and seventeen regional VA offices were to be closed forthwith — including the hospital in Miles City, Montana.

That's no way to make Brownie points with Congress. The roar of pained protest was instantaneous and deafening, and Mansfield's voice was among the most piercing, partly because of his position in the vanguard. The next morning he took the Senate floor to denounce the closings as "an appalling, backward and insensitive act." Ten days later he was still seething. In testimony before the Senate Labor and Public Welfare Committee he described the new economy move as "heartless" and "outrageous." Johnson did not react publicly to the characterizations, which he doubtless considered treasonous, but in meetings thereafter with Congressional leaders he flayed Mansfield with cutting sarcasm, to the great discomfiture of those in attendance. Mansfield characteristically did not reply in kind, but there was no question about his determination to thwart the Presidential will. In the end he was only partly successful. Johnson eventually did manage to close six of the hospitals, two of the homes, and nine of the regional offices. The Montana hospital stayed open.

Mansfield was never one to hold a grudge, and he had untold sympathy for anyone burdened with Presidential decisions. A year later, in a January 1966 meeting with Johnson and other Senate leaders during suspension of the bombing of North Vietnam, he read a meticulously drafted statement arguing against any resumption of the air raids. A few days later, after watching Johnson announce on television that the bombing soon would be resumed, he reacted not with resentment but with his habitual compassion. "I feel so sorry for him," he commented. "I can imagine what he's going through."

Similarly, in another meeting with Johnson in March 1968, the discouraged President asked what he thought of sending another 40,000 troops to Vietnam. Not much, Mansfield responded; instead, we should simply get out, since we "shouldn't have been there in the first place." The conversation lasted over three hours, with Mansfield holding the same position at the end as at the beginning. Toward the end Johnson said that he appreciated his friend's honesty, but — inserting his customary first person possessive pronoun — "Mike, I wish my leader would support me." Mansfield simply bit his tongue. He was, after all, dealing here with a man who could dominate the indomitable Hubert Humphrey. "I was not his leader," said Mansfield later. "I was the Senate's leader." Three days afterward Johnson announced that he would not seek reelection to the Presidency.

The Loyal Opposition

Johnson's replacement was even worse from the viewpoint of the helpless Indochinese. Nixon's "secret plan to end the war" had nothing to do with ending the war but was rather a program for reducing American battle casualties through "Vietnamization." The price for this laudable goal included bombing the daylights out of North and South Vietnam, Cambodia, Laos, and any other small country that happened to get in the way and couldn't bomb back.

Mansfield — whose reputation as an authority on the Orient included Indochina and who had gone there on fact-finding mis-

27

sions for every President from Roosevelt to Nixon — was of course in total sympathy with the withdrawal of American troops, gradual or otherwise. From the beginning, after the French defeat in 1954, he had been appalled at the notion of getting American land forces mixed in a logistically impractical Asian war, especially in the interest of preserving a native surrogate of French colonialism. He was generally unimpressed by the Westernized leaders of South Vietnam and, in an early report to Congress, questioned whether the U.S. should continue supporting, in any way, a regime that had not really demonstrated "the will and popular support necessary to fight for their national freedom." In 1969 he called for a ceasefire in Indochina, and in June 1971 he persuaded the Senate to adopt an amendment to the selective service bill that would have withdrawn all U.S. military forces from that bloody region within nine months, contingent only on the release of American prisoners of war. The amendment was killed in the House, but a House-Senate Conference Committee compromise was substituted which urged the President to set "a date certain" for such a withdrawal. At least, and at last, Congress was on record in favor of withdrawal from Vietnam. Now, Mansfield pointed out, the President could speed up the disentanglement without worrying about a partisan bombardment from Capitol Hill. Nixon cooperated in his usual vein, declaring that he would ignore any such amendment.

While he hated what Johnson and then Nixon were doing to Indochina, Mansfield never hated the men themselves. On the contrary, he showed great sympathy for them both, not being sure how he himself would hold up under the sometimes crushing burdens of the office. For many years he was close enough to the Presidency to know what a killing job it could be when things weren't going well, and he never let his outspoken opposition to policies interfere with his natural compassion for the fellow human being behind those policies. (He breakfasted with Nixon at least once a month, privately. "We're not intimate friends," he once told a Ralph Nader staffer, "but we get along.") He could be independent and stubborn and at times obstreperous. But, as Hubert Humphrey once observed, there was "no meanness in him."

With Republicans in control of the White House, Mansfield's

problems with the conservative coalition were compounded by more than eighty Nixon-Ford vetoes. Even after the heavily Democratic elections of 1974, the liberal Democratic group was still not strong enough to muster the two-thirds vote required to override Presidential vetoes. With the GOP members tending to close ranks behind Ford after the Watergate embarrassment, liberal Republican support grew less reliable than ever. Yet Mansfield & Co. were able to corral enough votes to override the vetoes of several unconscionably progressive bills, such as those on health care, aid to education, school lunches, and voting rights. In addition, Congress stood its ground against the Executive, forbidding the President to impound funds without its approval, restricting aid to Turkey after the invasion of Cyprus, resisting Executive efforts to linger in the Vietnam quagmire and to plunge into another in Angola, imposing Presidential election reforms, cutting taxes by $23 billion with no budget strings attached, phasing out gas and oil depletion allowances, extending unemployment compensation. It was not a period of lethargy, and certainly not of apathy. It kept Mansfield very busy, what with his meticulous preparations for the impeachment trial of a defendant who jumped bail at the last minute, and his relentless push for a Senate select committee to investigate government intelligence tricks and treats.

"When to Go"

But then he had been busy with the people's business for 33 years, and especially for the past 15. And so in March 1976 he formally announced that this would be his last year in the Senate. Perhaps he felt confident of a Democratic Presidential victory in November, which might lessen the need for his services in protecting the American people. Or perhaps he was simply underlining President Kennedy's observation that Mike knew "when to stay and when to go." Although in this case maybe he didn't.

He still had another year left as majority leader, and the announcement of his retirement by no means ended his influence. In the spring of 1976 it looked very much as though the Church committee's fifteen-month investigation into extracurricular intelligence activities was about to come to naught. In March, the

Government Operations Committee, responding to the Church committee's report, had proposed establishing a permanent Senate oversight committee to rigorously supervise all government intelligence operations, including the FBI's secret-police capers and the CIA's furtive meddling at home and abroad. The proposal not only drew heated criticism from the Senate's cloak-and-dagger romantics, but it also threatened the oversight authority (if not the responsibility) of the Armed Services Committee (over military intelligence) and the Judiciary Committee (over the FBI). Jealous of their long-standing if long-neglected prerogatives, the chairmen and some members lobbied hard against the proposal, and the conservative Rules Committee, in several 5-to-4 votes, responded not by killing the proposal but by performing extensive surgery that would have left the new watchdog committee "sans teeth, sans eyes, sans taste, sans everything." Liberal Senators, alarmed over the past and possible injuries to civil liberties, were in despair.

Then Mansfield moved in and wrought a compromise. The new committee could share its oversight powers with Armed Services and Judiciary, he proposed, but would have sole authority over the CIA, including funding authority. Further, all intelligence agencies would be required to inform the committee of their plans in advance, however innocent or nefarious. Against some strenuous objections, he insisted that the risk of leaks was an exaggerated and unavoidable price for the preservation of citizens' rights and for an open society.

Support for his compromise grew rapidly among reasonable conservatives and realistic liberals, and in late May the Senate established the committee by an overwhelming vote of 72 to 22. Mansfield named as chairman Hawaii's tough-minded Senator Daniel Inouye, his good friend and protege. He was confident that Inouye would not accept testimony uncritically. During the Senate Watergate hearings, the incredulous Hawaiian had reacted to one witness by muttering inadvertently into a live microphone, "What a liar!"

That, at least, is something that no one ever had reason to say about Mike Mansfield.

The Speeches

Even the laconic Mansfield could not avoid using millions of
words during 34 years of public service. As might be expected, the
Congressional Record provides a voluminous record of what he
had to say on a great variety of public issues. Selecting the "significant" speeches and other statements, and then further selecting their significant portions, is obviously a very subjective operation, though it need not be merely capricious. The excerpts that
follow were chosen primarily because of their relevance to
memorable events and to Mansfield's personality, professional
conduct, and political philosophy. Included also, at some length,
are remarks of other Senators about him and his long service as
majority leader.

Each selection is preceded by a brief exposition, or reminder, of
the context in which the various statements were made. As with
the rest of this book, these short introductions were not written in
a spirit of cold impartiality.

October 20, 1943:

On repeal of the Chinese exclusion laws

From his ten years of university teaching in Montana, Mansfield brought to Congress an expertise in the history, culture and social conditions of the Far East, an affectionate regard for the peoples of that part of the world, and considerable distaste for Western hobnailed interference. A respect for the rights and independence of other peoples, as well as of other people as individuals, marked his career from beginning to end. In March 1976, in his last year in Congress, he argued strenuously against the United States' saber-rattlings against Cuba because of Castro's adventure in Angola. Cuba, he pointed out, was a sovereign state with a right to conduct its own foreign policy. No interference by the United States was warranted, he mainted, except to protect its own vital interests – which did not lie in Africa.

In somewhat the same vein, in October 1943, in his first year in Congress, he argued that the United States should stop treating the Chinese as ignorant coolies and start showing that vast and civilized country the respect it deserved.

* * *

Mr. Mansfield of Montana. Mr. Chairman, China is the only one of our major allies with whom we all sympathize but about whom we do nothing . . .

We did not do China any real good at the time of the Boxer Rebellion. Our nationals as well as the nationals of other countries put in exorbitant claims which were later scaled down. We stole everything we possibly could of real value and transported a great deal of it back to this country. Some of it is still in the capital city of the United States today, where it does not belong.

We ought to wake up and realize that of all people the Chinese are the most tolerant. Every religion — Catholic, Jewish and Protestant — has been welcomed in China. Every people has been

32

welcomed in China. It is the occidental who is intolerant, not the Chinese.

When we think of our superiority, we ought to keep in mind the fact that Chinese culture is approximately 4000 years old, and maybe it will prove to be even older when we get through with our research in that particular field. China was a great and powerful nation long before there was such a thing as a Greece or a Rome. Those are the places which we consider as the foundation of our civilization, but, believe me, they cannot compare with China in antiquity, and we must not forget that fact.

Do we by any chance have the idea that we have treated China fairly, that our policy has been for the best? Do we favor the idea of extraterritoriality? Do we realize it was formally incorporated in a treaty — the Treaty of Wanghia — first by America? Do we derive any satisfaction out of the results of the opium war — the so-called First Anglo-Chinese War — which preceded that treaty? Do we uphold the idea of treaty ports? Do we uphold the idea of foreign concessions and compounds? Do we uphold the idea of having American consular courts in China, and a district court at Shanghai dispensing justice to American nationals on Chinese soil? No. We have a good many things to answer for, and this [repeal of the discriminatory exclusion laws] is one way that we can make good some things we owe our Chinese friends.

We must awaken from our lethargy about the Orient and put the manifest sympathy of the American people to a practical use. We must realize just how much we need China, not how much China needs us. We must never forget that we will have full need of all our energies, abilities, and real friends in our barbaric struggle with Japan. We must not forget our future lies, in large part, in the Pacific. A friendly and strong China will be a safeguard for us in that area. Let us recognize the situation as it really exists and do our share to keep China going so that American lives will be spared and the war shortened considerably. Not by words — which mean everything and anything — but by action now.

October 11, 1945:

On American involvement in the Far East

At the end of World War II Congressman Mansfield was saying what most of his fellow Americans would be saying thirty years later, at the end of the Vietnam disaster. He did not share in the giddy feeling of omnipotence brought on by our military victory in a two-front war. He was concerned particularly over the American military presence in the Far East. Serious military meddling in the internal affairs of countries across an 8000-mile-wide ocean would present staggering logistical problems – problems which, between 1965 and 1975, were to plague and ultimately defeat three Presidents and a long gaggle of frustrated military men. In addition, Mansfield was hewing to his line against interference in other countries, a line that he would maintain stubbornly throughout his career.

* * *

Mr. Mansfield of Montana. Mr. Chairman, what is our policy in the Far East going to be? This is a question which I have been mulling over in my mind ever since the surrender of Japan and to date, with the exception of our policy in Japan, I have been unable to find the answer. . . .

The continent of Asia today is a cauldron of unrest, and the questions affecting that continent are of tremendous importance to us and to the peace of the world. The questions are varied and many and, while I will not attempt to discuss all of them, I will list them and discuss those which directly affect us. They can be summarized as follows:

First. Syrian and Indochinese demands for independence from France.

Second. The Moslem-Hindu clash in India between themselves and their demands for freedom from Britain.

Third. The attempt of the Indonesians to escape from Dutch domination.

34

Fourth. Anglo-American rivalry for the oil of Arabia.

Fifth. Anglo-Russian sphere-of-control politics in Iran.

Sixth. The question of Kuomintang-Communist relations in China, the Sinkiang revolt, and the Yunnan incident.

Seventh. The question of Korea.

Eighth. The question of policy in occupied Japan.

There are many more questions affecting Asia which could and should be brought to your attention, but time does not permit a detailed analysis of each specific one. However, I do feel that the questions affecting the use of United States military forces in the Far East are of paramount importance at this time and should be discussed in the Congress of the United States. I bring this matter to your attention now because I am interested in my country above all things, and, in my opinion, the matter of our foreign policy in the Far East should be given the attention it deserves. Without going into great detail I would like to present my views on our policy in Japan, China, and Korea, and, to a lesser extent, in Burma and India.

In my opinion all of our troops should be under orders to withdraw from India and Burma at the earliest possible moment. We have no vital interests in those two countries now that the war is over except to make an agreement with the government of India and Great Britain covering our expenditures there. This agreement would cover the building of roads, railroads, and telephone lines, and the equipment we have expended in their construction so that we may recover an equitable share of our costs relative to our efforts. There is absolutely no need for retaining more than a skeleton crew of our armed forces in Burma and India at this time, as our job there has been completed.

In Korea it would be wise to allow Chinese occupation forces to move into that country, as they would understand far better than we the situation there. The traditional friendship between Korea and China, based on mutual understanding over the years, would do much to ameliorate the difficult situation which has confronted our forces since our occupation policy was promulgated. Korea was promised her eventual independence in the Cairo Declaration, and the one country which is in the most advantageous position to help her achieve that status is China.

In China itself our position is confusing, the say the least. There are too many powder kegs in that country, and we do not desire to become involved in any of China's internal difficulties. Fuses could easily be applied to such powder kegs as Manchuria, now under Russian control; Sinkiang, where a revolt has been in progress for many months; Shantung and Hopeh provinces, where our marines are stationed and our warships anchored; Hongkong, whose future status is by no means definitely established; and many others.

We should withdraw our soldiers, sailors, and marines as soon as possible from China, because the longer we stay there the more possibility there is that we may become involved in the internal Chinese situation. It was my hope that we would get out of China at the earliest opportunity once the war with Japan was ended. However, the opposite seems to be true, because with the defeat of Japan we are strengthening our forces in China and funneling more troops into that country. . . .

The landing of the First and Sixth Marine Divisions and the dispatch of the American cruisers to Chefoo constitute an unwarranted interference in the affairs of China, and, while these moves undoubtedly had the approval of Chiang Kai-shek, I feel that we are making a serious mistake in furthering this gunboat policy.

Surely there are no American business interests to be protected and no American civilian lives at stake. . . .

Summing up, there is, and will be for a long time to come, a need to keep a strong occupation force in Japan. However, there is no sound reason for maintaining all our troops in India, Burma, Korea and China, and certainly there can be no justification for sending additional marines and sailors to the Asiatic mainland. The best interests of the United States would be well served if we were to withdraw all our servicemen from these four areas at the first available opportunity. It is time that we called for an explanation of our policy in the Far East, so that we will not again become involved in hostilities in that area. With the exception of Japan, our military business has ended in the Far East, and the best procedure for us to follow would be to let the countries in that part of the world settle their own internal difficulties.

March 31, 1948:

On the priority of Europe in foreign aid

In the spring of 1948 the United States' political fancy turned to thoughts of foreign aid. Congress rang with debate over the European Recovery Program – the Marshall Plan – and aid to China, which was ringing itself, or tolling, with a bitter civil war. Support for the European aid program was widespread and generally bipartisan, largely through the efforts of Senator Arthur Vandenburg. There was a fly in the Republican ointment, however, for a group within that party believed that equivalent amounts of aid should go to China, or more particularly to the Nationalist government of Chiang Kai-shek, which was feverishly represented in Washington by the celebrated China Lobby. The Truman Administration, and particularly Secretary of State George Marshall, opposed this two-front proposal, somewhat in the spirit of the "Europe First" policy followed by Franklin Roosevelt and Marshall in World War II.

In the House, Mansfield, for all his Far Eastern bias, argued that while Europe gave every indication of being a low-risk client, China offered strong prospects of being a high-risk client, if not a bottomless pit. Although less than enchanted by Mao Tse-tung's violent revolutionaries, he declined to view Chiang's Nationalist government through the rose-colored glasses being liberally distributed by the China Lobby. He considered it incorrigibly corrupt, militarily incompetent, and socially neanderthal. He did not consider it a likely prospect for aid, as he made clear on the floor of the House in March 1948.

Mansfield could be partisan when he felt that the occasion called for partisanship. The effort to link Chinese with European aid was highly partisan, and in his speech he did not hesitate to treat it as such. He did so without virulence, however, and without indulging in personalities.

* * *

37

Mr. Mansfield. Mr. Chairman, I rise at this time in support of the amendment striking Title III from the measure now before us.

After reviewing the European situation very carefully — both in person and as a result of committee hearings — I have come to the conclusion that the Marshall proposal offers a possible solution to the difficulties of western Europe. I have based my decision in this respect on three factors: One, it is a humanitarian measure which will provide relief to people who are subsisting on a semistarvation basis and are not in a position to help themselves; two, it will provide for the economic rehabilitation of Europe, allow these nations to take their rightful places in the world's economy, and give employment, hope, and security to their populations; and three, it is necessary in the interests of our own national security to take this "calculated risk" so that these countries will not, on the basis of insecurity, hunger, and chaos, move into the satellite area through pressure and intimidation from minority groups whose real loyalties lie not with their respective countries but with the U.S.S.R.

This program, as it applies to western Europe, does not offer an assured success. It is, I repeat, a calculated risk, and we stand to appropriate a sum of between 15 and 20 billion dollars over a 4¼-year period in the hope that it will succeed. The alternative to this proposal is the loss, by default, of all of western Europe and the isolation of our country.

What will this alternative, this isolation, mean to us? It will mean that we shall have to spend much more than contemplated under the Marshall proposal in strengthening our own defenses; it will mean that our natural friends in western Europe will be lost to us, perhaps irretrievably; and it will mean depression at home, the possible rise of a state-controlled economy, and the loss of many of the privileges which we as Americans have always felt were rightfully ours.

On the basis of these arguments, because the sixteen nations of western Europe have made a real effort to evaluate their needs on a cooperative basis, and because I feel this program offers a road to real peace, I support the proposals of Secretary Marshall and the recommendations of the American committees which have considered and approved this program. . . .

We are now faced with a dilemma, and we will have to decide

the relative importance of Europe and the Far East in our diplomacy. We will have to recognize the fact that our resources are limited and that we will have to decide — as we did during the war — where to place our emphasis and greatest effort. Secretary Marshall has faced up to the same decision he encountered during the war, and he has stated that in his opinion western Europe is the most important and that, while economic assistance should be sent to China, military assistance should not. Just as in the war, the Secretary has had to put up with special pleaders for special areas, and, just as his judgment was sound then, so do I think it is now. First things must be met first, and China in the present instance is not first.

In my earlier remarks I indicated that ERP was a calculated risk with no assurance of success, but only a reasonable possibility. Do we want to include the rest of the world and thus make way for the stretching of our lines on an extremely thin basis, with the possibility of failure on all fronts rather than our possible success in Europe? Do we have the resources to carry on a world-wide program as contemplated in this measure?

Proponents of the China program have merit on their side when they cite the fact that the Communist leaders of China — Mao Tse-tung, Chou En-lai, Chu Teh, and all the rest — are out-and-out Marxian Socialists and intend eventually to create a Soviet state. They do not, I believe, have as much merit on their side when they compare China with Greece and say that because we have gone into the latter country we should, for the same reasons, go into China. Greece is a small country, with a small population, China is a country one-third again as large as the United States, with a population of 475,000,000. Our policy in Greece is costly and far from successful,; our policy in China will, if enacted into law, be far more costly and will have much less chance of success. I do not agree with those who always find fault with our State Department or with Secretary Marshall in their China policy, because they are interested in their country's welfare and are doing the best job they can in behalf of the United States. They are fully aware of the possible costs of a China adventure; they have no illusions about what may happen if we embark on this policy; and they know that, once started, the drain on us will be terrific and will have a snowball effect as the years go on. We should be under no illusion that we are supporting a democratic regime, and we should realize that many Chinese in Kuomintang China will not look upon us as deliverers nor will they welcome our participation in their affairs.

Our study of China should not be on a partisan basis. I should be more than happy to consider a China policy based on the Marshall program which would have a reasonable chance of success and which would give the Chinese people hope in their national future and security in their daily lives. ...

The Chinese government is operating under the double handicap of a civil war and a badly shaken deteriorating economy. These difficulties cannot be overcome by help from the outside alone but must be met and conquered largely by the Chinese themselves. Any American aid should be conditioned by adequate reforms instituted in fact, and not on paper, for the benefit of the Chinese people. ...

It has been stated that with additional American help the Kuomintang could win the civil war. This, I believe, is open to question. American-trained Chinese divisions have been wasted; political incompetents have been placed in charge of Chinese armies, and good military commanders have been deprived of their divisions. Furthermore, much American materiel has found its way into the hands of the Communists, and, perhaps in the last analysis, we will find that indirectly we have supplied a large portion of the war materiel they have used. The questions in my mind are: How much of our munitions and planes and supplies to the Kuomintang have been put to good use, and how much can we afford to waste?

The situation in China is not a pleasant one. We can argue here in this Congress from now till doomsday about the merits and demerits of the Chinese problem, but we will have to admit eventually that the solutions to China's ills will have to come from the Chinese themselves. When that day comes the United States can then embark on a program of aid and assistance which will have some hope of success. Then, on a mutually cooperative basis, the governments and the people of both countries will be able to respect and assist each other in the maintenance of peace in the Pacific and throughout the world.

In conclusion, I want to say that the European Recovery Program is based on the carefully worked-out plans of free nations for their own economic revival and is not, as in the case of China, a hit-or-miss proposition with little assurance of success. The time has come to decide whether the policy contemplated in this Congress is to be applied on a world-wide scale with little possibility of victory or if it is to be applied in wstern Europe, where we have a reasonable chance for success. The choice is ours.

Mr. Chairman, under unanimous consent granted to me earlier in the day, I am inserting at this point in my remarks a copy of a speech made by me before the Academy of Political Science in New York on November 12, 1947. The title of this speech is "The Chinese policy of the United States."

* * *

Mansfield's address to the Academy of Political Science was long, thoughtful and technical. Although it doubtless enhanced his growing reputation as a foreign-policy pundit, only a portion of it is relevant here. After discussing U.S. foreign policy in very academic terms ("objective, pattern, and technique," for example), and reviewing the history of American relations with China, he turned to the current situation.

* * *

We still actively support, internationally, the sovereignty of China and the government of Chiang Kai-shek. But with regard to the internal situation we have, in effect, retired almost completely to the sidelines to await further developments. If there is a clear indication that out of the chaos there is emerging a hope for the development of peace, unity, and democracy, we are pledged to move in actively with economic or any other aid necessary to support that hope. To date, that hope has not emerged. Civil war now rages throughout North China and Manchuria. Other areas are in a state of incipient separatism. The Communists are resorting to their old extremist tactics of brutal terrorism. And the administrative machinery of the national government, as General Wedemeyer has recently pointed out, is bogged down in a mire of unparalleled corruption.

41

That we regret this situation, that we sympathize with the Chinese people goes without saying. But it is equally true that there is little we can do, as our experience has shown, to alleviate their difficulties. Nevertheless, powerful and capable voices are heard in the United States urging us to project ourselves into the middle of this problem in China. Let us for a moment consider the views of those who object to the abeyant state of our policy in China. Many Americans have a deep and sincere affection for the Chinese. Among them there are those who point out that it is ignoble for us to forsake our wartime allies in their hour of need. Therefore, they insist, let us do something for China, and let us do it through the living symbol of China's resistance, Chiang Kai-shek.

Let me, first of all, make clear the extent of aid already made available to the National Government. I have alluded to the post-war military and international assistance which we have tendered to President Chiang. Mention should also be made of the American Army and Navy missions still in China to help establish a truly national military organization. Since 1941 total aid in the form of loans and grants is in the neighborhood of $2.5 billion. In addition, we have transferred extensive quantities of surplus property at a fraction of original cost. We have also turned over 271 naval vessels. This year the United States foreign-relief program probably will allot $30 million in medical supplies and food to China.

Furthermore, the United States stands committed to provide additional assistance for non-civil-war purposes as the circumstances permit. When there is some assurance that, instead of adding to the wreckage of the civil war and to the private fortunes of corrupt officials, our aid will assist in the restoration of the well-being of the Chinese people, its flow should increase. Those who are sincerely distressed over the plight of China need have no fear. The United States government will do all in its power to lessen the sufferings of the Chinese people but will firmly resist all ill-considered efforts to have it add to their distress. The great shortcoming of many who insist, vaguely, that we "do some-thing" for China is that they fail to realize the limitations on what we can do. We can stand beside the Chinese as sympathetic friends. We can help them through our private charities, our

Christian missions, our educational and cultural endowments, and governmental grants or loans to meet their most pressing needs. All these measures we have taken and will continue to take. But we cannot supply the spiritual spark which will release the capacities of the Chinese people and channel them into a reconstruction of their noble civilization. That spark can — and will someday — come only from the heart of China itself.

June 17, 1948: On women in Congress

The term "gentleman," like the title "Honorable," is of course used quite indiscriminately in Congress. When applied to Mike Mansfield, however, neither term is meaningless. If one mark of a gentleman is respect for the opposite sex, he offered his credentials officially as early as June 1948 on the floor of the House, long before the heyday of Women's Liberation. Although some of the more stridently female militants today might consider his comments an instance of condescending chivalry, he certainly couldn't be accused of Male Chauvinist Piggishness.

* * *

Mr. Mansfield. Mr. Speaker, the women members of the House of Representatives have made outstanding contributions to the political life of America. It is to be regretted that their numbers in this body are so few, and it is to be hoped that their numbers will increase so that the outlook of this body may be broadened and much needed legislation be brought into existence through their activities. It has been my privilege to work closely with such outstanding members as Mrs. Helen Gahagan Douglas of California, Mrs. Frances Bolton of Ohio, and Mrs. Edith Rogers of Massachusetts on the House Foreign Affairs Committee. Knowing them was to respect and admire them for their courage, intelligence, and sense of responsibility. The same can be said for Mrs. Margaret Chase Smith of Maine, Mrs. Mary Norton of New Jersey, Mrs. Georgia Lusk of New Mexico, and Mrs. Katherine St. George of New York. They have all contributed greatly to the dignity, intelligence, and understanding of the House, and it is my sincere hope that they will be with us for many years to come. We are proud of all of them.

January 30, 1950:

On U.S. entanglement in the Far East

The end of 1949 was also the end of Chiang Kai-shek's Nationalist government, which fled to Formosa, or Taiwan, in December, leaving the battle-scarred mainland to the Communists. In the United States a new, virulent religion of anti-Communism was taking root among the jingoes whose high priest, Senator Joe McCarthy, was soon to inject his own peculiar brand of venom into the body politic. In January 1950, when the "loss" of China was already being ascribed to traitorous maneuvering within the Truman Administration, Mansfield decided to stand up early and be counted. His speech at the Washington Town Meeting was a classic defense of the United States' postwar policy in China and a much needed warning against foreign entanglements, especially in the vast and distant recesses of the Far East. If its underlying thesis had been applied later in Vietnam, what pain and moral debasement might have been avoided is immeasurable.

The speech justifiably enlarged his reputation as an authority on foreign policy, although it could not stem the rising tide of corrosive fanaticism. It also put his name on McCarthy's enemies list. When he ran for the Senate in 1952, McCarthy came to Montana with his smear brush to warn voters against this coddler of Communists, and Mansfield was very nearly defeated. As might be expected, there is no record of Mansfield ever attacking McCarthy personally, even during the later censure proceedings in the Senate, but neither could he bring himself to warm up to such a reptilian personality. When McCarthy approached him on the Senate floor early in 1953 with a hearty, ol'-buddy greeting, "How are things in Montana these days, Mike?", Mansfield simply replied coldly, "Much better since you left."

44

Because the speech presented its case so well, drawing distinctions that were later badly blurred in the McCarthy madness, it is presented here in its entirety, as it appeared in the February 9th Congressional Record.

* * *

In any discussion of China policy, two premises ought to be agreed upon at the outset. Unless they are, we will end by obscuring the very issues which we are supposed to clarify.

First of all, China is not merely a group of political and military chieftains on the island of Formosa. Nor is it a few Chinese Marxist theoreticians in Peking or — as they are at present — in Moscow. We mean or should mean, when we speak of China, the 475 million Chinese people, who possess a very ancient and distinct culture and who, during the past half century, have come to develop an increasing awareness of their national unity. They constitute the China toward which the friendly hand of the United States traditionally has been extended. They are the China we have long sought to encourage in the direction of democracy and freedom from foreign control.

In the second place, we ought to agree that China policy is not solely a question of "to aid or not to aid" Chiang Kai-shek, but rather is the whole couse of action and inaction in our relations with that country. The question we must ask ourselves is whether the course we have set is the best that can be pursued under existing circumstances. Does it serve all the interests of the United States? Not merely our commercial interests in China, although they are of some importance; not merely our strategic interests in the Far East, although obviously those too are important — but the entire range of American concern with China, the Far East, and the rest of the world.

If we keep these two fundamental facts in mind, we shall find, I believe, that the policy followed in turn by General Marshall and Secretary Acheson during the administration of President Truman has been on the same bipartisan track pursued by administration after administration, Republican and Democratic, during the past half century. It should be kept on that track despite the efforts

45

of those who, for reasons of sentimentality or politics, would derail it.

So much heat and so little light has been shed on this policy by the debate of the past few years that I should like to review briefly just what we have done and what we have not done with respect to China.

During the war and immediate postwar period the United States extended both economic and military assistance to the Chinese. The amount of that assistance was not large enough to satisfy some people. It was much smaller than that which went to Russia or Great Britain. At the time, however, most of us were concerned not with dividing the American inheritance equally among our allies, but with using available resources in a manner best calculated to defeat our enemies. The fact that we are meeting here tonight seems to indicate that the decisions of our wartime leaders in this respect were at least reasonably correct.

Assistance given to China during the war, limited though it may have been, was the critical factor in saving a valued ally from collapse, and I think it is about time we stopped being ashamed of it. American interests were served by this aid in that we were able to share the terrible human sacrifices demanded by the war. China's interests also were served, for that country emerged from the conflict in a stronger and more independent position than it had ever before occupied in the modern world.

Partly to complete our wartime commitments and partly to equip China for its greatly enhanced and important international role, the United States continued aid to China during the months following the end of the war. The Chinese people wanted the removal of the 8 million Japanese remaining in China. They wanted internal stability and rapid economic and political reconstruction. And above all they wanted an end to civil war.

The intention of our postwar aid was to assist them in realizing these objectives; we were not concerned with furthering the interests of any particular group of Chinese officials. If we extended our assistance through the National Government, it was because the available evidence indicated that, at the time, most of the Chinese people still looked to the generalissimo, who had led them in war, to continue to supply them with leadership in peace.

General Marshall's mission similarly was in accord with the

wishes of the Chinese people. The general did not go to China to force Chiang Kai-shek to accept Communists into his government, as has been so recklessly charged by some in this country. He went to help achieve what the Chinese people clearly and desperately desired — what the generalissimo and the National Government had repeatedly proclaimed as their official policy — a settlement of the internal problem of unity by peaceful means.

When it proved impossible to achieve such a settlement, President Truman reiterated the traditional policy of the United States — that we would not become directly involved in a Chinese civil war. That decision was applauded by the people of China, who were overwhelmingly opposed to the suicidal conflict being precipitated among them. As the civil war spread, we sought ways to alleviate the suffering it caused and to prevent China from collapsing into utter anarchy.

The cost of the American effort to help the Chinese people has been great. An official calculation placed the total amount in excess of $2 billion in loans and grants since V-J Day. It is possible to argue about the exact amount, and millions of words have been wasted in proving that it was closer to one billion or to three billion.

The significant facts, however, are these. During the first few weeks after the defeat of Japan the United States transported by sea and air 400,000 to 500,000 National Government troops over and around the Communist forces to key sectors of East and North China. The purpose of this undertaking was to insure an orderly surrender, disarmament, and repatriation of the Japanese. Fifty thousand American marines held such vital cities as Peiping, Tientsin, and Tsingtao for months, thus preventing their seizure by the Chinese Communists. By the end of 1945 we had delivered sufficient tonnage to equip 39 divisions of National Government ground forces and an eight-group air force. Whatever Japanese equipment the Chinese Communists obtained with the facilitation of the Russians in Manchuria was offset by the Japanese equipment surrendered to the Nationalist forces in North, Central, and South China.

In December 1945 Chiang Kai-shek held a numerical superiority in combat forces over the Communists of five to one. He had a monopoly of heavy equipment and mechanical transportation and an unopposed air arm. Yet by December 1948, exactly three years later, this preponderance of strength had been so dissipated that General Barr, head of our advisory mission in China, was forced to conclude that without direct American involvement with combat forces the complete defeat of the Nationalist armies was inevitable.

What lies behind this colossal failure? We have the answer from General Marshall, General Wedemeyer, General Barr, and practically every other competent observer who has had the opportunity to view the situation in China at first hand. The failure was due not to any lack of arms and ammunition. The failure was due to the incredible ineptitude of the Nationalist Army command. It was to the inability or unwillingness of the Chinese government to take the necessary and repeatedly advised measures of social, economic, political, and military reform which alone could have retained for it the support of the soldiers and the common people of China. It was due to the downright corruption in official circles.

In the face of the mass of evidence, there are still people who cling to the theory that the Yalta agreement is at the root of all of China's difficulties. It follows, then, that since we participated in this dark and wicked conspiracy we are guilty of some sort of gross betrayal.

Let us see what this much-maligned agreement actually provided. Under its most pertinent clause, the United States committed itself to intercede with the Chinese government in order to obtain the return to the Soviet Union of certain limited port and naval concessions in Manchuria. They were substantially the same as had been lost by Russia to Japan in 1904. In return, the Russians agreed to enter the war against Japan. They also reaffirmed their recognition of China's sovereignty over all Manchuria, and consented to give assistance and support to China exclusively through the National Government.

Military considerations were largely responsible for the American decisions at Yalta. It is all very well, with the wisdom of hindsight, to ridicule these considerations. But at the time the war with Japan was still of uncertain duration. Without the unforeseeable impact of the atomic bomb on the outcome, hundreds of thousands of additional casualties might have been the price of the defeat of Japan. The administration wanted to share that toll as far as possible with other countries. No one, it seems to me, is justified in talking glibly of such a consideration.

The fact is that we could not have prevented, by any method short of war, the penetration of Manchuria by Russian imperialism, so we tried to limit it. The American people have never indicated a willingness to go to war for the elimination of non-Chinese control from Manchuria. Our traditional China policy has never countenanced such a step. We did not go to war when the Russians originally penetrated the area toward the close of the nineteenth century. We did not go to war when the Japanese replaced them in 1904. It was, as a matter of fact, President Theodore Roosevelt who arranged that first "Yalta" agreement. And in 1931, another Republican administration refused to lead us into war over this issue when the Japanese expanded economic concessions into political domination of all Manchuria.

We have placed on record in the past our conviction that Manchuria is Chinese territory. At Yalta we did so again. And we still believe Manchuria remains Chinese territory, regardless of the advantages taken by predatory neighbors in this time of China's weakness. But the task of restoring Manchuria to China in fact as well as in name is primarily the task of Chinese nationalism. It is not now and it has never been the responsibility of the United States armed forces.

Rather than speak of Yalta as a gross and iniquitous betrayal, I think it time to recognize it for what it was — the best possible chance, at the time, of preserving the long-term interests of both the United States and China.

Another bogey has now made its appearance in connection with the island of Formosa. This time the administration is accused, not of betraying the Chinese, but of betraying the Formosans, who, incidentally, are about 98 percent Chinese.

At the Cairo Conference in 1943, the United States pledged the restoration of Formosa to China. There was practically unanimous approval of that decision both in this country and in the allied world. When the war ended, the Formosan Chinese welcomed the return of the National Government as a liberator. Chen Yi, an old friend of Generalissimo Chiang Kai-shek, was appointed the first governor. Chen Yi found living standards on the island better than on the mainland. He found a populace both industrious and law-abiding. And he found no Communists. After a little more than a year of Chen Yi's carpetbagging maladministration, the island was rocked by a fierce uprising against the mainlanders. Chen Yi crushed the revolt with a ruthlessness that claimed several thousand lives. It is not surprising that many Formosans believe their lot — bad as it might have been under the Japanese — was preferable to what they have suffered under the National Government. Successive and more enlightened governors — Wei Tao-ming, Chen Cheng, and K. C. Wu — have not been able to wipe out the bitterness and hatred which the Formosan Chinese feel for their oppressors.

It is into thus ugly situation that we are now invited to project ourselves. Since a peace treaty with Japan has not yet been signed, a legal loophole exists whereby we might assume some sort of protectorate over Formosa. In this manner we might conveniently avoid or postpone in Chiang Kai-shek's interest the pledge given to the Chinese people at Cairo. This ignores the fact, however, that for three years we have not questioned Chinese control over the island and to do so now would be unabashed interference in internal Chinese affairs.

The "gunboat" policy for Formosa currently being advocated in some quarters is not a new one. It was first proposed a hundred years ago by Admiral Perry and decisively rejected by the American people then. If we were to follow it now, we might be able with superior force to discourage the present Communist masters of China from seeking to take the island. But in doing so we would give credence to the anti-American propaganda in the orient that charges us with using our power for imperialistic purposes. We would build, in the final analysis, a lasting heritage of hatred, just as the Russians are now busily doing in Manchuria, Sinkiang, and Mongolia.

The situation in Formosa points up the key difficulty involved in keeping our China policy on the right track. We must discriminate between what we can do and what we cannot do both in a material and an ethical sense. There is no virtue in acting in foreign affairs just to be acting, and there are times when inaction is more effective than action from the point of view of American interests.

The cardinal principle of United States China policy must remain what it always has been — recognition of the fact that the internal problems of the Chinese people, whether on the mainland or on Formosa, must be solved primarily by the Chinese people themselves. They do not want and they will not acquiesce indefinitely in solutions forced upon them by foreign intervention.

We cannot make ourselves responsible, militarily or otherwise, for a regime which has been abandoned by the Chinese people. To do so would be the certain way of diverting attention from the real threat to their nation arising in the north.

We cannot continue to supply armaments to a government which the Communist leader Mao Tse-tung has callously, but unfortunately with much accuracy, labeled his supply service for the delivery of American equipment.

We cannot, by conducting naval exercises in the path of an impending engagement in the Chinese civil war, find a cheap and involvement-free solution to the complex problem of Chinese policy. It is irresponsible and dangerous to threaten force unless you are prepared to use it. And I doubt that even those who advocate such a policy are ready to go to war over Formosa.

We cannot, on the other hand, give recognition to a Chinese Communist government which shows little regard for the rights of our citizens and little respect for even the most elementary international usages. There would appear to be little point, moreover, in our association with a regime which claims to speak with the authentic voice of China but which has the accent of the Soviet Union. At the conclusion of the present and unexpectedly long talks in Moscow we may know better whether that regime has abandoned the accent or China's fundamental interests.

What we can do in the present circumstances is maintain our faith in China — not in a handful of exalted figures but in the Chinese people themselves. We can continue to help those people with the limited means at our disposal, through public and private channels, in whatever regions remain open to us. The Chinese people will not forget acts of genuine friendship in their hour of trial.

We can, moreover, through the Voice of America, the United Nations, and other feasible ways, keep the attention of the Chinese and the world focused on the Soviet exploitation that is now going on in China's remote provinces. Through the United Nations we can also seek to prevent the present Communist masters from pushing the peaceful Chinese people into aggressive campaigns across China's borders.

By lending encouragement to legitimate nationalist aspirations and by extending practical economic assistance under Point 4 to the countries surrounding China, we can demonstrate our genuine interest in the progress of all Asia.

Finally, we can keep our thinking on general foreign policy flexible. Only in this way will we be able to act appropriately in any given circumstances. Above all, we must avoid the fallacy of believing that consistency in foreign policy lies in acting in precisely the same manner in every part of the globe. It is, for example, fantastic to suggest that what we have done in Greece we must also do in China, which has 58 times as many people, 60 times as great an area, and a vastly different set of political and strategic problems.

The only consistency we need be concerned with is the consistency with which we devote ourselves to the protection of the security and all the legitimate interests of the United States. That is the basic ingredient of the nonpartisan, nonpolitical approach. Beyond it let us exercise a little imagination and a lot of discretion.

July 8, 1954:

On U.S. policy in the Far East,

especially Indochina

In the spring of 1954 the French colonialists finally were ejected from Indochina, and nineteen nations participated in the Geneva Conference to settle affairs in Southeast Asia. Mansfield and many other Senators had objected to U.S. participation in the conference until some common-front position could be established among the non-Communist nations, to counter the much greater solidarity of the Communist bloc. Secretary of State John Foster Dulles, however, did not consult the Senate, and the Con-

ference left Indochina open to the unrelenting infiltration that was to be the pattern for the next two decades.

This irked Mansfield, as did Dulles' "agonizing reappraisal" of foreign policy and his reliance on "massive retaliation." The Senator could tolerate the persistent anti-Communist chest-thumping of right-wing Republicans in the political arena, but he objected to it as a formulation of U.S. foreign policy. Indeed, he was irked enough to indulge in some partisan sarcasm in a Senate speech in July 1954, and in some of the debate that followed.

He also offered some Cassandran remarks on U.S. military involvement in Indochina.

* * *

Mr. Mansfield. Mr. President, the war in Indochina appears on the verge of ending in a truce. The bloodletting of the past eight years will probably come to a close very shortly. There will be no more Dien Bien Phus, at least for the present. The danger of armed involvement of American forces in Indochina, once so close, has receded.

These are welcome byproducts of the Geneva Conference. There is little else. The situation in Korea, presumably the principal reason for our participation in the Conference, remains unchanged. Thousands of American soldiers are still committed there on the mainland of Asia.

With respect to Indochina, a serious defeat has been inflicted on American diplomacy. And in the process vast new areas have been opened for potential conquest by Communist totalitarianism.

Last spring, Mr. President, in two speeches in the Senate, I expressed the view that our consent to participate in the Geneva proceedings was a mistake. I did so because it was clear at the time that the Communists would enter the Conference, for all practical purposes, as a bloc; that the Communists, whether from the Soviet Union, Korea, China, or Indochina, would possess a singleness of outlook. It was not clear that the non-Communist nations shared any such unity of objective. The British wanted to stay out of Indochina, the French wanted to get out of Indochina, and for a while it seemed that we were on the verge of getting into Indochina.

In these circumstances, how could negotiations lead to anything but failure for the non-Communist powers? . . .

Thanks to the courage and wisdom of a sincere American and great Secretary of State, George C. Marshall, and thanks to the financial sacrifices of the American people, who bore the cost of the Marshall Plan willingly and generously, Western Europe had been able to lift itself out of the mire of a disastrous war. It had begun the long, slow ascent toward unity. It was on the verge of reaching the most elusive goal of all, the formation of a common European army. Had this goal been achieved, France and Germany would have ceased to revolve in age-old, separate, and suicidal orbits. The intelligence, the skills, the strengths of these and other great nations of Europe would no longer have been pitted against each other in senseless, destructive rivalry. They would have been united for mutual benefit and for the benefit of the entire world.

This was a dream worth having, and it was shared by great and small alike in Europe and in America. It was the hope of a century, and it stood on the very edge of achievement in the proposed creation of the European Defense Community, the common European army. But now the dream is fading, the hope is dimming.

These results were not expected when the Secretary of State, at the Berlin Conference last February, announced that this nation had been committed to the Geneva meeting. I say this without reflecting on the intentions or the capacities of the Secretary of State. The Secretary is an able and devoted public servant. Some have even waxed lyrical in their appreciation of his exceptional qualities. It has been said, for example, that it is "wonderful" to have at last "a Secretary of State who is not taken in by the Communists, who stands up to them."

I cannot hope to match such eloquence in the expression of my regard for the Secretary. That he did stand up to the Communists, however, is beyond doubt. The Secretary refused to participate in the Geneva Conference unless Mr. Molotov agreed that the Conference would in no way constitute recognition of Communist China. He refused quite correctly even to accept Mr. Molotov's word in this matter. He insisted that Mr. Molotov sign a piece of paper making clear that the Geneva meeting would in no way constitute recognition of Communist China. The Secretary fought

Mr. Molotov day after day at Berlin on this issue of the piece of paper. And finally, because he had refused to be taken in by the Communists, because he had stood up to them, the Secretary triumphed. Mr. Molotov capitulated. And in a climax worthy of the best of our current television dramas, Mr. Molotov signed the piece of paper.

The Secretary is to be commended for not being taken in by the Communists, for standing up to them, for obtaining this piece of paper.

We still have the piece of paper in our archives, I presume, and meanwhile the Communists have obtained at Geneva all that they set out to acquire at Berlin a few months ago. . . .

The Secretary of State used an eloquent phrase some time ago when he spoke of an "agonizing reappraisal." . . . This "agonizing reappraisal" of policy seems already to have begun. In my opinion, it has begun on a note of irresponsible partisanship. A few weeks ago the Postmaster General of the United States, a member of the President's cabinet, found time from his duties of delivering the mails to deliver some political remarks in Indiana on the subject of foreign policy. He began his reappraisal by going back a decade or more in search of the causes of the loss of Indochina. He discovered these causes, like long-lost letters, in such places as Yalta, Teheran, and Potsdam. . . .

A few days ago, in a different vein, in a responsible vein, the able majority leader (Mr. Knowland) raised the question of seating Communist China in the United Nations. He made clear his opposition to any such attempt with all the vehemence and eloquence of which he is capable. I have the highest regard for the sincerity and the consistency of the distinguished majority leader, and I can appreciate his sentiments in this matter.

But, with all due respect to the distinguished majority leader, I do not believe that a reappraisal of policy ought to begin with an even that has not happened. The President has not indicated, so far as I am aware, that he is about to change the policy pursued by the previous administration, the policy of opposing the seating of Communist China in the United Nations. That policy has kept the Peking government of Communist China from gaining a seat in the United Nations. . . .

It is true that some members of the Senate differed on one point with the administration. They would have preferred that the United States avoid participation in the Geneva proceedings, and said so in debate. Those of us who took this position — and there were a number of Senators on both sides of the aisle who did so — were not necessarily opposed to negotiations as such. Some of us were aware, however, that the free nations were divided and confused on the issue of Indochina. Before the United States participated in a conference with the cohesive forces of Communism, we wanted the division and confusion on our side eliminated. . . .

I do not know whether the President himself ever seriously considered committing this nation to an armed involvement in Indochina. Nevertheless, the air around him was full of military sound and fury just prior to Geneva. There was much talk of involvement, even though Indochina would have been in every sense a nibbling war.

The terrain of the Indochinese conflict — the flooded deltas, the thousands of scattered villages, the jungles — is made to order for the nibbling of mechanized forces. The French have been nibbled and chewed for eight years. . . .

A people, whether in Asia or in the Americas, can preserve their independence only if they have it in the first place and if they are willing to fight to keep it. Beyond this initial responsibility, which every nation must accept, nations can combine among themselves for a joint defense of freedom. If they are threatened by aggression, singly or jointly, they can seek recourse through the United Nations. But from the beginning to the end of this process of defense, the key factor is the determination of the people of each nation to defend their freedom. This factor was lacking in the Secretary of State's eleventh-hour attempt to set up an alliance to save Indochina. . . .

I make the following suggestions without in any sense regarding them as immutable. I make them with a full awareness of their imperfections and their inadequacies. I hope they will be challenged, debated, discussed, and improved, but I make them now in the hope that they will help to put up the guideposts that are so urgently needed.

First. Colonialism — Chinese Communist or any other — has no place in Asia, and the policies of the United States should in no

56

way act to perpetuate it.

Second. The United States should look with favor on governments in Asia which are representative of their people and responsive to their needs, but this nation should not intervene in the internal affairs of any peaceful country.

Third. The defense of freedom in Asia must rest in the first instance on the will and determination of the free peoples of that region.

Fourth. Systems of alliances for the defense of free nations in Asia against aggression must draw their primary and preponderant strength from the Asian countries; the association of the United States, if any at all, with such alliances should be indirect, through the machinery of ANZUS or similar combinations of non-Asian countries.

Fifth. The United Nations should serve as the only worldwide marshalling center for resistance, in the event of aggression or threat of aggression in Asia.

Sixth. The economic development of the nations of Asia is preponderantly the responsibility of the peoples of that region, to be pursued in accord with their individual national genius and objectives; any assistance rendered by this country, whether directly or through the United Nations or other agencies, should be peripheral and should be rendered only when genuinely desired. . . .

Mr. Fulbright. Mr. President, will the Senator yield?

Mr. Mansfield. I am glad to yield.

Mr. Fulbright. First, I should like to compliment the Senator on his magnificent speech and to associate myself with much that he has said. Of course, he is one of the best qualified men in the Senate and in government on the subject of Asia. . . .

The Senator from Montana agrees with the President, if I correctly understand him, that the determination which has been expressed in some circles, that under no circumstances at any time should Red China be admitted into the United Nations, is not in accord with a wise policy such as we pursue at this time?

Mr. Mansfield. It would be pretty difficult for us to follow such a policy because, as one Congress cannot bind the succeeding Congress, one generation cannot bind the next generation. When the time comes, those who are then in power are the ones who will have to make the deicison. . . .

Mr. Jackson. Needless to say, I am happy to join with my colleagues in commending the Senator from Montana for his outstanding contribution today to the subject of our foreign policy. . . .

Will the Senator agree that if we have learned anything from the situation in Indochina, it is that military assistance alone is no longer our contribution to the world?

Mr. Mansfield. I could not agree more heartily. . . .

Mr. Sparkman. . . . I should like to commend the able Senator from Montana for having given us one of the clearest and ablest discussions of some of our problems in the field of foreign relations that I have ever heard on the Senate floor. . . .

Mr. Cooper. First, I should like to say that I find much to commend in what the distinguished Senator from Montana has said. I have listened to most, if not all, of the speeches he has made on foreign affairs, and I have found them, without exception, constructive and scholarly. . . .

My friends on the other side of the aisle cannot have it both ways . . . Let me ask them now whether they favor intervention [in Indochina].

Mr. Mansfield. No, I was never in favor of intervention, and I am opposed to it now. I think it would be suicidal. I believe the worst thing that could happen to the United States would be to have our forces intervene in Indochina and then bog down in the jungles there. . . .

February 28, 1959:

On the new Democrats in the Senate

In the 1958 midterm elections the Democrats substantially increased their numbers in both houses of Congress. In February 1959 Mansfield, who was now the Senate majority whip, was chosen to give the keynote address at the Democratic "Victory" Dinner. (The association of politics with competitive sports is sometimes excruciatingly intimate.) It gave him an opportunity to engage in some partisanship for its own sake, but in his own gentle, light-hearted fashion.

The automobile industry is often described as the pace setter of American industry. In other words, it occupies a position in the American economy like the Democratic party in American politics. There's one difference. Last year the American people didn't go too well for the new cars. Last November they went, with real enthusiasm, for the Democrats.

So tonight we are having a victory dinner. You know, there are some people who think you can have too much of a good thing. They say, for example, "There's too many Democrats in the Senate. What's Lyndon going to do with them all?" Well, so far as I know, we don't have any Democratic unemployment in the Senate. The distinguished majority leader has put all the Democratic members to work, and they are beginning to produce. There's no such thing as an "acceptable" level of unemployment in the Democratic Senate, just as there oughtn't to be in the nation.

Personally, I don't think you can ever have too many Democrats at work — in the Senate or anywhere else. As a matter of fact, there's a shortage of Democrats. The country could use a lot more of them over in the other branch of the government. I don't know about the market for automobiles. But, as far as the Democrats are concerned, it won't be until 1960 that the supply will begin to catch up with the demand.

In the last few weeks we've been seeing the new automobiles on the streets of this city. They have clean, fresh lines. Some of the cars are conservative-looking. Others show liberal style changes. A few even have that futuristic look.

Not to be outdone by the automobile industry, we have our own display of 1959 Democratic models tonight. We've got four lines with us — not Fords, General Motors, Chryslers, and Ramblers. What we do have are Democratic Governors, Senators, Representatives, and Democratic Presidential possibilities. We've done something which Detroit hasn't been able to do for years. We've brought in a successful new producer — Alaska — with three new Democratic designs, all fully equipped with snowshoes.

Some of us have had an opportunity to preview the new 1959 Democratic models in the Senate. We've already looked under the hoods and tried the steering gear and the brakes. Take it from us, the new automobiles have nothing on them. These new Democratic models may not handle as easily — take, for example, the one produced in Wisconsin — but they all do have plenty of power. As a matter of fact, some of us older rattletraps, the Model A's, are beginning to wonder what the influx of these bright and shining new additions to the Senate is going to do to the used car market.

Nevertheless, we strongly commend them, all of them, to you. We urge you to take them to your hearts as we have done. They add luster, drive, safety and countless new extras to the Democratic Party and to the nation.

That is why I am delighted to participate in this victory dinner. It is true we are celebrating, in a general sense, the triumph of the Democratic Party in the 1958 elections. But in a special sense we are celebrating the victory of these new Senators, new Representatives, and new Governors. It is they who add up to the difference between an ordinary election and the great Democratic victory at the polls last November. Through them, the nation has made it clear what it expects of all of us.

I am very glad that the great leader of the Senate, Lyndon Johnson of Texas, is here tonight to help us interpret the meaning of this victory. I can tell you that his reputation as a skilled craftsman and mechanic in this trade is fully warranted. He knows his political automobiles. And out of his warm and responsive heart and his clear-thinking head, he knows something much more important. He knows that the function of the Democratic Party is to go, not to seem to go. It is to go not in starts and stops, not in bursts of power and sputtering stalls, but to go firmly and steadily in the direction which the American people, by giving us this great victory, have commanded us to go.

The late Senator Robert Taft said that the function of the opposition is to oppose. With all due respect to that great Republican leader, I want to say that for Democrats opposition alone is not enough. We Democrats will oppose when it is necessary to oppose. But we shall oppose responsibly and we shall try to contribute constructively to the security and progress of the nation whenever and wherever we can.

To do that, we have got to have clearly in mind what we cannot do, as well as what we can do, under our Constitutional system. The administration alone can lead in this country. True, it is a fact

60

that it is going to change in 1960. It is going to change, however, only if we do what the American people have commanded us to do; it is going to change only if we do what we can do, not what each of us thinks he would like to do. What Democrats can do, what they must do, is to point out a constructive path for the Republican administration to follow. We have got to keep it working when it would prefer to relax. For the sake of the American people we must hold the hand of this Republican administration when it is perplexed. We must try to guide it when it loses the way. We owe that to the people who have entrusted us with a large share of the responsibility for running this government.

In specifics, we have got to try, as we have been trying, to get it started on the road to policies which may lead to a more durable peace. We have got to improve the administration of foreign aid and restore the decent image of the United States in so many parts of the world. We have got to see to it that this Republican administration keeps its nose to the grindstone of the social and economic problems which plague large parts of the nation. You know those problems — inadequate education and other unequal opportunities for millions, a disgracefully wasteful agricultural policy which sees mountains of decaying surpluses side by side with millions of people without enough to eat, high prices, millions of unemployed, the decay of urban centers, a lagging science, an antiquated and inequitable tax system, and a neglect of our older citizens. These and similar matters are the problems which confront us. To boot, we have to try to deal with them within the framework of a sleight-of-hand budget from an administration which last year gave us another such budget along with policies that helped to produce a $12-billion deficit in it.

We Democrats have a duty to try to make this administration work, not for the benefit of one, but for all sections of the nation and for peace. We have a duty to try to make this administration work, not for the benefit of the few but for the welfare of the many.

That is the meaning of November 1958. That is what the American people have asked the Democratic Party to try to do. I do not know whether we shall succeed. It is a monumental task to try to do anything with a Republican administration. Speaking for those of us who are in the Senate, however, I can assure you that we shall try our best.

April 8, 1959:

On flexibility and firmness in foreign policy

*The Cold War was the first war in history, of whatever tempera-
ture, to threaten the extinction of human civilization, such as it is,
and perhaps of humanity in general; Albert Einstein, for instance,
had remarked that World War IV would be fought with sticks and
stones. Under these circumstances, American and Soviet foreign
policies were based on a kind of gingerly circumspection. Diplomacy, faced with unprecedented risks, required the alertness and
flexibility that would approach today's problems with something
besides yesterday's hypotheses. The United States could not surrender cravenly to Soviet intimidation, but neither could it afford
emotional luxuries, such as doctrinaire rigidity or unyielding
hostility, in its efforts to deal with Soviet maneuvering. Yet, for
many Americans, these were luxuries hard to renounce.*

*Mansfield renounced them. In the continuing debate on foreign
policy he argued against self-induced paralysis and for rational
accommodation. What he condemned, chiefly in opposition to
the jingoes, was a rigid militancy in dealing with Communist
nations, as illustrated in a small but significant way by Secretary
of State John Foster Dulles' celebrated refusal to shake the extended hand of Premier Chou En-lai. What he proposed was
flexibility, a realistic recognition of Communist power (growing)
and objectives (limited), and a more civil attitude that might lead
to a relationship that would later be called "detente."*

*In January 1959 Nikita Khrushchev called for a conference to
negotiate a German peace treaty, to be followed by a summit
conference with Eisenhower. In response, a conference of foreign
ministers was held at Geneva in May and June; it ended essentially in their agreement to continue their disagreements. As a
result, the Eisenhower-Khrushchev summit conference in September turned out to be little more than a social, and occasionally
antisocial, visit to the United States by Khrushchev, ending with a
statement by the two leaders that they'd try to do better in the
future.*

In April 1959, a few weeks before the Geneva Conference,

Mansfield gave an address on foreign policy to the alumni associ-
ation of the New York University Law School, and a week later his
fellow Senator from Montana, James Murray, entered it in the
Congressional Record. *Murray's introduction is included here as*
a backdrop.

* * *

Mr. Murray. Mr. President, my distinguished colleague,
Senator Mike Mansfield, made an address of world-wide signifi-
cance in regard to foreign affairs at the annual dinner of the
Alumni Association of the New York University Law School on
April 8, 1959.

Montana is justly proud of her distinguished junior Senator.
His great ability and attainments in the national legislative field
have not only been recognized in Montana for many years, but
here in the U.S. Senate by his designation as majority whip.
Senator Mansfield is equally qualified in the field of international
affairs. His approach to world problems is always well reasoned
and sound.

In his address, . . . Senator Mansfield has outlined the changing nature of our problems and our dealings with the Soviet
Union. He has urged that the United States approach negotiations
with the Soviet with flexibility and with new ideas. He has urged
that the United States not maintain a cold, rigid, and conse-
quently brittle position that could lead only to intensification of
the cold war and even to hostilities.

So that members of the Senate may have the full text of this
splendid address available to them, I ask unanimous consent that
it be printed in the *Congressional Record.* . . .

* * *

Justice Frank, Father O'Reilly, President Newsom, Senator
Murray, Judge Valenti, distinguished justices, Commissioner
Kennedy, members of the bar, and, if there are any here other than
myself, fellow laymen, I feel overwhelmed by the generous words
of introduction. I am deeply grateful for them even though they
are undeserved. The introduction was so kind as to suggest that,

for a moment, Justice Frank had doffed his judicial robes in order to serve as counsel for the defense.

I appreciate his summation on my behalf more than I can say. For, in the midst of this distinguished legal gathering, I am in need of counsel. You see, as a layman I share the layman's sense of awe in the presence of the law, or perhaps I should say in the presence of lawyers. That may seem strange to you since, as you know, I have been helping to make laws for almost twenty years. It is one thing, however, to write the law. It is another to be face to face with those who can tell you in no uncertain terms what it is you have written. . . .

In a few weeks a conference on Germany will be held in Geneva. It will be a conference of the foreign ministers of the Western nations and the Soviet Union. Free Germans of the West and Communist Germans of the East will be present. This conference is likely to be followed by another in the summer — a conference of President Eisenhower and other Western heads of state and Mr. Khrushchev. . . .

I believe it is reasonable to say that decent men and women — in Russia and in Poland no less than in the United States or the United Kingdom — are not interested in propaganda conferences or face-saving conferences. They are not interested in conferences which merely restate platitudes on the virtues of peace. They are interested in conferences which will get on with the business of peacemaking. . . .

For us, the origins of these talks do not rest in Mr. Khrushchev's recent statements. The need arises elsewhere. It arises from the vast changes which have taken place in the world during the past decade; more particularly the changes which have taken place on the European continent; specifically, the changes which have taken place in Germany. . . .

Can we suppose for a moment that these changes — these vast, immeasureable changes and others do not compel changes in the relationships among nations? It is obvious that they do; they alter the facts of the situation with which the policies of this nation, of all nations, must deal if there is to be peace. Obviously, policies devised years ago, in another setting, cannot serve in the new situation which is evolving.

It is true that there have been some adjustments in the policies of all the principal nations to these changes. The question is, are these adjustments sufficient? And are they coming in good time? Unless they are, not only is there little likelihood of a genuine peace being achieved, but even the unspoken truces which have, heretofore, cushioned the principal points of friction in the world, are endangered. In the light of the worldwide transition of the past decade these unstable truces must either be altered by reason, by negotiation, sufficiently and in time, or, sooner or later, they will give way in conflict.

One of these points of friction, of possible conflict, exists in Germany. In fact, it extends throughout Central Europe. It is in this region that the military power of the two nations capable of ultimate war, the United States and the Soviet Union, are in the closest of contact. It is in this region, too, that most of the residual injustices of World War II are to be found.

For years now an unspoken agreement, an unstable truce has existed in this region. The shaky peace has rested on the avoidance of military incidents which go beyond the point of no return. It has rested on the acquiescence of the Germans, no less than of the Western Powers and the Soviet Union in a divided Germany and a divided Berlin. It has rested upon the acquiescence of ourselves and the peoples of Eastern Europe in Soviet military domination of that region.

For years this has been the reality, despite talk of unification of Germany, despite talk of liberation of Eastern Europe, despite Soviet threats and blandishments.

It has been a tolerable, if not exactly a comfortable, arrangement. What we have failed to reckon with, however, or at least to reckon with adequately, is that the pressures of change in the world and, particularly, in Europe and Germany itself have been building around this point whether we have realized it or not, whether or not we and the Russians chose to look at this reality. We have waited a long time to face this fact. I deeply hope that we are prepared to face it now and that it is not too late to face it now, in peace. . . .

We will endanger our own position and the prospects for peace if we become obsessed with the fascinating game of interpreting the ever-changing charades of Soviet policy. These charades may mean peace. They may mean war. They may mean neither peace

65

nor war. We can only assume as certainty that at any given time they can mean any of these possibilities and that we must be prepared to face any of them. What we can do, beyond this, if we would increase the prospects of peace, is to get clear in our own minds why it is that we stand firm in Germany, as indeed we must. Standing firm is not an end in itself. We stand firm in order to go forward toward a durable peace. If there is to be peace we, no less than the Russians, shall have to put aside the dangerous toys of the propaganda war, and the chips-on-the-shoulder of the cold war. We shall have to put aside both the grins and the frowns. We shall have to examine, and examine deeply, the problems of peace and see what is possible to do with them in the light of the new realities in the situation which confronts us. We shall have to apply, to these altered problems, new ideas. We shall have to bring these problems a renewed determination to respond to the deepest desire of our own people and of all mankind, a new dedication to the search for progress toward a durable peace.

June 14, 1961:

On the neutralization of Berlin

A major factual difference between Lyndon Johnson's and Mike Mansfield's majority leadership positions was that during all of Johnson's term a Republican was in the White House. Mansfield probably was expected, with a Democrat in the Oval Office, to act as a kind of vending machine, producing Senate votes when his button was pushed and standing quietly in a corner when not in use. But any such expectation ran counter to his concept of the Senate as an independent deliberative body with its own set of responsibilities, including advice to and restraint of the executive branch, especially in matters of foreign policy.

Furthermore, he had a right and a duty as a Senator to partici-pate in the Senate's discharge of those responsibilities, whatever his role as majority leader. And so, in June 1961, on the Senate floor, he offered some unsolicited advice on Berlin. Because as majority leader he was widely assumed to be acting as a kind of puppet spokesman for the White House, his proposal was inter-

preted by many political seers as a trial balloon, but this was belied not only by his own intransigent denials but also by the consternation his speech seems to have caused at the American embassy in West Germany, where it was greeted by cries, in English and German, of anguished alarm.

For about two years Nikita Khrushchev had been insisting, with his congenital flair, that all four occupiers should withdraw from Berlin, turning the Western sectors into a single "free and demilitarized" city, ripe for incorporation into East Germany. The allies had simply refused in favor of the status quo. Mansfield, like many others, considered this mutual intransigence dangerous. In his June 1961 speech, therefore, about a week after a civil but quite inconclusive meeting between Kennedy and Khrushchev in Vienna, he proposed that the U.S. and its allies suggest a possible way out of the impasse. Once again, what he was arguing for was a little flexibility. But like so many sensible, if debatable, ideas in international politics, this one never received the serious consideration that it deserved.

* * *

Mr. Mansfield. Madam President, as anticipated by the President, the talks in Vienna . . . swept away the chaff. They revealed to both Mr. Khrushchev and Mr. Kennedy the hard kernel of the problem. They revealed, too, that the problem confronts us in substantially the same form as it did when it first appeared more than two years ago.

I suppose we may regard the fact that the situation in Berlin is unchanged after two years, and that the crisis has been postponed for two years, as some sort of achievement. In early 1959, a military showdown appeared imminent to me, as it did to most observers, unless the policies and attitudes of a decade and a half would begin to change. The showdown did not take take place.

It was forestalled by an almost continuous round of subsummit and summit conferences and visitings back and forth and hither and yon. The crisis has stirred again from time to time during the past two years but it has not erupted. Because it has not, does not mean that it will not. If the present positions of the parties concerned remain unchanged, sooner or later this crisis postponed, this crisis avoided will cease to lie dormant. . . .

In these circumstances, we owe it to ourselves to examine the position which we have assumed with respect to Berlin. The leaders of the Soviet Union are obligated to do the same. Both sides owe it to the people of the world. The responsibility which we have, Madam President, and which the Soviet Union has, is not merely to reassert positions already assumed and obviously irreconcilable. The responsibility is to seek to determine whether or not there is a third way on Berlin which corresponds more accurately to the needs of Germany today, Europe today, and the world today — indeed, a third way which meets more fully the contemporary needs of both the Soviet Union and ourselves. . . .

The Soviet Union intends to withdraw from its World War II occupational responsibilities in East Berlin, and it insists that the Western powers must do the same in West Berlin. It proposes to turn over East Berlin to the East German authorities, presumably as part of a separate peace treaty with the East German government. It offers to join a guarantee of a new status for West Berlin as a free city within that state. And if I am not mistaken, Mr. Khrushchev has added to this position a further contention that the Soviet Union will come to the military aid of the East German authorities in the event that the Western powers refuse to accept this change and continue to assert their present responsibilities in West Berlin in opposition to the wishes of those authorities.

These two positions, then, form the substance of the Berlin crisis which is now dormant but which, at any time, may become active. We insist, in effect, on the continuance of the status quo in Berlin for the present and, presumably, until such time as Germany is unified. The Russians are intent upon changing the status quo in a particular fashion in the near future, regardless of the eventual solution of the question of German unification. . . .

We prove our courage, our steadfastness, our determination when we insist, as insist we must with all that insistence implies, that we shall not permit the Russians or anyone else to dictate unilaterally the terms under which this nation and its allies shall discharge the responsibilities which were assumed in Berlin in the wake of World War II. We shall prove little more than the inertia of Western leadership, however, if we insist that the status quo in Berlin is sacrosanct. We shall prove little more than the sterility of our diplomacy if we insist that the status quo at Berlin cannot be changed even by mutual agreement leading to a new situation, which is neither that which now exists nor the alternative which the Soviet Union propounds. It seems to me, Madam President, that if we are to be not merely courageous but intelligently courageous, that is precisely the course we must pursue. We must seek a third way in Berlin which may better serve the interests of all the parties concerned — of the German people no less than other Europeans, of the United States no less than the Soviet Union, and of that great stretch of the world with its hundreds of millions of people to whom Berlin is but a name, if it is even that. . . .

I do not believe, Madam President, that the way to peace can be found either in the maintenance of the status quo in Berlin or in the change which Mr. Khrushchev proposes. A third way may lie in the creation of a free city which embraces all Berlin — the Communist East no less than the free western segment of that metropolis. Let this whole city be held in trust and in peace by some international authority until such time as it is again the capital of Germany. Let the routes of access to this whole city be garrisoned by international peace teams. . . .

I realize, too, Madam President, that this approach may evoke no response from Mr. Khrushchev. But do Mr. Khrushchev's reactions, whatever they may be, release us from our rational responsibilities to ourselves and to the world in this situation? Do not those responsibilities require us to explore fully and vigorously any and all avenues of peace even as we steel ourselves for what must come if the way to peace cannot be found?

I make these suggestions, Madam President, as one Senator from the State of Montana, and I make them on my own responsibility. I make them in full recognition of the present position of this government, which, if it is unchanged, will be my personal position when all the words are exhausted. I make them, however, in the belief that this present position is not enough, even as the present Soviet position is not enough. Our present position on Berlin, even if unchallenged by the Soviet Union, leads on in a circle endlessly repeated it continues to recede from the changing realities of Germany and Europe, until it now promises to become at best irrelevant and at worst a stimulus to catastrophe. . . .

April 2, 1962:

On U.S. support of colonialism in Africa

To a dismaying extent, the United States allowed itself during the Cold War to be maneuvered into the position of supporting colonial powers in their efforts to continue their suppression and exploitation of native peoples in Asia and Africa. To a similar extent the Soviet Union managed to portray itself as the champion of exploited peoples and the avenging scourge of a hastily retreating colonialism.

In the early sixties much of the action was in the Congo, where the native people were busy with expelling the foreign but resident burglars. In April 1962 Mansfield took the occasion to urge the Senate to consider the awkwardness of contemplated U.S. colonial entanglements in Africa and to work for a policy of allowing native peoples to solve their own problems and of helping them under the relatively nonpolitical aegis of the United Nations. His statement was both insightful and prophetic. It was also greeted as courageous by Vermont's Senator Aiken on the Senate floor.

Its effect on American foreign policy, of course, cannot be measured. That policy has shown more restraint in Africa than in Asia. But certainly the effect was not as great as Mansfield would have wished. In November 1964, in the final days of colonialism in the Congo, the United States supplied planes to evacuate the last-ditch white settlers out of the Congo that they had assumed they owned. And early in 1976 the Ford Administration managed to put the United States on the side of South Africa's unsavory white oligarchy in the fighting in Angola.

* * *

Hopes rise and fall with respect to developments in the Congo. A road to an orderly and progressive future for that region opens one day only to be blocked the next by seemingly insurmountable obstacles. The problems of the Congolese transition are dumped suddenly on the United Nations to the tune of universal acclama-

70

tion. Just as suddenly discordant notes are injected into the tune.

It is late in the day for this Congress to raise a question of this kind. I do so, however, because almost imperceptibly, but deeply and rapidly, this government is moving into involvement in the affairs of the Congo and Africa. Acts of the Senate are a factor in this trend in policy and, hence, the Senate shares in the responsibility for the form which the trend assumes. . . .

It is clear that colonialism is rapidly disappearing as a political system in Africa. What is not so clear, but what may be of even greater significance, is that colonialism as a political propellant has not yet left the scene. The word still has the capacity to evoke a militant nationalism, and even racism, in Africans. Its capacity in this respect may increase before it begins to decrease. That is likely to be the case so long as any part of the African continent remains under alien jurisdiction. It is likely to be the case so long as any independent nation of Africa, now dominated by European settlers, has still to evolve a workable system of government under which the peoples of varying races can live together in a reasonable acceptance of one another. It is likely to be the case until a free Africa persuades itself that it is a full and equal participant in the general affairs of the world.

The persistence of this political propellant may or may not be valid in logic. What matters from the point of view of policy, however, is that it exists in fact and is likely to continue to exist for some time. A policy which, in concept or administration, ignores its existence rests upon a most fragile foundation.

Beyond the persistence of the factor of colonialism, there are other political realities in the African situation with which our policies must reckon. It is now apparent that the stability of the colonial system was imposed from without at the price of a large measure of social atrophy within Africa. The basic mode of existence for great numbers of Africans today differs little from the pattern of an earlier time with its multiple tribes, multiple languages, multiple customs, values, and superstitions. Furthermore, the political boundaries which colonialism drew in Africa were more a consequence of power adjustments among European nations than expressions of natural divisions and of human forces within Africa itself. Yet it is within these boundaries that African nations today are emerging into independence.

71

I do not make these observations in criticism. What is past is past and cannot be undone. I point to these factors because they are significant in the unstable situation with which our policies must deal during this period of transition in Africa. There will be strong pressures to pull apart the outwardly imposed political unities and to revert to the schismatic earlier pattern. The sophisticated nationalism of a handful of African leaders will not easily be transferred to the many. These leaders themselves will have to search for ways to reorder boundaries into new political units, knowing as they do the requirements for a durable statehood in the modern world. To a considerable extent this search can be fruitful and beneficial. Other consequences, however, may also be anticipated if the search becomes aggressive or if African leaders pursue concepts of pan-Africanism on the basis of a militant racism.

That brings me to still another significant factor in the African situation with which we must deal in policy. To a degree perhaps unparalleled since the revolutions of independence in the Americas, the great political transition in Africa depends upon a handful of trained and experienced leaders. And unlike the simple world of the Americas at an earlier time, Africa is being propelled, in independence, into the modern world of instant communications, missiles, nuclear power, and complex bureaucratic organization.

Few Africans have been introduced as apprentices, and even fewer as managerial participants, in the affairs of the modern state, the modern economy, and the modern world. Yet many must learn rapidly if, to the bare bones of independence, there are to be added the sinews of economic and political organization which will give that independence beneficial meaning and durability for the people of Africa. The problem is not simply one of replacing the European colonial bureaucracies with UN and other bureaucracies and, then, with an African bureaucracy in the same form. However much replacements of this kind may be unavoidable for the present, the deeper problem is the development of responsible African government and responsible African management to guide the African peoples to a way of life suited to their needs, and, at the same time, capable of peaceful, free, and constructive cooperation in the general progress of mankind.

72

The task which confronts an emerging Africa is monumental. Much will depend on an understanding and patient hand from the rest of the world. But even more will depend upon the dedication, the wisdom, and the realistic restraint of those few Africans who are now assuming the reins of political power. They, more than anyone else, will make the decisions that set the patterns, for better or for worse, for the new way of life in Africa.

I turn now to the last significant factor in the African situation with which I wish to deal at this time. I have already noted that Africa's future is partially dependent upon an understanding and patient assist from the rest of the world. There appears to be a great, a universal eagerness to lend a hand in Africa. We see it clearly in the Soviet Union and China. We see it clearly in Cairo. We see it clearly in Europe. We see it clearly in this country and in the United Nations.

What we do not yet see clearly is the nature of this hand. Certainly there is a human and sincere desire — and I am sure it exists among the people of all countries — to help those who for too long have been cut off from equal participation in the mainstream of human civilization. But is that all there is in the extended hands? Is there not also a certain eagerness to project into Africa the many ramifications of the cold war and other power rivalries which now plague the rest of the world?

The field is wide open for that game at the moment. Africa is in transition, and its leadership has only limited experience. But transitions are not forever, and those who have learned the way to national independence are equipped to learn other matters. Most important, I believe the emerging African peoples have had enough of the role of pawns moved on the chessboards of others. They will not meekly assume that role again, and they will react against those who seek to return them to it.

It may be too much to expect, but it is not too much to attempt to insulate an emergent Africa from the international political and ideological storms which now sweep the rest of the world. In any event, I believe that policies, in concept or administration, that deliberately seek to project these storms into Africa will redound neither to the benefit of the African nations nor even to the long-range interests of those nations which pursue them....

If we in the United States are to deal effectively in policy not

73

only with the situation in the Congo but, in truth, with developments throughout Africa, not only must we see our interests clearly but we must pursue those interests in the light of significant factors of the kind I have been discussing today. Our interests are not hard to define. They arise, first and foremost, from the universal implications of the historic American doctrines of freedom. And men and women in Africa today are striving for freedom and its meaning for them. They may struggle awkwardly and ineptly, perhaps, and sometimes even blindly, but, nevertheless, the struggle is authentic.

Furthermore, American citizens have modest cultural and commercial ties with Africa, and the prospect for the improvement of the ties are good as Africa develops in freedom. These, too, constitute American interests.

Finally, we have an interest in human progress in peace in Africa. We have that interest in part because we cannot — and no people worthy of the name human can — close our eyes to the desperate travails of a vast segment of the human family. We have it, too, because the peaceful progress of Africa is interrelated with the peace of the people of this nation in this second half of the twentieth century. We have this interest because, if Africa can progress in freedom and peace, it will spare us the extension of the costly trappings of the cold war to still another continent. . . .

We cannot answer for others in this connection, but we can look to our own policies on Africa and their administration. In the light of the analysis which I have attempted today, I would suggest that our policies must flow from the following principles.

First. This nation should give its support, diplomatically and otherwise, to the end that independence and human equality will eventually be achieved throughout Africa. Our support must go, as it has begun to go under this administration, to those who work soberly in Africa for these ends. May I say, in all candor, that this principle grows easier to maintain with consistency and dynamism as the nations of Europe with whom we are associated in other matters increasingly espouse it in their own African policies. The difficulties, however, are great and will remain great in those areas in Africa of heavy European settlement, and I do not wish to make light of the task of those who must conduct our policies affecting those areas.

It seems to me particularly important that this principle find expression in the character and conduct of our expanding network of embassies in the new African republics. I hope that these establishments will be kept modest in size and character. I hope, further, that our official representatives will seek a fresh and full understanding of the situations which they encounter, based upon direct and broad contact with the peoples of these new nations. I hope, finally, that these embassies will be conducted in a manner which reflects the simple good will of this nation toward the new republics of Africa and our sympathetic appreciation of their struggles. In sum, it seems to me of the utmost importance that now, at the beginnings of contact with the new Africa, our official representation be kept free of those characteristics which would invite a deflection of the political propellant of colonialism to this nation.

Second. In the absence of overriding considerations to the contrary, this nation should use whatever influence it can against a centrifugal fragmentation of existing political units in Africa. However powerful the divisive forces of an ancient tribalism may still be, they are the forces of the dying Africa; they are not the strengths of the Africa that is struggling to come into being. May I say that to hold to this principle is not to stand against adjustments in present political boundaries. Such adjustments are to be anticipated and are to be encouraged if they lead to more practical political and economic units. We should resist these tendencies, however, if they derive either from a narrow tribalism or a sweeping racist pan-Africanism.

I realize that these particular problems must be dealt with primarily by the African peoples themselves. There is every indication, however, that the United Nations may be drawn increasingly into them. Since that is the probability, we must be prepared to exert our influence affirmatively in that organization on the side of modern political progress in Africa.

Third. We should recognize that the hopes for freedom and progress in Africa during this period of transition depend, perhaps, more on the caliber of men than on the forms of governments, and we should lend a most understanding ear to those African leaders who, with sincerity, personal dedication, and realism, seek to move their nations forward.

We must learn, quickly, as much as we can about the emergent African leadership, and, if we are to learn accurately, will eschew such inapplicable frames of reference as pro-Communist or pro-Western. The leadership that matters for the future of Africa will be neither the one nor the other. It will be pro-African in the finest sense of the term in that it will be dedicated to the welfare of its own peoples and will drive soberly but relentlessly to increase their capacity for survival and expression in the modern world.

Fourth. We should join with all nations so inclined in an effort to lend a genuinely helpful hand to the vast needs of Africa for training in modern skills and for prompt economic and social development.

If Africa is to make the most of this help and if the rest of the world is to gain from it in terms of peace, then it seems to me that this help must go to Africa free of any extension, expressed or implied, of the power conflicts and rivalries which divide the world. The challenge of Africa is not a call to greater propaganda battles between us and the Soviet Union. The challenge of Africa is to the world. It is a challenge to help open in peace the doors of modern life for the peoples of Africa, for their benefit and for the still unfathomed benefits which may flow to mankind from that opening. . . .

I do not know if it will be possible to bring into being the beginnings of a constructive and cooperative approach to Africa along the lines of the suggestions which I have advanced. There is little ground for sanguine expectations. Nevertheless, I believe we should make, in policy, an effort of this kind. We should make it with all diligence and all sincerity. We should make it in our own interests, and in the interests of the emergent African peoples, and in the interests of the peace of the world.

June 3, 1962:

On foreign policy and the

realities in Latin America

An area in which Mansfield developed considerable expertise, and for which he developed considerable concern, was Latin America. Although he could understand, and indeed shared in , the United States' preoccupation with pressing problems else- where, he consistently deplored the fact that this generally has been an area of unstudied neglect in the practice of U.S. foreign policy, with occasional and not always desirable exceptions like the "protection" afforded by the Monroe Doctrine, the acquisitive war with Mexico, the building of the Panama Canal, the inconsis- tencies in dealing with Cuba, the surface scratching of the Al- liance for Progress, and the undercover meddling in Chile. Partly as a member of several Senate delegations, he traveled exten- sively in Latin America, becoming familiar with the age-old prob- lems left over from the days of Iberian domination.

In June 1962 he gave a commencement address at Stonehill College in Massachusetts that demonstrated not only his intellec- tual grasp of conditions in Latin America's multifaceted society but also his very human sympathy for the plight and the aspira- tions of the destitute millions struggling under the suffocating burden of callous plutocracies. The address even included a thoughtful defense of physical violence, or at least a plea for an understanding of it, although violence, even verbal violence, was something that he assiduously avoided in his personal and polit- ical life, whatever the provocation. (It also included some rare personal remarks.)

* * *

I appreciate deeply your kindness in inviting me to be with you today and the honor which goes with it. You who have just finished four years of work will understand the special charm of a degree which is obtained without the completion of a single course requirement. In the circumstances, one might even forgive you a touch of envy, if the good fathers will permit me to say so.

In a more serious vein, I appreciate this opportunity to be with you for a personal reason. This visit evokes deep and poignant memories. Many of you, I am sure, were acquainted with Professor Brassil Fitzgerald. Years ago he taught at Montana State University even as in recent years he taught here at Stonehill. I came to him at a somewhat advanced age for a college student. I was 27 years old when I entered Montana University. It was not so much that I was a slow learner. At least I hope it was not that I was a slow learner. Rather, I think it was a case of stubbornness. In those simpler days of high rates of illiteracy, it was commonplace to believe that any youth over the age of 12 could learn at least as much outside of school as in it. It took many years to convince myself of the fallacy of that belief.

So I went back to school, somewhat sobered by hitches in the Army, Navy and Marine Corps, work in the copper mines, and an assortment of odd jobs. I might note that my greatest career advancement in all the years from dropout to back-in was from private to private first class in the Marine Corps.

Professor Fitzgerald was one of my teachers at Montana University. I do not know for what reason — perhaps because he was also stubborn; perhaps because he had a scientific interest in me as a prototype of the contemporary school dropout problem; perhaps because he sensed that I would tax his great abilities as an educator to the utmost — but, whatever the reason, he gave me far more than a formal education. He not only sharpened my grammar; he sharpened my wits. Most of all, he helped me to form a far more adequate perspective on human affairs and to develop a sense of self-discipline in participating in them. He drew on the wellsprings of his own good and great character in order to give me breadth, depth, and direction.

His counsel, in class and out, together with that of my wife, set the basic pattern of my career in public life. So in reality it is this early contact with Professor Fitzgerald to which my presence among you today may be traced. You will understand, then, the sense of sweet sorrow which I feel in being here, a feeling which I know Mrs. Mansfield, who was also taught by Brassil, shares. For my career, which Professor Fitzgerald did so much to launch, has now led me to this place where he ended his career just a short time ago.

In life, Brassil Fitzgerald gave me some of my most decisive experiences. In death, he leaves me some of my most enduring memories.

Among other things, Professor Fitzgerald encouraged my interest in Latin America. For a while I taught its history at Montana University. And in recent years I have traveled extensively in the republics to the south.

And so, partly in tribute to Brassil Fitzgerald and partly because Latin America is likely to be of compelling importance to you in the years ahead, I should like to turn your attention to that subject today. I have chosen Latin America, too, because it affords an opportunity to try to impart to you something of the kind of perspective in which Professor Fitzgerald helped me to view human affairs.

If, as most of us do, you skim the newspapers for your information on Latin America, you know that until recent years there has been very little news. Events in Cuba, of course, acted to enlarge the flow of information. Still the composite picture of Latin America which emerges from news coverage remains flat and two-dimensional. It is like a photographer's montage of a handful of candid camera shots. I am sure that, as I describe some of these photographs, you will recall them. The mishmash includes a naked Amazonian savage complete with poison darts. It includes a child obviously suffering from malnutrition and other diseases. It includes a band of bearded revolutionaries, a snow-covered peak in the desolate Andes, an old and beautiful Spanish cathedral, an Indian in high felt hat standing beside a llama, a family of downtrodden peasants huddled together outside a shack of a home, a student riot led by Communists, a military uprising, rhumba dancers, the futuristic city of Brasilia and, most recently, a Peace Corps volunteer helping to build what appears to be a well in a remote village under a sign which reads "Alliance for Progress."

Now there is nothing inaccurate in any of these flashes. Each one, taken individually, is a scene from life in Latin America today. But to be familiar with these flashes, to lump them together as Latin America, is to understand neither the region nor what is transpiring in it.

We must ask ourselves, first, have we, with these and similar mental flashes, seen all the elements in the situation or just a part of them? Second, we must ask ourselves, do these flashes, each of equal size and shape, give us an accurate sense of proportion with respect to the region?

Let me illustrate to you, first, the kind of elements which are not reflected in this usual concept of Latin America. To be sure, there is malnutrition in the region. The picture of the little child suffering from it portrays the plight of too many men, women and children who are its victims. And there is disease — all sorts of disease, a good deal of which goes untreated. And there is illiteracy. And countless millions are housed in rural or urban shanty towns. In short, people in great numbers in Latin America are exposed to a life which is a continuous and bitter struggle for mere survival, from birth to death.

But there is also another side of the coin. Millions in Latin America are well-fed — in some places, very well-fed. Particularly in the large cities, there are excellent public health services, medical facilities, thousands of first-rate doctors and nurses. As for schooling, while it is appallingly inadequate in many areas, in several countries it is good by worldwide standards, and in at least some instances it compares with the best. It may surprise you to learn that, in a region of so much illiteracy, there are in the neighborhood of 400,000 college and university students and upwards of 50,000 will graduate from these schools during this present year. Some will become teachers, doctors, lawyers, engineers, scientists, and so forth. In other words, life will unfold for them pretty much as it will for you, except that it will have more of a Latin accent and, perhaps, offer less numerous and diversified outlets and opportunities.

Take another element in the stereotype of Latin America; the naked Amazonian savage. It tells us that there is a primitive kind of existence in the region. But does it tell us how small a part of the population lives in it? Does it tell us that, for the most part, the people of Latin America are more fully clothed than some of the tourists who walk through the Capitol during a hot Washington summer?

Or look for a moment at the picture of the magnificent Spanish cathedral, so much a hallmark of Latin American guidebooks. Do we see behind the magnificent cathedral? Do we see the thousands of parish churches of these Catholic countries? Do we see the thousands of hard-working priests in these simple surroundings? Do we see them laboring in much the same way as do priests in this country and the world, trying their best to minister to much the same needs?

Or look, too, for a moment at the revolutionaries, the student rioters, the military insurrectionists. Look at the tableaus of terror and violence in which the newspaper accounts freeze these scenes from Latin American life. And then look deeper. Do not isolate them in an empty background as a camera does. Do not view them in terms of our experience, in which many avenues exist for the peaceful redress of grievance, for the assertion of popular will. Look at them rather — if you would comprehend their meaning more accurately — in the light of certain political facts of life in Latin America. View them in the light of tyrannical governments which brook no peaceful opposition. View them in the light of ineffectual government which countenances widespread economic and social misery and offers no hope of alleviating it. Or view them in the light of careless and corrupt government which exploits the many for the personal enrichment of the few. To see the violence, abhorent as it may be, without seeing these other factors is to see without depth.

These are but a few of the gaps and the distortions in a two-dimensional comprehension of the situation in Latin America. If all the gaps were filled, if all the distortions were set aright, I dare say a somewhat different concept of the region as a whole would emerge. It would contain all these flashes plus many others. In proportion, moreover, some would loom very large and others would hardly show at all. Indeed, what would emerge would be a kind of curve of distribution. It would embrace just about all of the elements which are found in life in the United States, but in different proportions. The segment, for example, which we regard as social advance would be smaller. There would be, in Latin America proportionately, a much higher number of people without adequate food and shelter and modern services for their health, personal education, and development. There would be, proportionately, a much larger number of people living on, working on, and depending on the land for their livelihood and getting very little return for their efforts. The urban poor, proportionately, would be more numerous, the rich more conspicuous, and all in between fewer and less favored. There would be, proportionately, a much more limited development of modern science and industrial technology and an even more limited distribution of its opportunities and benefits among the people. There would be, proportionately, less geographic and cultural integration but more racial and religious integration than in this country. There would be, proportionately, less diversified and less productive economies. There would be, proportionately, less effective institutions, less responsible government in a popular sense. There would be, proportionately, much more fear of internal political upheaval but much less concern with international conflict.

But let me say again that these and other differences are differences of degree, not absolute differences. Just about the same great diversity of human experience and human hope which we find in the United States is present in Latin America. Proportions alone provide the significant variance.

And in this great diversity there exists in Latin America an enormous potential for advance in every aspect of human hope and aspiration. It exists quite apart from what we may or may not do in our relations with that area. Generally speaking, Latin America is not going to go forward on the basis of what we do or, indeed, of what any other country does. It is going to move, stand still, or retrogress primarily on the basis of what the Latin Americans themselves do or fail to do.

The Peace Corps worker building a well in a remote village is a lonely figure and, alone, can have little significance in a continent of thousands of remote villages and millions of neglected human beings. It is obvious that if the future of these villagers depended primarily on Peace Corps workers we would have to find them, and pay for them, not by the hundreds as we do now, but by the thousands and tens of thousands. Similarly, a great dam built under a foreign-aid program at a cost of many millions of dollars is but a speck on the rivers and streams of Latin America. It is obvious that if light, power, and irrigation are to be brought to all the areas of present and future need in Latin America under the aegis of foreign aid alone, it would take not millions or hundreds of millions but billions of dollars.

Similarly, a Latin American military force based heavily on military aid from outside will not automatically insure the security of a Latin American country or the freedoms of its people. On the contrary, it can become a source of insecurity to both unless it has strong roots in its own peoples and serves them through an effective and responsible civil government. Similarly, a Voice of America explaining the evils of communism, no matter how powerful and repetitive, will not be heard in a nation driven to the threshold of massive revolt by years of neglect and oppression. A diplomacy of moderation, of patience, will have little influence unless it is coupled with strong links of mutual interest in commerce, cultural enrichment, and the maintenance of peace.

Now you will note that in mentioning the Peace Corps, foreign aid, military aid, the Voice of America, and diplomacy, I have mentioned most of the means by which the United States conducts its official relations with Latin America. To them might be added the unofficial relations — the business and investment contacts which we have, the tourist contacts, the highly significant private educational, labor, and religious contacts.

Yet, even when these are added, what the United States does or does not do will not be the primary factor in what transpires in most of Latin America.

Do I mean to suggest, then, that these contacts are unimportant? Not at all. They are immensely important, to us as well as to Latin America. But I think it is essential that we see their role in proper perspective. It is essential that we recognize that, for the most part, they are peripheral to the situation in most Latin American countries. They are not, of themselves, the key to Latin America's future.

The key lies within Latin America itself and the inner forces, the native forces which play upon each national situation. You young people will understand that perhaps better than anyone else. You are subject to all sorts of influence from outside. Sometimes it is welcomed. Sometimes it is not. Sometimes you react favorably to it. Sometimes you do not. But, in the last analysis, it is from within yourself, from what you are and what you hope to be that your future will unfold.

In a somewhat similar fashion the Latin Americans will welcome guidance and advice from outside in some matters, and sometimes they will not. Sometimes they will welcome assistance and proffers of friendship, and sometimes they will not. Sometimes they will be misled by outside nations, and sometimes they will not. But in the last analysis what they do with their nations and societies will be what they themselves decide. In the long run, no other nation can make these decisions.

Once that fundamental reality is appreciated, we can place our own role in proper perspective. Without the conceit of assuming ultimate responsibility for what ultimately transpires in Latin America, we can do many constructive things in Latin America and together with Latin America. In many Latin American countries, there is a strong will to close the time gap in social and economic modernization as between themselves and the United States and other Western nations. There is a strong will to have done with long, sorry histories of oppressive, corrupt, and ineffectual governments and to evolve a new tradition of stability, responsibility, and responsiveness in government, a new tradition of dedicated public service for the benefit of all rather than the few.

Where such a will exists, it is not a question of whether change will or will not come. It is already in process. The significant question is whether it can come in orderly, evolutionary channels. If the pressures for change are great and the resistance to change is powerful, the prospects are for revolutionary explosions with unpredictable repercussions and reverberations. Cuba is an example of what can happen elsewhere in Latin America. Indeed, we have seen just in recent months situations of dangerously high pressures for change and dangerously high resistance to change in Venezuela and Argentina, and we are likely to see others. The balance is still uneasy and is likely to remain so in much of Latin America for a long time.

Do I suggest, then, that there is no role for us? On the contrary, I would suggest that the Alliance for Progress and other elements of our Latin American policy can be of the greatest importance. But I stress that they can be constructive, in any significant sense, only when the efforts of the Latin Americans themselves are clearly directed toward evolutionary progress. Then our policies and our actions may indeed provide a decisive margin. But to plunge into every situation in an indiscriminate fashion, on the assumption that it all and always depends on us, is as fallacious as to evade our responsibilities on the assumption that what we do really doesn't make any difference at all.

What we do does matter a great deal, for better or for worse. And we must try to make it matter for the better. For we have a great stake in what occurs in Latin America. There is a trade of many billions of dollars involved. There are very substantial investments. There are political and cultural ties which have much to do with whether this hemisphere and we as a part of it remain reasonably secure in a most insecure world.

But, beyond all others, we have a deeply human stake in the efforts of the peoples of these other American republics to build the institutions through which to fulfill, in order and stability, the promise of freedom.

We will be able to help Latin America, we will be able to act for better rather than for worse as we refine our perception of the realities of that region rather than beguile ourselves with the superficial. We will be in a better position to safeguard our interests as we act with a mature and sober restraint on the dictates of these realities.

I hope, certainly, that you will bear in mind this need for a deepening of our understanding of Latin America in the event your futures should carry you to that area in some official or unofficial capacity. I hope you will remember it even if your future association with Latin America should be limited to newspaper reading. For, as you deepen your understanding, you will be in a position to appreciate and to sustain those who have the heavy responsibility of trying to preserve and to strengthen inter-American relations for the benefit of all Americans, north and south, in the Western Hemisphere.

January 19, 1963:

On the responsibilities of Senate Democrats

Throughout his life Mansfield was loyal to the two-party sys-tem and to the Democratic Party within that system. He resisted any balkanization of American politics (such as Senator Eugene McCarthy and others in later years would try to introduce) on the premise that a democracy is viable only in an atmosphere of compromise – and that it can be suffocated in an atmosphere of doctrinaire intransigence such as characterized, for example, the chaotic French Third Republic.

His leadership of the Democrats in the Senate, therefore, was positive and conciliatory, according full recognition to the differ-ences bound to be expressed in a deliberative political institu-tion, but always stressing areas of consensus that would permit concerted action. All this was illustrated in the moderate tone of his brief address to the Democratic National Committee in January 1963, after the November 1962 midterm elections had somewhat increased the Democratic majority in the Senate and maintained the majority in the House. He was not seeking to turn adversaries, in either party, into enemies.

* * *

I am delighted and proud to be here with Democrats from the North, South, East, and West.

We represent the only real national party and, because of that, we represent a wide divergence of views.

It is our job to overcome, or at least alleviate, our differences to the end that the Democratic Party can remain a cohesive whole and our nation can continue to advance along the path of great-ness. To do that we must all work together to the end that we can elect our candidates at the city, county, state, and national levels in the years ahead.

This is what we must do in our own behalf, and the responsibil-ity rests not on you alone but on all of us, no matter what part of the country we come from.

We begin the 88th Congress with a Democratic President and an administration which has received the nearest thing to a popular vote of confidence that is possible under our system in a non-presidential year. It was not an overwhelming vote but it was a healthy Democratic vote, let there be no mistake about it.

To be sure, there were local and state issues which loomed large in it. But just about everywhere the Kennedy administration was an articulated and an implied issue. And the answer is clear. Throughout the nation, the people want the kind of government — a mixture of idealism and realism, the sensitivity to human needs and human possibilities — which the President himself personifies.

I know of no higher goals which the Congress, a Democratic Congress, can aspire to than to give the President every possible assistance through legislation in leading the nation in the direction which he indicated in his State of the Union message a few days ago. Certainly, as the Democratic leader of the Senate, elected by my Democratic colleagues from all sections of the country, that will be my primary purpose. We shall not try to steamroller the President's program. We shall not ask Senators to suspend their critical faculties. We could not do so even if we were so inclined, which we are not. There are still major differences with some elements of the President's program on the part of Democratic members of Congress, let alone insofar as Republicans are concerned. But there is also a great area of common agreement among Democrats with the President. That is the area which the leadership will seek out and encourage with a view to realizing as much of the President's program as possible.

Our goals in this Congress will most certainly center on the tax cut. The President has laid great stress on its need both in terms of its benefits to each American family and, even more important, in terms of putting a surge forward into the nation's economy. Conditions have been good in the nation but they have not been good enough. They have not been good enough to raise our sights to new possibilities and standards of excellence for all our citizens.

That is what is involved in a tax cut of the kind the President seeks, and in the Senate we shall do what we can to get it into legislation.

Beyond the tax cut, we must turn our attention to the special needs of older citizens and young people. In these areas there is too much callous neglect. In the case of older citizens we shall set out legislative goals to the end that they may live their years out not only free from the want of food and shelter but also free from the fear of impoverishing illness.

And as for young people, we shall do what we can to establish creative outlets for their energies both in terms of constructive service to the nation and constructive development of their capacities for their own sake. The key here is to open equal opportunities for education throughout the land, so that all young people may be educated in excellence to the limits of their capacity and determination. What it takes in the way of legislation to achieve these ends, that is what we shall seek.

Looking beyond the immediate, the legislative goals of the Democratic Party in Congress, as in the administration, shall be to seek in every possible way to bring this nation closer and closer to its ideals of equal opportunity for all Americans whoever they may be and wherever they may be in this nation.

And while we seek this goal we shall also endeavor to do our part in bringing this nation and the world closer and closer to a more secure peace. For it is upon peace in this nuclear age that all else depends. The President leads in this matter. He leads with intelligence and courage and restraint. In Congress we can perform no greater service than to support him in every possible way in this fundamental task of the nation and of all nations. A great President deserves no less.

May 23, 1963:

"A debt yet to be redeemed."

In May 1963 New York City's East Coast Memorial to the missing of World War II was formally dedicated, and among the speakers were the President of the United States and the senior Senator from Montana.

Mansfield's speech, characteristically, had less to do with dedication of a memorial than with the dedication of Americans to a firm resolve that "these dead shall not have died in vain."

It was the last such function that he and his good friend Jack Kennedy would participate in together.

* * *

It was not a long time ago, as time goes. It was scarcely twenty years ago when it all took place.

In the dawn and in the dusk and through the day, men and women went forth from this nation — to Africa, to Asia, to Europe, to the South Pacific, and to all the far places of the world. Week after week they went, and month after month, and year after year. . . .

They came, these men and women in the armed forces, from the farms, the mines, the desks, the work benches. They came from slum and suburb, from country and town. They came from Utah and New York, from Puerto Rico and Georgia, from all the States and places in the land. They came from the long-rooted strains of Americans and from those so new that even the English language was still halting on the tongue. They came in all colors, all faiths, all creeds. And they were welcome in all colors, faiths, and creeds. . . .

In the end, it did not matter who they were, what they were, what they did, where they had come from, or why. They became, all of them, the sinew and bone and muscle of a mighty arm of a nation. The nation's purpose was their purpose, and it was they who bore the great costs and dangers of that purpose through the long years of the war.

A common human hope joined these Amercans with others — the English, the Russians, the Chinese, the French, and many more. In the end, this massive force swept, like a great wave, over the ramparts of the tyrants. It tore loose a deadly weight from the minds and backs of hundreds of millions and flung it into the cesspools of history. . . .

Countless Americans were among those who did not see the bright flash of freedom and peace which swept the earth when the conflict ended. They died in all the places and in all the ways of war's death. Today most of them lie here in the earth of America or in a plot in other nations which is of this nation because they are there. But for others we cannot provide even a grave with a cross or a star to mark their last traces.

These are the missing, and it is they who have summoned us.

How much do we know of these missing men, we who stand here today? We know their names. We know the numbers they bore in the Army and Air Force, in the Coast Guard, the Navy and the Marines. But what do we really know of them? Do we know them as a wife, a mother, a father, a sister, brother, or friend might know them? For those close to them, each life lost was a star whose light was bright for a while and then, in a moment, ceased to burn.

We cannot know that world, we who stand here, that closed but infinite world of each man's circle. What we can know, what all in this nation can know, and all the world's people should know, is that these deaths are a debt yet to be redeemed. And those whom we could not even bury are of its pledge.

Let us not delude ourselves. We do not pay the debt with these words today. We do not end it with these stelae of granite pointed toward the sky nor with names struck upon stone.

We seek the words to praise these men, and they are wanting. We search to express our thanks to these men, and even the genius of the sculptor is not enough.

The debt remains unpaid. What we do and say here today is not needed by these men whom we honor. It is needed by us, ourselves. It is needed to remind us that the debt is unpaid, for these men whose names we record, and the countless others throughout the world whose passing was marked or unmarked, did not die for words of praise or memorials of stone. They died that those who lived might have a chance to build this nation strong and wise in justice and in equity for all, in a world free at last from the tyrants of fear, hate and oppression.

It was a long time ago, as time goes, that they died. It was not twenty years but fifty years ago — or a century, or a millenium. For they died not only on the Normandy beachhead but also at Verdun, at Gettysburg, at Valley Forge, in all the places and in all the times that the human right to be human has been redeemed.

If we would honor these dead, then — all of them — if we would praise them, if we would repay them, let us ask ourselves what we have done with this chance which they have given us. And let us

90

ask ourselves again and again what we have done until there is, in this nation and throughout the world, the need to ask the question no longer.

September 4, 1963:

On the nuclear test ban treaty

By the early fifties the nuclear-test fallout problem had come to a head in all but the densest of heads. Atmospheric testing of nuclear weapons was fouling the earth's technologically irreplaceable blanket of air with such lethal isotopes as strontium 89 and 90, cesium 137, iodine 131, carbon 14 and tritium, most of which were turning up in the world's water, milk, meat, fish and vegetables. The Eisenhower Administration had been seeking a treaty with the Soviet Union and others to prohibit all but underground testing, and in 1952 both the Republican and Democratic party platforms contained strong pledges to continue the effort.

The aversion to atmospheric testing, however, was by no means unanimous. Some influential people in the military-scientific-industrial complex, or cabal, and their spokesmen in Congress argued that the contamination was a small price to pay for testing weapons that might possibly, perhaps, conceivably give the United States military "supremacy" for the forseeable future. They were therefore appalled when, in July 1963, the U.S., the Soviet Union and Great Britain agreed on a treaty banning all nuclear testing except underground.

In the U.S. the treaty had to be ratified by the Senate to take effect. It fell to Mansfield, after weeks of grueling committee hearings, to sum up for the defense. He did so in a carefully organized and reasoned yet wit-sprinkled floor speech described by Senator Hubert Humphrey as "one of the most definitive, moving, and persuasive statements that I have heard during all the many days of testimony and the many years of hearings relative to the possibility of a treaty to ban nuclear tests."

In addition, Mansfield's experienced understanding of the throes of decision-making led him to open with an oblique state-

91

ment on that process. In its expression of sympathy for both sides of the debate and its recognition of the fallibility of human judgment, it could well serve as required reading for the young, inexperienced and doctrinaire. (The treaty went into effect in October 1963.)

* * *

Mr. Mansfield. Mr. President, for several weeks the Senate has had the proposed treaty on nuclear testing. The question has been examined intensively not only by the Committee on Foreign Relations but also by members of the Armed Services Committee and the Senate members of the Committee on Atomic Energy, all of whom were invited to participate in the hearings, and all of whom collectively comprise more than one-third of the membership of the Senate.

There has been in process, in short, a very thorough Senate consideration of the proposed treaty. The specific questions have already been asked and answered, as far as it has been possible to answer them. The specific doubts have been raised and, as far as possible, laid to rest.

We are now approaching a point at which we must put the penultimate question in solitary conscience. It is this decision which will produce the final vote by which the Senate will either give or withhold consent to ratification of the proposed treaty. . . .

This penultimate question which confronts us is simply stated: Does the proposed treaty serve, on balance, the interests of the people of the United States, when those interests are considered in their totality? Or to put it negatively: Is the proposed treaty, on balance, inimical to the interests of the people of the United States?

If it is inimical, obviously, the President should not have had the treaty signed in the first place, and certainly the Senate should not now consent to its ratification. But if the treaty passes even a minimal test, if reason tells us that, on balance, the treaty is not inimical to this nation, then that alone would seem to be sufficient grounds for approving it. For if we mean what we say when we speak of supporting the leadership of the President, irrespective of party, in his great national responsibilities in foreign relations, we must mean at least that in matters of this kind we are inclined to give him the benefit of those vague and residual hesitancies by which each of us in his own way may be possessed.

And may I add, Mr. President, that I do not see how any Senator can vote either for or against this treaty with a sense of absolute assurance. In any major essay in foreign relations there are bound to be, and there should be, hesitancies. They would be there if we debated the proposed treaty, or any major issue, a month, a year, or a decade.

There were doubts and hesitancies when a Republican Congress voted a Marshall Plan under a Democratic President. There were doubts and hesitancies when a Democratic Congress voted a Middle East resolution under a Republican President. The doubts are there year in and year out when Congress considers the foreign aid program. For the simple truth is that there are no certainties, no absolutes in significant matters of foreign relations.

Indeed, were there no doubts on this question of a nuclear test ban, that in itself would be cause for the deepest concern. For the absence of any doubt would suggest either a dangerous delusion or an insipid insignificance in the treaty. . . .

Mr. President, the search for a nuclear test ban treaty was clearly a cardinal element in the foreign policy of the nation during the second Eisenhower administration. When Mr. Kennedy assumed office, he did not have to continue that search. He could have abandoned it. He could have ignored the efforts of the previous administration. He could have turned his back on the affirmations in favor of a nuclear test ban treaty, as they were contained in the platforms of both parties during the 1960 Presidential campaign, and upon which Mr. Kennedy and Mr. Nixon stood for office. That is a prerogative of the Presidency, and Mr. Kennedy could have exercised it had he judged, after a full examination of all relevant information, that the policy was detrimental to the interests of the nation.

But Mr. Kennedy did not so find. On the contrary, he pursued the matter even as Mr. Eisenhower had done before him. And he continued to pursue it in spite of repeated setbacks and frustrations not unlike those undergone by his predecessor, until an agreement was at last initialed by his distinguished agent, the

Under Secretary of State, Mr. Averell Harriman, on July 25, 1963. . . .

Further, Mr. President, when members of the Committee on Foreign Relations and the Committee on Armed Services and the Senate members of the Joint Committee on Atomic Energy probe every word, comma and period of the text of the treaty, when they examine every conceivable implication of the treaty for days on end, when they hear countless relevant witnesses from the executive branch, including the Secretary of State, the Secretary of Defense, the Joint Chiefs, the Chairman of the Atomic Energy Commission, and the Director of the CIA give sober but unmistakable support for this treaty, when the committees summon for testimony not only the advocates of this treaty but also its most articulate and competent opponents — in short, when the treaty is subjected to the most stringent Senate committee scrutiny and the great preponderance of informed testimony is favorable — there is strong presumption that the treaty is in the positive interests of the United States. . . .

And yet, Mr. President, a strong presumption is not enough in a matter of this kind. Each Senator has an individual responsibility to examine this treaty for himself in the light of his own conscience and his own concept of the interests of his state and the nation.

The Senator from Montana has done so, and he has just returned from reporting to the people whom he represents on his position on this treaty, which will be before the Senate very shortly. And having done so, he is persuaded that the proposed treaty does no violence to, but on the contrary serves, the interests of the people of his state and the nation.

It serves those interests, immediately and tangibly, in matters of public health as they may involve a resident or a child yet to be born in Montana or in any one of the fifty states. I refer, Mr. President, to the question of radiation which, as an uninvited but ever-present spectre, has haunted these hearings of the past few weeks. To be sure, there may be a lack of certainty among scientists and doctors on the precise effects of manmade radiation on health and the human species. But let there be no mistake about it. There is a minimal concept of the dangers of radiation from which reputable scientific and medical opinion does not depart. It is

94

expressed very clearly in the unanimous report of the United Nations Scientific Committee on the Facts of Atomic Radiation, 17th Session of the General Assembly, 1962. . . . It is a most conservative statement, and one must question the sobriety of anyone who would pass off the factor of radiation damage as irrelevant or propagandistic in the consideration of the proposed treaty. It is of central importance. For what the statement says, in effect, is that we do not know precisely how harmful manmade radioactivity is but we are certain that it is not good for human health or for the genetics of the human race. It is not good, in short, for men, women, and children — and particularly children — in Montana, Arizona, Ohio, Washington, Nevada, Mississippi, Utah, or Missouri any more than in London, Paris, Moscow, Peking, or Tokyo. What the statement says, in effect, is that radiological technicians in hospitals do not wear heavy protective clothing and dentists do not shelter themselves for the fun of it when they take X-rays. They do so because the stuff of X-rays, as of nuclear bomb tests, is insidiously dangerous. What the statement says, in effect, is that it is highly inadvisable to put even minute quantities of strontium 90 or 89 into milk or to add other radioactive isotopes such as iodine 131 or cesium 137 to bread, as though they were vitamin A, B, C or D. They are quite the reverse in their effect on human health and on the human species. The statement says, in short: Handle manmade radioactivity with extreme care, or, preferably, do not handle it at all.

Yet we have been compelling our own people to handle it, as well as the Russian people and others, and the Russians have been compelling their people as well as ours and others to handle it. That has been the consequence of bomb tests because, beyond the radiation released in proximity to a test site, the phenomenon of fallout results in a wide distribution throughout the world from each detonation, wherever it may occur. And radioactivity is both ideologically neutral and wholly indifferent to national boundaries. When carried in the air currents and clouds of the atmosphere it places free peoples, Communist peoples or whatever, all on this planet, in the same radioactive boat. . . .

Mr. President, it is clear that, however small the effects appear to be in the statistical computation, nuclear bomb testing has already caused damage to human health and its continuance is potentially a great danger to human health. It is so clear that it can be said in this Senate that we will not find one reputable scientific voice that will advocate the continuance of bomb tests on the grounds that they are a kind of fillip for human health or a genetic stimulant for the improvement of the human species.

Therefore the fundamental, if unspoken, assumption of the treaty must be that neither this nation nor the Soviet Union seeks the dubious distinction of being the foremost contaminator of the earth's physical environment with radioactive substances. It is the assumption that the Russians are at least rational enough and human enough to be concerned with this menace to the health of their children and their grandchildren as we are with respect to ours.

Those may be erroneous assumptions. It may be, I suppose, that the Russians are so obsessed with being first that it is all the same to them whether the race has to do with the Olympic games, the moon, economic growth, the ballet, or radioactive contamination. It may be that this obsession is so strong that they are prepared to sacrifice even their progeny to it.

Even if it were so, even if the Russians were indifferent to the pollution of their own place, along with every other nation's place, in the earth's environment, then all it would signify is that this treaty has little meaning. It would signify that the treaty will not do much good. But then, with the safeguards which are provided and assured, neither will it do much harm.

For what would happen, Mr. President, if we ventured on the assumption that the Russians did not wish to menace the health of their own people any more than we, and then events proved us wrong? At some point in the future the Russians would resume atmospheric and marine testing. But would they not be able to do that in the absence of a treaty? What is to stop them? And if they resume this dubious process of denaturing the physical environment of mankind, what is to stop us from joining in this macabre competition once again? Not this treaty, Mr. President. There is nothing in this treaty which would stop us in those circumstances. And it has been made very clear in the hearings that we intend to rejoin this competition on very short notice if it is forced upon us. . . .

To be sure, Mr. President, there are other nations — France and

China in particular — which, health factors notwithstanding, have already announced that they will not adhere to this treaty. Such states will remain legally free to test nuclear weapons in any environment. But without this treaty such would still be the case. Even at the worst, these countries cannot conceivably pose, for many years, anything remotely resembling the kind of threat to human health which is implicit in a resumption of unrestricted nuclear testing by the United States and the Soviet Union. With the treaty effectively maintained between the United States, the Soviet Union, and the United Kingdom, we will have at least a period of respite which in itself will be of some worldwide health benefit. And with the adherence of the great bulk of the civilized nations of the world — over eighty nations have already signed the agreement — there will be an opportunity for a vigorous and concerted search for additional ways to make the treaty universal in its application.

Mr. President, let me emphasize that there are no grounds for sanguine expectations that this treaty, even if it is ratified by this nation, will bring an end to the more dangerous types of nuclear testing. It is a tangible hope, that is all. But against that tangible hope there is certain despair. In the absence of this treaty, the process of radioactive contamination of the environment by bomb tests will continue and in all probability intensify. Past experience indicates that deploring these tests in speeches and party platforms will not end them. Introducing Senate resolutions against them will not prevent them. Passing resolutions in the UN General Assembly will not inhibit them. Voluntary moratoriums will not stop them. All these experiences, short of a treaty, have been tried and they have not succeeded. The inescapable fact is that not only this nation but every nation is still completely free at this moment to wreak damage not only on its own heritage of the earth's environment but on that of every other people. And the inescapable fact is that the fear of losing a technological military advantage or the hope of gaining one — this terrifying fear and this elusive hope — which in the past have impelled the Russians no less than ourselves to overlook the hazards to human health in these tests will almost certainly compel us to do the same in the future. We shall be so impelled, and they shall be so impelled, unless this treaty enters into force and is scrupulously maintained on both sides. The likelihood — I venture to say the certainty — is that, without this treaty, the danger to the health of all Americans, of all human beings, from bomb-made radioactivity will multiply. Neither an embarrassed silence nor a soft-pedaled evasion of experience and fact changes the reality one iota. . . .

There is one ground, one ground alone, on which the Senator from Montana would be prepared to go home and tell the people who sent him to Washington and tell them that these tests in the atmosphere and in the seas must go on despite the great potential threat of their continuance to their health and their children's health. . . . To ask them to accept the health risks, he would have to find, in the total record, specifics for concluding that the risks of military attack would be significantly increased by our adherence to this treaty. He would have to find, in specifics, affirmative answers to the following questions.

First. Is there some nation other than the Soviet Union — Communist China, for example — which, by not adhering to this treaty, is likely to develop a nuclear technology which will approximate ours in the next decade, another nation which could close the nuclear gap solely because it tested and we did not? The answer is "No."

Second. If the Soviet Union, then, is the one nation which poses a nuclear threat to the United States in the next decade or more, has that nation already achieved a substantial advantage, on balance, over the United States in the military technology derived from nuclear physics, the kind of advantage which we might neutralize by continuing aboveground tests on our side, even though they also continued to improve their techniques through such testing on their side? The answer, insofar as it is possible to answer the question, on the basis of fact, knowledge, and the overwhelming judgment of the most highly skilled and qualified witnesses in the nation, is "No."

Third. Is there any reason to assume that our advances in nuclear science and its applications to military technology will be hampered to a greater degree than those of the Soviet Union in the complete absence of atmospheric and marine tests on both sides? The answer is "No."

Fourth. By the terms of this treaty, will the Soviet Union be legally authorized to do anything which we are not also authorized to do? The answer is "No."

Fifth. By the terms of this treaty are we legally forbidden to do anything which the Soviet Union is not legally forbidden to do? The answer is "No."

Sixth. Is there any other than the most remote possibility that the Soviet Union could engage in significant but prohibited tests without detection? The answer is "No."

Seventh. If the Soviet Union were to engage in a clandestine test and if it were identified, or if we had very valid reason to believe that such a test had occurred even if not identified, would we ourselves still be bound to forego a resumption of testing above ground? The answer is "No."

Eighth. Is there a significant possibility that a single Soviet test suddenly sprung upon us could so alter the balance of military forces between the two nations as to increase the risk of military attack upon us? The answer is "No."

In short, the answer to every specific doubt which involves the possibility of the Soviet Union or any nation gaining some unique or significant military advantage as against ourselves in this treaty is not "Yes," but "No." For this reason I cannot in good conscience ask any citizens of Montana to accept the heightened risks to the health of their families which will be inevitable in the absence of the ratification of this treaty by the United States.

If there are not specific grounds of unique disadvantage to the military defense of the nation for rejecting this treaty, what other grounds can there be? One detects in the few articulate opponents of this treaty a consistent theme which suggests a basis for the remaining doubts and hesitancies. It is, apparently, the belief that our scientific-military complex is so superior to all others that, if not subjected to any limitation as to nuclear testing, it will produce an amazing advance in nuclear military technology. The complex, it is suggested, will achieve some incredible breakthrough so as to widen, once and for all, the gap between ourselves and the Soviet Union. That the Soviet Union, of course, in the absence of a testing limitation, will also be free to seek a similar breakthrough is either overlooked or regarded as of little consequence. That there are dangers to health in the continuing process of uncontrolled testing by both sides, of course, is either overlooked or regarded as of little consequence.

Mr. President, I have the highest respect for our nuclear physics, our industrial technology, our military leadership, and our capacity to merge them into a powerful complex for the purpose of the nation's defense. This complex is second to none in the world. But the admiration and respect for these capacities do not and must never compel the elected officials of this nation to accept the dictum of this complex as to what is best for the people of the United States.

The fact is that this treaty will introduce no curbs upon the creativity and dynamism of the complex which are not also placed equally upon such complexes in the Soviet Union and elsewhere in the world. That men of scientific genius or highly developed technological specialization may find such curbs irksome or burdensome is understandable. But there is too much at stake here, for the nation and for the world, for the Senate to be persuaded by individual considerations of that kind.

Indeed, reason and experience must lead us to question most seriously the course of policy which flows from such considerations. It is the course which assumes that if we will only continue to debar any restraints on testing, if we will only continue to throw considerations of public health to the winds, our scientists and our technicians will create that decisive nuclear gap, that ultimate military gap, which will insure the nation's security. . . .

So we must ask ourselves, Mr. President: What has happened in all these years of unrestricted testing? Has the gap widened with the free rein which has been allowed to the scientific-industrial-military complex? Have we gained the absolute advantage, the ultimate advantage which will guarantee the nation's security? The truth is that the gap has not widened. On the contrary, it has narrowed almost to the vanishing point. It has narrowed both in terms of the basic knowledge of the sciences involved and in terms of the application of that knowledge in military technology. Once no nation, except ourselves, could have inflicted on any other tens of millions of nuclear deaths in a matter of hours. Now we ourselves, no less than others, are subject to a catastrophe of this magnitude. . . .

Do not, Mr. President, look for miracles from this treaty. There are none. This nation, the Soviet Union, and the world are destined to live for a long time with feet dangling over the grave that beckons to the human civilization that is our common heritage. Against that immense void of darkness, this treaty is a feeble candle. It is a flicker of light where there has been no light.

The Senator from Montana will vote for this light, and he will hope for its strengthening by subsequent acts of reason on all sides. He will vote for approval of this treaty because it is, on clear balance, in the interests of the people of his state and the United States. He will vote for it because it is a testament to the universal vitality of reason. He will vote for it because it is an affirmation of human life itself.

October 25, 1963:

On compromise in a democracy

Mansfield's loyalty to the two-party system was, of course, only a facet of his loyalty to democracy and of his faith in the art of compromise as essential to democracy's survival. While he would not advocate pusillanimous compromise with such extreme dangers as the blitzkrieg intimidation of an Adolph Hitler, the aggressive tyranny of a Joseph Stalin, or the sneak assault tactics of an Hideki Tojo — or, indeed, the savage slanders of a Joseph McCarthy or the lawless gameplans of a Richard Nixon — he had steadfastly maintained that no short cuts from the route of compromise could be justified except as a last, unwelcome resort.

A willingness to compromise, in Mansfield's view, comes from a recognition of realities, of what can and cannot be done within what today is called the cost-benefit ratio. More importantly, he insists, it also arises out of a sincere respect for the patriotism, integrity and intelligence of those who happen to hold other, and even opposite, positions on problems demanding solution (except in the face of incontrovertible evidence to the contrary, a rare eventuality). He could wax quite eloquent on the subject, as he did in a speech to the Montana Education Association in October 1963.

* * *

It is with great personal pleasure that I meet with you today. I have enjoyed a long affinity with the Montana Education Association, as a teacher in fact, and in retrospect over the years.

When I was asked to speak today, several topics were suggested. The one entitled, "Compromise in a Democracy," caught my attention at once. That is not strange, since the word "compromise" is very often associated with the word "politics" as equally noxious terms. But if that view had predominated in our history, this nation would not have known an orderly evolution. Indeed, without the constant exercise of compromise, a popularly responsive and responsible government such as we know could not exist.

We have learned through experience that compromise is an essential ingredient of a government by consent. The history of our own state is a good example. The tradition of our early years, as you well know, is accented with violence. Many of our pioneers were veterans of the Civil War, and our early history reflects some of the vindictive aftermath of that conflict. Vigilante law and the quick draw, not compromise and due process, were an early and accepted way of dealing with differences. In honesty, however, I suspect that the actual casualties which resulted from this approach in all the early years of the state's settlement do not equal the current output of death by violence in a week of TV westerns.

We have come some distance since those early days. Officeholders today are no longer removed by hanging but rather by the more refined, and presumably less painful, process of the ballot. I, personally and understandably, regard this as a great achievement.

One of the keys to this transition has been the general recognition that an orderly society is inconceivable in the absence of the will to compromise. To say this is not to defend those instances in which compromise represents an abuse of public power and a violation of public trust. But I do say that the view which tends to hold compromise in contempt is a most unfortunate one. And it does not matter whether this view is applied in a local setting, in state or national politics or, indeed, to international problems. For it is but one step from the disdain of compromise to the application of the opprobrium of appeasement or "sellout" to all who practice this essential art of political, indeed of all, human relations. And to cast aspersions upon the efforts to solve, by compromise, problems which defy the simple solution is to invite chaos. And along with that chaos would come a return to the law of the vigilante and the quick draw — this in a world in which the first quick draw, in the final analysis, may be the last.

If there is anything which I have learned in more than two decades in Congress, it is that issues which have only two sides — and which can be disposed of largely on the basis of all right or all wrong — are for the most part either unimportant, old and settled matters or, more rarely, new questions which often have tragic implications. The declaration of war against Japan, for example, was passed in less than a day and with only one dissenting vote in both houses of Congress. It was a clear-cut issue, but it was also a tragic issue.

In Congress today most defense measures are also passed by nearly unanimous vote. The necessity for them is clear-cut and long established and remains essentially unchanged in the absence of significant change in the world situation. In every Congress, of course, we also pass many minor bills unanimously. But for the most part they involve the relief of a single citizen who in some way or other has suffered some obvious injury at the hands of the government or other matters of very limited implication.

But with respect to significant new issues, quick and unanimous agreement is unusual. There are just too many millions of persons in this country, too many groups and subgroups, whose interests are affected by the passage of legislation. Here are some of the more obvious divisions within our society.

There are ten distinct geographic divisions and countless subdivisions in the United States, each with its own peculiar problems and interests.

The last census showed 125 million people living in urban areas and 54 million in rural areas. The former stress that the government's resources and energies should be directed toward cleaning up slums, improving mass transportation systems, and a thousand other worthwhile goals. The latter call for greater investment in conservation, more emphasis on strengthening the agricultural and livestock industries, and so forth.

Over 20 million Negroes and numerous whites of almost every religious denomination ask for equality of treatment for all

Americans in all walks of life and demand that it be given today. Other millions resist this effort and urge, in effect, that there be a slowdown in the process of applying with greater equity the promise of the Constitution to all citizens.

There are more than 18 million persons over 65 years of age, many of whom are living out their final years in poverty and fear of financially catastrophic sickness. They ask that the rest of the nation consider their past contributions, if not the future to which we are all headed, by providing a self-respecting and adequate system of insurance against the major financial hazards. Yet there are some — and I would hope not too many — Americans who would begrudge any such system to older citizens, especially if it is under the general control of the Federal government. But how, otherwise, it might be adequately provided is not made clear.

On the other end of the age spectrum, there are some 70 million persons under the age of 20. Their needs, if we are to look to a stable national future, include adequate access to higher education, commensurate with ability. They include in many parts of the nation sufficient classrooms and teachers at all levels of education. And they include action to open up jobs, to end ill-advised or avoidable school dropouts, and to develop a sound, well-rounded national approach to the mounting delinquency problems of our young people. And no one knows better than educators that the term "juvenile delinquency" covers a complex multitude of factors which will not be dispelled simply because we have assigned them this glib name and then wrung our hands and deplored the name.

There is, too, as still another aspect of our national diversity, the endless conflict of industrial interests among themselves and with agricultural interests. Poultry raisers in Georgia and beef producers in Montana and their Congressmen and Senators, including me, watch with growing concern the rising imports of their products into the United States. Detroit workers who owe their living in part to the export of automotive parts fear that tariffs which we impose will bring retaliation against them.

The government sustains prices for raw cotton production in order to help one set of farmers. The cotton is disposed of at bargain terms abroad in order to keep the stockpiles from mounting too high. The bargain-term cotton is manufactured into various textiles abroad and, when some of these are exported to the United States, we face the complaints of our own textile producers in New England or, indeed, in the same states where the cotton is grown. And so it goes. We do the best we can to deal with these inconsistencies while at the same time, through compromise, we seek to strike some measure of equity for all parts of the land and for all groups in the economy.

In the political arena, the monopoly by the Republicans and Democrats leads some to suppose that there are only two well-defined parties in the nation. But there are other political and quasi-political bodies competing for public acceptance, and there are repeated divisions and alignments within each party. It is significant, for example, that in the vote in the Senate on ratification of the Nuclear Test Ban treaty, 25 Republicans joined 55 Democrats in support of the treaty while only 8 Republicans joined 11 Democrats in opposition.

Anyone who has had the opportunity to travel the length and breadth of this great land cannot but be amazed by the tremendous vitality in its diversity. This quality contributes much to our strength and our greatness. At the same time it is a major souce of the need for compromise. All of the diverse interests must somehow be contained within a broader concept of national interest. For, in the last analysis, there is no future for agriculture in this nation unless there is also a future for industry, and the reverse is true. There is no future for the Negro if there is not also a future for the white, and the reverse is true. There is no future for Montana if there is not also a future for the other states, and the reverse is true. In short, the diversities of interests must in some way find, through compromise and mutual restraint, a common meeting place in the national interest and a common hope in the nation's future. Unless they do so, the immense strength and vitality of the whole may be exhausted in the bitter schisms of the parts.

The nation has grown great and is great, in short, precisely because we have learned the art of compromise. It has given us a powerful unity which undergirds our position as a nation in the world and provides stable progress at home. Throughout our history, only the Civil War yields an example of the overwhelming and devastating rejection of the process of compromise. That one exception came when the passion of various groups for their own point of view grew so overweening as to foreclose rational reconcilation among them. And, even today, we are haunted by this failure of a century ago. Problems which otherwise might long since have been resolved are still with us. And we have still a difficult way to go before the racial and sectional fears and suspicions and misunderstandings — the grim heritage of that one great failure — are finally laid to rest, as one day they will be.

We would do well to consider some of the factors which complicate the art of mutual accommodation and make more difficult the tasks of this nation. There are two which stand out and which have a special urgency for us today. I have touched upon one of these already. It has to do with the apparent compulsion of some to insist that the simple solution can be applied to every problem — no matter how complex it may be. The other is the tendency of many Americans to question the motives or loyalty of those with whom they disagree. Both tendencies have long existed in mankind. But the complex life of the twentieth century has sharpened them — and at a time and under conditions when the nation can least afford them.

The shrinking of distance, the greater mobility and forced association of peoples who a short time ago would never have come into contact with one another, the increased urbanization, the growing population, and the increasing impersonalism of our economic organization have all contributed to an atmosphere of greater anxiety and insecurity. And over all hangs the ever-present specter of devastating nuclear conflict, although just a few weeks ago we witnessed a glimmer of hope in this connection with the signing of the Nuclear Test Ban Treaty.

It is not surprising, then, that there is a nostalgic desire on the part of many to cling to the belief that a return to simpler days, days of the relative isolation of individuals, communities and states, is a choice still open to us as a nation. I can understand this desire. Indeed, there are days when I share it. But the front page of any morning's newspaper is enough to dispel it. The added pressures within the nation and the awesome dangers from without make it more imperative than ever that we seek solutions that take full cognizance of the complexities of modern life in this nation and in the world. If we are to succeed in finding solutions, we must draw into a common pool such wisdom and sensitivity as

106

may be available in all parts of the nation, in all political parties.

We cannot read any able citizen out of the community simply because we do not happen to agree with him politically. We cannot arbitrarily decide, as some have done, that an American as distinguished in his service to the nation as former President Eisenhower or his Secretary of State, John Foster Dulles, were not only useless but even worse — virtual enemies of America. If these men were not worthy of bearing the name Americans, then I am not and no person in this room is worthy of it. Who, then, is worthy?

The truth is that no single individual, no single group, no single political party has a monopoly on virtue or patriotism. None can lay claim to sole possession of all that is necessary to make our nation work. None has all the answers. But all are Americans, and each in his own way has a contribution to make which can be made only if we have a measure of mutual respect and mutual restraint and accommodation.

The democratic process, the practice of compromise, does not necessarily provide perfect answers. But it has supplied and will continue to supply suitable answers, and the only answers suitable, to a free people.

It does not matter whether the place where these answers are sought happens to be the Congress of the United States or the City Council of Missoula— or, for that matter, the PTA or the MEA. The problems facing Congress may be more complex. The decisions made by it may affect far more people. But, in the final analysis, in the House of Representatives it is almost 440 men and women, and in the Senate it is 100 men and women, meeting in a face-to-face situation, trying to do the best they can to serve the interests of the states and the people whom they represent. There is nothing to keep Senators from pulling the government apart in this process — nothing, that is, except self-discipline, mutual respect, tolerance for the views of others, and a willingness to compromise. The system is far from perfect, and the answers which it produces are not necessarily always the best. Nevertheless, the institution is bound together by the desire to safeguard and advance particular interests in the context of the total national good. It works largely because individual Senators are prepared not to press their concept of what is 100 percent perfect 100 percent of the time.

When a Senator is elected to the Senate leadership, he remains the Senator from Montana or Minnesota or Illinois or California. His primary responsibility is unchanged. Unless he serves the people whom he represents, he cannot serve the nation.

To put it another way, leadership responsibilities in the Senate are not assumed at the expense of state responsibilities. They are an addition, not a subtraction.

The function of leadership in the Senate is to help to operate a principal branch of the Federal government and to keep it geared into the other branches on behalf of the people of all fifty states. In practice, this means a great deal of work in concert with the President and with the Speaker of the House in an effort to see that what needs attention gets attention from all concerned. It means regular conferences every Tuesday morning with the President, and other meetings as critical issues of foreign or domestic policy arise. It means planning with the other Senate leaders — minority and majority — with committee chairmen, and with individual members for the legislative program. It means cooperation, understanding, and accommodation with my distinguished Republican counterpart, Senator Everett Dirksen of Illinois, because, if this is not forthcoming, the Senate would find it difficult to function as effectively as it has. The leadership's first function is to communicate the President's sentiments to the Senate and to make known the Senate's tendencies to the President. The follow-through involves the process of achieving the practical. It means riding herd on legislative measures, from their inception through the committees to the Senate as a whole and, long hours thereafter, on the floor until some disposition is made of these measures.

Presidential proposals may be voted up or down or modified in the Senate. But significant issues presented by the President warrant, as a minimum, the courteous but independent consideration of the Senate, and a decision one way or the other. To bring this about, the leadership has only the persuasiveness of the Presidential proposals themselves, the patriotism and the reasonableness of the members of the Senate, and the interest of the people of the states in the President's program. The leadership has no special powers to lead. It has only such respect and cooperation as may be freely bestowed upon it by the Senate as a whole.

Power is widely diffused in the Federal government, and it is widely diffused in the Senate. Each Senator, including the majority leader, has one vote, no more and no less, on every issue. Insofar as the Senate is concerned, it operates 99 percent of the time on the basis of the procedural cooperation of every member. The 1 percent of the time when it does not so operate accounts for almost all of the ridicule and criticism which from time to time throughout history has been directed at the institution.

By changes in the rules it may be possible that operations in the Senate could be improved. But, in the last analysis, the key to its effectiveness will remain where it always has been — in the voluntary restraint and the courteous behavior of each member and, where necessary, accommodation and compromise. There is no other way to function in a body of such individualistic men and women, each equal in his Constitutional power. On the whole, the Senate has functioned effectively by this process. In the last Congress a great deal of significant legislation was considered and disposed of. Before this Congress expires, the great bulk of the program now before us will be considered by the Senate, and much of it will be enacted. The achievement will reflect credit not on the leadership but on the members of the Senate of both parties and on the way of life of the nation which has produced a capacity for a cooperative unity and accommodation in diversity in its great institutions no less than in our society as a whole.

I have emphasized the legislative branch of the government because it is most familiar to me. But these observations apply, to a considerable degree, to the executive branch of the government. Too often we forget that the President of the United States is only a human being faced with a superhuman task. Every time he makes a significant decision, a thousand and one pressures are directed upon him from all parts of the nation as well as from abroad. And he, too, must think in terms of the accommodation of these pressures to the end that the nation stays on an even keel and moves in an orderly and unified progress. The President, too, does the best he can on the basis of patriotic dedication to the nation — and that applies, may I say on the basis of my personal observation for two decades, no less to President Eisenhower than it does to President Kennedy and to the Presidents who preceded them.

109

In these remarks I have tried to emphasize that the words "compromise" and "politics" are not in themselves unsavory terms, but rather that they are the staff of freedom. Successful compromise is as necessary as the air we breathe. This is true for all aspects of government, from the smallest community in Montana to the Congress and the Presidency of the United States.

I have every confidence that we will continue to exercise the good will toward one another and the moderation which have done so much to make this nation great. And while the TV westerns will continue to awaken a warm and an understandable nostalgia for the simpler days of the frontier — especially since we do not have to bear their hardships in the comforts of our living rooms — I have every confidence that Americans also recognize that the real frontiers of our modern world now lie on the fringes of outer space. We will think and act as we must in order to live and prosper in this changed setting even as the frontiersmen thought and acted in consonance with the realities which they encountered and with which they lived and prospered.

As educators, I can think of no way in which you might better prepare the youth of the state for a responsible, useful and satisfying life than to help them to understand what the nation and the world today are really like, and to emphasize to them the place of compromise, mutual accommodation, and tolerance in making both run in freedom.

November 5, 1963:

On the factions in South Vietnam

After 1957, in Vietnam it grew increasingly clear that the political leftovers from the French colonial cuisine tended to stick in the craw of the Vietnamese man in the street and in the rice paddy. One need only recall the contrast between the ascetic-looking Ho Chi Minh and Premier and Mrs. Nguyen Van Thieu, who in 1975 escaped from Saigon with ten tons of treasured luggage, to remember the United States' uncanny knack for picking the wrong end of the horse.

An earlier entry was Ngo Dinh Diem, another spiffy dresser who also gave the impression of being simply a dark-skinned, olive-eyed Frenchman. When his regime was dealt a series of military reverses in the early sixties and the people of South Vietnam began to grow restless, the real Diem crept out from behind his democratic facade and set up a police state, complete with martial law and news censorship. And so, on November 2, 1963, he was killed in a military coup which introduced four years of musical chairs played by similarly Frenchified panjandrums. At the time American military personnel numbered about 15,000 — three times as many as a year before, though only 3% of the number to be reached five years later.

Mansfield, with his devotion to self-determination and his anxiety over the risk of quagmire entanglements, urged that the U.S. government not indulge in any paroxysm of retribution over the elimination of Our Boy, as Diem was thought of by some of the more devout believers in Manifest Destiny. Diem was not our boy, Mansfield hastened to assert shortly after the coup, and the United States should beware of identifying itself with any particular Vietnamese political faction. South Vietnam, he contended, could not be sustained indefinitely through an umbilical cord 8000 miles long.

* * *

Mr. Mansfield: Mr. President, the recent events in Vietnam are tragic events. It is tragic that a leader who began by accomplishing so much that was constructive with so little, that a government which began with so much promise, in the end crumpled in military coup and violent death, a situation which I deeply and personally regret.

When news of these events first reached this city, it seemed to me that their primary significance to the United States was clear. They were a clarion call for a reassessment of U. S. policies with respect to Vietnam and southeast Asia. For the government which fell, up until a few months ago, had been generally regarded for years, I so felt, as indispensable in the structure of American policy in southeast Asia. We will fail to heed this call only at the risk of great danger to the future of our relations with all of Asia.

111

We will not serve the interests of the nation if:

First. We regard the overthrow of the Diem government as a victory or defeat for this country. It is neither. It is more an inexorable development in the tragic postwar history of the Vietnamese people.

Second. If we reassume that the successor military-dominated regime is an automatic guarantee of a permanent improvement in the situation in Vietnam. This successor authority in Vietnam is, at this point, at best a promise of something better. But if the Korean experience is at all relevant, it is apparent that such promises can be undone in short order.

If these tragic events of the past few days are to have constructive significance for this nation as well as for the Vietnamese people, we would be well advised to recognize that the effectiveness of our Asian policies cannot be measured by an overthrow of a government, by whether one government is "easier to work with" than another, by whether one government smiles at us and another frowns. In the last analysis, the effectiveness of our policies and their administration with respect to the Vietnamese situation, and indeed all of southeast Asia, can only be weighed in the light of these basic questions:

First. Do these policies make possible a progressive reduction in the expenditures of American lives and aid in Vietnam?

Second. Do these policies hold a valid promise of encouraging in Vietnam the growth of popularly responsible and responsive government?

Third. Do these policies contribute not only to the development of internal stability in Vietnam but also to the growth of an environment of a decent peace and a popularly based stability throughout Asia — the kind of environment which will permit the replacement of the present heavy dependence upon U.S. arms and resources with an equitable and mutual relationship between the Asian peoples and our own?

This is indeed an appropriate time, Mr. President, for the executive branch to reassess policies for Vietnam and southeast Asia in these terms. It may well be that few changes, if any, are required at this time. But if that is the case — if indeed the problem in Vietnam has been primarily one of an inadequate government — then, Mr. President, we should begin to see results in the year

112

ahead. We should see

>*first*, a reduction in the commitment of U.S. forces and aid in Vietnam and southeast Asia;
>
>*second*, the emergence in Vietnam of a responsible and responsive civilian government attuned to the needs and the reasonable aspirations of its people;
>
>*third*, an improvement in the relations of Vietnam with Cambodia and Laos; and
>
>*fourth*, a growth in mutual commercial, cultural, and other friendly intercourse between the people of this nation and the various Asian peoples.

These are basic tests, Mr. President, and it remains to be seen how they will be met not only in our own relations with the successor authority in Saigon but with all the nations of southeast Asia. From the point of view of this nation, it would appear appropriate to reiterate at this time what the Senator from Rhode Island (Mr. Pell) and the Senator from Delaware (Mr. Boggs) will recall that we stated on our return from a visit to Vietnam and southeast Asia less than a year ago:

>It must be clear to ourselves as well as to the Vietnamese where the primary responsibility lies in this situation. It must rest, as it has rested, with the Vietnamese government and people. What further effort may be needed for the survival of the Republic of Vietnam in present circumstances must come from that source. If it is not forthcoming, the United States can reduce its commitment or abandon it entirely, but there is no interest of the United States in Vietnam which would justify, in present circumstances, the conversion of the war in that country primarily into an American war, to be fought primarily with American lives. It is the frequent contention of Communist propaganda that such is already the case. It should remain the fact that the war in Vietnam is not an American war in present circumstances.

That conclusion, Mr. President, in my judgment would apply to the successor government in Saigon no less than to its predecessor.

November 6, 1963:

Senator Dodd on Senator Mansfield's leadership

Everything has its price. The price of Lyndon Johnson's dazzling manipulation of the Senate as majority leader was an ever-growing resentment against his tactics, which included his use of the leader's presumed prerogative to keep the Senate in session until exhaustion won the day for his viewpoint. It was not uncommon, especially during filibusters, to see Senators of all ages and physical conditions answering quorum calls at all hours of the night and in various stages of dishevelment, some with pajamas showing under their outer clothing. Twisted arms were not so conspicuous, but they were there.

Mansfield as majority leader was temperamentally and philosophically unable to use such demanding tactics. He had too much respect for the dignity and the deliberative role of the Senate, too much concern for his colleagues (some of them old and unwell), to act like a headmaster of a school for juvenile delinquents. For him, humane goals could not justify inhumane means. The price for this viewpoint, of course, was a reduction in Senate "discipline," which became most noticeable whenever the Senate lay becalmed in the legislative doldrums. Such occasions are especially frustrating because Senate doldrums can be accompanied by high winds, but winds too directionless to budge the ship of state.

To a large extent this was the situation in the 88th Congress early in November 1963. The 87th Congress in its first ten months had passed nearly 700 bills, a record for which Mansfield had received no resounding plaudits. In the equivalent period the 88th had passed only about 250 bills. This quantitative difference was dismaying to many Senators, especially to mavericks like Wayne Morse of Oregon, Jacob Javits of New York, William Proxmire of Wisconsin, and Thomas Dodd of Connecticut.

On November 6, at the end of the legislative day, the Senate was coming to the end of eight enervating days of debate on the foreign aid bill. President Kennedy had asked for $4.5 billion, which had been laboriously whittled down to $3.8 billion only to be cut *another $75 million in a liberal revolt led by Morse. Everyone was tired and edgy and ready to go home.*

Senator Dodd – a Democrat and a Lyndon Johnson fan who was to be censured four years later for allegedly using political contributions for personal expenses – picked this moment of general prostration to launch an attack on the leadership not only of Mansfield but also of the minority leader, Everett Dirksen of Illinois. Neither leader was in the chamber, and the teapot tempest had to be contained by the two whips, Democrat Hubert Humphrey of Minnesota and Republican Thomas Kuchel of California. Dodd, whose sole answer to Senate stalemate was longer hours on the floor (prostrate or otherwise), began his verbose and rambling discourse (much abbreviated here) with praise for Morse's role in the debate on the foreign aid bill.

* * *

Mr. Dodd . . . . In my judgment, the Senator from Oregon has rendered the Senate a great service. I consider him to be one of the intellectual bright lights of this body. I want him to understand that I am in no way critical of what he is doing. I believe he would be the first one to say that I am right, and that the Senate should be sitting longer hours. Many times in my service in this body the Senate met at 10 in the morning and sat through until 12 midnight. Why are we not doing so tonight?

I am conscious of the fact that my statement will be construed as criticizing the leadership; and indeed I am. I wish the Senator from Montana were present. He should be leading the Senate. The Senate should be in session longer hours, and be working harder.

Mike Mansfield is a gentleman, Senators, we are of one mind about that. There is not a kinder, more gentle, or more understanding member of this body than the Senator from Montana.

But I worry about his leadership. He must assume it. If we are to accomplish the business of the Senate, he must behave like a leader. Because a leader is one who leads. He must say "No" at times; he must say "Yes" at times. But he must be a leader.

I remember when the present Vice President, Lyndon Johnson, stood there.

I used to tell my friends in Connecticut, when they asked me,

115

"What kind of a leader is he?" that he reminded me of an orchestra leader. He stood up and blended into a wonderful production all the discordant notes of the Senate.

I am not critical of my friend from Montana in a harsh sense. I am critical in a gentle and, I hope, helpful sense.

One cannot be a leader and be every man's leader. One must say "No" sometimes. He must say "Yes" even when it hurts to say "Yes." I wish our leader would be more of a leader and lead the Senate as it should be led.

I am willing to have the Senate sit longer hours. I am confident my colleagues are.

Let us sit Saturdays. Let us sit nights. Let us get the people's business done. Let us stop the Wall Street attitude of 9, or 12, to 4 or 5 or 6.

We are not doing the people's business. We are being frivolous with the people's business. No wonder the Senate has been denigrated.

The whole Congress has been denigrated. The hounds who do not believe in free government or in the importance of the legislative branch are at our heels. We are worried about scandals that beset us. We are worried about criticisms that confront us. Our business is to revive in the people's minds the idea that the Senate is the best body in all the world to protect a free people.

That is my complaint . . . .

I repeat again, I wish the majority leader were present, because I know this will be construed as a criticism of him. It is meant to be. It *is* a criticism of him. I do not think he is leading the Senate as he should; and I believe we should have leadership.

Until we have, we shall go on dribbling our way through the legislative session, instead of doing what we should. . . .

I worry about the opposition. The opposition has become so complacent, so soft, that it does not make any sense. Most of the opposition I have made, to my own administration, should have been made on the other side of the aisle. But it is not made any more. The Republican opposition is so soft, so cozy, that it does not count for much. . . .

I believe the Senate should sit longer hours, and should start earlier. We should be fulfilling our promise to the American people. . . .

Mr. Kuchel. Mr. President, I do not have a better friend in the Senate than the Senator from Connecticut. I consider him an able Senator. I do not sit on his side of the aisle; I sit here with the Republicans. . . .

Because of a statement or two which my colleague from Connecticut made, let me on this occasion briefly say that no defense is necessary for the Republican minority. The minority, through its leadership, is trying publicly to tell the nation, each week, by our comments in the Senate, our position on public questions. . . . I am thankful that there are no straitjackets in use in the Senate. . . .

I said to our able majority leader the other day, when I observed my Democratic colleagues not at each other's throats, but certainly rather vigorously contending conflicting points of view, that I noticed an ideological disarray, which was being exacerbated during this debate. But let this *Record* be crystal clear as to my position on the majority leader. Mike Mansfield is a splendid American and an able exponent of the point of view of his party. And I salute him as the leader of his party in the Senate. He is not responsible for the cross-purposes at which our colleagues on the majority side labor on occasion. . . .

Because my counterpart on the majority side, my dear friend from Minnesota, the Democratic whip (Mr. Humphrey), desires to comment briefly — I underscore "desires to comment *briefly*" I yield to the able Senator from Minnesota.

Mr. Humphrey. Mr. President, I thank the Senator from California. . . .

I speak for one purpose, as I have indicated to the Senator from California. I wish only to say that Senators are really very fortunate in having as their leader a man of complete integrity, a man who has an outstanding personality of leadership, not with the stick, but with the mind, with the spirit, and with the educated, trained, experienced hand of a legislator.

I wish to be quite clear. There are many ways in which people can lead. Sometimes one leads through sheer dominance of personality. Others lead through the respect in which they are held by their colleagues; through the sense of affection and loyalty that comes from a warmth of personality and from understanding.

I know that others of my colleagues, on both sides of the aisle, would agree with me when I say that Senator Mansfield graces the Senate by his brilliant mind, his keen intellect, his unusual understanding of the legislative process, his sense of forbearance — which the position of majority leader requires more than any other position I can think of — and his deep appreciation of the many problems which each Senator has and which each Senator brings to his attention. . . .

Mr. Sparkman. I desire to make a comment in connection with the remarks of the Senator from Minnesota. I join him in what he has said. In the consideration of the bill now under consideration, the majority leader has given the Senate a demonstration of the very finest qualities of leadership. This has been a difficult bill to handle. Speaking of diversity of opinion, there has been a diversity of opinion throughout the Senate. There has been excellent leadership on both sides of the aisle. . . .

Mr. Dodd. I am greatly encouraged by the remarks of the distinguished assistant minority leader. I think we can look for more opposition. I am more encouraged by the remarks of the assistant majority leader, who assures us that we will have longer sessions. So something has been accomplished for the people. . . .

November 7, 1963:

Senator Mansfield on Senator Dodd's mutiny

On the following morning Mansfield and Dirksen entered the Senate chamber after reading Dodd's critique in the Congressional Record. The difference in their reactions is evident in the following excerpts from the Record for that day, the 7th. Dirksen, never one to welcome criticism eagerly, had been in an auto accident on his way to the Hill; his wife's foot had been injured, his hand had been lacerated, and his eyeglasses had been broken. His copy of the Record was waiting for him in his office; and reading it, as best he could, did nothing to restore his equanimity. As for Mansfield, he exercised his customary restraint throughout the colloquy, except fleetingly in a response to Senator Javits. At one point he even rose to Dodd's defense.

Mr. Mansfield. Mr. President, the work of this Congress would be no further advanced if, beginning in January, we had gone in at 8 a.m. every day, including Saturdays. It would be more likely to be less advanced because under the rules of this body the committees might well have been stopped from meeting while the Senate was in session.

The Senate Calendar, which represents the bills reaching the Senate floor and not disposed of, has not during this entire session contained more than a bill or two of great significance at all times. As the bills have reached the calendar, it has been the policy of this leadership to stay with them until they are cleared; and in this respect we have received the wholehearted cooperation of the Senate as a whole.

The work completed on the Senate floor has been substantial during this session.

Those who complain of the total legislative output would do well to look elsewhere than the Senate floor. On the Senate floor, the leadership — majority and minority — has a primary responsibility which it must discharge without any greater authority enjoyed by any other single member of this body.

Allegations have been made that the leadership is "dull and dreary." I must admit to the accuracy of that charge insofar as it involves the majority leader alone. Glamor is not the hallmark of the Senator from Montana. But I must say that the Senator from Montana, in twenty years or more of experience in the Congress, has operated on the principle that it is not the headlines, but the results, that count. And the results of the two sessions of the 87th Congress and the Senate's output to date in the first session of the 88th Congress require no apologies whatsoever.

I believe I speak with some experience when I say that the hours on the floor have been perhaps long and tedious, but not unproductive. No member who has been here consistently to attend to his primary legislative responsibility needs to apologize for the time he has put in this session — and without time-and-a-half for overtime. A Roman circus may make good newspaper copy, but it does not necessarily make for greater or better legislative output. So long as the Senator from Montana has anything to say about it, the operations on the Senate floor will be those of a body of mature men and women charged with a serious national purpose.

We will work on the floor when there is work to be done — when the calendar tells us there is work to be done. But we will not arrange sideshow sessions of the Senate for the edification of the press or in order that this body may give the appearance of being busy for the purpose of impressing the boss, the American people.

Mr. President, may I say that, if I had had my way — and I do not speak defensively — the Senate would have remained in session longer last week and this week than it did; and as long as there are amendments to be offered and amendments to be voted on, the Senate can and should be prepared to remain in session until late hours in the evening.

Mr. Dirksen. Mr. President, conforming to the suggestion of the majority leader, I shall say very little about the incoherencies that I have found, this morning, set out in the *Congressional Record.*

The brave crusader from the Nutmeg State on his white charger has great zeal for being here and getting on with the business, and he is not here. If he does not know that the Senate is in session, he ought to know it. So I will be prepared to suggest the absence of a quorum and see if he can find his way to the Senate chamber where the business is done. I shall withhold my suggestion of the absence of a quorum long enough —

Mr. Mansfield. Mr. President, will the Senator yield?

Mr. Dirksen. I yield.

Mr. Mansfield. The Senator to whom the minority leader has referred has been most assiduous in his attendance. He has been present as much as any other Senator, to the best of my knowledge. The *Record* ought to make that very clear.

Mr. Dirksen. Mr. President, what I said still goes.

Mr. Morse. Mr. President, I rise to speak in defense of the majority leader's record in the Senate.

I believe that the record is clear that on substantive issues from time to time the majority leader and I may be in opposition as to our positions on the merits of controversial proposed legislation. But there is nothing to which anyone can point that shows that the majority leader and the Senator from Oregon are in any conflict whatsoever in regard to the operation of the Senate under the able leadership of the Senator from Montana. I wish the *Record* to show that the Senator has extended to the senior Senator from Oregon unfailing courtesy, unfailing cooperation, and unfailing good will at all times.

Mr. President, I wish to speak for a moment about some of the accomplishments of the present session of the Senate about which the Senator from Montana is too modest to talk. We have made a good legislative record as far as Senate business is concerned in connection with proposed legislation that has reached the calendar. For unanswerable proof of the comment I have made, all one would have to do would be to take a look in the Senate calendar as of this morning. Yesterday I had printed in the *Congressional Record* the calendar of the Senate. As of yesterday the calendar contained a listing of fourteen bills. Not a single one of those bills could be considered a major bill which would call for long, major discussion in the Senate other than the foreign aid bill, which we were then dealing with and are still dealing with.

In fact, aside from the foreign aid bill, I do not believe there is a bill on the Senate calendar that would call for consideration in the Senate for more than two or three hours at the most. We could clear up the entire Senate calendar in a couple of days of sessions if we went down the calendar. That speaks more than I believe anything that can be said about the leadership of the Senator from Montana in handling the business of the Senate.

What that means — and he did not specify it, but I think it was clearly implied in the remarks of the majority leader — is that we should not look to the floor of the Senate to find out what is wrong — if anything is wrong in regard to the legislative record of the present session of Congress. I suggest that we look to the committees, where there are some major pieces of proposed legislation that have not yet been reported from committee. . . .

We have taken through the Senate, with the able assistance of the majority leader, a higher education bill and a bill on the vocational education that represent weeks of work of the Senate Committee on Labor and Public Welfare and long debate in the Senate. So today I rise in complete and total defense of what I believe has been a remarkable job of fine leadership that the Senator from Montana has given to this body at the present session of Congress, as he has given in the past.

Mr. Gruening. Mr. President, I believe neither the majority

121

leader nor the minority leader needs any defense. Although I am a comparatively recent comer to the Senate, I heartily approve of the character of leadership given the Senate by our majority leader and the quality of cooperation, and occasionally effectively presented dissent, given by the minority leader. I think it is unfortunate that any doubt as to the ability of the leadership of those two men should have been raised. I dissent from it completely. On the contrary, we have had a fine example of leadership. It is the kind of leadership that the Senate should welcome. It is a leadership that involves respect for the wishes of individual Senators and recognizes that their function in the Senate should be left to their consciences. That has been the policy of our distinguished majority leader. . . .

Mr. Javits. Mr. President, I should like to address a question to the majority leader based upon his statement that the calendar is clear. About three weeks ago we all understood that the Committee on Commerce has reported the so-called public accommodations section. All of that intervening time has gone by. It seems to me that an opportunity should be afforded to test out the time when the Senate should go into the civil rights debate, which opportunity could be afforded if that report were filed.

I should like to join my colleagues in saying to the majority leader and the minority leader that I do not believe there is any question about their good faith or their dedication to the tasks at hand in their endeavor to accomplish the business of the Senate, but I have a very strong difference with the majority leader as to when debate on the civil rights issue shall begin. . . .

Mr. Mansfield. Mr. President, in response to the question raised by the distinguished Senator from New York, may I say that even if the public accommodations bill is reported from the Committee on Commerce, it is not my intention to call it up. I repeat again what I have previously said. When the Senate faces the civil rights bill, it will face as whole a civil rights bill as possible. If a fragment of the civil rights bill is reported, we shall be here until doomsday.

Again I wish to say that I will not engage in any kind of Roman holiday or sideshow. When the Senate faces the issue, it will face it as a whole.

Mr. Javits. I should like to say to the Senator that if other

Senators differ with him, they should have the right to endeavor to call up the committee bill. If the bill is reported, as propriety would require, it seems to me, it would therefore appear on the calendar. Without its being on the calendar, we are deprived of an opportunity to call it up. The calendar may appear clear, but the fact is that there is a critically important bill in the wings which the Senate should have the right to decide whether it wishes to take up or not. The Senate may not agree with the majority leader. Knowing him as I do, I am sure he would be the first to say that the democratic processes which the Senate rules afford should at least be followed through.

Mr. Mansfield. Mr. President, if the Senator from New York wishes to take over the leadership of this body, he is welcome to do so, but as long as I happen to be the leader on this side, I have announced what the procedure will be, and it will be that as long as I am leader. . . .

Mr. Javits. The Senator from New York has no desire to take over the leadership. I believe that is a completely different question from the question of an opportunity to test out this very serious question. I hope that we shall see the bill to which I have referred placed on the calendar. I understand that it is fully ready for the calendar. I am very much puzzled by the fact that the report has not yet been filed.

Mr. Mansfield. I am not interested in a headline or an issue. I am interested in results. And if we want results — if it is at all possible to get results — the Senate will wait for the whole bill, and not merely a part of it. If we want a sideshow or a Roman circus, we will take up one segment of the civil rights bill and then let everything take its course.

Mr. Proxmire. Mr. President, I have not in past years been reluctant to criticize the previous leadership of the Senate. I have done so, and I have done so vigorously. But I believe that the present distinguished majority leader is absolutely right when he points to the calendar and says that if we dispose of the foreign aid bill we shall not have other pending legislation before us on which we could act for very long. I do not believe we can blame only the majority leader for holding up action in the Congress. . . .

Mr. President, I suggest that, if there is no one to blame here, we

123

certainly should get the facts and find out why proposed legislation is taking so long to reach the Senate. I believe that, under these circumstances, we always indulge in a round of back-slapping, and we say that no one is to blame, that everyone is doing a fine job.

I believe we have two wonderful gentlemen as leaders, both Democratic and Republican. The majority leader has been very courteous, friendly, and helpful to me on many occasions. But I believe all Senators should get the facts and find out what the situation is, and then move — not to remain in session interminably and be unable to finish our program competently.

Mr. Kuchel. Mr. President, sometimes, after most Senators have gone home in the evening, a few of us remain here, and strange things occur. I must say, very frankly, that I regret some of the comments which were made in the chamber last night.

Let me try to be constructive for a moment. Mr. President, do Senators know what is wrong with the Senate today? It is the archaic rules under which we operate. . . .

What is the situation? There still remains a miserable, despicable rule of filibustering, under which one or two or three or four or more Senators can frustrate the business of the U.S. Senate. It is because of the power that one or two or three or four Senators can exercise that even if we could put Paul the Apostle in the majority leader's seat he could not conduct the business of the nation in the Senate in the absence of general, perhaps unanimous, consent to go forward. We also lack, for a limited time each day, a rule of germaneness which would put each Senator on notice that the full attention of the Senate would be devoted to the pending business, whatever that might be.

I recognize that in the situation such as we have been in last week, yesterday, and now today in this chamber, there are honest divergences of view. We have on occasion similar divergences on this side of the aisle. . . .

Last night some of the divergences of view came forward. I am a Republican, and I want my Republican Party to do what I believe it is doing; that is, to act constructively . . . .I want my party, the Republican Party, to follow the leadership of this or any other administration when our party believes that leadership on a particular question represents the best interest — the national interest, the public interest — of all of the American people. That is what we have done in this debate. That is why I salute today, as I did last night, these two Americans — one a Republican and one a Democrat — one on our side and one on the other side — who are uniquely equipped by experience to know what they are doing, who arrived at a proposal that was so overwhelmingly — indeed, unanimously — approved yesterday in the Senate so that for the first time in many days some progress was made in this chamber. . . .

Mr. Dodd. Mr. President, I should like to call to the attention of the distinguished minority leader the fact that I am present.

Unfortunately, I was at a meeting and was unable to be present at 12 o'clock. I say this merely to show that I have been reasonably faithful in my attendance, commensurate with other duties.

I am not one who enjoys the role of critic, particularly when the object is the majority leader, or the minority leader, both of whom I respect and admire, and for whom I have deep affection. I join with all my colleagues who have made reference to their great characters, strong personalities, and generosity. I am well aware of it. I said it last night in this body. I could not say it too often.

That has nothing to do with the subject I discussed last night, which I should like to discuss at this time for five minutes. . . .

I believe that any objective appraisal of the Senate record will bear out my criticism. . . .

Look, first of all, at the routine business of the Senate which is transacted every year, the appropriation bills. Thirteen appropriation bills were supposed to have been passed by July 1, but here we are on November 7, and only five appropriations have been enacted into law. Virtually the whole government is operating on borrowed time.

Of our four major objectives of this session — a tax bill, a civil rights bill, a general aid-to-education bill, and a medicare bill, in my judgment — none has a real chance of enactment this year.

So Senators may make whatever defenses they wish of our performance and, when they are through praising it, when they are through making emotional defenses of the leadership, I ask them to look again at the record, at the box score. They will see a record not only of unfulfilled promises, but a record of failure even in meeting the routine statutory obligations placed upon the

125

Congress. .

I have, therefore, spoken out to try to kindle some sense of urgency in carrying on the public's business. I think we should come into session early in the morning, stay late at night, work weekends, holidays, day in and day out, until we get the people's business done, and I want the *Record* to show this.

Mr. Dirksen. Mr. President, I would be the last Senator ever to use the Senate chamber for a glorified wailing wall. I would be the last Senator ever to express publicly his own ineptitude to discharge his responsibilities. . . .

It is astonishing that a Senator, who ought to know the rules of the Senate if he does not know them, who ought to know the working hours of the Senate if he does not know them, should come here at night and emotionalize about staying in session until midnight, and castigate the majority leader because the Senate adjourned at 4 o'clock, 5 o'clock, or 6 o'clock. I have not seen a 4 o'clock adjournment, except when there were extraordinary circumstances which justified it. I believe the Senate has been very diligent.

It may be that the distinguished Senator from the Nutmeg State does not have anything to do in his office. I do not know whether he has or not. I am three days behind with my mail now. That is only a fraction of the mail I see. I spoke to the press this morning. I reminded them of the briefcase that goes home every night. Every morning, on the ride to the Capitol, I read mail and keep up with my chores; every weekend I sit at my desk; and that happens even on Sunday, when one ought to be enjoying God's sunshine.

Perhaps the Senator from Connecticut does not do that. I believe we owe to every Senator ample time to discharge the manifold responsibilities of his office — the departmental work, the claims, the protests, the mail, the detail, the people. I do not know how many people come to the offices of other Senators. My office is always full. I have to put them off and put them off, to make deferred arrangements to see my constituents, people who are taxpayers, who are entitled to see me.

When I read the Senator's comments in the *Record* this morning, I thought it was a bundle of incoherence that should never have appeared in the *Record*. I will let my comment stand at that point. If ever there is to be an answer, I will answer the distinguished Senator from Connecticut, and he will know well that he will have been answered when I am through.

Mr. Dodd. I would be happy to have the Senator make his answer.

Mr. Dirksen. I will answer in my own good time.

Mr. Dodd. I hope the Senator will have the courtesy to let me know.

Mr. Dirksen. It will not be at midnight, when the Senate session is over.

Mr. Dodd. The Senator may choose his own hour.

Mr. Dirksen. It will not be when the Senate session is over. We had excused all Senators last evening, and told them to go home, with the announcement that there would be no more votes.

Mr. Dodd. I did not hear that.

Mr. Dirksen. The Senator is not around enough. I can prove it with the Senator's committee record and with his record of attendance on the floor. If the Senator wishes to stay here until midnight, we can keep him here.

Mr. Dodd. That is all right. If the Senate has business to do, I will be here. A number of Senators were on the floor last evening. It was about 6:30, and the Senator from California had made reference to his amendment. I expected the Senate to vote on it.

Mr. Dirksen. Then the Senator did not know what was going on.

Mr. Dodd. I think I did, as much as any other Senator does; and I think I know as much as the Senator from Illinois does about what is going on.

Mr. Dirksen. It could be.

Mr. Dodd. Of course, I am not privy to some of the secrets. I do not share them with him. However, he does not frighten me, if that is his purpose with his menacing words addressed to me, and the implications. I shall be glad to hear his answer at any time he likes. I said what I think is so. I do not intend to be frightened out of it by anyone. I assure the Senator from Illinois that I particularly mean him. So I say to the Senator from Illinois, "Come on with your answer. I will be here too."

Mr. Dirksen. The answer will come, but I will not come to the floor with a 20-page effusion, first having delivered it to the press, to make it appear what a great crusader the Senator from Connecticut purports to be, emotionalizing on a 24-hour Senate day. . . .

* * *

With this edifying exchange the debate, which had been losing steam, now petered out. That night Dodd took the floor briefly for a graceful, face-saving capitulation. His lapels were quite smooth and his arm was not in a sling.

* * *

Mr. Dodd. Mr. President, I shall be brief. I felt this morning somewhat like a skunk at a lawn party.

I do not want to appear to be a spiteful or hateful man. I do not like the role of critic. I am not of that nature.

I wish to relate to the Senate what, I suppose, is the best experience I ever had.

About 6 o'clock this evening my telephone rang, and a voice at the other end said, "Tom, this is Mike Mansfield. I want to come down and talk with you."

I said, "Oh, Mike, you can't come down and talk with me; I will go up and talk with you."

We had a couple of exchanges about that, and I went up and talked with him.

I am not going to relate the conversation, because I do not want to "spill over" about it. But I want to say again what a gentle, decent, honest, great man Mike Mansfield is. He showed toward me a kindness and a generosity that I shall never forget.

I said, "You make me feel about the size of a pin. I wish I were as big as you are."

Because he is big. He is a very great man. He is a very great Senator.

I fear I was harsher than I meant to be last night toward him — and, I might add, toward my friend, Everett Dirksen, whom I really like and for whom I have affection. Both of these men are great men. I hope they will understand that what I said was not said out of malice. I spoke out because I was upset about the delays, about our lack of progress. But I want to tell the Senate that we have wonderful men leading us.

Mike would never tell this. It is not in his nature to do so. But I tell it.

I publicly tell it because I want it on the record that this great soul, this noble character, this fine human being, this great Senator, should have thought to humble himself.

But it was not he who humbled himself. He humbled me, and I am grateful to him.

I want him to know that he has not only my affection and devotion and admiration, but, as well, my loyalty. (Applause).

Dodd's capitulation restored him to the club, more or less, but his censure some four years later, in 1967 (in which Mansfield took no leading role), was a fatal blow. When he came up for reelection in 1970, he was defeated. He died in July of the following year. Mansfield, as majority leader, delivered the Senate eulogy.

* * *

Mr. Mansfield. I rise today to express my sorrow at the death of Senator Thomas Dodd and wish to extend my condolences to his family.

Thomas Dodd made many contributions to the people of this country. As a prosecutor at the Nuremberg trials after World War II, he helped establish the principle that citizens of any country have the highest moral duty to their fellow men; and that this duty in times of war as well as peace comes before duty to governmental dictate. As a member of the Armed Services Committee, he helped assure, through his dedication and foresight, that this country would be prepared to defend itself against any aggressor. And, most importantly, he showed high purpose and courage when he introduced and successfully sought the passage of a significant gun crime measure. Utilizing his experience as a former law enforcement officer and maintaining an independent stance against heavy organized pressure, he persuaded many of his Senate colleagues of its wisdom.

A man's achievements are his best testimonial, and Tom Dodd

has many proud achievements to his credit. Our society will continue to benefit from his efforts long after any words are forgotten.

I express my deepest regrets to his wife, Grace, and the members of his family.

November 25, 1963:

Eulogy to John F. Kennedy

Mansfield had known Jack Kennedy for many years. He had worked with President Kennedy closely for almost three years. The two men and their families were good friends.

The assassination shocked Mansfield and moved him deeply. He was struck particularly by Jackie's symbolic gesture of removing her ring and placing it in the coffin with her husband's body. The Senator's eulogy during the ceremony in the Capitol rotunda, on the day of the funeral, was remarkable for its simple, touching eloquence. Jackie later described it as moving "as a Pericles oration."

* * *

There was a sound of laughter; in a moment, it was no more. And so she took a ring from her finger and placed it in his hands.

There was a wit in a man neither young nor old, but a wit full of an old man's wisdom and of a child's wisdom, and then, in a moment, it was no more. And so she took a ring from her finger and placed it in his hands.

There was a husband who asked much and gave much, and out of the giving and the asking wove with a woman what could not be broken in life, and in a moment it was no more. And so she took a ring from her finger and placed it in his hands, and kissed him and closed the lid of a coffin.

A piece of each of us died at that moment. Yet in death he gave of himself to us. He gave us of a good heart from which the laughter came. He gave us of a profound wit, from which a great leadership emerged. He gave us of a kindness and a strength fused into a human courage to seek peace without fear.

He gave us of his love that we too, in turn, might give. He gave that we might give of ourselves, that we might give to one another until there would be no room, no room at all, for the bigotry, the hatred, the prejudice, and the arrogance which converged in that moment to strike him down.

In leaving us — these gifts, John Fitzgerald Kennedy, President of the United States, leaves with us. Will we take them, Mr. President? Will we have, now, the sense and the responsibility and the courage to take them?

I pray to God that we shall, and under God we will.

November 27, 1963:

On the Senate leadership

The Kennedy assassination interrupted the debate on the character of leadership in the Senate. Mansfield recognized, and explicitly acknowledged, that Dodd had performed a service in bringing cloakroom scuttlebutt and grousing out into the open. The Senator from Connecticut also had struck a nerve with his remarks about working hours (which he equated with in-session hours), for one of Mansfield's early reforms had been to get himself and his colleagues home for dinner on most evenings. Through the middle of November 1963 the majority leader and his staff therefore had been busy with (among other things, as always) a response to the charge of Senate lethargy and ineffectiveness. It was a strong statement that went beyond its particular subject, touching on the nature of leadership among equals and on Congressional cooperation with the Executive. It also showed a surprising talent for gentle sarcasm in emphasizing favorite points.

The statement was ready by Friday, November 22. That afternoon Mansfield scheduled it for delivery on Monday, the 25th. A few minutes later he received news of the assassination. When the

Senate reconvened on Wednesday the 27th, he could not bring himself to deliver the statement but asked rather that it simply be printed in the Congressional Record. This act of self-effacement unfortunately weakened the effect of a vigorous yet thoughtful apologia.

The statement incorporated lists of actions taken by nine Congresses, the 80th through the first session of the 88th. The last two lists are included here for those who feel that Congress never earns its salary, as well as for those who consider the Senate to have been ineffective under Mansfield's leadership. It must be remembered that all these measures involved controversy and debate. As they should have.

* * *

Mr. Mansfield. Mr. President, minutes before the tragedy last Friday, I asked the Senate for unanimous consent that I might be recognized on the following Monday at the conclusion of the morning hour for the purpose of making a statement on the Senate and its leadership. The remarks which I had already prepared at that time were intended to set forth a few facts on the Congress, in order to set straight some of the generalizations and the illusions about the Senate which had been coming from a variety of informed quarters. It was a statement of what has been achieved, not by any genius of the leadership or by some Senate establishment, but by the 100 members of this body working in cooperation and in mutual respect. The statement is, I repeat, the record of 100 Senators. We all share in the responsibility for achievements as well as for shortcomings, and both are recorded in the statement, I hope, in useful perspective and on the basis of fact. I have recorded on the basis of what is tangible in the legislative record, not on the basis of what the Senate looks like at 8 o'clock at night, or whether the members are driven or herded or function at their own collective pace and of their own will. After a while, what the Senate appears to have been in any given period will be noted, if at all, only by the scholars. What the Senate does in a legislative sense in any given period will be felt for a long, long time by all the people of the nation. We are not here as actors and actresses to be applauded. We are here as Senators to do the business of government. It is not we, but it is that alone, in the end, which counts to the nation.

So, Mr. President, the remarks which I had intended to deliver on Monday last, in the nature of an interim report on the Senate and its leadership, now become, because of this overwhelming tragedy, a final report on the Senate and its leadership during the Presidency of John Fitzgerald Kennedy and an indication of what remains to be done under the administration of President Johnson.

In the light of what has happened, I have no heart to read this report to the Senate. I ask unanimous consent, therefore, that the statement, "The Senate and Its Leadership," unchanged from the form in which it was prepared for delivery in the Senate on Monday, November 25, 1963, be printed as though read at this point in the Record. (There being no objection, the undelivered speech appeared in the Record as follows.)

Mr. President, some days ago blunt words were said on the floor of the Senate. They dealt in critical fashion with the state of this institution. They dealt in critical fashion with the quality of the majority leadership and the minority opposition. A far more important matter than criticism or praise of the leadership was involved. It is a matter which goes to the fundamental nature of the Senate.

In this light, we have reason to be grateful because, if what was stated was being said in the cloakrooms, then it should have been said on the floor. If, as was indicated, the functioning of the Senate itself is in question, the place to air that matter is on the floor of the Senate. We need no cloakroom commandos, operating behind the swinging doors of the two rooms at the rear, to spread the tidings. We need no whispered word passed from one to another and on to the press.

We are here to do the public's business. On the floor of the Senate, the public's business is conducted in full sight and hearing of the public. And it is here, not in the cloakrooms, that the Senator from Montana, the majority leader if you wish, will address himself to the question of the present state of the Senate and its leadership. The Senator from Montana has nothing to conceal. He has nothing which is best whispered in the cloakrooms. What he has to say on this score will be said here. It will be said to all Senators and to all members of the press who sit above us in more ways than one.

How, Mr. President, do you measure the performance of this Congress, of any Congress? How do you measure the performance of a Senate of 100 independent men and women — of any Senate? The question rarely arises, at least until an election approaches. And then our concern may well be with our own individual performance and not necessarily with that of the Senate as a whole.

Yet that performance, the performance of the Senate as a whole, has been judged on the floor. Several Senators, at least, judged it and found it seriously wanting. And with the hue and cry thus raised, they found echoes outside the Senate. I do not criticize Senators for making the judgment, for raising the alarm. Even less do I criticize the press for spreading it. Senators were within their rights. And the press not only was within its rights but was performing a segment of its public duty, which is to report what transpires here.

I too am within my rights, Mr. President, and I believe I am performing a duty of the leadership when I ask again : How do you judge the performance of this Congress, of any Congress? Of this Senate, of any Senate? Do you mix a concoction and drink it? And if you feel a sense of well-being thereafter, decide it is not so bad a Congress after all? But if you feel somewhat ill or depressed, is that, then, proof unequivocal that the Congress is a bad Congress and the Senate a bad Senate? Or do you shake your head back and forth negatively before a favored columnist when discussing the performance of this Senate? And if he in turn nods up and down, then is that proof that the performance is bad?

With all due respect, Mr. President, I searched the remarks of the Senators who have raised the questions. I searched them carefully, for I do not make light of the criticism of any member of this body. I searched them carefully for any insight as to how we might judge accurately the performance of this Senate, in order that we might try to improve it.

There is reference, to be sure, to time-wasting, to laziness, to absenteeism, to standing still, and so forth. But who are the time-wasters in the Senate, Mr. President? Who is lazy? Who is an

134

absentee? Each member can make his own judgment of his individual performance. I make no apologies for mine. Nor will I sit in judgment on any other member. On that score, each of us will answer to his own conscience, if not to his constituents.

But, Mr. President, insofar as the performance of the Senate as a whole is concerned, with all due respect, these comments on time-wasting have little relevance. Indeed, the Congress can, as it has — as it did in declaring World War II in less than a day — pass legislation which has the profoundest meaning for the entire nation. And by contrast the Senate floor can look very busy day in and day out, month in and month out, while the Senate is, indeed, dawdling. At one time in the recollection of many of us, we debated a civil rights measure 24 hours a day for many days on end. We debated it shaven and unshaven. We debated it without ties, with hair awry, and even in bedroom slippers. In the end, we wound up with compromise legislation. And it was not the fresh and well-rested opponents of the civil rights measure who were compelled to the compromise. It was, rather, the exhausted, sleep-starved, quorum-confounded proponents who were only to happy to take it.

No, Mr. President, if we would estimate the performance of this Congress or any other, this Senate or any other, we will have to find a more reliable yardstick than whether, on the floor, we act as time-wasters or moonlighters. As every member of the Senate and press knows, even if the public generally does not, the Senate is neither more nor less effective because the Senate is in session from 9 a.m. to 9 p.m., or to 9 a.m. the next day. In fact, such hours would most certainly make it less effective in present circumstances. . . .

There has been a great deal said on this floor about featherbedding in certain industries. But if we want to see a featherbedding to end all featherbedding, we will have the Senate sit here day in and day out, from dawn until dawn, whether or not the calendar calls for it, in order to impress the boss, the American people, with our industriousness. We may not shuffle papers as bureaucrats are assumed to do when engaged in this art. What we are likely to shuffle is words — words to the President on how to execute the foreign policy or administer the domestic affairs of the nation. And when these words pall, we undoubtedly will turn to the court to give that institution the benefit of our advice on its responsibilities. And if we run out of judicial wisdom, we can always turn to advising the governors of the states or the mayors of the cities or the heads of other nations on how to manage their concerns.

Let me make it clear that Senators individually have every right to comment on whatever they wish and to do so on the floor of the Senate. Highly significant initiatives on all manner of public affairs have had their genesis in the remarks of individual Senators on the floor. But there is one clear-cut, day-in-and-day-out responsibility of the Senate as a whole. Beyond all others, it is the Constitutional responsibility to be here and to consider and to act in concert with the House on the legislative needs of the nation. And the effectiveness with which that responsibility is discharged cannot be measured by any reference to the clocks on the wall of the chamber.

Nor can it be measured, really, by the output of legislation. For those who are computer-minded, however, the record shows that 12,656 bills and resolutions were introduced in the 79th Congress, in 1945-46. And in the 87th Congress, in 1961-62, 20,316 bills and resolutions were introduced, an increase of 60 percent. And the records show further that in the 79th Congress 2117 bills and resolutions were passed, and in the 87th Congress 2217 were passed. . . .

If these figures tell us anything, they tell us that the pressures on Congress have intensified greatly. They suggest, further, that Congress may be resistant to these pressures. But whether Congress resists rightly or wrongly, to the benefit or detriment of the nation, these figures tell us nothing at all.

There is a refinement in the statistical approach. It may have more meaning than the gross figures in measuring the effectiveness of a Democratic administration. I refer to the approach which is commonly used these days of totalling the Presidential or executive-branch requests for significant legislation and weighing against that total the number of Congressional responses in the form of law.

On this basis, if the Congress enacts a small percentage of the executive-branch requests it is presumed, somewhat glibly and impertinently, to be an ineffective Congress. But if the percentage is high, it follows that it is classifiable as an effective Congress. I am not so sure that I would agree, and I am certain that the distinguished minority leader and his party would not agree, that this is a valid test. The opposition might measure in precisely the opposite fashion. . . .

In any event, the statistics on this score are not calculated to give aid and comfort to those who are in a hurry to mark off this Congress as a failure at the midway point. . . . In sum, Mr. President, 79 of the requested 137 executive-branch measures, or 58 percent of the program, has in effect cleared the Senate. As a Democratic Senator who needs to make no apology to any member on this side of the aisle for his voting record in support of the President, I nevertheless find nothing to brag about in these figures. But neither do I find any grounds for apology as majority leader. I ask any member to search the *Record* and find in the postwar years a basis for deprecating the work of the 88th Congress on a statistical basis of this kind. The 88th Congres has yet to run its course, but about 60 percent at the midway point is not in any sense an inadequate statistical response to the President's program. . . .

But there is still another test which persuades me that the previous Congress under this administration was — and, before it is completed in 1964, this Congress will be — more than adequate. This test, admittedly, is a subjective one. Yet it may provide a more accurate insight than statistics into what really matters most in any Congress. I refer to the test of history. I refer to the capacity of the Congress, any Congress, to produce what might be called significant legislation of adjustment, legislation which is in consonance with the forces of change which are at work in the nation and in the world of its time. . . . When all else recedes into history, when the newspapers of the times yellow on the library shelves, when all years roll into the good old days, these are the measures, beyond the routine, which will count in terms of the shaping of the nation and of its place in the world. And it is largely on the basis of this legislation of adjustment that the historical judgments will be made. The number of significant measures is not great in these pre-Kennedy Congresses. The range is from 7 or so in the two years of the 80th Congress to a high of 13 or so during the two years of the exceptional 85th Congress under the leadership of the distinguished Vice President, Mr. Johnson. For the most part, each two years witnessed the enactment of a total of 8 or 9 items, most of them elaborations or variations on themes already set in preceding years.

We come now, Mr. President, to the record of the 87th Congress, the first Congress of the Kennedy administration. Here, then, is the comparable list.

First. It passed the omnibus farm bill to reduce surpluses and to provide for a new land use adjustment program.

Second. It authorized a program of health aid for migrant farm workers.

Third. It extended unemployment benefits an additional 13 weeks.

Fourth. It provided a program of aid to dependent children of the unemployed.

Fifth. It increased minimum wages from $1.00 to $1.25 and extended coverage to several million additional workers.

Sixth. It established the area redevelopment program.

Seventh. It increased old-age insurance benefits and provided for the retirement of men at 62 and liberalized disability payments.

Eighth. It authorized almost $5 billion in new funds under the Omnibus Housing Act.

Ninth. It extended the efforts to control water pollution.

Tenth. It established the manpower training program.

Eleventh. It accelerated the public works program by authorization of $900 million.

Twelfth. It made a significant revision in the tax structure.

Thirteenth. It authorized direct loans for housing for the elderly.

Fourteenth. It provided for voluntary pension plans under the tax laws.

Fifteenth. It enacted the trade expansion program.

Sixteenth. It passed the communications satellite bill.

Seventeenth. It established the Peace Corps.

Eighteenth. It established the U.S. Arms Control and Disarmament Agency.

Nineteenth. It created the U.S. Travel Service.

Twentieth. It authorized the purchase of UN bonds to save that

138

organization from bankruptcy.

Twenty-first. It initiated a Federal program on juvenile delinquency.

Twenty-second. It provided a program for aid for educational TV in the schools and colleges.

Twenty-third. It ratified the Treaty of the Organization for Economic Cooperation and Development.

Twenty-fourth. It approved a Constitutional amendment abolishing the poll tax.

Twenty-fifth. It passed a substantial foreign aid bill.

Twenty-sixth. The Senate invoked cloture for the first time in several decades. . . .

It is not the record of the majority leader or the minority leader. It is the Senate's record and, as the Senator from Montana, I for one will not make light of these achievements in the first two years of the Kennedy administration. And the achievement is no less because the 87th Congress did not meet at all hours of the night, because it rarely titillated the galleries, or because it failed to impress the visiting newsmen and columnists.

And now, Mr. President, we come to the 88th Congress, and particularly to this Senate. We have come to this Senate, which some have already consigned to the wasteheaps of history. We come to its leadership, which some find is to be pitied, if indeed it is not to be scorned.

Here, Mr. President, I will include the list — in the list of the significant legislation of adjustment — not only the measures which have cleared the Congress but also items which have at least cleared the Senate and are awaiting final action. Congress is not for one year. It is for two. What this Congress will in the end produce we cannot say until this Congress comes to an end some time in 1964. But to date in this Congress and in this Senate, here is the list:

First. It has initiated a program which begins to recognize the full dimensions of major health problems of the nation and to come to grips with them — mental illness and mental retardation.

Second. It has expanded Federal aid for maternal and child health services for crippled children.

Third. It has acted to forestall what would otherwise have been a crippling railroad shutdown.

139

Fourth. It has acted to provide for a vast expansion in training and research facilities in medicine, dentistry, and related sciences.

Fifth. It has acted to expand academic facilities in higher education through grants and loans for construction.

Sixth. It has acted to expand vocational education and extended for three years the National Defense Education Act and the impacted areas program.

Seventh. It has acted on the problem of mass transit.

Eighth. It has acted to establish a domestic Peace Corps.

Ninth. It has acted to establish a system of Federal public defenders.

Tenth. It has acted to create a Youth Conservation Corps.

Eleventh. It has acted on a water resources research program.

Twelfth. It has acted to preserve wilderness areas.

Thirteenth. It has acted to expand the area redevelopment program.

Fourteenth. It has acted on the problems of air and water pollution.

Fifteenth. It has authorized a substantial foreign aid program.

Sixteenth. It has given consent to the ratification of the nuclear test ban treaty. . . .

However this midway Congress may compare with what has gone before, the leadership would be the first to recognize that there are inadequacies in it. And the most serious, in my judgment, are neither the status of the civil rights bill nor the tax bill. The most serious, in my judgment, have to do with the day-to-day financial housekeeping of the government. We have got to face the fact that if we are going to have an orderly fiscal administration of this government, we cannot long continue with the practice of raising every few months, as a ritual, the legal debt ceiling. Nor can we expect a rational administration of the vast and far-flung activities of the executive branch of the government if the basic appropriations bills do not become law until months after the fiscal year begins. . . .

That is the story of the legislative state of the Congress during the Kennedy administration and particularly of the Senate, as the majority leader sees it. It is a barebones story, without embellishment. It is a story written by all the members and not by the leadership. It is a story of the facts, the significant and enduring facts, as one Senator sees them at the midpoint of the 88th Congress. . . .

I turn, finally, to the recent criticism which has been raised as to the quality of the leadership. I do not question the right of anyone to raise this question — certainly not the right of the Senate and the press to do so. I regard every member with respect and esteem, and every member in his own way has reciprocated that sentiment, and I am sure that no member intends to do me ill. As for the press, it has been invariably fair, even kind, in its treatment of me personally. I have never been misquoted on any remarks I have made in the Senate, and only on rare occasions have I been misinterpreted — and, even then, understandably so.

Of late, Mr. President, the descriptions of the majority leader, of the Senator from Montana, have ranged from a benign Mr. Chips, to glamourless, to a tragic mistake. I have not yet seen "wetnurse of the Senate," but that, too, may not be long in coming.

It is true, Mr. President, that I have taught school, although I cannot claim either the tenderness, the understanding, of the perception of Mr. Chips for his charges. I confess freely to a lack of glamour. As for being a tragic mistake, if that means, Mr. President, that I am neither a circus ringmaster, the master of ceremonies of a Senate nightclub, a tamer of Senate lions, or a wheeler and dealer, then I must accept that title also. Indeed, I must accept it, if I am expected as majority leader to be anything other than myself — a Senator from Montana who has had the good fortune to be trusted by his people for over two decades and who has done the best he knows how to represent them, and to do what he believes to be right for the nation.

Insofar as I am personally concerned, these or any other labels can be borne. I achieved the height of my political ambitions when I was elected Senator from Montana. When the Senate saw fit to designate me as majority leader, it was the Senate's choice, not mine, and what the Senate has bestowed it is always at liberty to revoke.

But so long as I have this responsibility, it will be discharged to the best of my ability by me as I am. I would not, even if I could, presume to a tough-mindedness which, with all due respect to those who use this cliche, I have always had difficulty in distinguishing from soft-headedness or simplemindedness. I shall not don any mandarin's robes or any skin other than that to which I am accustomed in order that I may look like a majority leader or sound like a majority leader — however a majority leader is supposed to look or sound. I am what I am, and no title, political facelifter, or imagemaker can alter it.

I believe that I am, as are most Senators, an ordinary American with a normal complement of vices and, I hope, virtues, of weaknesses and, I hope, strengths. As such, I do my best to be courteous, decent, and understanding of others, and I sometimes fail at it. But it is for the Senate to decide whether these characteristics are incompatible with the leadership. . . .

And finally, within this body I believe that every member ought to be equal in fact no less than in theory, that the members have a primary responsibility to the people whom they represent, to face the legislative issues of the nation. And to the extent that the Senate may be inadequate in this connection, the remedy lies not in the seeking of shortcuts, not in the cracking of nonexistent whips, not in wheeling and dealing, but in an honest facing of the situation and a resolution of it by the Senate itself, by accommodation, by respect for one another, by mutual restraint and, as necessary, adjustments in the procedures of this body.

I have been charged with lecturing the Senate. And perhaps these remarks will also be interpreted in this fashion. But all I have tried to do is state the facts of this institution as I see them. The Constitutional authority and responsibility does not lie with the leadership. It lies with all of us individually, collectively, and equally. And, in the last analysis, deviations from that principle must in the end act to the detriment of the institution. In the end, that principle cannot be made to prevail by rules. It can prevail only if there is a high degree of accommodation, mutual restraint, and a measure of courage — in spite of our weaknesses — in all of us. It can prevail only if we recognize that, in the end, it is not the Senators as individuals who are of fundamental importance. In the end, it is the institution of the Senate. It is the Senate itself as one of the foundations of the Constitution. It is the Senate as one of the rocks of the republic.

May 29, 1965:

On new roles for women

Clarke College is a noted college for women in Dubuque, Iowa. In May 1965 it awarded one of its former students, Maureen Hayes Mansfield, an honorary LL.D. In his commencement address the Senator considered the expanding role of women in our society, and especially in politics. In the process he demonstrated that chivalry can heighten a man's respect for women, and need not debase it into a form of condescension.

In a long aside he also discussed the importance of a free press in American society. Although a free press in general is a democratic luxury that many politicians and bureaucratic satraps would just as soon dispense with, and although much of the American press had been less than generous in criticizing his Senate leadership, his support of the Fourth Estate was, as always, unqualified. His comments would prove worth remembering later, when the media reporting of Vietnam and Watergate was to come under savage attack from the most subversive Presidential cabal in the country's history.

* * *

Before I begin my remarks to you, I should like to pay tribute to the one person who, more than any other, is responsible for my being here today. I refer to Maureen Hayes Mansfield — who spent seven happy years at Clarke, who has so many friends here and who is responsible for my being referred to, on occasion, as the third Senator from Iowa.

It is not too difficult for a man in public life to gain recognition, provided he is lucky enough to share his private life with an exceptional wife. All too often the women who stand with public figures go unnoticed and unsung. But I know, and I am delighted to acknowledge, that if I had not had Maureen Mansfield by my side through the years, these years of public life would not have been possible. If I had not drawn strength from her patience, if I had not found courage in her understanding, if I had not had access to her wisdom, I would not be with you today. You would

143

not have had occasion to invite me, for the simple reason that I would not have had very much to say to you.

So, for making it possible for me to be here, for her enormous assistance to me in a life of public service which has brought me much personal fulfillment, I should like to add, to the public honor which you have bestowed on Maureen Mansfield, a public expression of my deep affection and gratitude to her.

Ladies of the graduating class of 1965, distinguished members of the faculty, parents, relatives, and friends, I am grateful for the privilege of sharing in this graduation ceremony. . . .

To you graduates, your diploma is the capstone of your college career. It is for you at once the beginning and the continuance — the commencement — of what might be called "Women's Journey in the United States."

That journey began with the very beginnings of the nation. And through the years it has been marked by change. In the earliest days, the change was slow and scarcely perceptible. But in what historians eventually will record as a relatively brief period of time, three factors have been instrumental in creating startling change in the role of women in our society. These factors are expanded educational opportunity, expanded economic opportunity, and expanded political opportunity.

Almost from the beginning, an elementary school education has been available to both boys and girls in this country. But the door to a secondary school education for a girl opened more slowly. Nevertheless, by the end of the 19th century, twice as many girls as boys were being awarded high school diplomas because, for work reasons, males constituted a higher percentage of school dropouts.

At the higher education level a real distinction between educational opportunities for males and for females has existed until very recent times. It was almost 200 years after Harvard University was founded to provide higher education for men that Oberlin College in 1833 broke ranks to provide instruction at the advanced level to what was referred to as "the misguided and neglected sex." In spite of this breakthrough, it was a long time before the concept of free choice for women in educational pursuits received any general acceptance. Even 50 years ago, for example, it would have been pointless for a girl to prepare for a career in politics or international affairs.

As soon as women were given a fair crack at educational opportunities, they proved that they did indeed possess brainpower equal to that of men. Nowadays women earn one-third of all B.A.'s, one-third of all M.A.'s, and one-tenth of all Ph.D.'s. Virtually no profession is closed to a woman who is capable and trained. What is of the essence, of course, is this nation's general and growing recognition that an equitable educational opportunity should be available to all, regardless of the individual's color or sex or the station in life in which he or she was born.

As with educational changes, expanded economic opportunity also has brought about a significant transition in the role of women in our society. In the relationship of women to work outside the home, statistics reveal that in the span of 60 years, from 1900 to 1960, the number of American women earning paychecks increased almost fivefold. Today more than half of the women who are working are married, and one in every three workers in the United States is a woman.

It is clear that some women must work to support themselves and their dependents. And some women work to supplement family income. But increasing numbers of married women are working because they find they can successfully blend the responsibilities of a family life with those of a part- or full-time job. After her children are grown up, many a married woman has virtually a second adult lifetime which may be dedicated to self-development, the use of talents and skills, and service to family and community in its broadest sense. . . .

One area in the United States where a change in the role of women has been particularly significant is the field of politics. Today, only 45 years after ratification of the suffrage amendment, women occupy political offices at all levels of government. They serve as mayors and on town and city boards. They are members of state legislatures and occupy state elective and appointive posts.

Women are active also in political party councils. As you have doubtless noticed on television, women are much in evidence at political conventions, where they act as delegates, speakers, contributors to party platforms and, last but not least, occasionally as a Vice-Presidential or a Presidential candidate. As a Democrat, I do not wish to be in the position of advising the Republican Party, but it is no secret that I favored Senator Margaret Chase Smith as that party's candidate for the Presidency in the last election. The Republicans did not heed my advice, and you know what happened last November.

My state of Montana sent the first woman to the U.S. Congress in 1917. Since then the role of women has continued to expand in national politics. Over sixty women have been members of the House of Representatives, and ten currently serve in that body. Ten women have been members of the Senate. Currently Margaret Chase Smith, a Republican from Maine, and Maureen Neuberger, a Democrat from Oregon, make a great contribution to the Senate and the nation.

They do so because they are intelligent, wise and immensely skilled Senators and equally because they are charming and gracious women. . . .

Anything men can do in politics, women can do, and in many instances better. Through participation in politics, you graduates can make your voices heard and your views felt in our democratic system of government. Politics offers you a way of helping to promote good candidates for office, to keep good officials in office, and to insure good government across the board. Politics offers you a way of translating into political action your own ideas and thoughts. Politics offers you a means of influencing public attitudes, governmental policies, and world events. I trust you will accept those offers and make them at least a part of your contract with life. . . .

What are some of the ways in which you increase understanding of the world in which we live and enhance other people's understanding of us? You can keep yourself informed on international affairs. You can become an active participant in one or more of any number of volunteer or professional organizations that study specific foreign policy issues or engage in other activities related to foreign affairs; you can communicate to your elected representatives any ideas you have; you can take foreign visitors sightseeing or invite them to visit your homes.

Most important, you can make intelligent use of the unparalleled sources of information which are available in this nation, particularly the press. Newspapers, large and small, those printed in the metropolitan centers of our country and those that abound in smaller cities, have done an outstanding job of supplying the facts and informed opinion on national and international developments. They have helped to keep government on its toes. They have served to bring to the public an independent picture of our national policies at home and abroad.

And while I am on this subject, I want to say a word of praise for the American men and women who report the news. They do an excellent job, even if I may sometimes suffer personally at their hands. The reporter's job is to turn the light on, regardless of the inadequacies in government which may be exposed. Management of news by government can never be squared with our continuing and growing need for a fully informed and alert public. It can never be squared, in other words, with the needs of a democratic society. . . .

We will never safeguard this nation by deprecating, in the name of national policy or of a superior governmental wisdom, the free press which is one of the principal institutions by which freedom is maintained. Government officials are almost always inclined to think — and understandably — that they know better than the press what is transpiring in the world or any segment of it, and what to do about it. But time and again events have indicated that on many occasions they do not. In this connection I think, for example, of the work of American correspondents in Vietnam and the Dominican Republic, which has been outstanding in every respect. One sometimes has the impression that the accuracy of the press reporting and some of the press analyses in both places may very well have been greater in many instances than the great flow of information which has come to Washington through official channels.

I want to say, too, as a member of the Foreign Relations Committee, that over the years, in secret or public sessions, the flow of information from the executive branch to the Senate on the international situation is more copious but many times no more revealing or lucid than that which has been carried in the great newspapers of the nation.

In short, I want to stress to you the indispensable service which the press of the nation performs in our society. It must continue to reflect the truth as it sees the truth, directly, with its own eyes, and not as it is reflected in the retina of official positions. The two may

147

be and often are identical. That is fortuitous when it is the case. But, when it is not, there must be no forced convergence in the name of a national unity. For that kind of unity can never be more than skin deep. It is not a source of strength. Rather, it is a source of a dangerous and delusive weakness.

The basic work of the press leads to the asking of the incisive questions which in a democracy need to be asked by the people and answered by their government. And so, as in the case of the situation in Vietnam and the Dominican Republic, the press provides the impetus and stimulus for a searching and continuing public debate which is likely to go on and should go on until there is a satisfactory resolution of critical national questions.

Speaking of the press, the other day I read a magazine description of the composite American woman. She was portrayed as "good-looking, youthful, energetic, capable, independent, restless, confused, frustrated, spoiled — lucky." I shall reserve comment on that characterization on the grounds that I might otherwise incriminate myself. But I think you graduates and I would both agree that you have been lucky in having the opportunity to attend this institution of higher learning where the pursuit of excellence is emphasized and the quest for truth is encouraged.

Moreover, I think you are lucky to be living in the 20th century, a century of unfolding opportunity, unprecedented demands, and unparalleled hope. Of you women, much will be asked. You will be expected to possess capacity for change, clarity of thought, and courage of conviction. You will be expected to work hard. You will be expected to have purpose and to be willing to commit yourself to service in useful articulation of the needs of your family, your community, your country, and the world. . . .

I should like to leave you with my hope for your part of the women's journey in the United States which you start today, a hope expressed in an old Gaelic blessing:

> May the road rise to meet you.
> May the wind always be at your back.
> May the sun shine warm upon your face
> And the rains fall soft upon your fields.
> And, until we meet again, may God hold you
>   in the hollow of his hand.

January 31, 1966

In defense of President Johnson

The year 1965 proved critical for the United States' involvement in Vietnam. In February, in response to Vietcong attacks on U.S. installations in South Vietnam, the Air Force began bombing North Vietnam in deadly earnest. At this time there were some 27,000 American troops in Vietnam. In April the Soviet Union clumsily bolstered the cause of American war hawks by threatening to send troops to Indochina, thus reinforcing the notion of a monolithic Communism about to engulf Southeast Asia. Meanwhile North Vietnamese troops were infiltrating the south in growing numbers, encouraging the Vietcong rebels to conduct ever bolder adventures. Meanwhile, American ground forces were pouring in from across the broad Pacific, and August brought the first major attack on the Vietcong conducted solely by U.S. troops. In November word came from North Vietnam that President Ho Chi Minh considered any settlement impossible until all the American troops in Vietnam — by then numbering close to 200,000 — had been totally withdrawn.

Mansfield, as we have seen, had been warning against any such American entanglement for several years. In early January 1966 he and four other Senators (Aiken, Boggs, Inouye and Muskie) issued a report to the Senate Foreign Relations Committee decrying the lack of popular support in South Vietnam for the ruling French leftovers; the five dismayed Cassandras also foretold the futility of American military intervention.

In the escalating hawk-dove controversy over Vietnam, Mansfield had long been and still was in the forefront of the dove contingent; yet, as majority leader and a longtime friend of Lyndon Johnson, he was in an acutely uncomfortable predicament. Some of us today may look back on Johnson's attitude toward the war in Vietnam as that of a backwoods ruffian nailin' coonskins to the wall, to use his own unhappy metaphor. Mansfield, however, worked with him intimately, saw him almost daily, and could see at first hand what the war was doing to him. It was a

149

painful thing to watch.

Mansfield's closest friend in the Senate was Republican George Aiken of Vermont, whom Senator Paul Douglas of Illinois once called "the saint of the Senate." The two friends, both early risers, almost always had their workday breakfasts together, fortifying each other to face the rigors of another legislative day. Aiken, who labored under none of the leadership restrictions that bedeviled Mansfield, had long been an outspoken critic of the burgeoning U.S. role in Vietnam. At the end of January 1966 he delivered a major speech on the subject on the Senate floor. It is noteworthy that Mansfield used his leadership prerogative (giving him precedence in recognition by the presiding officer) to assure Aiken of whatever time he needed to finish his speech. Yet, after agreeing wholeheartedly with Aiken's position on the issues, he rose to the defense of the increasingly beleaguered Johnson.

The selection given here begins with excerpts from the latter part of Senator Aiken's address. This colloquy occurred on January 31, some hours after Johnson's decision to end the 37-day halt in the bombing of North Vietnam.

* * *

Mr. Aiken . . I trust that those who make the decisions for our country will bear in mind that while the war of democracy versus communism cannot be won in southeast Asia, it can be lost there.

In fact, communism will not be defeated on the battlefield anyway, except on the battlefield of men's minds.

If any phase of the conflict between these two ideologies must be fought with arms, we should not let our enemies choose the battleground.

From now on our Number One concern must be the preservation of the United States and its institutions. There can be no half-hearted effort in this respect.

Our people, regardless of whether or not they support the acts of this administration, must be prepared for extraordinary sacrifice.

Mr. Mansfield. Mr. President, I ask unanimous consent that the distinguished Senator from Vermont may have as much time as he may desire, and that the time be extended to allow other Senators to participate in discussing this momentous speech.

150

Mr. Aiken. I thank the majority leader.

The Acting President pro tempore. Without objection, it is so ordered.

Mr. Aiken. Mr. President, this sacrifice will have to be paid in terms of resources, freedom, and life itself.

There may be a chance that a world nuclear war can be avoided. There may be a chance that we may escape the devastating effect of a general land war in Asia, the kind of war we are least likely to win.

We cannot proceed on the hope for miracles, however. Therefore we must be prepared for the worst, and without delay.

President Johnson has asked for some $13 billion with which to increase the tempo of the war in Vietnam. This $13 billion is only the first drop in the bucket. Common sense and experience should tell us that. . . .

The President asks us to rescind the tax cut on telephone charges and automobiles in order to help us meet this cost. It is ridiculous to expect that the income from these recisions would even begin to pay the cost of an escalated war.

If President Johnson means business — and I believe he does — he will ask for the suspension of the General Tax Reduction Act of two years ago. He will ask to have the loopholes of overgenerous deducations and special tax privileges plugged. And he will ask for such new taxes as may be necessary.

There is no sense in waiting until after the election to recommend the inevitable. Lives are more precious than votes.

Secretary of Defense McNamara asks for an increase of 113,000 men in the armed forces. Whom does he think he's kidding?

Winning a guerilla war requires a ratio of ten to one on the side of the law, and the enemy already has 200,000 men in the field. The Secretary knows that an escalated war will require universal conscription.

To wait until after the election to announce this is just another attempt to lull the people. . . .

Since the Vietnam war began to escalate rapidly three years ago, I have repeatedly tried to make clear my belief that a major war would have disastrous results for the United States either militarily or in the loss of personal liberty at home.

Although I have at all times recognized the responsibilities of the United States for the people of South Vietnam, I never for an instant regarded my vote for the concurrent resolution of August 1964 as a vote to give the President authority to wage war at will in southeast Asia.

I opposed as strongly as I could the start of a new war in North Vietnam. And I believe the President has erred in taking new steps which may lead to a cataclysmic world conflict.

It appears, however, that my voice has been ineffective and that the President has decided to take such steps. The most that is left to me now is the hope that the President is right and that I have been wrong.

Mr. Mansfield. Once again, the distinguished Senator from Vermont has performed a public service. I say "once again" because that has been his forte down through the years, regardless of the issue which was being discussed.

There has been a good deal of reference in the press in late months to the categories of the dove and the hawk. Personally, I do not pay much attention to those designations. What I think the Senator from Vermont typifies and personifies, if I may use the word, is the owl. He is the wise man, the man who looks ahead, the man who is unswerving in his support of the United States, but who is also aware of the dangers which confront us in any given situation. . . .

The Senator from Vermont has mentioned something about the possibility of nuclear activity. The very use of the word "nuclear" makes me shudder, and I hope that those who are in favor of the use of such weapons — and unfortunately there have been some who have so stated — will not be taken too seriously, because I do not believe such advocacy represents the feelings of the administration, of Congress, or of the American people; nor does it, for that matter, represent the feelings of the peoples of the world. . . .

May I take this occasion, if the Senator will allow me to do so, to express my wholehearted sympathy and support for the efforts, covering 37 days, made by the President of the United States to seek an avenue or a door to the negotiating table.

I think I probably know Lyndon Johnson as well as any other member of this body knows him. I have been closely associated with him for 24 years. I know how deeply concerned he is about Vietnam. I know the agonizing days and nights he goes through. I

152

know of his intense desire to bring this most difficult of all situations which has ever faced an American President to some sort of honorable conclusion. . . .

This is a most serious situation, and I applaud the President for the many avenues he has sought and tried, for the many doors on which he has knocked, for the many times he has had conversations and conferences, for sending ambassadors all over the world and for the instructions which he gave to the ambassadors — all to try to bring this situation to the conference table so that a satisfactory solution and conclusion might be reached.

It is therefore no fault of the President, as the distinguished Senator from Vermont has said, that these attempts have failed over the past 37 days. He has tried. He is concerned deeply. I do not think it is so much a matter of his place in history as it is a matter of finding a way by which he can, under honorable conditions, bring this most difficult confrontation to a satisfactory conclusion.

The American people must know the truth. They must know the potential involved in southeast Asia. They must be made to know all of its ramifications. We in the Senate, regardless of our views, whether we are called doves, hawks, or owls, have a responsibility. That responsibility is being lived up to, and I am sure it will be lived up to even more in the future.

This is a grave time for the nation, and it is a grave time for the President, who, under the Constitution, has this awesome responsibility. He cannot shove the buck to us. He knows that. He knows that, in the final analysis, there is only one man in this republic who can make the decision. He is subjected to that responsibility as Commander in Chief of the Armed Forces of the Republic and as President of the United States of America.

I repeat: So far as the Senator from Montana is concerned, he will do his very best to give the President of the United States as much in the way of support as he possibly can.

I thank and commend the distinguished Senator from Vermont for laying out what he thinks should be done and for making the Senate, both sides of the Senate, more aware of the difficulties inherent in the situations which faces us and by making it known, in his simple, logical manner, to the American people as well.

June 16, 1966:

On seeking an accommodation with Peking

Despite General MacArthur's humbling experience with Chinese intervention in Korea, despite Soviet threats to put troops in Indochina, in the summer of 1966 bellicose voices were heard in the land demanding an all-out effort for a "final" victory in Vietnam, to the tune of General William Westmoreland's persistent refrain, "Give Me More Men!" Mansfield in response argued that, instead of thus risking untold additional losses of blood and treasure in Asia, we should intensify our efforts to come to some accommodation with Peking. Even the current military commitment, he maintained, could hardly be justified, since it was being fulfilled in the interest of Saigon's ever-scrimmaging warlords at the bloody expense of the suffering Vietnamese people, both north and south.

In June 1966 he expressed these views in a speech at New York's Yeshiva University. It is ironic that his plea for a more direct and conciliatory approach to Red China was to be partially heeded years later by, of all people, Richard Nixon.

* * *

I welcome the opportunity to share this day with the Class of 1966. For the most part, you are among the last to have been born during World War II. Hence, you are among the first to have received the pledge of peace of the United Nations in 1945. The preamble to the Charter, you will recall, contains this solemn statement of purpose: "To save succeeding generations from the scourge of war."

The pledge has stood for twenty-one years. Commencement addresses this year might well ponder the adequacy of its fulfillment. It is a fitting theme for graduating classes, not only in the United States, but also in the Soviet Union, China, Britain, and elsewhere.

The Class of 1966 has been witness, since birth, not to a growing peace in the world but to a procession of crises and conflicts. This class has come to maturity in an atmosphere which for two decades has been heavy with war and the threat of war. This class graduates directly into the face of the bitter war in Vietnam.

Yet the words remain: "To save succeeding generations from the scourge of war."

Therefore I address your attention today to the problem of peace in Vietnam. I ask you to consider this problem in the context of the limbo in which, for more than a decade and a half, have reposed the relations between China and the United States. The two questions — peace in Vietnam and peace with China — are very closely interrelated, if not, indeed, inseparable. . . .

We are engaged in war against the North Vietnamese, the Vietcong, and the National Liberation Front of the south. But the elements of leadership in South Vietnam who have the greatest stake in that effort are engaged in a quasi-war among themselves. This inner conflict has produced pressures for instability in the south which have little to do with the war in which we are engaged. In the light of these pressures, it is unrealistic to describe the situation in South Vietnam in a clear-cut ideological context. It has never been, in fact, that kind of simple situation.

To view the conflict as wholly one of an aggression of the north against the south also does not do adequate justice to the perplexing realities of Vietnam. The war is more than a clash between two nations or hostile strangers. It is also a rending of long associated cultures — north, central, and south — which contain relatives, friends, and enemies for whom the 17th parallel is a division of dubious significance and durability.

It is illustrative, in this connection, to note that the leader of North Vietnam, Ho Chi Minh, was born much farther south in Vietnam than the present leader of South Vietnam, General Nguyen Cao Ky. Ho Chi Minh, the Communist, was educated extensively in what is now anti-Communist South Vietnam, while Nguyen Cao Ky, the anti-Communist, received his training in what is now Communist North Vietnam. And if that leaves you confused, think for a moment what it must do to the Vietnamese people who must live with the confusion.

What I am suggesting by this digression is that, while Vietnam may be two houses in conflict, it is at the same time one house not only divided but also united in many ways. What I am suggesting, too, is that events of the past few weeks represent the surfacing of but a few of the complex difficulties of the Vietnamese situation.

It seems to me that these difficulties have grown more intractable and the solutions more difficult since the tragic assasination of President Ngo Dinh Diem in 1963. Coup has followed coup until the count has been lost. In the process, the leadership of South Vietnam has been sundered and weakened, the rivalries have grown, the mutual antipathies have increased. And, in the process, the Vietnamese people have suffered greatly in consequence of these developments, as well as from the war.

In all frankness, so, too, has this nation suffered from these developments. The instability among the South Vietnamese leaders has meant a steady increase in our involvement in Vietnam, and especially our military role. There is no question that the armed services of the United States have provided a growing margin of power without which a Republic of Vietnam could not have survived. To them has fallen the task of filling the defensive gap left by the growing strains on the South Vietnamese authorities. On them has fallen the principal burden of meeting the increased military pressures from the north. These tasks, which have been assigned to them by the nation's policies, have been discharged with great dedication and at great personal sacrifice.

The increase in the American effort in Vietnam has been and will continue to be very costly. During the past year and a half our ground-forces commitment has grown from about 25,000 to 267,000. By year's end this figure will be much higher. The deployment of American naval and air power has been of a very great magnitude. It has brought to bear on Vietnam the impact of tens of thousands of additional highly trained men who have unleashed a level of destructive power which may approach or even surpass that which was set loose during the Korean war.

At the beginning of 1965, the United States forces were incurring casualties at the rate of about 6 per week. Now, upwards of 500 Americans are killed or wounded each week. For the past five or six weeks in succession, the casualty rate for Americans has surpassed that of the South Vietnamese armed forces.

In monetary terms, the current cost of Vietnam to the United States has been estimated at an annual rate in the neighborhood of $13 billion and is continuing to rise. In early 1965 the costs were

156

perhaps $1 or $2 billion.

I wish that I could tell you that this powerful injection of American resources had brought the war nearer to a conclusion. But I can only repeat what I said at the outset of my remarks: the end of the war in Vietnam is not in sight.

It has been suggested of late — perhaps "inferred" is more accurate — that the war can be ended quickly by a further expansion of the American military effort and, particularly, by more and better-placed bombing. That is an appealing suggestion, and I have no doubt that it will be heard more frequently between now and November. It wraps up, in one simple thought, a criticism of the present political leadership, a promise of a less painful war, an expectation of victory at a relatively small increase in cost. In short, it suggests that there is an easy exit. Let us underscore one point here today: There are easy ways to plunge more deeply into this situation; there are no easy ways out of this situation. . . .

The field of battle was confined largely to South Vietnam when the expansion of our military effort began. Air and sea bombardment has now extended the arena of conflict throughout almost all of North Vietnam. The war has spread sharply into Laos. More and more, it verges on Cambodia and threatens to spill over into Thailand. . . .

Is the war, then, to continue to intensify? Is Vietnam, both north and south, to be reduced to a charnel house amidst smoking, silent ruins? Indeed, is that to be the fate of great areas of southeast Asia and regions beyond?

Experience requires us to recognize that this danger exists in the conflict. Prudence compels us to recognize, moreover, that the terminal point may not be reached until and unless the war has involved China directly. . . .

I can give you no assurances on these questions. The answers depend not only on our wisdom and restraint but also on that of the Chinese. I can only stress to you that the relentless search for affirmative answers is a most solemn responsibility which rests especially upon the leadership of this nation and of China but concerns also the United Nations, the Geneva powers, and the entire world.

There is little doubt that this search is hampered by the long hiatus in United States relations with China. . . . The direct

157

human contact between the world's most populous nation and the world's most powerful was reduced to formal and routine meetings in Warsaw between an American and a Chinese ambassador which, over the years, have averaged out to about one a month.

In the past few weeks members of the administration have sought to make clear in public statements that this nation seeks to restore some "bridges" to China. . . . What is needed most, at this time and in the light of the danger, is an initiative for a direct contact between the Peking government and our own government on the problem of peace in Vietnam and southeast Asia. This problem is of such transcendent importance, it seems to me, that it is a fit question for face-to-face discussion between China and the United States at the highest practicable level. . . .

What a conference at this time must be concerned with is, in the first instance, a curb on the expansion of the war and a prompt and durable termination of the tragic bloodletting in Vietnam.

It must be concerned with insuring a choice free of coercion of any kind to the people of South Vietnam over their future and on the question of the reunification of Vietnam.

It must be concerned with how the independence and the territorial integrity, not only of Vietnam but of other small nations of southeast Asia, can be safeguarded in peace.

It must be concerned, finally, with how foreign bases and foreign military forces can be promptly withdrawn and excluded from Vietnam and other parts of the southeast Asian mainland.

These are fundamental questions. Answers to these questions must begin to be found. And, in the last analysis, they must be concurred in by China and the United States. Those are the essentials if conflict in Vietnam is to end and if a reasonable and stable peace is to be established in southeast Asia.

Let me make clear that I am not sanguine as to the possibilities that these questions will be faced in conference in the near future. Even less is it to be expected that answers to these questions are going to be found very quickly. The chasms are deep, the walls are high.

Nevertheless, at some point these questions will have to be faced and answers will have to be found. It seems to me that we must continue to try to take those first faltering steps toward peace in Asia. We must try to take them now, before the tragedy which is

Vietnam is compounded many times over. That is the great responsibility. It rests on the Chinese. It rests on this nation. It rests, finally, on all the nations of the world.

September 21, 1966:

On compulsory school prayer

In June 1962, a U.S. Supreme Court ruling forbade states to require prayer recitation in the public schools, thus negating the bias that for decades had supported institutional religious practices with public money. One reaction was to introduce a Constitutional amendment overturning the Court ruling and thus restoring the pressure on children to conform regardless of their own parents' wishes, in a spirit somewhat reminiscent of the Roman emperors' demands on the early Christians.

The opponents of this compulsory prayerfulness, somewhat ironically, shared the distaste expressed by Jesus Christ (Matt. 7:21) for the mere saying of "Lord, Lord," especially in demanding it of others regardless of objections. Their opposition was based, of course, on the First Amendment's injunction against "an establishment of religion," which they strongly felt should not be repealed. Since there was merit on both sides, the dispute was, and is, largely a matter of giving the benefit of the doubt to freedom of conscience or to piety by prescription.

Mansfield had no hesitancy in choosing between these alternatives. In September 1966 he argued forcefully on the Senate floor against "the Dirksen Constitutional amendment." But, typically, he ended on a note of compromise.

* * *

Mr. Mansfield. Mr. President, since June 1962, when the Supreme Court prohibited the State of New York from composing and prescribing a prayer for recitation in its public schools, there have been about 200 resolutions introduced in the Congress in an attempt to remedy this apparent reversal to religious training. All the sponsors of these various proposals are genuinely concerned

159

with the growing deemphasis of religion in our modern society. When a topic of casual conversation is whether "God is dead," the concern is real, and the remedy must be appropriate.

As I read the First Amendment to the Constitution, it says in nonlawyer language that the government — Federal, state, or local — shall keep out of the field of religion. I consider this prohibition as wise today as it was 180 years ago. I think the Supreme Court was merely enforcing this "no trespassing" sign when it forbade the reading of a state-composed prayer or a passage from a Bible in a public school. Those of us who believe strongly in the consolation of prayer and the wisdom of the teachings of the Bible cannot understand how anyone could fail to appreciate the redeeming value of these practices. But we must not forget that our beliefs are personal and free— and this freedom is also extended by our Constitution to the nonbeliever.

When President Kennedy was asked to comment on the Supreme Court's prohibition of the New York regents' prayer, he said, "We have in this case a very easy remedy, and that is to pray ourselves. And I would think that it would be a welcome reminder to every American family that we can pray a good deal more at home, we can attend our churches with a good deal more fidelity, and we can make the true meaning of prayer much more important in the lives of all our children."

I agree fully with this statement of our late President. The manner of worship must be the free choice of the person; it is a personal and family responsibility that should not be surrendered to any public body. With the daily problems of society becoming more complex and the government at various levels taking a more active role in so many facets of our daily lives, I think it imperative that we protect fully and without exception the free and personal choice of religion and emphasize the responsibility of the person and the family in these matters of delicate choice. We must do nothing to upset the neutrality of government in religion; it is clear to me that with the authoritative position of state government in the public school system, this neutrality can be maintained only by a policy of abstention. I think that anything less would render a body blow to the proven American doctrine of the separation of church and state.

One's religious practice is a response to the individual conscience; it is too personal, too sacred, too private to be influenced by pressures for change each time a new school board is elected to office.

I support the First Amendment as it now exists. I believe that we should continue to separate all manners of worship from the public schoolroom. I strongly believe that we should preserve our public academic institutions from a function they cannot justify — a function that could be destructive of their purpose.

Finally, I agree that a period set aside for silent meditation in a public schoolroom would not abuse the personal choice of prayer or the private nature of worship. I believe such is consistent with the First Amendment. I urge all members to give serious thought to any proposal that seeks to change any of our Bill of Rights. I hope that, after serious consideration, you will agree that the remedy for irreligion in our society is in the home — not in the Congress.

January 18, 1967:

On a proper majority to end filibusters

The Constitution offers many safeguards against a dictatorship of the majority, among them the two-thirds voting rules for Congress in overriding vetoes and passing Constitutional amendments for ratification. An extrapolation of this is the Senate's tradition of unlimited debate, under which any Senator may hold the floor so long as he, and his surrogates to whom he yields the floor, can continue orating, or until the rest of the Senate invokes cloture. The cloture rule was introduced in 1917 and amended in 1959 to permit two-thirds of the Senators present and voting to limit floor speeches to one hour and thus to end unlimited filibustering.

Left-wing liberals in the Senate were very impatient with the two-thirds majority requirement largely because filibustering had been used so successfully by Southerners in blocking civil rights legislation. In 1959 South Carolina's Strom Thurmond had proved his manhood by setting an individual filibustering record

161

of 24 hours and 18 minutes against a civil rights bill, and a filibuster had delayed the Civil Rights Bill of 1964 for three irksome months. (The liberals were not above filibustering as the occasion demanded; Senator Wayne Morse had held the previous individual record for protracted logorrhea.)

In January 1967 Senator George McGovern introduced a rules change that would have permitted a simple majority of those present and voting to invoke cloture. Mansfield, who for a long time had been urging that the two-thirds requirement be reduced to three-fifths, stoutly opposed this effort to override minority objections. At the very least, he maintained, the actual adoption of the change should require more than a simple majority, for the continuity of the Senate as a unique American institution was involved. He was successful in his opposition, although it was not until March 1975 that his three-fifths proposal was finally adopted.

* * *

Mr. Mansfield. Mr. President, the motion of the Senator from South Dakota (Mr. McGovern) demands cloture by a simple majority; it thereby denies the continuing nature of this body. It is imperative that all of us clearly understand the full implications of this issue. It has much more significance than a direct and easy way to extricate the Senate from the parliamentary maze in which it finds itself now and at the beginning of each new Congress. The questions posed by this motion reach to the very heart of the Senate as an institution.

The underlying question is the motion to proceed to the consideration of Senate Resolution 6, a resolution to change Rule 22 to require three-fifths of those present and voting, instead of the present two-thirds, to close debate. I have always favored this proposition — not because I believe that there is anything magical about the choice of three-fifths but because I feel it draws an equitable balance while still protecting the rights of a minority position in the Senate. . . .

This biennial dispute for a change in the rules has brought to issue the question of the Senate as a continuing body. The concept is really symbolic of the notion of the Senate in our scheme of

162

government.

Numerous reasons are given to support the continuity of the Senate: the fact that two-thirds of its members carry forward from one Congress to the next; the fact that committees of the Senate meet even after *sine die* adjournment of a Congress; the fact that states themselves by their own laws require the filling of vacancies in this chamber even after *sine die* adjournment; the fact that the Senate itself by an overwhelming vote in 1959 attested to the continuation of the rules from one Congress to the next — and 47 members who voted for that proposal are still serving in this chamber. But these reasons, though compelling, have not resolved the issue. They do demonstrate, however, that the Senate as an institution is very different from the House, that its function in our scheme of government is distinct and unique. What should be considered is whether the motion at hand, the motion for simple majority cloture, would destroy the character of the Senate as a parliamentary body.

Our consideration should be directed, therefore, to the destructive effect the pending procedure would have upon these distinct and historical features which distinguish the Senate as an institution.

First of all, the motion to cut off debate immediately has never been used in the Senate. This fact does not in itself make the motion improper, but it does justify questioning why the Senate has never before chosen to cut off debate in this manner. If a simple majority votes to sustain the availability of this motion at this time, it necessarily means that henceforth on any issue, at any time, and during any future session of any Congress a simple majority, with a cooperative presiding officer, can accomplish any end they desire without regard to existing rules of process and without consideration of or regard to the viewpoint of any minority position.

Unquestionably, majority rule is basic and vital to our democracy. And a simple majority should and does decide on the merits of virtually every issue raised in this body — including a change in our rules. But that is not the question here; the question is whether the simple majority can cut off debate in the U.S. Senate. And because of the earnest zeal of the advocates for a change, and their frustration in facing a prolonged debate, they insist that in

163

this case debate must be shut off by a simple majority so that a majority can rightfully accomplish a proper change.

I think the issues are distinct. I simply feel that the protection of the minority transcends any rule change, however desirable, if attempted in this manner.

The issue of limiting debate in this body is one of such monumental importance that it reaches, in my opinion, to the very essence of the Senate as an institution. I believe it compels a decision by more than a majority. I believe it ranks with other fundamental issues which by their very nature are elevated to a level above the dictates of a majority. This is not a novel concept. This is not heresy. Our Constitution itself specifies that nine distinct issues shall require more than a majority for adoption. The Constitution of the United States is not undemocratic. . . .

In 1964 a great majority of the present members debated and resolved one of the most comprehensive pieces of legislation enacted in this century, on an issue which generated deep emotions and conflicting convictions. The distinguished occupant of the Chair, the Vice President, played an essential and leading role in that great debate on the Civil Rights Act of 1964. You will recall that the debate proceeded on this Senate floor for 83 days.

I cannot but wonder what would have been the result if a majority could have imposed cloture on that debate. I know it could have been accomplished in a month or less. I doubt very much that the bill would have been nearly as comprehensive. I do not believe that this law's observance today would be nearly as uniform, nearly as great a source of pride for all Americans without that comprehensive debate. The Senate then demonstrated its unique and distinct character. The conflicting convictions were expressed in an atmosphere of open and free debate, where the result was not by any means a foregone conclusion. Attention was focused on this body as the safety valve for an emotionally charged issue in our scheme of government. The country as a whole regarded the Senate as the one institution that would test, for all, the urgency and propriety of that measure. The fact that the law is now fully observed in all parts of our country attests abundantly to the vital service performed in this chamber. After all, any law is only as good as its observance. I think the Senate as an institution should continue to play this critical role on issues of

164

this nature, when emotions are so highly charged. It provides the only forum where calmness, coolness, and reflection may be demanded of even a majority. The experience of 1964 and 1965 removes, in my opinion, a great deal of the sting from the urgency for a change in Rule 22. I do not mean to say that a change to three-fifths would not strike a more equitable balance and still preserve the institution of the Senate in our governmental system. At the same time, there is no basis for belief that such a limited proposal would assuage the demands for further change. However, I do not agree that the basic nature of the Senate should be destroyed in reaching the end. I urge each member to consider carefully the implications of his vote.

March 13, 1967:

On inflexibility in foreign policy

The United States, like any other country, has its complement of hardcore stand-patters. In foreign policy a knot of worshippers can always be found at the altar of the status quo, sometimes wrapped piously in silent intransigence, sometimes feverishly flinging imprecations against the proponents of change.

If Mansfield was anything in arguments on foreign policy, he was a proponent of change, or flexibility and variety in responses to developing situations. In March 1967, in an address to the University of North Carolina Forum, he pointed out that U.S. policies in Europe and toward China were some twenty years out of date and that the American failure to explore every possible avenue in the United Nations toward peace in Vietnam, whatever the far-right objections to that organization, might well be responsible for the intolerable blood-letting in that ill-fated land of colonial abuse.

* * *

Prior to my coming to Congress a quarter of a century ago, I thought my stock of solutions to the questions of foreign policy was quite adequate. In fact, as a teacher of history at the University of Montana, which I was, I had a touch of what Senator Fulbright might call the arrogance of brain power. In more common idiom, there were times when I thought I knew it all. That, may I say, is a failing common to exceptional historians, from Herodotus to Schlesinger.

As a new member of Congress, I found my background in history to be highly useful. I also discovered, however, that my knowledge of international affairs did not go very far. It did not begin to provide much of an understanding of, let alone answers to, the critical issues which were emerging as World War II drew to a close. In those days, most of us in government suffered from serious imperfections in our notions of the outside world and widely held but unfounded hopes for an automatic postwar peace under the United Nations. . . .

To this day, a student I have remained; an expert I am not; and teaching is the profession to which, at some point, I may return. In the latter connection, I should note that my name is still carried, on leave of absence, on the roster of the University of Montana. Moreover, thanks to a seniority system in college teaching, second not even to that of Congress, I now hold the rank of full Professor of History.

I am constrained to point out that teaching and legislating are the two outstanding examples in American society of the application of a major tenet of Confucianism: that the accumulation of years is to be equated automatically and unquestioningly with the accumulation of wisdom. This principle, I know, is insufferable to the young, tolerable to the middle-aged, and a comfort to those full of years. At this point in time, I must confess that I find a system of seniority tolerably comfortable.

For the present, I have no hesitancy in invoking the authority with which seniority endows me, in order that I may speak to you on what seem to me to be the central concerns of contemporary American foreign policy. . . .

It used to be that we tended to stand apart and aloof from the affairs of the rest of the globe. Some have called that period of our history which led up to World War I the age of isolation. The characterization is glib and somewhat misleading. We were not so much isolated as we were insulated by a fortuitous geographic endowment. The greater part of the nation's historic energies,

166

therefore, could (and fortunately did) go inward, into the development of a rich, ample, and sparsely settled land. We had little need or inclination which would stimulate us to look much beyond this endowment for our needs and, if I may use the term, for our kicks. . . .

Since World War II, however, we have found ourselves plunged, hands, feet, and head into the mainstream of the world's affairs. We did not seek this role. We did not want it. Most of us still find the clothes of a great international power costly, ill-fitting and uncomfortable. Nevertheless, we are unable to get out of them. There is even the probability that some of us have learned not only to tolerate this new garb, but to like it.

In any event, as a sequel to World War II, this nation has come onto the center of the stage of international affairs. In this leading role we have expended an immense amount of resources, energy, and money for a great variety of purposes. We have developed all manner of costly intelligence and informational Services. We have developed towering military services whose annual cost is now around $70 billion.

We have fought one war in Asia and are now engaged in a second. We have narrowly missed involvement in several other peripheral clashes elsewhere. More than twenty years after World War II, we still have something on the order of agreements for mutual security with forty or more nations. These agreements, in effect, are commitments to military action everywhere on the globe, except perhaps the Antarctic. The strategic air force is on a minute's alert. Intercontinental and other missiles are preset for instant retaliatory launching. Day and night the American navy patrols the seven seas. American soldiers are stationed in many nations abroad; in Europe and Vietnam, they number in the hundreds of thousands.

These far-flung commitments have been questioned from time to time. In my judgment, it is most proper that pertinent questions be raised about them. Not only do they involve great expenditures of public funds; they carry, at all times, immense implications for the very survival of the nation and civilization. As I see it, we have undertaken so many and such widely scattered defense obligations that any need for the simultaneous honoring of a group of these commitments would find us hard-pressed to provide even a limited response. For that reason, if for no other, it seems to me that we would be well advised to look closely at these military commitments and activities and to weigh carefully their contemporary value ...

I speak in all candor when I say that there have been tendencies, under both Democratic and Republican administrations, for foreign policy to lag behind the realities. Until recently a kind of inertia, for example, has existed with regard to one of the central concerns of American foreign policy — the United States and Soviet confrontation in Europe. Until recently we have been most reluctant to bring ourselves to face, in policy, the changes which have taken place on that continent.

To be sure, President Eisenhower sought in his administration to restore at least a measure of civility in the conduct of U.S.-Soviet affairs, by his personal associations with the leaders of the Soviet Union. To be sure, President Kennedy, in the Nuclear Test Ban Treaty, removed a rigidity which for years had decreed that agreements should not be concluded with the Soviet Union. It has only been in the last year or two, however, that as a nation we have begun to explore fully the implications of change in Europe and to react to its potentialities in terms of our interests and world peace.

Yet substantial change has been manifest for some time in inner developments in both Eastern Europe and Western Europe and between the two regions. In Eastern Europe, the immediate postwar isolation from the West was a severe one. It was compounded of political and war-born vendettas, ideological parochialisms, reciprocal fears, and the inturning of human energy to meet the massive demands of postwar reconstruction. Especially since the death of Stalin, however, there has been a general loosening of the ideological and other strait-jackets throughout Eastern Europe. There has also been a growing response on the part of governments there to consumer needs, the satisfaction of which involves greatly expanded commerce with the non-Communist world.

As indicative of the breadth of change, communications, travel, cultural exchanges, and other contacts have grown rapidly between Eastern and Western Europe. The rise in trade levels between the two regions has been very pronounced, and it should be noted that, Berlin Wall notwithstanding, West Germany leads all other non-Communist nations in commerce with Eastern Europe.

For those who read the tea leaves of official sociability, moreover, I would call attention to the recent visits of President Podgorny of the Soviet Union to Italy and the first reception of a Chief of that State by the Pope, as well Premier Kosygin's warm receptions in Paris and London. One may attach such values as he chooses to these events. The facts of change in Europe, however, speak for themselves. The talk of war subsides; the sounds of intra-European cooperation are heard more clearly on all sides. The European detente has not only begun, it is already well advanced.

For many years, six divisions of American forces have been consigned to NATO in Western Europe. These forces and their dependents involve a U.S. military establishment in Western Europe of well over half a million Americans. It is an undertaking which represents an expenditure of billions of dollars of public funds each year. Yet I would not begrudge one cent of these funds if I were persuaded that the six divisions were as essential to peace in Europe today as they were believed to be when dispatched there years ago. . . .

It is now very evident that the United States alone has felt deeply the need to sustain the full military burden of the earlier common commitment to NATO. Our allies in Western Europe are much closer to the firing line; yet, in a period of unprecedented prosperity, they are most unwilling to carry their pledged share. In effect, the Western Europeans have made adjustments in their commitments to NATO to reflect over-all changes in Europe, and they have made these adjustments unilaterally. . . .

In all frankness, I find it difficult to acquiesce in Executive Branch fears for Western Europe's safety, which are obviously far greater than the fears of Europeans themselves. In all frankness, I find some lack of dignity in the lengths to which these fears have carried our diplomacy. We have begged, badgered, and buttered Western Europe in an effort to stimulate a greater contribution to NATO. In all frankness, I did not relish this nation having been placed in the position of wearing out its welcome in France. I should not like to see that experience repeated elsewhere in Europe. Yet it may well be repeated unless there is a willingness to make timely adjustments.

I have therefore joined with 43 other Senators in the introduction of a resolution which recommends to the President that the Executive Branch make substantial reductions in the present deployment of our forces in Western Europe. Personally, I have felt for several years that two or three, rather than six, divisions would be more than sufficient to underscore our adherence to the North Atlantic Treaty. That figure is in line with estimates of present need which have been advanced by General Eisenhower and General Gavin, both of whom have had a long association with this question. I find it most difficult to comprehend why two divisions are any less affective than six in serving notice that we regard the pledge of the North Atlantic treaty as binding and our national security as inseparable from that of the North Atlantic region. To talk of six divisions as a manifestation of international resolution and two divisions as an indication of a revived isolationism is to reveal how irrelevant, if not downright misleading, these terms have become.

On the other side of the globe, in Asia, there looms another central concern of American foreign policy. It is the confrontation with China, across the littoral states of Korea, Japan, Taiwan, and Vietnam.

Almost two decades have passed since the collapse of the national government on the Chinese mainland and its retreat to the island of Taiwan. That event, which occurred when most of you were too young for it to be noticed, was cataclysmic in its consequences. It sundered the fabric of Chinese society and, almost overnight, brought about the disintegration of a main pillar of postwar American foreign policy. In the rubble, the watchword became "wait for the dust to settle" before doing anything about China. . . .

Within China there have been momentous events which have also added to the difficulties and uncertainties of developing a cohesive policy toward the Chinese mainland. The Chinese have exploded nuclear devices at Lop Nor in the western Asian desert of Sinkiang. Recent ideological conflicts have sent great tremors through the whole of the inner political structure of China. There has been, finally, the great cleavage in Sino-Soviet revolutionary solidarity which has torn apart almost all of the relationships between the two giant nations of the Eurasian continent.

170

In the context of these events, it is not surprising that the dust, for the settling of which American policy has waited for 18 years, is heavier than ever. The obscurity, moreover, is not likely to be dispelled in the near future. There is nothing in the recent history of China which suggests that it will be easier tomorrow than it is today for us to see clearly a direction for effective policy. Whatever the course of American relations with China, it will have to be pursued in spite of the dust with which the situation is covered. . . .

We can also note, from afar, the serious difficulties between the Soviet Union and China. . . . Whatever the possibilities, if any, of more effective adjustment of our policies in the light of this and other trends, however, we are inhibited from their pursuit by our current approach or, rather, non-approach to mainland China.

Let me turn, finally, to the immediate and overriding problem of policy, the situation in Vietnam. Vietnam affects every other aspect of our foreign relations, and particularly the two central concerns. It diminishes our capacity to deal constructively with the United States —Soviet confrontation in Europe. To put it mildly, it multiplies the problems of the confrontation with China in Asia. . . .

I must say, with great regret, that signs of a settlement in the near future are lacking. There is, instead, the fact of an ugly war of spreading devastation. All the while, the options are running out; the alternatives which might lead to negotiations grow fewer.

Many proposals have been put forth and many have been explored. As an example, over the past year or more I have publicly called attention to these possible easements of the situation and for eventual settlement:

1) in lieu of aerial bombardment of North Vietnam, the sealing off of the borders of the 17th parallel, through Laos;

2) a reconvening of the Geneva Conference on the basis of the 1954 and 1962 agreements by call of the cochairmen, the United Kingdom and the Soviet Union, or by any participating conferees;

3) an all-Asian conference at Rangoon or Tokyo, or any other suitable location, to consider the conditions of an honorable peace;

4) the inclusion in any peace conference of whatever

belligerents may be necessary to bring about a termination of the conflict in Vietnam;

5) an enlargement of the Manila Conference of 1966 into a follow-up conference, to include friend and foe alike; and

6) a face-to-face meeting of the Secretary of State, Dean Rusk, and the Foreign Minister of the Peking government to discuss the restoration of peace in Vietnam.

In addition, I have urged that the closest consideration be given to informed French views on Vietnam and to the views of the Cambodian Premier, Prince Norodom Sihanouk. I have urged that the proposals of U Thant and Mrs. Ghandi be considered. I have endorsed various statements of the President, Secretary Rusk, and Ambassador Goldberg, all of which have made clear that not only our proposals but also those of Hanoi and the People's Liberation Front might provide a basis for settlement. I have recommended that there be not just a cessation of the bombing of North Vietnam but that all killing stop, on both sides, in a cease-fire and stand-fast, on the ground and in the waters adjacent to Vietnam as well as over Vietnam, to the end that efforts may be made to initiate talks.

In some of these proposals the President has concurred and has had them pursued by his diplomats. He has examined all of them and, if they have not been pursued, I can only conclude that there have been sound reasons for not pursuing them. Suggestions for peace have come from many sources; the actual pursuit of peace in the past year, however, has been by diplomacy, and largely by secret diplomacy. Indeed, that is the case even with the efforts of the distinguished Secretary General of the United Nations, U Thant. In his attempts to bring about a peace in Vietnam, U Thant has acted in his personal and diplomatic capacity rather than in his Secretarial capacity of carrying out organizational decisions of the United Nations. . . .

It seems to me that the cause of a peaceful and honorable settlement may possibly be advanced — certainly it cannot be hurt— by modest recourse at this time to the procedural machinery of the United Nations. In my judgment, this nation should consider seeking a face-to-face confrontation of all belligerents at the United Nations. Following the Korean precedents, it seems to me eminently desirable that this government give every consideration to a possible initiative which would bring to a vote in the Security Council two resolutions along the following lines:

> 1) that the Security Council invite all belligerents, direct and indirect, including China and North Vietnam, to participate in an open discussion of the conflict in Vietnam and ways and means of ending it; and

> 2) that the Security Council request the International Court to render an advisory opinion on the current applicability of the Geneva Accords of 1954 and 1962 and the obligations which these agreements may place on the present belligerents in Vietnam.

Whether or not there is much prospect of a positive response from others in no way lessens the desirability of offering these resolutions in good faith and bringing them to a vote. In my judgment, an American initiative of this kind serves not only our interests but the interests of peace in Vietnam.

Let me conclude by clarifying one point: the conflict in Vietnam cannot be settled from the Congress or from the campus. In the end, if it is to be settled honorably, there is only one Constitutional officer of your government who can speak for you and for the entire nation in its foreign relations. Whether we agree with him or not, whether we like him or not, whether we abhor him or love him, that man is the President of the United States.

In a government such as ours, a Senator lives with a Constitution, a constituency, and a conscience. All three considerations underlie the suggestions respecting Vietnam which have been made here today and which have been expressed on other occasions. President Johnson and all the Presidents who have gone before him have listened to advice from many sources, including the Senate.

It is the President, however, who makes the fundamental decisions of foreign policy. These decisions are of an immensity which enjoins upon us all a high respect for the burdens which a President must bear, and a responsibility to tender to him every support which can be given in good conscience. In the end, these decisions will determine — insofar as it lies within this nation to determine — the moment of peace in Vietnam and Asia.

May 30, 1967:

On the megastatistics

of the war in Vietnam

As of January 1967, the numbers of American soldiers killed and wounded in the first six years of the conflict in Vietnam (since the formation of the Vietcong) were 6,700 and 38,000, respectively. Before the end of that year the figures were to reach 15,000 and 100,000; in that single year there would be more American casualties than in the preceding six. Small wonder that the use of the word "escalation" was escalating in American political conversation, from sea to shining sea.

In a Memorial Day commencement address at Haverford College in Pennsylvania, Mansfield tried to add some meaning to the tragic statistics of the war. The greatest tragedy, he feared, might be a lessening of sensitivity, among his fellow citizens, not only to what was being done to Americans but also to what Americans were doing. The "megastatistical" part of his speech is given here; the rest, devoted to recommendations for pursuing peace, largely recapitulated his talk at the University of North Carolina three months earlier.

* * *

...I expect that what you expect from me is to make some sense on the question of Vietnam — on the war and its prospects and your prospects in the light of it. I do not know that I can live up to those expectations if what you seek is a punchcard computation of satisfying answers. I do not have that sort of information, and I do not know how to run the computers. As one Senator, I have only the personal estimates and attitudes which come from a long effort to understand what is involved in the problems of Vietnam and Asia. I have only the concerns which I share with young people as to their personal future in the light of this persisting difficulty. I have only an awareness of the curtain of uncertainty

174

which Vietnam has drawn across the pursuit of happiness in this nation and the prospects for continued civilized survival everywhere in the world . . . .

The fact is that the war bewilders. The sensitivities of our society are changed. Figures totalling billions of dollars tend to be regarded now with the noncomprehension of scores in a sport in which we are not interested. Unless affected directly by personal considerations, we tend to accept the grisly casualty counts with the same non-thought as the regular morning cup of coffee. In the growing demands of war there is a tendency to consign to a limbo pressing domestic problems and other issues of foreign policy. . . .

It might be possible to appreciate what $25 billion a year for war in Vietnam means if the figure is compared with the annual cost of certain other Federal programs. On the basis of the President's budget requests in January for the coming fiscal year, for example:

Fourteen weeks of war expenditures in Vietnam would fund all Federal transportation proposals, including our huge highway construction program and the development of such items as high-speed railroad and commuter services and the supersonic passenger airplane.

A year's costs of veterans' benefits and services growing out of all past wars could be met with 12 weeks of current war expenditures in Vietnam.

Eight weeks of military expenses in Vietnam equal all of the Federal monies sought for education — elementary, secondary, higher, vocational and international — and the special funds for improving education in city slums and depressed rural areas.

The costs of all housing and urban affairs programs of the Federal government, including slum clearance and other efforts to make the nation's cities safer and more satisfying places for human habitation represent 6 weeks of the cost of the Vietnamese war.

The entire Food for Peace program, which feeds millions of hungry people abroad, is supported on the equivalent of less than 4 weeks of war costs in Vietnam.

The international activities in which we participate for the purposes of humanitarian and economic goals, and above all a more stable peace, can be expressed in similar stark contrasts. The

175

annual level of U.S. appropriations, for example, for the inter-American Alliance for Progress, much of which is repayable, represents only about 6 weeks of war costs in Vietnam. One economist has estimated that a redistribution of farmland to peasants throughout India, Pakistan, the coastal areas of Asia, and all of Latin America could be brought about, equitably and without confiscation, for about $5 billion in total cost. That would be the equivalent of 10 weeks of war expenditures in Vietnam. Finally, a look at United Nations costs suggests that the entire annual U.S. contribution to the regular budget and to all other programs of that organization — such as the peace-keeping missions in the Middle East, Cyprus, and elsewhere — comes to 80 hours, or 3 days, of war expenditures in Vietnam. . . .

Whatever the economic implications, however, the fundamental tragedy of Vietnam lies not so much in those considerations as in the toll of human life and hope. Already the overall casualties are more than one-third those of the Korean war.

It is grim to speak of human suffering by way of statistics, yet some numerical comparisons are necessary if we are to understand the dimensions of Vietnam. In the first three weeks of April, for example, 518 Americans were killed in action. These young men joined 10,000 others who have lost their lives since U.S. troops were committed to Vietnam. So far the number of young Pennsylvanians alone who have been killed in Vietnam is about equal to the entire student body of Haverford College.

In addition to the dead, there have been over 60,000 Americans wounded in Vietnam. To give this figure of 60,000 some sense of the pain it has entailed, note that it would be the equivalent if every man, woman and child in the city suffered an injury in some sudden and appalling disaster in Haverford. . . .

The hostile military forces against whom we are pitted have also been hard hit. Official sources list the combined total of North Vietnamese and Vietcong killed in action as 149,000 for 1966, with weekly totals at times in excess of 2000. These figures are indicative of the great destructiveness of the repertoire of modern weapons which has been drawn upon for use in Vietnam. Yet enemy forces continue the struggle and actually are growing in numbers. The latest Pentagon figures show enemy strength at record levels — 287,000 today as compared to 239,000 a year ago.

This increase is in the face of an estimated loss of half a million in the war to date. . . .

Much has hapened since Dienbienphu. Many persons have been involved, Communists and non-Communists, Americans and foreigners, Democrats and Republicans. Mistakes have been made. Good intentions have been distorted. At this late date, the question is not "Who got us here and why?" but rather "Where do we go from here, and how?"

In connection therewith, I hope that I have at least made the point that as one American, as one Senator, I believe without reservation that it is in the interest of the United States and all others involved in Vietnam and the world to scale down these hostilities as quickly as possible. I believe it is in the common interest to get to the conference table without delay, to bring this war to an honorable end, and to begin using the immense energy and resources which are now preempted by the conflict for the constructive works of peace.

August 24, 1967:

"In a Montana Mood"

By the mid-sixties Mansfield's reputation as an outstanding Congressional authority on international relations was solidly established. In 1967 it was figuratively carved in Montana granite when the University of Montana Foundation inaugurated a series of lectures on foreign relations to be known as the Mike Mansfield Lectures. In an August address to Foundation representatives in Washington, D.C., he responded by demonstrating how lyrical he could be about the grand and rugged state which, after a quarter of a century of working and living in Washington, he and Maureen (to whom he here again paid tribute) thought of as their only real home.

It has been said that the two great loves of my life are the University and the study of foreign affairs. I readily acknowledge a lasting liaison with the first and a deep absorption in the second.

The University and foreign affairs are indeed great loves. But there is another which is greater and comes before both. That is the State of Montana — the Land of the Shining Mountains and the High Plains — and its people.

For a quarter of a century Montanans have trusted me, as one of them, to represent their concerns, first in the House and then in the Senate of the United States. I have tried to sustain that trust by following the basic principle: If I do not forget the people of Montana, they will not forget me.

So, for a quarter of a century, Montana's people, regardless of politics, position, power or profession, have come first with me. That is as it always has been. That is as it always will be.

That bond that ties me to Montana is woven of many strands. But, before all else, it involves my personal feelings, as a citizen of the state, for its beauty, history, and people. For you who are not of Montana, let me try to tell you why the bond is inseparable, insofar as I am concerned. Let me try to explain to you why Montanans who are outside of Montana are always homesick for Montana.

To me, Montana is a symphony.

It is a symphony of color. It is painted by a thousand different plants and shrubs which set the hills ablaze — each with its own kind of inner fire — during spring and summer. Montana is the intense blue of the Big Sky reflected in the deep blue of mountain lakes and the ice-blue of tumbling streams. It is the solid white of billowing clouds and the haze-white of snow on a hundred mountain peaks. It is the infinite theme of green in mile after mile of farm-rich valleys and in millions of acres of forests.

We who are of Montana know the color harmony of a springtime of millions of wild flowers — the orange poppies, purple heather, yellow columbines, red Indian paintbrush, beargrass, and purple asters in the mountains; the tiger lilies, dogtooth violets, Mariposa lilies, bitterroot and kinnikinnick in the foothills; the shooting stars, daisies, larkspur, yellow bells, and sand lillies in the plains.

And in the long winter we know the muted music of the snows

which blanket the state. A theme of hope runs through these snows because they are the principal storehouse of the state's great natural resource of water. In one year the amount which will flow out of the mountains and rush down the hills is enough to fill Montana from boundary to boundary to a depth of six inches. And bear in mind that Montana's 54 million acres make the state as large as the entire nation of Japan with its hundred million people.

Montana is a symphony. It is a symphony of color and it is a symphony of sounds. Listen for them for a moment, in the names of places. There are mountain ranges called the Beaverhead, the Sapphire, the Ruby, the Bear Paws, the Highwoods, the Snowies, the Beartooths, the Judiths, the Crazies, and the Big Belts. And, incidentally, there are also the Little Belts as well.

There are streams whose names sing: the Silver Bow, the Flathead, the Kootenai, and the Sun; the Jefferson, the Madison, the Gallatin, and the Musselshell; the Milk, the Yellowstone, the Tongue, the Powder, the Blackfoot, and the Boulder.

And when the roll of Montana's cities and towns is called, you hear: Eureka, Chinook, Whitefish, Cut Bank; Circle, Hungry Horse, Absarokee, Butte, Wolf Point, and Great Falls. And you hear Lodge Grass, Lame Deer, Deer Lodge, Crow Agency, Big Fork, and Twodot.

These and a hundred others like them are strains in the history of the state. Each has a story, and together they sing the story of Montana.

It began in a mist of time, with Indians — with the Crows, the Blackfeet, the Assiniboine, the Flatheads, the Chippewa-Crees, the Sioux, and the Northern Cheyennes. Then came Lewis and Clark and the great fur-trading companies. When the boom in pelts died, the gold rush began. At Grasshopper Creek in 1862, the find was so rich it was said that miners could pull up sage brush and shake a dollar's worth of dust out of the roots. The town of Confederate Gulch grew on gold. In six years the population jumped from zero to 10,000 people. In the seventh year, the gold was gone, and only 64 lonely souls remained.

Indians, fur and gold echo in the overture to Montana's history, and throughout runs the beat of the famous and infamous, the hunted, the haunted, the violent and the pacific and the politic.

179

There was, for example, the notorious Henry Plummer who, as Sheriff of Bannack, engineered the bushwhacking murders of 102 of the citizens he was supposed to protect before he was hung by the vigilantes. But there was also the Methodist minister, Wesley Van Orsdel — Brother Van — who got off a steamer at Fort Benton in 1872 and went directly to the Four Deuces saloon to preach his first sermon; and the saloon closed, respectfully, for one hour for the service. . . .

Silver came after gold. It was struck rich in places like Argenta, Butte, Granite, Castle, Elkhart, Monarch, and Neihart. But when Congress discontinued the purchase of silver in 1892, the silver camps were added to the ghost towns which dotted the lonely gold trails.

Then it was copper's turn, at Butte and Anaconda in western Montana. The struggle for copper was of such proportions that it set off political and economic reverberations which are felt even today not only in the state but also in the nation and throughout the world.

While some dug into Montana's earth for wealth, others sought it from what grew out of the earth. Stockmen filled the rolling, grass-covered high plains of central and eastern Montana with cattle and sheep. In scarcely ten years the cattle population rose from a few thousand to over a million. Then the cruel winter of 1886-87 froze 90 percent of them into grotesque ice sculptures on the plains, and another Montana "boom" went "bust."

Beginning in the 19th century, railroads run through the symphony of Montana. Sledges in the gnarled hands of a hundred thousand immigrants pounded down the parallel steel ribbons, mile upon mile. The iron horses came rushing out across a continent. The Great Northern advertised free government land in a region of "milk and honey" to lure settlers to its line. They came in eager droves from Scandinavia, Germany, Mexico, Poland, Yugoslavia, France, Italy, Spain, and the United Kingdom, Ireland, and a score of other countries. They made agriculture, mining and lumbering the state's chief industries. But the great drought of 1917 took away the milk and honey and left only a parched and stricken land and a hurt and wiser people.

Montanans drove, tumbled and stumbled into the 20th century. The state has picked itself up and started over again many times.

Its history is of a people drawn from many sources, headed toward the glowing promise of the Western frontier. It is of a people who have known the collapse of hope and the renewal of hope. It is of a people who have lived in intimacy with fear as well as courage, with cruelty as well as compassion. It is of a people who have known not only the favor but the fury of a bountiful and brooding Nature. The history of Montana is the song of a people who, repeatedly shattered, have held together, persevered, and, at last, taken enduring root.

Now the 20th century moves on toward the 21st, and the ups and downs of the past yield to the more stable present. The state has grown out of a dependency upon a single extractive industry. The old threat of spring flooding and summer drought grows dimmer as Yellowtail, Canyon Ferry, Hungry Horse and other dams — great and small, public and private — have risen to discipline the rushing waters. The cold temperatures — a reading of 70° below zero has been recorded at Rogers Pass — have yielded to modern heating. And the hot temperatures — it once reached 117° above in Glendive — are tempered in Montana as elsewhere by air conditioning to match its cool nights. Plane travel cuts the huge distances and the immense isolation. Indeed, the virtues of Montana's space, clean air, and clean water, scenery and unparalleled recreational opportunities are becoming better known and look ever more inviting to the rest of the nation.

Modern transitions notwithstanding, something remains in the state that is durably unique and uniquely durable. It is to be found in the character of the people. Montanans are formed by the vastness of a state whose mountains rise to 12,000 feet in granite massives, piled one upon another as though by some giant hand. To drive across the state is to journey, in distance, from Washington, D.C., north to Toronto or south to Florida. In area, we can accommodate Virginia, Maryland, Delaware, Pennsylvania and New York, and still have room for the District of Columbia.

Yet, in all this vastness, we are far less than a million people. In short, Montanans have room to live, to breathe, and, above all, to *think* — to think with a breadth of view which goes to the far horizon and beyond. Vast and empty space and high mountains may isolate a population, but they open the minds of a people. The minds of Montanans dwell not only upon community and state,

181

but upon the nation and the world and on the essential unity of all. And this sense of unity is buttressed by the harsh uncertainties of an all-powerful environment which has taught us to draw together in a mutual concern for one another and to be hospitable to all who come from afar.

So, in a sense, a lecture series on international relations which is proposed to be initiated at the University of Montana will be doing what comes naturally to Montanans, because it promises to open up new channels of understanding between us and our unseen neighbors on this globe. The series will stimulate, I am sure, deeper insights and greater comprehension of the nation's relationships with the people who live on all of its horizons.

I need not tell you that the realization that this process will be taking place under the aegis of my name fills my heart to the full. It is far more than I ever expected when I came to Washington to represent Montana in Congress a quarter of a century ago. It is far, far more than I deserve.

Indeed, I should like this honor to go where it is most due — to the woman who set out with me from Butte so long ago and who has remained a wise counsellor and steadfast inspiration through all these years. Without her, I would not be in the Congress of the United States. Indeed, I should not have reached the University of Montana or for that matter even received a high school certificate. A more appropriate title for the lecture series, therefore, would be "The Maureen and Mike Mansfield Lectures."

May I suggest, too, that if the response to the effort on which you have embarked is a good one, a modest maximum should be established for the capital of the Fund for the lectures on international affairs. If any additional monies should become available beyond that maximum, I should like to see the excess go into scholarships for the children of Montana's, and the nation's, first Americans, who have not always had the benefit in equal measure with the rest of us from Montana's development and the nation's progress. I refer to my friends and brothers — the Northern Cheyennes, the Crows, the Flatheads, the Assiniboines, the Blackfeet, the Chippewa-Crees, the Landless, and all the others who live with us in Montana.

I suggest this procedure because the lecture series by its very nature turns our attention to the world beyond our borders and to the promise of a fruitful future for Montanans and all Americans. It is good that our attention is so directed *provided* we are also prepared to look inward and backward, and so remember what it is we are building upon; and to try to fill the gaps and to heal the hurts which may have been opened in the process of arriving at where we are. In that way, we shall better tie the past into the present and open wider the horizons of the future. In that way, we shall better bind together, into a greater nation, all who live in a great state and in a blessed land.

I wish that, tonight, I could have more adequately conveyed to you the thoughts on my mind and the feelings, the deep feelings, in my heart. But words are inadequate when the mind and the heart are too full.

September 7, 1967:

On counterviolence in the cities

In July 1967 Newark, New Jersey, was the scene of riots in which 20 people were killed and over 1000 wounded; in riots in Detroit, 43 people died, nearly 2000 were injured, and 5000 were left homeless in a paroxysm of burning and looting. In response to these and other incidents, cries of law and order echoed throughout the land, delivered generally in the same hard accents as the demands that the United States win, win, win in Vietnam. Generally, too, these same accents marked the complaints against profligate government spending on nonmilitary boondoggles like urban renewal. There were a lot of bumper stickers calling vaguely for support of local police but none for raising their pay.

Merely applying more force, Mansfield countered prophetically, would prove as futile in the cities as it was proving in Vietnam. In September 1967, at a meeting of the Missouri Bar Association, he pleaded his case for rejection of counterviolence as a solution to the misery in the American ghettos and in Indochina. Whatever the answers might be, he argued, that surely wasn't one of them.

183

There are, I am advised, about a thousand lawyers at this conference. A lot of lawyers. But, if my calculations are correct, this large gathering forms only 0.3% of the legal profession in the United States.

To a nonlawyer who happens to be a lawmaker, the thought of 300,000 lawyers gives rise to a most uncomfortable question. How can we in the Congress, who are so few, generate so much business for so many? I find even more appalling the possibility that the necessity for so many lawyers may be related to the quality of the product of the lawmakers.

Be that as it may, I do know that lawmakers and lawyers share a common endeavor and a common hope. We work to strengthen the nation and the freedom and well-being of its people within a framework of law.

This joint effort is confronted in 1967 with a challenge whose character is peculiarly of our own times even if it has been of many times in the making. We are living through a long night of violence both at home and abroad. A harsh antiphony of hostility is heard throughout the nation. It rises out of the ordeal of Vietnam and is echoed in the turbulence of the nation's cities.

The sound of violence does not set well with me or with you who are trained to seek peaceful and orderly solutions to disputes. Nevertheless, as a nation we have become so jaded by the continuous violence of our times that the sense of indignation appears dulled except at moments of fierce fury when a great city goes up in flames.

It takes a Detroit to arouse the nation. But Detroit took a toll of 43 dead and brought injury to more than 1000 people, many of whom were peaceful bystanders. For five days the overall casualties in Detroit ran at a higher rate than those which, of late, have been suffered by American forces in Vietnam.

While Detroit burned, it was not uncommon to hear expressed, as a remedy for rioting, less coddling and more cudgeling. That remedy on a massive scale is thought by some also to provide a way out of the difficulty in Vietnam.

Experience has demonstrated, however, that it would be as futile as it is dangerous to yield to any easy indulgence of that kind at home or abroad. In the urban areas of the nation no less than in Vietnam, an abject reliance on force is a formula not so much for solutions as for stretching a summer of seething disorder into an autumn of simmering discontent, and so on from season to season and year to year.

The cure of urban ills involves something more than force, even as force is essential in the restoration of an order which has broken down. On that subject let me say that for too long we have expected too much for too little from the police of the nation. The police are more often than not underpaid, underprivileged, over-used and over-abused. Indeed, it is not unusual to hear the cry of "police brutality" while a policeman is being hit over the head. . . .

It is one thing to reject rioting. It is another, however, to turn our back on the difficulties of the urban areas because riots have occurred in them. Those difficulties were there before the riots. They were there during the riots. They are there now. The nation's responsibility for confronting these difficulties existed before the riots. It existed during the riots. It exists now. . . .

That is not to say that an effort has not been made, in a paraphrase of the words of John Fitzgerald Kennedy, to "get the cities moving again." We owe a great deal to him for his efforts in this direction. We owe a great deal to Lyndon B. Johnson for continuing and expanding the effort, and also to his insistence that the effort be realistic in a financial sense. Under his leadership, and in cooperation with Congress, many Federal stimulants have been applied boldly and broadly in an effort to revive the urban centers.

These efforts have cost a great deal of money. They are going to cost more. We are properly concerned with these costs and with the effectiveness of the efforts. We can properly inquire into the great number of programs which have been put into operation within the last few years. May I say that I have advocated for several years a more vigorous exercise of legislative review by the Congress in this connection. And various Senate committees are proceeding with the job of evaluating, adjusting and improving this vast body of legislation.

It will help to keep a perspective in this process, however, if we note that the cost of the Federal programs which are directed heavily at the urban and other social ills of the nation run to billions a year less than the cost of the Vietnam war and are but a fraction of the budget of the Department of Defense, which now reaches an overall annual figure of about $70 billion. As we have been prepared to make the effort for the security of others abroad, and particularly the security of Vietnam, we must also be prepared to act for the inner security and stability of the nation. . . .

The long night of violence in Vietnam will know no dawn until the world community can end the diplomatic inertia which has characterized its reaction to Vietnam. Until the war is brought to an end, moreover, the hope of removing the roots of disorder in our cities may well remain beyond our reach.

February 23, 1968:

On "winning" in Vietnam

High on the list of many Americans' sacred cows is the competitive sport. Its simple ideals of superiority over rivals and of totally artificial "team loyalty" may be harmless enough on the playing fields, where muscle-headed aggression generally harms only muscles and superfluous heads, but such simple fantasies can be devastating, as illustrated in the Vietnam and Watergate competitions.

In early 1968 there were still plenty of war-games fans bent on "winning" the war in Vietnam. The scorecard often descended to listing comparative casualties. The unsavory President Thieu, whose concern for the people's needs and desires was modeled on that of Louis XIV, was our s.o.b. and therefore deserved America's loyal support, at the cost of thousands of lives and unimaginable suffering. Ho Chi Minh, even if he was personally frugal and had wide popular support, was nevertheless one of them. This cheerleader approach to the problem of Vietnam was already poisoning discussions of an "honorable" withdrawal from Vietnam. Under Nixon and Ford, whose notions of honor apparently were derived from Vince Lombardi, it was to delay complete withdrawal until long after the game was over.

Mansfield touched on this sports-fan's view of the Vietnam

186

controversy in a speech at Indiana University in late February 1968, just five weeks before Lyndon Johnson was to concede final political defeat. One reason for this defeat doubtless was that the Texas warrior had now almost completely lost the support, though not the sympathy, of his former Senate whip in the debate over Vietnam.

The Indiana speech was introduced into the Congressional Record on March 1 by Senator Clairborne Pell of Rhode Island. Part of his introduction is included here.

* * *

Mr. Pell. Mr. President, the problem of Vietnam and what we should do in achieving a decent resolution to our involvement in that wartorn, unhappy land is a problem that looms over the thinking, the plans, and the aspirations of us all.

There is no Senator among us who is more familiar and knowledgeable concerning this problem than the senior Senator from Montana, whose knowledge of the area and whose experience with its people is great.

The distinguished Senator from Montana made a singularly perceptive and forthright speech at the convocation of the University of Indiana a week ago today. . . .

I call the speech to the attention of my colleagues. . . .

* * *

The struggle in Vietnam has turned grim, pitiless, and devastating. The casualty figures are staggering. The physical damage is enormous. Men, women, children, soldiers, guerillas, weapons, machines, cities, towns, and villages — all are thrown together in an inferno of destruction.

It is not surprising that the situation has been interpreted in some quarters as approaching some sort of climax. It may well be, as has been suggested, the beginning of the end. The question is, what beginning and what end? Peace by military victory? Peace by negotiations? With whom? For what? There is no certainty at this point as to what will emerge in Vietnam or, for that matter, whether the end of this war is to be found in Vietnam.

I have no desire, therefore, to indulge today in what has become a kind of parlor game called "Who's winning in Vietnam?" It is offensive to me, as I know it must be to you, to hear this deadly conflict treated as some sort of athletic contest. The lives of too many young Americans are on the line in Vietnam. Too many bewildered men and women and children are being burnt, bloodied and broken by this war. Too much is in ruins. Too many lie dead. Vietnam is not a game. There can be no winners; there are only losers, and the longer the war persists the greater are the losses of all concerned. . . .

A restoration of peace is imperative for the welfare of the people of Vietnam; they have been fought over for so long that, in the millions, they are torn from their ancestral places, seeking refuge where there is no refuge. For us, too, an honorable solution is of the utmost urgency. The war in Vietnam has been deeply divisive in its effects on this nation. It has diverted energy and resources from the great needs of our own society. The vast difficulties of the urban areas, for example, cry out for attention, but the cry is barely heard above the din of the distant conflict.

The nation's economic equilibrium is in danger of being thrown out of kilter by the immense demands of the war. In this connection, we have already suffered a significant degree of inflation. Furthermore, we are confronted with what can only be called the embarrassment of having to discourage the travel of Americans abroad because of difficulties which the war and other foreign commitments have introduced into the nation's balance of payments.

In our relations with the rest of the world, the war in Vietnam has placed formidable blocks in the way of further progress in international cooperation. It has brought in its wake new threats to the stability of peace, as in the case of the U.S.S. Pueblo incident, which may be but the precursor of others. In these pinpoints of instability, moreover, there are ever-present threats to the frail defenses of the world against nuclear catastrophe. . . .

Whatever the outcome of the present battles, the basic military problem is as it has been from the outset. The war remains open-ended, and escalation continues to rise with escalation. The National Liberation Front remains omnipresent, from the demilitarized zone at the 17th parallel to the southern tip of the peninsula. Its regular forces and guerillas are obviously steeled to accept great privation and to make enormous sacrifices. The Vietcong remain entrenched and virtually untouched in their traditional strongholds: the swamps, the paddyfields and hamlets of the Mekong Delta, from which they are able to dispatch forces to reinforce units which, as is now apparent, honeycomb Saigon and other cities.

It is dangerous to presume that either the forces of the National Liberation Front or North Vietnam are nearing the end of their rope. Actually, Hanoi has committed to the war in the south considerably less than a quarter of the forces of General Vo Nguyen Giap, who is generally credited with masterminding the current military strategy in the south. And beyond North Vietnam lies the untapped manpower of China and the supply sources of both China and the Soviet Union. . . .

This nation is deeply committed in South Vietnam, but let us not make the mistake of interpreting that commitment as compelling us, in the name of victory or whatever, to see to it that every last member of the NLF is either dulled, dead, captive, or in flight. That course leads not to an ending but to an endless succession of violent beginnings.

An inextricable involvement of American forces in Vietnam may meet the needs of some, but it accords with neither the interests of the United States nor those of the people of Vietnam. In this connection President Johnson has repeatedly stated that the nation's objective is ". . . only that the people of South Vietnam be allowed to guide their own country in their own way." He has stated that he is willing to move at any time in negotiations which might bring about that result. He has stated that we are prepared to move out lock, stock, and barrel in a matter of months after a satisfactory settlement is achieved.

It should be clear, therefore, to all concerned — Americans and Vietnamese in Washington, in Saigon, and in Hanoi, and to whomever, wherever — that that is the accurate measure of this nation's commitment. There is no obligation to continue to pour out the blood and resources of this nation until South Vietnam is made safe for one Vietnamese faction or another. On the contrary, there is an obligation to the people of the United States to conserve that blood and those resources; and, to the people of Vietnam, there is an obligation to avoid the destruction of their land and society even in the name of saving them. . . .

March 29, 1968:

On rapprochement with Red China

In 1956 the government of Communist China suggested an exchange of journalists with the United States. But in those days there was still feverish talk of "unleashing" Chiang Kai-shek, as though the leash were holding him in rather than holding him up. The Chinese suggestion was curtly rejected by Secretary of State John Foster Dulles, whose foreign policy was much given to the uninformative but righteous glare. When State Department bureaucrats later sought to accept the suggestion on sober second thought, they found that it had been withdrawn.

The incident typified the United States' lack of communication with the government of the world's most populous country, which was already experimenting with nuclear bombs. By 1968 the situation had become so obviously ridiculous and deplorable that even Richard Nixon was tentatively recommending a change. In March of that year Mansfield, who had been urging a change for years, returned to the subject in the first of the foreign policy lectures to be given under the auspices of the Maureen and Mike Mansfield Endowment at the University of Montana.

* * *

Vietnam is heavy on the heart of the nation. The Vietnamese war is a tragedy. It is a tragedy in the American lives which it claims. It is a tragedy in the death and devastation which, in the name of salvation, it has spread throughout Vietnam. . . .

What I have to say to you today touches only indirectly on Vietnam. My remarks are intended to go beyond Vietnam to what may well be the roots of the war. In this first lecture of the series on

190

international affairs, I wish to address your attention to what is the great void in the foreign relations of this nation — to the question of China. . . .

China needs peace if the potentials of its culture are to be realized. This nation needs peace for the same reason. In this day and age, the world needs peace for civilized survival. You young people have the greatest stake in peace. For that reason, I ask you to look beyond Vietnam, behind Korea, to what may well be the core of the failure of peace in Asia — to the U.S.-Chinese estrangement of two decades.

In 1784 Robert Morris, a signer of the Declaration of Independence, sent the first American clipper ship to trade with China. The year that President George Washington took the oath of office, 1789, fourteen American ships were riding at anchor in the Pearl River off Canton in south China.

There are no American ships in Chinese ports today. There have not been for almost twenty years. In twenty years, hardly an American doctor, scientist, businessman, journalist, student, or even a tourist has set foot in China.

Across the Pacific Ocean, we and the Chinese glare at one another, uncomprehendingly, apprehensively, and suspiciously. In the United States there is fear of the sudden march of Chinese armies into Southeast Asia. In China there is fear of a tighter American encirclement and American nuclear attack . . . .

We and the Chinese have not always looked at one another with such baleful mistrust. The American images of China have fluctuated and shifted in an almost cyclical way. There has been the image of the China of wisdom, intelligence, industry, piety, stoicism, and strength. This is the China of Marco Polo, Pearl Buck, Charlie Chan, and heroic resistance to the Japanese during World War II.

On the other hand, there has been the image of the China of cruelty, barbarism, violence, and faceless hordes. This is the China of drumhead trials, summary executions, Fu Manchu, and the Boxer Rebellion — the China that is summed up in the phrase "yellow peril." . . .

At the end of World War II, admiration was displaced by disappointment and frustration, as the wartime truce between Nationalist and Communist forces collapsed in cataclysmic in-

191

ternal strife. This nation became profoundly disenchanted with China, a disenchantment which was replaced abruptly in 1949 by hostility.

The hostility was largely a reaction, of course, to the coming to power of a Communist regime on the Chinese mainland. We did not interpret this event as a consequence of the massive difficulties and the vast inner weaknesses of a war-torn China. Rather, we saw it almost as an affront to this nation. We saw it as a treacherous extension of the Soviet steamroller policies which had reduced eastern and central Europe to subservience at the end of World War II. . . .

Still, the press of events continued relentlessly. In June 1950 the North Koreans launched a sudden attack on South Korea. The Chinese forces intervened in the war in November of that year. The United States was brought into a major military confrontation in which, for the first time, the Chinese were enemies and not allies.

After these events, the assumptions of American policy toward China were revised. An effort was made to meet both the concern and the outrage respecting China which existed in this nation and the revolutionary militancy of the new Chinese regime in Asia. Policy was cast anew on the premise that the government on the Chinese mainland was an aggressor which, subject to directions from Moscow, would use force to impose International Communism on Asia. Conversely, it was assumed that if the endorsement of the free nations were withheld, this regime, which was said to be "alien" to the Chinese people — some sort of overgrown puppet of Moscow — would wither and eventually collapse.

On this basis, recognition was not extended to Peking. The official view was that the National Government, which had retreated to the island of Taiwan, continued to speak for all of China. We cut off all trade with the mainland and did what could be done to encourage other countries to follow suit. In a similar fashion, we led a diplomatic campaign year after year against the seating of the Chinese People's Republic in the United Nations. We drew an arc of military alliances on the seaward side of China and undergirded them with the deployment of massive American military power in bases through the western Pacific.

Much has happened to call into question the assumptions in

which the policies toward China have been rooted. In the first place, the People's Republic has shown itself to be neither a part of a Communist monolith nor a carbon copy of Soviet Russia. The fact is that, of the numerous divisions which have arisen within the Communist world, the differences between Moscow and Peking have been the most significant. They remain so today, although the more rasping edges of the conflict appear somewhat tempered by the war in Vietnam.

At the same time, the government on the mainland has not only survived, it has provided China with a functioning leadership. Under its direction, Chinese society has achieved a degree of economic and scientific progress, apparently sufficient for the survival of an enormous and growing population, and sophisticated enough to produce thermonuclear explosions. . . .

If the People's Republic, then, is here to stay, what of the other assumptions on which this nation's policy respecting China has long been based? What of the assumption that the Chinese government is an expanding and aggressive force? That it is restrained from sweeping through Asia only because we have elected to meet its challenge along the 17th parallel, which divides the northern and southern parts of Vietnam?

In recent years the present Chinese government has not shown any great eagerness to use force to spread its ideology elsewhere in Asia, although Chinese armies have been employed in assertion of the traditional borders of China. To be sure, China has given enthusiastic encouragement and has promised to support wars of national liberation. However, China has not participated directly in these wars, and support, when it has been forthcoming, has been limited and circumspect. . . .

Of course, there is an immense potential danger in China; but there is also an immense potential danger in every other powerful nation in a world which has not yet learned how to maintain civilized survival in a nuclear age except on the razor's edge. Insofar as China is concerned, the fundamental question for us is not whether it is a danger, real or potential. The fundamental question is whether our present policies act to alleviate or exacerbate the danger. Do we forestall the danger by jousting with the shadows and suspicions of the past? Do we help by a continuance of policies which do little, if anything, to lift the heavy curtain of mutual ignorance and hostility?

Like it or not, the present Chinese government is here to stay. Like it or not, China is a major power in Asia and is on the way to becoming a nuclear power. Is it, therefore, in this nation's interest and in the interest of world peace to put aside, once and for all, what have been the persistent but futile attempts to isolate China? Is it, therefore, in this nation's interest and in the interest of world peace to try conscientiously and consistently to do whatever we can do — and admittedly it is not much — to reshape the relationship with the Chinese along more constructive and stable lines? In short, is it propitious for this nation to try to do what, in fact, the policies of most of the other Western democracies have already long since done regarding their Chinese relationships?

I must say that the deepening of the conflict in Vietnam makes more difficult adjustments in policies respecting China. Indeed, the present course of events in Vietnam almost insures that there shall be no changes. It is not easy to contemplate an alleviation with any nation which cheers on those who are engaged in inflicting casualties on Americans. Yet it may well be that this alleviation is an essential aspect of ending the war and, hence, American casualties. That consideration alone, it seems to me, makes desirable initiatives toward China at this time. . . .

I urge you to think for yourselves about China. I urge you to approach, with a new objectivity, that vast nation, with its great population of industrious and intelligent people. Bear in mind that the peace of Asia and the world will depend on China as much as it does on this nation, the Soviet Union, or any other, not because China is Communist but because China is China — among the largest countries in the world and the most populous.

Mao Tse-tung remarked in an interview several years ago that "future events would be decided by future generations." Insofar as his words involve the relationship of this nation and China, whether they prove to be a prophecy of doom or a forecast of a happier future will depend not so much on us, the "Old China Hands" of yesterday, but on you, the "New American Hands" of tomorrow.

June 8, 1968:

On the death of Robert Kennedy

Robert Kennedy was shot soon after midnight on June 5, 1968. A few hours later Mansfield arrived at the White House. In A White House Diary Lady Bird Johnson describes him as coming "with a staring look in his eyes. He said, 'What is happening to the country?'"

Three days later he still seemed to be in a state of near-shock as he delivered a commencement address at Seton Hall University. In these times of the generation gap, young people weren't high on the Establishment's list of favorites, but this was a prejudice that Mansfield did not share.

* * *

I shall be brief because of the death of Senator Robert F. Kennedy, which has made all words inadequate. The remarks which I had intended to make to you are prefixed now with a deepening concern which I have long felt with respect to the nation's direction. The tragedy in Los Angeles has added another dimension to our urgent national difficulties.

These are, indeed, times that try men's souls. I grieve for Senator Kennedy and his family. I grieve even more for my country.

There is something wrong, very wrong, when the attempt of reason and understanding to cope with grave national problems is ripped apart time and again by the bullets of irrationality and hatred. Senator Kennedy was among the most civilized and sensitive of political leaders, and one of the nation's most thoughtful. His death lights up the threat to the very survival of freedom which is posed by this orgy of political violence. It has already brought down political and social and other leaders of the quality of President Kennedy; Medgar Evers; Martin Luther King, Jr.; two young Marine lieutenants in Washington, D.C., this week, one of them from my own state of Montana; and now Senator Robert F. Kennedy. These are rare men. As a nation, we could not afford the untimely loss of any of these men. We can afford no more.

This epidemic of horror, this pathology of political and social violence strikes at the very heart of the American structure — we will either put an end to it or it will put an end to American freedom.

I look to you young people of today in the hope of glimpsing a better tomorrow for America. It may be that you will be able to make that decisive contribution that will turn the crises of today into the resolved problems of yesterday. . . .

That the questions which young people are asking sometimes show a disdain for conventional and entrenched approaches to our national problems is not surprising. It in no way alters the importance, the necessity, of trying to find the answers. That was what Robert F. Kennedy was seeking to do.

If you who are young tend to look at the long-accepted and dogmatic descriptions of the world scene with a degree of healthy pragmatism, it is perhaps because you are not bound by the furies, fixations, and fears of the past twenty years. It may be, and I hope it is, that your thought processes are still flexible enough to permit you to perceive an obvious need for adjustments in the policies of this government in the light of the way Yugoslavia and Albania, not to mention China and Vietnam and most recently Romania and Czechoslovakia, have undercut the old theory of a Russian Communist monolith.

Whatever the reasons, it seems to me that you know enough to insist upon more than patent-medicine responses to the problems of international life in these closing decades of the 20th century. You know enough, too, to insist that this government assume a direct responsibility in the face of unrest and violence at home with at least as great a determination as it has sometimes displayed in taking on responsibilities for the curbing of unrest and violence abroad. In short, what your questions add up to is a call for a continuing appraisal of the premises of our foreign policies, particularly in the light of changes abroad and urgent needs at home. To a considerable degree Senator Kennedy succeeded in setting in motion that kind of appraisal in his all too brief years in the Senate and in these past few weeks as a candidate for the Presidency. He knew, as I believe all of us sense, that there is an intimate association between the achievement of peace abroad and the realization of peace at home. . . .

Let me close these remarks on the same note with which I opened them. This commencement finds the nation entering upon a time of testing. Our difficulties are underscored, personified, and emphasized by the tragic death of Senator Kennedy. We must face up to the question of violence within the nation. We must face up to the threat which it poses to an orderly, peaceful, and free political structure in this nation.

To deal with this difficulty, and others which plague us at home and abroad, involves material resources. Far more than material resources, however, the very survival of the nation, I believe, cries out for the resolve and the ingenuity, the wit and the integrity to face firmly the situation which confronts us. It requires us to look long and hard at the bitter experiences of these past few years. It compels us to search in the unspeakable and barbaric tragedy of Vietnam, in the assassinations of American leaders, and amidst the burnt-out cities of the nation, for clearer definitions of the evolving problems of our times and to develop new approaches and new policies which look to their solution.

In that pursuit the participation of the young people of this nation is essential. I ask you to join your fresh courage, your fresh conviction, your fresh concern and your fresh outlook to the longer experience of the rest of us. Together we can repair the weaknesses in the nation's society and mend the fences that have broken down. Together we can cut out the dry rot in our policies, both foreign and domestic. Together we can act to shape a new society in a new world. Far more than words of eulogy, a dedication of heart and mind to that purpose would be a fitting tribute to the late Senator Robert F. Kennedy.

Will you give it?

March 2, 1970:

On spreading the war in Indochina

In the fall of 1969 the Laotian government troops, with strong U.S. air support, took the strategically located Plain of Jars in northern Laos, ending five years of occupation by the pro-

Communist Pathet Lao forces. As might have been expected, the Pathet Lao were not hospitable enough to accept the continued presence of these uninvited guests. Soon the plain was under massive counterattack, in which Soviet-built PT-76 tanks conspicuously participated. By late February 1970 the surviving guests had departed southward, and the plain once again was under Pathet Lao control.

In the 1968 campaign, Richard Nixon had promised to "wind down" the war in Vietnam. The following year did see some winding down, the new buzz word being "Vietnamization." Yet Nixon had never been noted for a special devotion to unrestrained candor, and Mansfield was concerned that the Administration's response to events in Laos might be to carry the war offensively beyond the western border of Vietnam. Early in March 1970 he warned on the Senate floor against any such adventure in Laos. Less than two months later, American and South Vietnamese troops invaded not Laos, but neutral Cambodia. Nixon evidently was indeed bent on winding up the winding down.

* * *

Mr. Mansfield. Mr. President, I take the floor of the Senate at this time because of the serious situation in Laos. I do so not to criticize but, if possible, to be constructive, to be helpful, and to wave a warning flag about this area which might perhaps be helpful in preventing our becoming involved too deeply and in too costly a manner. When I speak of costly, I do not mean in money alone, but the total cost, including manpower. . . .

Perhaps the Pathet Lao and their North Vietnamese allies may stop the offensive on the Plain of Jars, short of the cities of Vientiane and Luang Prabang; that would be in the pattern of previous operations. Then again, they may push forward against these two capitals and press to the border of Thailand. Only time will indicate what plans and objectives may be involved. In any event, the question of the "nonwar" or the "secret war" or the "interlude war" in Laos cannot be avoided any longer.

Notwithstanding the Geneva accord of 1962, the North Vietnamese are deeply involved in this military situation. So, too, is the United States. Press reports indicate that the Thais may also be engaged. The involvement is so transparent on both sides as to make less than useless the effort to maintain the fiction of the accord or even to exchange charge and countercharge of violations. We are both in it — North Vietnamese and Americans — and we are in it up to our necks.

What disturbs me is that it is not only that both nations are forbidden by the Geneva agreement to use forces in Laos but that the President has also made clear that he does not desire to see the U.S. forces used in Laos. May I add that I have every confidence in the President's intentions. Yet the presence of American military advisers and others in Laos cannot be camouflaged any longer. . . .

It needs to be recalled at this time, therefore, that the full-scale U.S. involvement in Vietnam evolved from much smaller beginnings. First it was a little more aid and a few more military advisers, then it was the supply of transportation, then air support, then GI's.

I am sure that the President does not want that sequence to be repeated. The Defense Department has been at pains to gainsay it. In that respect, this President's intentions are not unlike those of his predecessor at the beginning of the Vietnamese involvement; the protestations of this Secretary of Defense also have a not unfamiliar ring. Nevertheless, a parallel can develop in Laos. Will we hear next what became the fateful rationale of the war in Vietnam? Will we hear next that a larger war is not up to us but up to them? Will we submerge in that rationale, once again, our responsibility to decide where and when in consideration of the national interests we shall risk the lives of Americans? Will we affirm that fundamental responsibility or leave it to others who have no reason to use it for this nation's well-being? . . .

The North Vietnamese have long since moved troops into the border areas of northeastern Laos to guard the so-called Ho Chi Minh trails. These are the routes by means of which men and supplies move down into South Vietnam. By the same token, American planes have long since been bombing the trails. The bilateral violations of the Geneva accord in this case at least have been directly related to the war in Vietnam.

Of late, however, both Americans and North Vietnamese have

expanded military activities further into Laos, in the region of the Plain of Jars. There are reported to be something on the order of 45,000 to 50,000 North Vietnamese now on the northern border of Laos. According to reports, not only has manpower increased but antiaircraft missiles have been implanted. On the part of the United States the bombing of Laos is reported to be heavier than it was in North Vietnam, with perhaps as many as 20,000 sorties a month.

In short, the war seems to be pouring out of South Vietnam through the Laotian panhandle into the rest of Laos and into the rest of Indochina. Even Cambodia, which has wisely sought, behind the wall of neutrality, to hold back the jungle of war has felt, of late, the intensified pressure of this flow of destruction.

As in 1965, the events in Laos caution that the threat of a continuing inclusive involvement in Southeast Asia remains unchanged. Indeed, it may be enlarging to embrace Laos. If the military seesaw goes down in Vietnam only to rise in Laos, our situation will not have improved; it will have worsened. In my judgment, only the utmost vigilance — on the part of the responsible officials of this government, of the President, of the Senate in particular, and of the press — will counteract this inevitable tendency. . . .

The time is short. The time is now to face up to the implications of this worsening situation in Laos. The danger of our overextended commitment in Southeast Asia needs to be considered frankly and without delay. The fact is that the President and the Congress have still not corralled an open-ended military involvement in a part of the world which is not directly vital to our security, in a part of the world in which the involvement was a misfortune to begin with, and every day of its continuance is a tragedy.

March 11, 1970:

On extending the vote to 18-year-olds

The Vietnam war, in which young men were fighting and dying so bloodily, brought increasing demands for lowering the voting age to 18. The Administration proposed that this be done by

Constitutional amendment. Mansfield, who for years had been submitting proposals for a lowering of the voting age, thought that this procedure would simply mean more delay. The Congress had the authority to extend the franchise under the 14th Amendment, he maintained in a floor statement in mid-March 1970, and should avoid further procrastination by simply adding a rider to the Voting Rights Act then under consideration.

This was done, and the Act was signed by Nixon in June. In December, however, the Supreme Court ruled that the vote-for-youth provision was constitutional only for Federal elections. In the spring of the following year the 20th Amendment to the Constitution, which finally did lower the voting age to 18 for all elections, made it through two-thirds of both houses of Congress and three-fourths of the states in less than three months.

* * *

Mr. Mansfield. Mr. President, this amendment would extend the right to vote to every citizen of the United States who is 18 years old and older. It would afford that right in every election — Federal, state and local. Much has been said lately about seeking to extend the ballot by statute. I am not a lawyer. For that reason, I felt compelled to consult distinguished members of the bar on this subject. In this connection, I contacted Professor Paul Freund of Harvard, one of the nation's leading Constitutional authorities. On Monday I inserted in the *Record* his letter explaining the Constitutional basis for lowering the voting age by public law. In this connection also, I reviewed the testimony of former Solicitor General Archibald Cox. Speaking before the Subcommittee on Constitutional Amendments last February 24, he said such a matter was fully within the power of Congress.

I shall not be so presumptuous as to sum up the fine points of the legal arguments. I will say, however, that the 14th Amendment states most clearly that the equal protection clause shall be implemented by Congress by appropriate legislation. . . .

I happen to think that Congress believes that those between 18 and 21 are excluded unreasonably from the ballot box. I happen to think that the record of such discrimination is clear beyond doubt. Most recently it has been established in hearings before the Subcommittee on Constitutional Amendments.

A) At 18, 19 and 20, young people are in the forefront of the political process — working, listening, talking, participating. They are barred from voting.

B) Eighteen is the age when young men are told to fight our wars even though they themselves may have no right to choose the officials who make the policies that lead to war.

C) At 18, they become young adults and are treated so by our courts. They are deemed legally responsible for their actions — both civil and criminal — and must suffer the full penalties of the law.

D) Eighteen-year-old men and women marry, have children, and need not obtain the consent of parents or guardians to do so.

E) Young adults of 18 hold down full-time jobs.

F) They pay taxes at the same level as everyone else; yet they have no voice in the imposition of those taxes.

G) Those 18 to 21 are simply denied a full voice in the political process to which they are fully subjected and for which they are fully responsible.

To withhold the ballot from them in such circumstances is an unreasonable deprivation. Congress can make that determination. It is a co-equal branch of the government. And to do so would only be stating the facts.

I ask that the Senate approve the ballot for 18-year-olds at this time, in this fashion and on this, the Voting Rights measure. As a political forecaster, I possess no extraordinary capacities. But I am aware of the public reports by some in opposition to the extension of voting rights — by any method — to 18-year-olds. I believe that the overwhelming majority of Congress are not in accord with that sentiment. The Congress should be permitted to express itself on this issue on this bill. It is my judgment that if the vote is not extended to 18-year-olds now on this particular vehicle — the Voting Rights Act — it will not be achieved in this Congress.

May 27, 1970:

On the imperial Presidency

In 1968 the Republicans won the Presidency but not the Congress. In 1969 Vice President Spiro Agnew, described by Senator Eugene McCarthy as "Nixon's Nixon," opened the midterm election campaign of 1970 with an unremitting series of splenetic speeches designed to appeal to the lowest Republican denominator. To enhance that appeal, he garnished his divisive oratory with labored epithets dredged from his ever handy thesaurus of polysyllabic invective.

In May 1970 Mansfield gave a brief speech at the Democratic Congressional campaign dinner. In it he responded not merely to the Agnew brand of light-hearted viciousness but also to the growing danger of Presidential imperialism, which had burgeoned under Johnson and was now becoming quite alarming under Nixon. As usual, his remarks were impersonal, mild and affirmative.

* * *

We meet in an hour of deep national distress.

It is a time not of war diminished but, again, of war expanded.

We meet at a time when the nation's economy is gripped in the dead hand of war, when Americans are caught in the cross-currents of inflation and recession. Jobs disappear. Profits shrink. Pensions can be stretched no further. Not prices, but production falls. Public problems — pollution, crime, transportation, education, drug addiction, health and a hundred others — cry out for attention. The cry is lost in the costly cacophony of war.

It is a time when dissension divides the land, when young are separated from old, when black is riven from white, when soldier is shunted from civilian. Yet there are those whose response to this national shame is still the rhetoric of denunciation and inflammatory division.

Let me say to those who compartmentalize the nation as they generalize their private hostility: Democrats will not join in dividing America. . . .

We must work together to strengthen the legislative branch of the government. The great issues of war and peace have slipped too far out of the hands of the representatives who are closest to the people of the nation. The responsibilities of the Congress must be reasserted.

It is the Congress this year and the next and the next which is called on to provide the critical balance-wheel in the Federal system. It is the Congress which must act to restore good sense to foreign policy and stability to the economy. It is the Congress which must heed the many voices of the nation, reconcile them, and then move to reorder the priorities of public commitment.

With this Republican Administration, the balance-wheel is a Democratic Congress. That there is little of the joy of a political gathering tonight does not stem from our political fortunes. It is due to the nation's misfortunes. It matters little what happens to us as Democrats. It matters greatly what happens to those Americans in Indochina whose lives are on the line. It matters greatly what happens on the streets of America, on the campuses, on the farms, and in the factories of America.

The purpose of Democrats in this critical year cannot be merely to retain control of the Congress. Our purpose must be to strengthen that control and consecrate this party to a new dimension of national leadership.

June 9, 1970:

On Presidential powers

to commit U.S. troops abroad

The invasion of Cambodia, beyond the controversy it provoked about Nixon's real intentions in Southeast Asia, resurrected a much older, deeper controversy about the President's authority as Commander-in-Chief as against the Congressional authority to declare war. The now notorious Tonkin Gulf resolution of 1964, which in effect gave President Johnson carte blanche in Indochina (as he decided to interpret it), was in very bad odor by 1970, partly because the Senate had been cozened into it by

Executive flimflam. In an effort to restore Congressional authority over serious foreign military commitments, Kentucky's Republican John Serman Cooper and Idaho's Democrat Frank Church got together in the spring of 1968 and introduced legislation that (1) required the President after June 30 to obtain Congressional approval for any foreign military action and (2) barred funds for such action in Cambodia after that date. To enhance its chances of enactment, they attached it as an amendment to a foreign military sales bill. Administration spokesmen in the Senate, such as Minority Leader Robert Griffin and Robert Dole of Kansas, countered by getting Robert Byrd of West Virginia to join Griffin in proposing an amendment to the Cooper-Church amendment. The ensuing argument, as can be seen in the excerpts given here, centered on Mansfield's contention that the Byrd-Griffin amendment, if broadly interpreted by the President, would require him to seek Congressional approval only if he wanted to, thus rendering Cooper-Church totally ineffective. During the debate in June 1970, Griffin conceded that it would indeed do just that but solemnly assured the Senate that the President, being a man of conspicuous honor, would never take advantage of the situation.

The Senate had been once burnt, however, and now was at least twice shy. The Byrd-Griffin amendment was defeated and replaced by a harmless sense-of-the-Senate substitute. The Cooper-Church amendment was approved later that month — only to be killed in the House some three weeks later. But in January 1971 Cooper-Church was tried again and this time was signed into law, by an unenthusiastic Nixon, as part of the defense appropriations bill. And in November 1973 a law requiring Congressional approval for simply committing U.S. armed forces abroad was passed, after nine attempts to gather the two-thirds majorities needed to override an earlier Nixon veto.

* * *

Mr. Mansfield. . . . Mr. President, it is not for me to question any Senator's motive with respect to the Cooper-Church amendment. Each Senator will determine his own position on this legislation. I would merely express the hope that we will be able to

205

dispose of the entire matter in the near future. With the cooperation of the Senator from Michigan there is now an agreement to
vote Thursday on the Byrd-Griffin modification. With his further
cooperation, perhaps, some accord might soon be reached to
bring the Cooper-Church question to a close.

The Senate should face up to this matter without further delay
because what began as a debate has shifted to an extended discussion and for some days has verged on a filibuster. It hardly reflects
credit on the Senate to obfuscate the question by prolonged resort
to the indulgent procedures of the Senate rules.

The issue will not go away, no matter how long it may be
debated. It will not be swept aside, whether the Cambodian adventure is held to be a military success or a failure. It will not be
laid to rest in the Senate because it cannot be laid to rest in our
consciences. . . .

Beyond military success or failure, the issue posed by Cooper-
Church is fundamental. For too long we have skated on the thin
ice of Constitutional expediency in matters of war and peace. For
too long, the Senate has shrouded its Constitutional responsibilities in the skirts of Presidential authority.

To be sure, it has been easier to say, "Leave it to the Commander
in Chief" or "trust the Commander in Chief" or "blame the Commander in Chief." When all has been said, however, there is still
the involvement in Vietnam. There is still the involvement in
Laos. There is still the involvement in Cambodia. There is still the
ever rising level of dead and wounded young Americans in Indochina, a level which now stands at 330,000. . . .

To be sure, the Senate's intentions have been of the best. For
many years, we have seen our role in matters of war and peace
largely as one of acquiescence in the acts of the executive branch.
If we have had doubts, we have swallowed them. Since President
Eisenhower's administration, at least, we have time and again
deferred to the executive branch in international matters. The
executive branch has presented us with decisions. We have gone
along. We have rocked few boats. . . .

That is the explanation of the Tonkin Gulf resolution of 1964. In
that act, the Senate joined the House in deferring to the President.
Then, too, the Senate gave assent to what the Executive had done,
was doing, and might do in the future in the way of committing

the nation's armed forces in Vietnam.

Why did we do it? Why did the Senate adopt the Tonkin Gulf resolution in short order and with only two dissenting votes? Were we fearful of exercising an independent judgment? Was it because we accepted assurances that we were strengthening the hand of the President in protecting American forces already in Vietnam? Were we persuaded that a show of unity here would secure freedom in South Vietnam? Were we convinced that what was tantamount to a post-dated declaration of war would so frighten the North Vietnamese as to forestall the further spread of the war and, hence, our deepening involvement?

Such were the reasons for the Tonkin Gulf resolution that were propounded at the time. Such were the judgments of the executive branch. That was almost six years ago. The Senate passed the Tonkin Gulf resolution. The Senate acted, we thought, to protect American servicemen already in Vietnam. The Senate gave the green light to go further into Vietnam in order the more quickly, we thought, to withdraw from Vietnam.

The rest is history. . . .

I do not recall this history without a painful awareness of the Senate's part in its writing. Yet it must be recalled. It must be recalled because the Senate is again face to face with another Tonkin Gulf resolution. I refer to the Byrd-Griffin modification which is now pending to the Cooper-Church amendment. . . . The Byrd-Griffin modification says that Cooper-Church will not apply unless the executive branch decrees that it should apply. Under Byrd-Griffin, the statutory wall of Cooper-Church against the spread of our involvement into Cambodia stands or falls on a word from the White House. . . .

The Byrd-Griffin modification is a direct descendant of the Tonkin Gulf resolution. The clay carries the same imprint. The door to further involvement in Cambodia is not closed by Byrd-Griffin. Byrd-Griffin opens the door wider. It sanctions an in-and-out entanglement in Cambodia. It sanctions a direct or indirect entrapment in Cambodia. It sanctions an *ad infinitum* involvement in Cambodia even as the Tonkin Gulf resolution did the same for the open-ended involvement in Vietnam. . . .

We have spilled too much of the nation's young blood in a wasting and mistaken war in Indochina. We have spent too much of the nation's strength in alien lands for an ill-starred purpose. We have thought too much of saving face and not enough of saving lives. All the while, the troubles within our own borders have multiplied. All the while, flashes of new dangers streak across other horizons. All the while, the nation remains bound in Southeast Asia, where fundamental interests are not engaged but great national resources disappear in an endless flow.

The hour is late, very late.

The Byrd-Griffin modification, in my judgment, is the critical vote on this issue. Reject it, and the Senate will say that the way out of Vietnam is not by way of Cambodia. Adopt Byrd-Griffin to Cooper-Church, and the Senate will still say that the way out of Vietnam is not by way of Cambodia, but only if the executive branch also says the same thing.

The Constitutional message of Cooper-Church without this proposed addition is clear. The Senate acts in concert with the President's expressed determination, but under its own legal responsibility, in an effort to curb the further expansion of the war in Indochina. The Byrd-Griffin modification clouds that message.

In my judgment, the Senate should keep the Cooper-Church amendment free of distortion. The credibility of the Senate demands it. The urgencies of the nation require it.

Mr. Church. Mr. President, I wish to say to the distinguished majority leader that I think he has delivered the most moving and persuasive argument against the pending amendment offered by the Senator from West Virginia and the Senator from Michigan yet made in the Senate. I hope every member of the Senate will read the Senator's statement with great care and give to it the attention it richly deserves.

Mr. Griffin. Mr. President, I have listened with close attention to the remarks of the majority leader. With the greatest respect for him — and he knows I have great respect for him — I must say very candidly that he has reached a long way to fashion an argument against the Byrd amendment. His characterization of the Byrd amendment is somewhat colorful but entirely inappropriate. The Byrd amendment is only a qualification or limitation of the Church-Cooper amendment. It could reach no higher in terms of authority than would be the case if there were no Church-Cooper amendment at all.

I wish to emphasize that the Byrd amendment touches only one of four subsections of the Church-Cooper amendment; so it could not be said that it goes so far as to nullify the Church-Cooper amendment. But even if one were to give the widest and most far-reaching interpretation to the Byrd modification, the most that could possibly be said is that it would nullify the Church-Cooper amendment. Certainly to nullify the Church-Cooper amendment is not to adopt a Gulf of Tonkin resolution, which the majority leader indicated was tantamount to a declaration of war.

So I respectfully suggest that the characterization is most unfair and most unreasonable under the circumstances.

I think it is very important to look at what the Byrd amendment provides. It would add language to that one particular subsection having to do with the retention of U.S. troops in Cambodia. It states: "Except that the foregoing provisions of this clause shall not preclude the President from taking such action as may be necessary to protect the lives of United States forces in South Vietnam or to facilitate the withdrawal of United States forces from South Vietnam."

Surely the distinguished majority leader, I know, does not object to that last clause reading "to facilitate the withdrawal of U.S. forces from South Vietnam."

It is very difficult for me, of course — and I respect our differences — to see how he could oppose recognition of the Constitutional power of the Commander in Chief to protect the lives of American forces in South Vietnam."

Mr. Mansfield. Nobody is opposing that, may I say. That is the first time I have heard that question raised on the floor of the Senate during this debate.

Mr. Griffin. I say it is very difficult for me to understand opposition to language which would recognize the authority of the Commander in Chief to protect the lives of American forces in South Vietnam. I think it is clear that that is the purpose of the Byrd amendment.

Mr. Mansfield. May I point out that this question has been raised time and time again: to safeguard American lives, to further the withdrawal of U.S. troops from Vietnam. Nobody in this chamber is against that. All 100 members of the Senate are for it. The chief proponents of the Cooper-Church amendment have said that time and time and time again, but the question is always raised.

I am willing to take the word of a Senator — certainly the chief proponents of an amendment when they are asked a question and they give an answer — because who knows more about it than the proponents, and who are more qualified to answer the questions?

If the Senator will yield further, I wish to point out that the President has unilateral Constitutional powers as Commander in Chief to take measures to protect the lives not only of U.S. servicemen in Vietnam but also of U.S. citizens, including servicemen, anywhere in the world. He does not need Congressional sanction for that purpose because he already has that power, authority, and responsibility. But the executive branch does not have the unilateral Constitutional power to commit this nation to an involvement which requires a continuing input of men and money in a country even in the name of defending U.S. forces, or for some other objective in a second country. That interpretation is underscored by the national commitments resolution which the Senate endorsed earlier in this Congress.

If the executive branch does make such a broad commitment on its own in Cambodia, directly or indirectly, it treads on highly questionable Constitutional ground. Furthermore, if it were to make such a commitment on its own — if and when Cooper-Church, as is, is enacted — the executive branch would break the law.

It would tread then on the most dangerous Constitutional grounds. But if it wished to act unilaterally, should Byrd-Griffin be enacted, then the executive branch could do what it pleased in the way of a broad commitment in Cambodia — forces, aid, or whatever — without further reference to Congress. Indeed, the Senate would have given its approval in advance to whatever the executive branch did in Cambodia, whether it was wise or foolish, necessary or unnecessary, responsible or irresponsible, whether it led to a wider war or not, provided what was done was done in the name of withdrawing U.S. forces from Vietnam or protecting U.S. forces in Vietnam. . . .

Mr. Griffin. Of course, the differences between the majority leader and the junior Senator from Michigan go to what are the Constitutional responsibilities of the President and what are the

Constitutional responsibilities of the Congress. I am one of those who believe the Senate should exercise its Constitutional responsibility to the fullest. However, I am convinced that the Church-Cooper amendment goes too far and seeks to get the Senate involved in what are essentially battlefield decisions. The proposed amendment would tie the hands of the Commander in Chief and would play into the hands of the enemy, making it more difficult for the President to carry out his objective of getting American troops out of Vietnam and bringing them home.

This administration is not sending more and more troops to Vietnam. This President is bringing troops home. This President needs and deserves the good faith and support of the Congress, and I sincerely believe he would have a much better chance of achieving the objectives we all want if we would give him our support.

Mr. Mansfield. . . . What we are trying to do is to strengthen the President's hand, to give him added stamina, added muscle, to give him a place to which he can come for recourse, a body in which he served for over eight years, among people whom he knows. We are trying to counterbalance the pressures which are on him constantly, which are on any President, to give him a chance not to act precipitately, but to think a little while before making a move, to discuss this matter with his friends in the Congress and to give recognition to the fact that under the Constitution the Congress of the United States is a coequal branch in the government, along with the executive and the judiciary. . . .

Mr. Fulbright. Mr. President, I just wanted to congratulate the Senator from Montana for a rare and brilliant speech. I think he has outlined some of the issues very well indeed.

The reference that has been made here to the Gulf of Tonkin resolution, of course, has overlooked what I believe to be the most important point in that case, which was that the facts which purported to justify it were misrepresented to the Senate; also, the fact that President Johnson has said publicly that he did not rely upon the resolution for what he did, that he considered he had the authority to do it without the resolution.

The present President has stated, in a letter to the Committee on Foreign Relations, that he does not rely upon the resolution for doing what he is now doing.

There has developed a new theory that I was not aware of before, of the right to protect the troops, that this is a right without limit, that it can be applied without any limit that we can think of, and in this case, to justify going into Cambodia. At least there has been reached a very serious question about the limits of that right. . . .

Mr. Dole. I appreciate the Senator from Montana yielding.

Since his characterization of the Byrd-Griffin modification as another Gulf of Tonkin resolution, I have reread the Gulf of Tonkin resolution, for which I voted as a member of the other body. Everyone in Congress, with the exception of two members of this body, supported the Gulf of Tonkin resolution.

Section 1 says that Congress approves and supports the determination of the President, as Commander in Chief, to take all necessary measures to repel any armed attack against forces of the United States and to prevent further aggression. . . .

I, for one, trust the Gulf of Tonkin resolution is repealed. As I understand it, that could be the next order of business when this one is concluded — if — when it is concluded. (Laughter)

If the Senator from Montana can enlighten me on how the Byrd amendment can be characterized as another Gulf of Tonkin resolution, it would be helpful.

Mr. Mansfield. I shall do my best. I thought I did so in the course of my remarks. I am delighted that twice the Senator from Kansas has indicated he is in favor of repealing the Gulf of Tonkin resolution. It will be brought up expeditiously and appropriately after the pending business is out of the way.

Now, relative to the question raised, the Senator is aware of the fact that if the Byrd-Griffin modification of the Cooper-Church amendment is agreed to, the President can, on the basis of his judgment only, without coming to Congress, make any kind of decision affecting Cambodia that he desires. . . .

I tried to make that point during the course of my remarks. I feel that it will be another resolution or amendment that can be pulled out of the Presidential pocket and looked at and shown to everyone in the room every ten minutes, every half hour, or every hour, as the Gulf of Tonkin resolution was. . . .

Mr. Dole. As I recall the Gulf of Tonkin resolution, it was a signal to the world that we were beginning a period of escalation.

212

There is no doubt about that. When Congress passed the Gulf of Tonkin resolution, President Johnson acted in concert with Congress and did escalate, as the Senator from Montana pointed out, from 20,000 men to a high of 545,000 American forces in Southeast Asia.

Mr. Mansfield. Under a Democratic administration.

Mr. Dole. Yes, I am not disputing that point.

Mr. Mansfield. I want to bring that out.

Mr. Dole. And I appreciate it, too, but now we are in a different situation. . . .

This is a different time in Southeast Asia, a time of deescalation compared to a time of escalation when the Gulf of Tonkin resolution passed the Congress, in record time, with only two dissenting votes.

It seems we strengthen the position of the Senate, we strengthen the position of Congress, and we give support to the President by adoption of the Byrd amendment. Adoption of the Byrd amendment would be a recognition of the powers of Congress under the Constitution and at the same time recognition that the President has an inherent right under the Constitution to protect American forces.

Thus the question I ask is: If the President has that power, what harm does it do the Cooper-Church amendment to adopt the language of the Byrd-Griffin modification?

Mr. Mansfield. I have tried to explain that. Now I shall turn it over to one of the principal cosponsors of the amendment, who will repeat what many of us have said many times.

Mr. Church. I thank the majority leader.

Mr. Mansfield. With perhaps some additions.

Mr. Church. Mr. President, I understand that the argument of the Senator from Kansas is that we need have no fear that the adoption of the Byrd amendment will be treated as a blank check by President Nixon to return in force to Cambodia or to enlarge the war, because he is in the process of deescalating the war, because his intentions are good, and because the situation is quite different from what it was when the Senate adopted the Gulf of Tonkin resolution.

I cannot accept that reasoning. I do not believe it is accurate to say that the Gulf of Tonkin resolution was passed by Congress to signal escalation of the war. Indeed, quite the opposite was the case.

The Tonkin Gulf resolution was asked for by the President as a warning to North Vietnam, just as Cambodia was supposed to be a warning to the enemy. President Johnson at the time argued that the resolution would help prevent us from becoming involved in a wider war in Southeast Asia. Congress, it should be remembered, debated the resolution in the aftermath of an attack upon American destroyers at sea. . . .

Mr. President, that is our experience. I am sure that President Johnson was sincere in his intentions at the time Congress enacted the Tonkin Gulf resolution. But we were careless enough to give him a blank check which permitted him later to change his mind and commit us to a major land war in Asia without having to come back to Congress for authority.

We do not want to do that again. It is not a question of the good intentions of President Nixon, or of what he has done up to now. It is the certainty that circumstances change. Presidents are human, Presidents change their minds, Presidents change their policies.

Our job is to take the present policy, defined as the President has defined it, and to say that after the present Cambodian operation has ended, if the President later decides to return to Cambodia, he must come to Congress, present his case, and ask Congress to lift whatever limitations it has imposed.

It seems to me that the argument offered concerning the good intentions of President Nixon is not relevant to the issue or to our experience with the Tonkin Gulf resolution. . . .

Mr. Dole. Mr. President, I point out briefly that I do not disagree with the general statement of the Senator from Idaho, and certainly not with the statement of the Senator from Montana.

I think the Senator from Montana made it clear at the outset that no Senator questions the motives or patriotism of any other Senator, nor do we question the desire of 100 Senators to disengage our country from military activities in Southeast Asia as quickly as possible. That is the general feeling of the Senate and the general feeling throughout America.

But again underscoring the record made the by present occupant of the White House, we are not seeing a period of escalation but one of deescalation and, therefore, there cannot be any relationship between what happened in 1964 at the time of the passage of the Gulf of Tonkin resolution and what may happen this Thursday at 1 o'clock when we vote on the Byrd amendment . . . .

Mr. Mansfield. Mr. President, we are poles apart in our interpretation of the modification of the amendment, if agreed to. But let me say that I join the Senator in honoring President Nixon for the withdrawals which he has made.

I would not go so far as to say that there has been no escalation, because the air activities in Laos, for example, have increased tremendously — many, many times over. And, to me, an enlargement, an extension of the war into a country like Cambodia is in itself a form of escalation.

So, with those minor provisos, I would like to join the Senator in saying that, up until Cambodia, the President was moving in the right direction — out — but not fast enough to suit me. However, it was in the right direction of reversing the process from escalation to deescalation.

As the Senator has said, I was not at all remiss in expressing, publicly and otherwise, my appreciation of what President Nixon was doing in that respect. However, with me, Cambodia created an entirely different situation. And, as I recall, I believe the distinguished Senator from Kansas himself, when he got hold of the news, was somewhat discomfited and disturbed, to put it mildly. . . .

I anticipate without question that (President Nixon) will get all U.S. troops out of Cambodia by the end of this month, if not before. I do not question his statement about that. I do not think that he wants to go back into Cambodia.

I think that what we ought to do is to try to help him, not give him power which would add to his already enormous authority, but rather hold out the hand of friendship and cooperation and see if together, in the best interests of the republic, we cannot work in concert.

June 17, 1970:

On spending money for bombs over there or for people over here

One of the notions nurtured and then killed by President Lyndon Johnson was that the United States had practically unlimited resources, more than enough to provide plenty of both guns and butter. He killed it by simply driving it into the ground. It was to die officially in the spring of 1975, after the abrupt and undignified departure of the Americans and their assorted Vietnamese lackeys and victims from the scene of the final eviction from Indochina.

Mansfield had never suffered from guns-and-butter hallucinations. On the contrary, he perennially opposed the perennial billions for the Pentagon precisely because he wanted the money thus saved to go instead into less belligerent, longer-term investments like health, education, housing, employment, school lunches, milk for poor children, and other such programs so vulnerable to Republican Presidential vetoes. In June 1970, in testimony before Senator Proxmire's Subcommittee on Economy in Government, he once again attacked the thesis that government spending should be channeled to hungry generals but not to hungry children.

* * *

Gentlemen, I first wish to thank you for extending me this opportunity. There is no single expert when it comes to assigning priorities or even for defining all of the various problems that confront us as a nation both at home and abroad. I do, however, profess certain notions about the order of things. And I prefer to look at them in terms of balance, of emphasis and choice.

Today we face perhaps the gravest choices of all. To be sure, militarily we are a strong nation. We are a nation that has produced a stockpile of weaponry sufficient to destroy the earth many times over. Since World War II, we have spent $1250 billion

216

on national defense. But the security of a nation cannot be measured solely by the amount of money spent on military hardware — even if each dollar spent were spent for weapon systems that worked. The decision to allocate so much of our resources for military might — in many cases purchasing military white elephants with a billion-dollar price tag — has cost us dearly in terms of satisfying what to me are the essential ingredients of a healthy and secure society — good education and health, decent living conditions for all, a safe and clean environment and the absence of poverty. Over the years, as we continued to build militarily, we allowed the cities to rot, we allowed the slums to grow and the ghettos to simmer and erupt. Only recently have we realized that the whole fabric of our society has begun to unravel at the seams. Only recently have we begun to talk in terms of shifting the emphasis, of establishing a better balance with respect to these fundamental needs at home and our continuing involvements abroad. . . .

If my memory serves me correctly, the Chairman of this Committee made a statement a few months ago to the effect that the overcost on weapon systems, conservatively estimated and on the basis of information furnished by the General Accounting Office, was somewhere in the vicinity of $21 billion. Now, one expects a certain amount of waste, but surely when contracts are let which indicate such a tremendous overcost — and in some instances the government bailing out some of the contractors — then I think it is time for all of us to sit up and take notice.

That is not to say that the elimination of waste alone is enough. It is not. What is needed is change in basic attitude by government at all levels but especially at the Federal level, where the real meaning of a safe and healthy society must be considered anew.

The clear awareness that our resources are not unlimited, that our wealth is not endless, is finally being understood. If it has proved anything, the war in Southeast Asia has established that fact beyond all doubt. That is why, also, the Congress last year went at least part of the way in attempting to respond both to the question of priorities and to the matter of our limited resources. First of all, it cut $5.6 billion from the President's overall budget requests for fiscal year 1970. Most of those cuts came out of programs sought by the Pentagon and the military requests for

217

more weapons and weapon systems. It reduced the foreign aid program by the same sum. In turn, Congress added a small fraction of the savings, about $1 billion, to health and welfare and education programs, to antipollution programs, manpower programs, and the like. This was not enough — not enough in terms of the areas where the reductions were made or additions granted — but it was a beginning; it was an indication that the Congress, and especially the Senate, had begun to take the lead at long last in what I think is the right direction. Congress demonstrated that it was willing at least to face the issue of priorities.

But, to complete the whole story, it should be said that not everyone was in agreement. After Congress had endeavored to face the issue of priorities by slicing sharply the Defense budget and rechanneling a small fraction of the savings into health, welfare, educational and environmental needs, the administration struck down the action with a veto of the vital additions for our most pressing domestic needs. That, gentlemen, is the real dilemma that we in the Congress confront.

For it is one thing to grasp the question of balance and emphasis. It is another to implement a new order of priorities. We are only now recognizing those areas of domestic concern that have for too long been ignored in favor of a global concern based on a costly network of international agreements, commitments and policies established decades ago for circumstances that were then only marginally relevant and that today serve no purpose whatsoever. There are currently over 3 million Americans in uniform around the world. Secretary Laird recently stated that perhaps a 1-million-man reduction could be achieved. There is simply no justification for the fact that about 1.5 million Americans are stationed overseas at more than 3000 installations and bases. . . .

If we are told a missile system is necessary — but can't be assured it will work — we must be willing to judge independently its necessity and demand reasonable assurance of its operational capability or else be willing to eliminate it. If it means that a veto must be overridden, then we must override the veto. In any event the same measure of cooperation, dedication and devotion that has characterized past investments in military programs and hardware must be applied with the same resolve and effect to the programs of human investment that are so vital now and for the future. . . .

Let us as a nation make a contract to clean our rivers and our air, a contract to assure every American child a quality education, to assure every American pedestrian a safe street in which to walk, and every American a decent home in which to live. Let us assure all of the training and the skills needed for a decent job and then, Mr. Chairman, let us withstand the overruns on these contracts and commitments that will surely provide America with the security it has sought these past three decades. Thank you very much.

June 24, 1970:

On Nixonomics

In June 1970 President Nixon, in a televised address to the nation, urged Congress to "join in holding down government spending to avoid a large deficit budget," although Congress, and particularly the Democratic majority, had already cut a great deal out of the budget that he had submitted. His sly and by no means ineffective tactic drove many Democrats up the wailing wall, and during the next several days there was a great furor over the injustice of "unequal time" on the boob tube. Mansfield characteristically felt that the President, whatever his party, had a right to disproportionate time for reporting to the people. "I think it's getting out of bounds," he commented later on the chorus of protest. "Every time the President makes a speech, somebody wants to answer it."

Ironically, it was he who was drafted to reply to the President's appeal, about a week afterward. He replied in his own way, with reason and restraint and with emphasis on the need for initiatives from the executive branch with which the legislature could cooperate. But he flatly declined to let Nixon get away with blaming Congress for Administration apathy at home and overexertion abroad, especially in Indochina. And once again he called attention to the distortion of national priorities.

219

* * *

It is unusual for a member of Congress to report in this fashion to the people of the nation. I do so because the circumstances are unusual and so, too, are the times. The matters to which your attention is directed affect every American. They hang over every deliberation of the Congress.

The Congress, I might say, was established by the very first article of the Constitution. Along with the executive and the judiciary, it is a coequal branch of the government of the United States. Your representatives in Congress, members of the House of Representatives and the Senate, are there to do a job for you. In the main, it consists of writing the laws. You have a right to know how that job is being done.

I speak to you today as the elected leader of the majority of the U.S. Senate and with the concurrence of the majority leadership of the House of Representatives. In recent days you have heard from the President on the state of the nation's economy: inflation, unemployment, and war. Whether the term is used or not, these words spell recession. That is today's fact. It is not a political fact. It is an economic fact. . . .

In short, the things which should be going up — home building, take-home pay, and real economic growth — are coming down. At the same time, the things that should be coming down — such as interest rates, the cost of living, and unemployment — are going up.

Congress shares the responsibility for correcting these discouraging economic trends, which started under previous administrations. To be sure, the Congress has not concurred completely in the President's approach to them. Nor has the President responded to all the actions of the Congress. That is neither unprecedented nor undesirable. Each branch has its separate responsibilities even as each branch shares in a common obligation to the people of the nation. When there are differences, insofar as the majority leadership is concerned, it will not waste time in political recriminations. It will concentrate, instead, on doing what can be done in the Congress.

In my judgment, much of what can be readily initiated by Congress to improve the economic situation has been forthcoming. Congress has required no prompting from any quarter, for example, to make cuts in the administration's budget as a counter to inflation. Overall spending for this fiscal year was reduced by $6.4 billion. To repeat: Congress did not increase the administration's budgetary requests; Congress made a $6.4-billion reduction.

Acting on its own, Congress passed a selective credit control law last December. The law gives the administration authority which can be used to bring down home mortgage costs. I do not know why that authority has not been used by the administration; nor do I know, if the legislation is unsatisfactory, why a legislative alternative to reduce mortgage rates has not been requested by the administration.

Acting on its own, Congress last year passed a general Tax Reform and Reduction Act. Tax loopholes of $6.6 billion were closed. These savings were converted into lower taxes for all Americans. Millions of persons on low and fixed incomes will get the principal benefit of these changes, which will begin to take effect in the months immediately ahead. This initiative was at first ridiculed as impossible to achieve, and then its enactment was resisted. Now the Tax Reform and Reduction Act is embraced. The fact is that its benefits will be no laughing matter as they begin to flow to persons dependent on moderate salaries or other fixed incomes.

Congress can cooperate with the administration in dealing with the problems of the economy. We have done so and we will continue to do so. We can provide the President with specific authority to take action. We have done so and we will continue to do so.

We can support the President if he wishes to use the persuasion of the Presidency, for example, as a means of discouraging excessive price and wage increases. That persuasive power has yet to be tried. Its effectiveness was demonstrated in 1962 when prices were rolled back in a basic industry by the determined efforts of the President at that time. As a result, other industries held the price line, and the economy avoided inflation and experienced a sound and dynamic growth. By contrast, without Presidential intervention, prices in that same basic industry have been raised four times already this year — and the year is only half over. Other

221

industries follow suit. The dollar loses value both at home and abroad. Millions of Americans are caught in a vise of higher prices and declining incomes.

Congress has already given more authority to the President than he wishes, apparently, to use against the rise in prices. That is his option. I do not criticize his decision. But the record should be clear. Congress has been ready and stands ready to cooperate with the President. . . .

In short, Congress can — and, I am confident, will — support initiatives of the administration which are designed to reverse the whole psychology of inflation.

The willingness of the Congress to work with the President reaches far beyond efforts to stop the downward drift in the economy. The fact is that the economic uncertainty today is only a reflection of a deeper concern. The root of our economic difficulties lies in the distorted use of the nation's resources. We are casting vast quantities of these resources, for example, into the continuing war in Southeast Asia — the estimates are over $26 billion a year, not to speak of the tragic loss of young lives.

We are using our resources at a reckless rate and with dubious wisdom in other places and in other ways.

Government spending, to put it bluntly, is seriously out of date. It is not how much is being spent. It is how it is being spent. Priorities are still determined largely by yesterday's fears and fallacies. They scarcely meet today's urgencies. They only begin to perceive tomorrow's needs.

If there is an overriding imperative, it is to readjust these national priorities, these allocations of government expenditures. . . .

Nations may be attacked from without. They may also crumble from within. For five years we have put great emphasis on protecting the nation from the inhabitants of Vietnam, Laos, and now Cambodia. In the meantime, what of the attacks on the very livability of our cities and their surrounding suburbs? What of the growing pollution of the environment? What of the mounting array of domestic difficulties? Crime? Transportation? Railroads? Drug addiction? Power shortages? Educational needs? Racial tensions? Health? Have any of these difficulties yet been brought under reasonably secure control? Will they stand still, awaiting some undefined solution to the war in Vietnam when, presumably, sufficient resources will be released to permit them to be dealt with without inflation? Will they remain quiescent, to the end that the United States may first be enclosed in a web of antiballistic missiles, at a cost of billions of dollars, which may or may not act to protect us from a missile attack which may or may not come before the system is obsolete?

Every dollar spent by government, whether for Vietnam or weapons or whatever, come from you, the taxpayer. For every man, woman, and child in the United States, the administration now requests about $1000 in spending. How and where each $1000 is spent sets the nation's priorities.

For the coming year, of each $1000,

about $7.00 is requested for health and mental-health research,

about $7.50 for elementary and secondary education,

about $5.00 for urban renewal for our cities,

about $4.50 for air and water pollution control;

about $1.40 for vocational education,

about $0.50 for education for the handicapped,

about $2.40 to assist state and local governments in their fight against crime, and

over $375 for military defense.

Consider that just the cost overrun for a single airplane, the C5-A cargo plane — that is, what was actually paid above what was quoted to the Congress as the initial price tag — has cost each American $10. Consider as well that it costs every American today $70 a year to back and maintain in Europe the several hundred thousand U.S. forces and their dependents who are still there — 25 years after World War II.

These illustrative examples clearly demonstrate where the emphasis in Federal spending has been placed for many years. For too long, we have pursued the nation's security all over the globe. For too long, we have forgotten that national security begins at home. It has taken the tragic war in Indochina to show us that our resources are not unlimited. Our wealth is not endless. Inflation and recession are a part of the price of this overdue insight.

As I have noted, Congress has begun to deal with the reality of our limited resources by reducing Federal spending by $6.4 billion. I must say also that the President reduced expenditures by $3 billion, and I commend him. By far the greatest share of the Congressional cut was taken from defense spending and the foreign aid program. Foreign aid alone was cut by $1 billion. Of the $32 saved for each American, Congress attempted to reallocate $5 to pressing needs in health, education, and the protection of the environment.

That is what has been labeled in some quarters as inflationary and irresponsible. Let the most be made of the labels. For those reallocations, there will be no apology from the Congressional leadership. Nor will the Congress be deterred from trying to meet essential domestic needs of this kind by charges of isolationism or neoisolationism. . . .

Within these premises, the majority in the Congress will give the most respectful consideration to whatever the President may propose to halt the inflation and high interest rates, to reduce unemployment, and to terminate our involvement in Vietnam. To that end, the President has had the cooperation of the Congress in the past. He has it now. He will have it in the future. He has it in good conscience — without ifs, ands, or buts.

The republic deserves no less.

June 23-25, 1970:

Tributes to Mansfield on his
record term as majority leader

Talk is what the Senate is all about. It is the "parli" in "parliament," for which the Senate was instituted. As a result, not many of its members could be called laconic. Logorrhea is an occupational disease. Further, in practice the talk has become encrusted with barnacles of meaningless (though not necessarily useless) flattery: "distinguished," for example, has long been a traditional nonword on the Senate floor. Indeed, most Senatorial "courtesy" seems about as thoughtful and premeditated as a preoccupied belch.

Any string of heady compliments delivered on the Senate floor, therefore, must be taken with stabilizing doses of salt to ward off giddiness. But even the most jaundiced discounting cannot deaden the ring of sincerity in Senatorial tributes to Mike Mansfield, especially when one cocks an ear for content rather than style. (Indeed, the style is often excruciating.)

Listen. It's Tuesday, June 23, 1970. Mansfield is absent from the floor.

* * *

Mr. Byrd of West Virginia. Mr. President, I take the floor today to announce that the able majority leader has, as of June 18, last week, held the office of majority floor leader of the U.S. Senate longer than has any other individual since the Senate began meeting in 1789. . . .

I am very proud to serve under the able leadership of Senator Mansfield. At all times during my twelve years in the Senate, he has been eminently fair and most, most considerate and never, never heavy-handed in his role as leader. He has always been a just man, an even-minded man, and he has commanded the respect of members of both sides of the aisle. He has performed in a most excellent way as majority leader. . . .

Mr. Fulbright. I should like to associate myself with the sentiments the Senator has expressed so well. Of course, I have worked closely with Mike Mansfield for as long as we have been in the Senate together. He has been a member of the Committee on Foreign Relations. Before that we served in the House together.

I agree with the Senator from West Virginia that there is no man under the pressures he endures in that office who could better maintain his equilibrium and be as fair and as kind as he is. He is just as fair with those who disagree with him as he is with those who agree with him. In fact, sometimes, in his effort to be fair, he may lean over backward to be a little fairer to those who disagree with his views than to those who agree with him. But he has brought great wisdom, calm, justice, and fair play to this body — which, after all, is the essence of this institution. If it is to be a constructive force in our democracy, it has to be led in that fashion. . . .

Mr. Allen. Mr. President, I wish to express my thanks and appreciation to the distinguished Senator from West Virginia for the fine remarks he has made about the service of our distinguished majority leader. . . .

It was not until I came to the U.S. Senate in January 1969 that I had the pleasure of meeting Senator Mansfield, but since then I have been greatly impressed by his ability, sincerity, and dedication. He has been extremely fair and impartial. We have not always voted alike, and, I suppose, if a label were to be applied to the majority leader, he would have to be classed as a liberal, whereas if a label were applied to me it would probably have to be that of a conservative.

Nevertheless, whether I have agreed with Senator Mansfield or not, I have always found him to be most fair and always willing to give each side of any controversy an opportunity to be heard to present its case before the Senate.

On at least two occasions the Senator from Montana cast votes with which I agreed wholeheartedly. Very vividly do I recall the first such vote. It occurred in January of 1969. I believe it to have been the most important vote that has been taken in the Senate during the 91st Congress. That was the vote on the appeal by the distinguished senior Senator from Florida (Mr. Holland) from a ruling of Vice President Humphrey.

The then Vice President had ruled that, at the opening session of a Congress, a majority of the members of the Senate could apply cloture to debate on a motion to amend the rules; and more than a majority did vote to apply cloture to the debate on that motion to amend the rules.

The then Vice President ruled that the cloture motion had carried because more than a majority had voted in its favor. An appeal was taken from the ruling of the Chair, and I remember that, on that vote, I was impressed very much when Senator Mansfield, the Democratic leader of the Senate, voted to overrule a Democratic Vice President on a ruling which, in my opinion, was clearly erroneous. The Senate did overrule the ruling of the Chair on the cloture motion to cut off debate on the motion to amend the rules to provide for cloture on a three-fifths vote of a quorum of the Senators present.

That vote by the distinguished Senator from Montana impressed me very much. Then, again on the Stennis amendment, which sought to achieve uniformity in the application of Federal criteria and guidelines for desegregation of public schools throughout the country (a very important amendment), we found the dis-tinguished Senator from Montana voting in favor of the amendment. The distinguished majority leader votes his convictions and lets the chips fall where they will.

The majority leader of the Senate, as I found when I came here, controls the flow of legislation to be considered by the Senate. That, of course, makes him the most powerful single Senator. But in my observation, that power has not been misused by the majority leader in a single instance, because everyone receives an opportunity to speak, and everyone gets an opportunity to have his bill considered by the Senate if it reaches the calendar. . . .

Mr. Metcalf. Mr. President, I, too, wish to join in congratulating Montana's senior Senator on achieving the distinction of having served as majority leader for a longer consecutive term than any of his distinguished predecessors.

Early in 1961, as my first official act as a newly elected Senator, it was my privilege to nominate Mike for the first time as majority leader. This may have been the most significant nomination I have ever made.

After more than nine years of Senator Mansfield's leadership, we have all come to appreciate the Mansfield technique. We know we have a majority leader who regards every Senator as an equal in a peerage that he respects. He enjoys the profound respect and deep affection of all who have served — not under him, the majority leader — but with him.

He is fortunate in that he has effectively combined the duties of Senator from Montana with those of the majority leader of the Senate, whose principal job is directing a national legislative program to enactment.

This honest, unassuming, and decent man has demonstrated what Senator Smathers said a few years ago, "Nice guys may finish last in baseball, but in politics nice guys are winners."

Our nation and the free world are the beneficiaries of nine years of devoted service by Mike Mansfield, one of the nicest guys I know.

Mr. Young of North Dakota. Mr. President, during my lifetime in the Senate, which has spanned quite a number of years, I have

227

seen many Senators come and go, many of them able and hard-working and most of them very personable. Some, of course, were more effective than others as legislators.

One of the most effective members during my time is our beloved friend from Montana, the distinguished majority leader, Mike Mansfield. His is an assignment that is far more difficult than most people realize. It requires great ability, good judgment and, above all, understanding and patience in working with all members of the Senate on both sides of the aisle.

I oftentimes marvel at the patience of our friend Mike Mansfield. If he is greatly disturbed — and I know that sometimes he is, and has reason to be — there is little outward manifestation. I know that sometimes he has a virtual storm within himself. His patience, understanding, and friendly attitude toward every member of the Senate are among the major reasons why he has served longer than anyone else as majority leader.

I am amazed at how Mike has been able to maintain himself in this difficult assignment for so many years. Oftentimes he has to take issue, and sometimes rather sharply, with powerful and influential members of the Senate. More often than not, they are his best friends.

I cite these examples, Mr. President, because I think they are unique in Mike Mansfield's personality and they speak louder than any words I could utter as the reason for the great record he has established.

No leader of the Senate, Republican or Democrat, has been more considerate and understanding of any problems I have had. Mike just does not turn people away if he thinks they have a reasonable cause. There is much more that could be said about our friend, but, to sum up, may I say that he is one of the most honorable and decent men I have ever known. . . .

Mr. Kennedy. Mr. President, as has been pointed out earlier, our distinguished majority leader, Mike Mansfield, last week surpassed, in time served, all previous records of service as majority leader of the U.S. Senate.

On June 18 he had served 9 years and 155 days as majority leader, exceeding the record previously established by Alben W. Barkley of Kentucky.

It is my intention, as assistant majority leader, to exercise such authority as the leader will permit, to set aside on Thursday of this week, some time shortly after 3 p.m., when Senators will be invited to participate in expressing their esteem and affection for this man, whom many have acknowledged to be the greatest of living legislators.

I make this statement to give notice to all Senators who wish to take part.

I have mentioned this also to my colleague, the distinguished Republican leader, and he has expressed full support for the idea. I make this proposal without the knowledge of my distinguished leader because I am sure he would be most reluctant to set aside any of the important business of the Senate which is now before us. But I think it would be appropriate, for a short period of time, to take this opportunity to express our appreciation to our distinguished majority leader.

Mr. Scott. Let me say to the distinguished acting majority leader that I concur wholeheartedly in what he has just said.

We are all aware of the modesty of the distinguished majority leader. We may have a little trouble getting him here, but I think we should ask him to listen to his colleagues on this occasion, because we have something to say that we want very much to say.

* * *

June 25, 1970

Mr. Scott. Mr. President, I offer a resolution on behalf of myself, the distinguished assistant majority leader (Mr. Kennedy), the distinguished assistant minority leader (Mr. Griffin), the secretary of the conference of the majority and Senator from West Virginia (Mr. Byrd), and I ask for its immediate consideration.

The Presiding Officer (Mr. Bellmon). The resolution will be stated.

The assistant legislative clerk read as follows:

S. Res. 423

Whereas, on June 19, 1970, Senator Mike Mansfield completed 9 years and 167 days of service as Majority Leader of the United States Senate, and;

Whereas, said period of service exceeds in length that of any previous Majority Leader in the history of the United

229

States, and;

Whereas, the Senate recognizes that Mike Mansfield has fulfilled this service to his country and to his State with consummate parliamentary skill and unfailing courtesy and consideration for his colleagues during a most crucial period in the nation's history, and;

Whereas, such service has been of exemplary example to his Nation and to the Senate; now

Therefore, be it resolved, that the Senate extend to Mike Mansfield its deep gratitude and admiration for this outstanding performance as a Senator and as Majority Leader.

The Presiding Officer. Is there any objection to the present consideration of the resolution?

There being no objection, the Senate proceeded to consider the resolution.

Mr. Kennedy. Mr. President, for the first time in the year and a half of my service as assistant majority leader, I have schemed behind the leader's back to touch his power. It was not easy, Mr. President, to outmaneuver the majority leader. I can say to the Senate, whose members know it is not possible to outsmart him, that it is equally difficult to outflank him. Because of the problem posed by the necessity of obtaining unanimous consent to set pending legislation aside, it required two quorum calls, a diversionary route through the Republican cloakroom, and a pretended scrutiny of the ticker tapes to clear the way for me to announce this colloquy.

Probably there have been few times in the history of the Senate when this body has been engrossed in deliberations more crucial to our future, or more far-reaching in effect, than we are in at this moment, as we debate the question of war and peace. But there are times when, in moments of stress, it is well to pause and reflect upon our sources of strength. As so it struck me as most appropriate on this occasion that we take time from the Senate's busy night-and-day schedule, to deliberate briefly upon the subjects of distinguished public service, of dedication to country, of decency, integrity, and ability as their are personified by the distinguished majority leader.

May I say to the members of the Senate that I spoke with the able Republican leader, Mr. Scott, in this regard, and he agreed wholeheartedly with the proposal, as did the managers of the pending legislation. . . .

As a legislative leader, Senator Mansfield is unique. In a body of men of ambition and aspiration, he is calm and deliberate and without pretension. In him is exemplified the noblest tradition of high public service. He is honest — intellectually, professionally, and personally. Because of his complete integrity and sense of fairness, trust flows to him. His power and influence in this body far exceed those vested in him by his party caucus at the beginning of each Congress. No Senator has ever claimed that Mike · Mansfield abused his confidence.

He is a man spare with words. He is a delight to watch on a television program, or to stand next to, as I do just prior to the opening of each day's session, when the reporters come onto the floor and "have at" the leadership. Most politicians, when they are asked a question, will say, "Now I want to make one thing perfectly clear." Others will say, "Now, I am glad you asked that question." And some will say, "Now, let me say this about that." But Senator Mansfield's answers are economical and always the best. His five best are "Yep," "Nope," "Maybe," "Could be," and "Do not know."

One of the most personally rewarding honors which I have received was when, this spring, I was invited to deliver the Mansfield lecture at the University of Montana. In spending two days on that campus and in the city of Missoula, I found that Senator Mansfield's constituents feel about him the way every Senator wishes his own constituents felt. They have full and unreserved faith in their Senator. The trust they put in him is, of course, not only well-placed but is the kind of trust that is becoming more and more unusual in American political life today. If Mike says it, it is right. For they and he are one — one in their sense of morality, one in their understanding of America, one in their dreams and hopes for the future. . . .

Mr. Aiken. Mr. President —

> There was a time ten years ago,
> If Republican Senators wanted a show,
> They would toss a needle across the aisle
> And then they'd all sit back and smile.

231

The Democrats' leader was Lyndon then,
Who was mighty with sword, and sometimes pen.
He was quick to respond to the needle's touch
And never refused a challenge as such.
The show would go on — the air get torrid —
Though Lyndon never said anything horrid.
But Barnum and Bailey could take a rest
When Lyndon was functioning at his best.
And whene'er we'd tense up with talk of taxation,
We could look to Lyndon for relaxation.

Then disaster struck us and Lyndon went on.
And with his departure went most of our fun,
For the Democrats made a new appointment
Which for Republicans spelled disappointment.

They had chosen a man from the Golden West,
Where every kid knows his country is best,
Where they shoot from the hip, whether right or wrong,
And ride off from their victims singing a song.

Of course Mike Mansfield would be such a leader,
Eating needles and darts like steers at a feeder.
He would give us the uplift Republicans need
And meet every challenge by word and by deed.

Did I say disaster struck us this time?
Just another understatement of mine.
For Mike had been leader only a week
When John J. Williams got up to speak.
For John, who was feeling a real good fettle,
Addressed the new leader somewhat like a nettle
And every Republican, one by one,
Sat back in his seat to enjoy the fun.
But, oh, the agony of what followed.
We might as well have arsenic swallowed.
For Mike got up to give John his reply
With such a reproachful look in his eye
That I thought John Williams would like to die.
And never since then do Republicans smile
When a needle is tossed across the aisle,

For we found that Mike is as square as a die,
With a mind as broad as Montana's sky.

It's now ten years that we've worked with Mike,
And during that time we have learned to like
The fairness and candor with which he acts,
And the way when speaking he deals with facts.
So let us be thankful that we serve with one
Whose honor and fairness are second to none.
And since we would miss him on this Senate floor,
I earnestly wish for him six years more —
As minority leader, of course. (Laughter)

Mr. Scott. . . . The qualities which we admire in him, I think, center in the one word, "character," and within that framework of character we find that we need so much for the amiable disposition of the traumatic seria which sometimes afflict the Senate, because within that great vise of character are gripped the qualities of fair-mindedness and integrity, of amiability and of economy of language.

Some may be proud of their articulateness, and others of their oratory, and some others of plain long-windedness (heaven forbid!), but Mike Mansfield's answers are straight, true, and direct to the point, and you know where you stand with him at all times. . . .

So, Mr. President, it is an enormous pleasure to be a party to this resolution, and to say these few words, every one of which, however, seems to have been longer than Mike Mansfield would have used in reference to similar situations. I hope that he is around. We have been trying to lure him into the chamber; but when he learned that his own name was going to be taken — and not in vain — I am afraid he has absented himself. . . .

Mr. Sparkman. . . . I have known quite a number of leaders here in the Senate. Some of them may have been more voluble than he. In fact, I think one of his remarkable talents is that which has been referred to already as his brevity in dealing with almost any matter. He can pack more into a few words, I believe, than anyone else on the floor of the Senate. Some of the leaders may have been more flamboyant, but none has been of greater ability, greater character, greater integrity, or greater success in getting things done than Mike Mansfield. I am glad that I have had the privilege of serving with him, and I am glad to pay tribute to him as a great leader. . . .

Mr. Prouty. Mr. President, I am happy indeed to join both my colleagues in saluting the distinguished Senator from Montana, whose length of service as majority leader now exceeds that of all his predecessors in that exalted office.

No one in this body commands or deserves greater respect than Mike Mansfield. Gentle, courteous, and always considerate of the problems of others, he is perhaps the antithesis of the typical majority leader. And yet it is these qualities which have enabled him to become an effective and strong leader, because they have gained for him the confidence and cooperation of all members of the Senate.

I am proud indeed to claim him as a friend and to serve under his inspired and compassionate leadership.

Mr. Randolph. Mr. President, as a member who has had the privilege of serving with Michael J. Mansfield of Montana in both bodies of the Congress — as far back as January 1943 in the House and since November 1958 in the Senate — I say that no man has deserved to hold the championship for continuous longevity in the office of Senate majority leader than has our esteemed colleague, Mike. . . .

Our quiet, earnest, nonflamboyant majority leader has been as consistently fair, as constantly patient, as congenially friendly, as carefully considerate, and as scrupulously honest as any man with whom I have had experience in the Congresses in which we have worked together.

What more can I say about Mike Mansfield than, Mr. President, to state emphatically: It has been much more than a privilege — indeed, it has been a real joy — to have served with Mike Mansfield and to have experienced the fair but forthright, prudent but progressive, and convivial but impartial leadership he has provided for those of us who have been his colleagues during his brilliant but benevolent tenure as majority leader — and for the years before that when he served as the assistant majority leader on this body.

Mr. Bible. Mr. President, like all of my colleagues, I have many enduring memories of events which have taken place on the floor of the Senate. There have been some great moments here, moments so absorbing that we can recall them, to the finest detail , many years later. I think this is one of those moments.

Any tribute to the distinguished Senator who serves us ably as the majority leader must necessarily be phrased in superlatives. Indeed, it is difficult to find words which do justice to the remarkable achievements of Senator Mansfield as a lawmaker and as a leader. . . .

By any objective yardstick, the 1960's were one of the most challenging periods in our nation's history, if not the most challenging of all. Someone has observed that more major laws shaping the destiny of human events were enacted during the 1960's than in the entire previous history of the American legislative process. Few would quarrel with that observation because, in fact, the volume and the impact of legislation written during the last decade were enormous. Congress engaged and acted upon a wide spectrum of problems, ranging from social injustice to preservation of the environment. It wrote and rewrote hundreds of laws to improve education, housing, medical care, transportation, law enforcement, recreation, and a hundred other areas of vital concern to every American citizen.

The contribution of Senator Mansfield to this unprecedented record of legislative achievement was inestimable. Perhaps it is enough to observe that without his personal qualities of tact and diplomacy, without his wise counsel and unfailing good judgment, without the inspiration of his positive leadership, it is doubtful the Congress could have approached this standard of achievement. Thus, if one must be chosen as a symbol of the vision and progress of Congress in the 1960's, Senator Mansfield is that man. . . .

Mr. Cotton. Mr. President, others have spoken of Mike Mansfield the majority leader, the statesman. I want to say just a few brief sentences about Mike Mansfield the man.

It was my privilege to serve for eight years with him in the House of Representatives and then, when I came to this body sixteen years ago, to serve with him throughout all that time — a total of 24 years.

Whenever I think of Mike Mansfield, I think of him on the first

235

occasion that he impressed himself upon me. It was, and I suppose still is, the custom in the other body each year to hold a memorial service for the members who had passed on during the preceding year; and a member is selected each year, alternating between the sides of the aisle, to deliver the memorial remarks. I always think of the first time I really came to get a vision of what Mike Mansfield is like, which was when he was selected and he mounted the rostrum and gave one of the most simple, direct, but most spiritual utterances I have ever been privileged to hear either in public bodies or in church. It was simple because he is not a man to wear his emotions or his spirituality on his sleeve. But on that day, because of the occasion, he opened up, and I caught a glimpse of the real spirit of Mike Mansfield.

During all the years since, when I have had the privilege of serving with him and under his leadership, that analysis has never changed. His kindliness, his courtesy, his sincerity, his integrity, his warmth, and his sympathetic understanding are known to every member of this body and the other body who has served with him. . . .

Mr. Pell. Mr. President, Senator Mansfield became majority leader of the Senate on January 3, 1961, the same day that I first took my oath of office as U.S. Senator.

I shall always remember the courtesy, consideration, and friendship which the majority leader extended to me as a brand new member of this body. And each year that I have served in the Senate has deepened my respect and affection for Mike Mansfield. He is honest, with himself as well as others; he is fair and even-handed, and — perhaps most important to the work of the Senate — he has an unfailing ability to find a way for the Senate to work its will on even the most controversial of issues.

In serving the Senate so well, Senator Mansfield serves also our entire nation. His is a voice of reason that is heard and heeded not only in the Senate but also throughout our country. He is sparing, too, in the use of his voice. In fact, he is one of the few of us who never lapses into loquaciousness.

To change ideas into events and to help people is the proper pursuit of all of us in politics. But in achieving these ends, Senator Mansfield excels.

Finally, it is as a man, as a gentleman, that I have come most to

236

respect our majority leader. His word is his bond. His honor is irreproachable. His faith and trust in the Senate are complete — and are fairly returned by our faith and trust in him.

There is no man in our nation, much less in this chamber, whom I would rather see as majority leader than Mike Mansfield, and I pray that he may long continue to occupy this position.

Mr. Eastland. Mr. President, while I rise to address the Chair, the feelings of my heart flow toward the occupant of the first seat on the right of the center aisle. . . .

He is a gentle man as well as a gentleman. He is fairminded. Without diluting the tenets of his own beliefs, he is fair to his adversaries as well as his friends. With this man one may disagree violently, but one never feels anger or resultant rancor.

I well remember his remark, when he took over the leadership, that though he may be the leader, he was only one of 96 Senators. His humility enshrouds those around him, quieting, soothing, and gentling raw nerves. With compassion he consoles friend and foe alike. He is a builder of men and ideals. He is in fact a Senator's Senator.

His brand is on this chamber and on his colleagues. The diverse beliefs of the 99 other legislators who make up this body cause us to support different causes and to follow various banners. I am certain, however, that every man here would be proud to wear an "I Like Mike" button every day.

As a committee chairman, I am well aware of the sensitivity with which this man handles the legislative reins of the Senate. We have had many differences throughout the years, and I can tell this chamber that he catches more Judiciary flies with his honey than other leaders have with their vinegar — often to my chagrin. Veritably, this is a man to go to the well with.

He cherishes our Senate traditions; though in a position of power, he treats power gingerly; he reveres the institutions of the other branches of our government; he is awed and abashed at the burdens of the White House; he knows not charisma, but charisma must certainly know him.

I wish this man well and Godspeed. I am honored to have known him, for he possesses the milk of human kindness. . . .

Mr. Church. Mr. President, compliments may be brief. Mine shall be — in keeping with the sparse, succinct, well-knit speaking style of Mike Mansfield, whom we honor today. I do hope, however, that our words will convey to our "Iron Mike" the deep respect in which I hold him, both as a leader and as a person.

All Senators on both sides of the aisle would agree, I am sure, that Mike Mansfield has the patience of Job, the persistence of Hercules, and the strength of Atlas. His sincerity of purpose and his steadfastness under pressure are two conspicuous traits that impressed me when I entered the Senate fourteen years ago. His kindness to newcomers is something that Senators will always treasure.

He has served, I am told, as majority leader for 9 years and 165 days. By my calculations that totals more than 3450 days during which he has borne the burden of leadership. His legislative days are kaleidoscopic ones, consisting of thousands of assigned chores, dictated messages, knowledge applied, legislative battles orchestrated, directions given, and, despite the bruising political struggle, objectives sought and gained.

Of course, I do not know whether we 99 Senators — persons of assertive views and not without idiosyncracies — have disappointed Mike Mansfield. I think we may have on occasion. Nevertheless, on this day we can perhaps help make his difficult task a bit lighter by pausing from our legislative work long enough to say "thank you." ...

Mr. Young of Ohio. Mr. President, . . . it is with pleasure I join my colleagues in expressing my deference and devotion to the distinguished majority leader, Senator Mike Mansfield of Montana, a great American, a great leader and, perhaps most important, a marvelous human being. His qualities of leadership have been well and amply expressed by Senators who have preceded me today. There is little that I can add to their praise.

However, I recall a speech Mike Mansfield made a few years ago in which he recalled the years when, as a young man, he labored in the mines of Montana. He spoke of how, before dynamite was exploded to disgorge the copper, the miners yelled "Tap 'er light." He related how this phrase, meaning "Take it easy" or "Play it soft," has become part of the folklore and language of his state. Perhaps that expression, "Tap 'er light," most succinctly characterizes this great leader from the West. A man of great force, energy, ability, and intelligence, he has always "tapped 'er light"

238

in applying those qualities to problems confronting himself and the nation.

As those with whom he has engaged in legislative combat well know, beneath his calmness, his gentleness, and his patience, there is a quality of great personal and moral courage. . . .

Few people are born leaders. Leadership is achieved by ability and by a willingness to accept responsibility; by getting along with people; by an open mind and a clear head in times of stress. The greatest asset in leadership is courage. Cowards never lead. Leadership requires tact, fairness, and confidence. Leadership implies consideration of those who follow. It requires communication that works both ways, from the bottom up as well as from the top down.

Mike Mansfield has all of these qualities in abundance and throughout the years has displayed them profusely to the great advantage of the nation. He understands the problems of those he leads. I can truly say, as I know all Senators can, that he has never once asked me to take a position that he knew would be in conflict with my responsibilities to the people of my state or with my conscience.

Mr. President, our nation has passed through many trying times. However, not since the Civil War have Americans been more sorely divided than we are today. I am confident that with the grace of God we shall emerge from this precarious era successfully and with renewed greatness and vigor. When historians of the future recount our times, it is certain that they will write that America was blessed with the leadership of the Senate of the United States in the hands of Senator Mike Mansfield. . . .

Mr. Jackson. Mr. President, it is rather difficult to add to the remarks that have been made here this afternoon in praise of our distinguished majority leader. . . .

We all know about the character of this man. Mike Mansfield is a kindly man, always a gentleman, a selfless individual. If there is any meaning to modesty, Mike Mansfield, more than most other individuals, is entitled to that descriptive term.

Having said this, Mr. President, I must let no one get the impression that Mike Mansfield is not a strong, determined man. Behind his kindly approach and interest in the well-being of all his fellow citizens, as well as his deep concern for the Senators on both sides of the aisle, there is a dedicated determination to stand by his deep-seated convictions, whatever the issue may be. This quality of firmness obviously comes from his great integrity as an individual.

We could not deny the fact that in the Senate from time to time we have our disagreements. But Mike Mansfield is a genius at being able to disagree without being disagreeable. More than any other leader I have ever served under, in either the House or the Senate, he has an absolute genius for being able to work his will to get a program through, without leaving battle scars in this chamber.

Mike Mansfield's record as a majority leader has covered a period of great ferment and turbulence in our history; and much of the accomplishment in the Senate is the result of his great leadership. All of us on both sides of the aisle owe him, and the country owes him, a debt of gratitude for his ability to bring us together on issues vital to the nation and to the world. . . .

Mr. Ribicoff. Mr. President, as of last week, Senator Mike Mansfield had served the U.S. Senate as majority leader longer than any man in the history of our country. In this body of 100 complex, independent men, this record is a great tribute to his sensitivity and leadership.

His decade as majority leader has been an exciting one, filled with upheaval and change. Thanks largely to his leadership, the Senate has kept pace with these rapid and almost dizzying changes by enacting an unprecedented number of landmark pieces of legislation.

It was particularly appropriate that, only a few days ago, the President signed a bill giving 18-year-olds the right to vote. This legislation would not have passed without the guidance and support of the majority leader.

In times such as these, emotions often run high and differences of opinion can become dangerously divisive, yet Senator Mansfield's special sense of fairness has harmonized disparate beliefs. His firm commitment to what he believes is right, coupled with an inexhaustible supply of patience and understanding of his fellow Senators, has made possible a truly impressive record of legislative accomplishment.

The accomplishments include three major acts extending the

protection of the Federal government to our black citizens, expansion of aid to education, the establishment of extensive manpower training programs, the establishment of the Department of Housing and Urban Development, and the passage of Medicare and Medicaid.

It is indicative of Senator Mansfield's statesmanship and sensitivity that he would be among the first to recognize the needs of the whole nation and then take a strong role in fulfilling them through legislation.

As a member of the Committee on Foreign Relations, Mike Mansfield has taken the lead in reestablishing the powers of Congress in the difficult field of international relations. Mike's knowledge and understanding of the intricacies of affairs in the Far East is unsurpassed in the Senate.

In the process of these accomplishments, no other Senator has earned the level of respect and admiration that is accorded to Senator Mansfield from both Democrats and Republicans alike. Whether on his side or another, each Senator knows that the actions of the majority leader will be wholly based on the principles of integrity and fairness.

One is tempted to talk at length about Mike Mansfield, but verbosity would be a particularly inappropriate tribute to the majority leader.

Through the past decade Mike Mansfield has been quietly, but firmly, effective. We are all acutely aware of his great contributions to both the Senate and our country as majority leader. I therefore take this opportunity to congratulate Senator Mansfield upon reaching a great milestone and to thank him for the effective and selfless leadership he has provided to the Senate and to the nation. . . .

Mr. Gore. Mr. President, throughout my service as a Representative and as a Senator, it has been my privilege to be the colleague of the distinguished senior Senator from Montana, our beloved majority leader. . . .

What manner of man is this that stands so tall amongst us, that bestows upon each of us, Republican or Democrat, conservative or liberal, irrespectively, an affection, who inspires in each of us a devotion and a respect?

He is a man of kindness and humility, of understanding and

241

compassion, of vision and courage, of leadership potential *par excellence.*

What manner of leader is he? A leader of conscience, a leader for the good of all, a leader of patriotism.

What manner of patriotism does he exemplify? A broad concept, a concept of patriotism that embraces not narrow chauvinism but rather the love of humanity, of his fellow man, of his state, of his country, and of the world.

Mike Mansfield exemplifies the stature, the statesmanship, the dream, and the aspiration which make this country great. He does not drive, he leads; he does not command, he persuades; and in all this he has the power of accomplishment given to but few men. . . .

Mr. McClellan. Mr. President, I am proud to have the privilege of sharing in the sentiments of my colleagues on this occasion and to have this opportunity of paying tribute to our distinguished majority leader, who is today one of the outstanding statesmen and leaders in our nation. . . .

Of all the leaders with whom I have served, all of them great men, I have served with none who was more considerate and more understanding; I have served with none who was more cooperative and helpful when the opportunity was presented. I have served under no leader who was more sincere and more dedicated to his task and to the principles and ideals upon which our government was founded and upon which our liberties rest.

A particular trait that I admire so much in Senator Mansfield in the performance of his duties as leader is that he never undertakes to apply what could be termed "pressure," sometimes referred to as "arm twisting," to influence a vote of his colleagues. Instead, Mike Mansfield employs the persuasion of logic and reason to influence others. I have never known him to reflect or manifest the least resentment toward any member of this body, particularly any Democrat who might disagree and who might vote contrary to the position of the leadership on a given issue. He respects others and their right and prerogative to disagree with him.

In fact, I have found Senator Mansfield, as the leader, to be a person with whom, when I disagree with him, I could disagree most pleasantly; and when, as in most cases, I could wholeheartedly support and follow his leadership, I could do it with much enthusiasm and confidence.

Mr. President, I say in conclusion that my experience in the Senate and my service have been greatly enriched, and my labors have been more pleasant and enjoyable, by reason of having served under and worked with such an able and effective leader as Mike Mansfield, a man who has the admiration of every member of this body because of his ability to influence and to command the respect and admiration of all those with whom he labors. . . .

Mr. Cooper. Mr. President, I am sure that Senator Mike Mansfield, wherever he may be just now, although appreciative of the tributes which he so richly deserves, nevertheless is rather embarrassed, for one of the most certain qualities of Senator Mansfield is his modesty. . . .

Senator Mansfield not only is a leader of his party, but he is a leader in the Senate. He is a leader in the Senate because he is a man of his word, a man of integrity, a man who is fair and just.

It is only natural that other qualities attend him, qualities of mind and heart, of conviction, of firmness, and of honor. Many of us have recognized his strain of poetry when he has spoken of his state of Montana and when we heard him speak in the Rotunda at the memorial service for the late President John F. Kennedy. He deserves, with his wife Maureen, the honor of the Senate and the country. . . .

Mr. Jordan of Idaho. Mr. President, I am pleased to join in the plaudits for the senior Senator from Montana. . . .

In this body of competitive and frequently sharply diverse interests, it is frequently difficult to maintain cordial relations with our colleagues, sometimes even within the same state.

But Mike Mansfield has that breadth of human character, that unshakable sense of fairness, and a demonstrated capacity for honesty and integrity that has won for him through the years the respect and support of his colleagues in this body.

All who know Mike appreciate that his word is not given lightly and that his word, once given, can be depended upon like the rugged granite peaks of his native Montana.

This outpouring of bipartisan praise and support is deep and sincere because Mike the political leader is first and foremost a dependable friend, a stalwart man, and a Senator's Senator.

Mr. Dole. Mr. President, let me say, as a junior member of this body, that I have great respect and admiration for the distinguished Senator from Montana, the majority leader, Mike Mansfield.

When one first comes to this august body he is impressed by various members, for various reasons. Freshmen members, both Republicans and Democrats, were impressed by Senator Mansfield because of his sincerity, his candor, and the many kindnesses and courtesies extended to us as freshmen members of this body. I can recall a number of personal instances in which Senator Mansfield has been helpful to the junior Senator from Kansas. I can say, on behalf of all the freshmen members of the Senate, that we appreciate and we respect leaders like Senator Mansfield. . . .

Mr. Allott. Mr. President, there is an old saying that it takes all kinds of people to make a world. When one thinks of great leaders, I am afraid that one is often prone to think of people who bluster into a room and speak in deep, ponderous voices and dominate the scene, at least with their words. But that is not true of the man whom we are honoring this afternoon. We have set aside this hour to congratulate Mike Mansfield as the majority leader who has served the longest in that capacity in the history of the Senate.

My words shall be very brief, but they are from the heart. I shall always remember Senator Mansfield for his sincerity, his intrinsic honesty, and the fact that during his conduct as leader of the Senate, his word has always been good under any circumstances.

There have been many times when people make agreements, and then later, because of pressures from some source or another, they are prone to modify or put a different meaning on the words they used when the agreement was entered into. There have been times when such situations were presented to Senator Mansfield, and if there ever was a question, he always resolved the question in favor of keeping the agreements in the way and in the manner the person with whom he made an agreement thought it was meant to be.

I know of nothing greater that can be said of a man than that he has conducted the leadership of the Senate — which certainly is one of the most trying of positions — in a way that clearly shows his sincerity and his complete honesty. These great personal attributes are constantly reflected in the manner in which Senator

244

Mansfield has always kept agreements with members of the Senate and respected them when he made those agreements. . . .

Mr. Baker. . . . Senator Mansfield has done what no other person before him has done in serving this length of time as majority leader; but he has done much, much more. He has set a tone for the conduct of the Senate, for the dispatch of its affairs, and for the handling of its requirements in difficult, tedious times. He has served under Republican and Democratic Presidents with equal dedication to duty. He is to be commended on this anniversary occasion, and I am pleased to add my accolade to those of our colleagues on this occasion.

Mr. Curtis. Mr. President, . . . Mike Mansfield's service as majority leader of this body stands out for several reasons, the least of which is the number of years he has served. The mere passing of time itself is not an overwhelming tribute in any activity; it is what you do while the time passes. Senator Mansfield has performed his job well. He has been a patient, understanding leader. His actions are never irritating. He takes into account the rights, the wishes, and the desires of every other Senator, and from that point tries to work out the program of the Senate.

Without a doubt, he experiences many trying times. There is no question in my mind but that the majority leader has to go through an ordeal, many times, in dealing with the rest of us in getting the program under way, and in advancing the legislation.

Yet, throughout all of this, Mike Mansfield is a perfect gentleman, with unfailing and unending courtesy and consideration for others. His grasp of public questions and his understanding of procedures are the best. I am happy to be among those who today go on record in testifying to his outstanding service as majority leader of the Senate.

Mr. Williams of Delaware. Mr. President, as one who has had the privilege of serving with Mike Mansfield for the past eighteen years, I am proud to join my colleagues in paying tribute to this man whom I consider to be one of the most able majority leaders of the Senate with whom I have had the privilege of serving.

The most required characteristic for successful leadership is integrity, and Mike Mansfield is Mr. Integrity. Men may agree or disagree with some of his decisions, but no man who knows him has ever questioned the fact that Mike's word is his bond and that every decision he makes is in what he considers to be the best interest of his country. . . .

Mr. Hart. Mr. President, what makes an effective Senator and leader? In quiet moments that is what all of us have asked ourselves. For the answer we have but to look at the majority leader: a man of principle and integrity, a man of quiet resoluteness, a master of the legislative process — and a friend of unfailing personal loyalty.

His bold and imaginative understanding of a political system that often seems to defy mastery and generate only frustration was brought clearly into focus just a week ago. The House had passed the extension of the Voting Rights Act. And included in it was the provision for the 18-year-old vote.

As I noted on the floor of the Senate that day, the credit for that achievement belongs to the majority leader. But, of perhaps greater significance today as we pay tribute to Senator Mansfield, is what that provision on the 18-year-old vote said about his leadership.

When the suggestion was made, I was reluctant to attach that proposal to the voting rights extension. I could see all kinds of hazards and began to speak and voice caution and reservation about it.

I had not finished three paragraphs before the majority leader announced, without any adjectives and in about two sentences, that he thought it was a great idea and that it was going to go on the bill.

He had in that short time determined with pointblank accuracy that the 18-year-old vote could be approved by both bodies. That is boldness and creative politics at its finest. And the fact that it was accomplished is a tribute to his skill as a legislator and to his hard work on behalf of all the people.

I have wondered from time to time, as I have seen that firm profile rise to report with those sparsely phrased sentences, how an artist might record Mike Mansfield. To catch the real personality he would have to take into account the moments of wry humor, the flashes of firm determination, and that genuine sensitivity to people.

Most of all, he would have to find a way to express what it means to the people of this nation in this time of flaying, divisive

246

rhetoric to be represented by a man of Mike Mansfield's calmness and reason. We are fortunate to be served by his leadership.

Mr. President, one of the qualities of which mankind is in perennially short supply is civility. Yet civility is an absolutely essential element in our dealings with one another if the measure of freedom within which we seek to live is to be maintained.

One of the reasons that young people may tend to reject civility is that they have very few examples of civil, gentle men making any impression on the community or the nation. We are fortunate that, especially when any young person begins to despair of ever persuading anyone to do anything unless he first hits him over the head, we can point to Mike Mansfield. Here is a man who is not frightened of admitting that his judgments have to be tentative about a great many things. All he is doing, of course, is demonstrating wisdom, because most of the things we are asked to pass judgment upon are so complex that it is only a very imprudent person indeed who would jump up all the time and announce that he knows exactly what to do.

Senator Mansfield is never under any compulsion to avoid giving an answer such as "I do not know; I will try to find out."

So we can point the concerned American youngster to Senator Mansfield and suggest that one need not be shrill, that certainly one need not be abusive, in order to be persuasive and effective. Ultimate power is not in force but in ideas; and no man in this body more clearly exemplifies his clear understanding that our survival hinges on our ability to develop prudent ideas, responsive in time to a myriad of complex problems that trouble not just the young man on the campus, but all of us.

Mike Mansfield is indeed a gentle man in the liberal sense; and, together with my colleagues, I am very grateful to be permitted the opportunity to serve with him, to see him, and to draw from him the strength that comes from quiet reserve, thoughtfulness, and self-discipline — all of the characteristics that make a really effective leader but which, in this turmoil today, we tend almost to discount as unimportant, as almost handicaps.

I thank the people of Montana, for the people of Michigan and the people of the country, for sending Mike Mansfield to the Senate.

Mrs. Smith. Mr. President, I am pleased to join in the richly

247

deserved tribute to the majority leader, who is a model of understanding, patience, dignity, tolerance, and even empathy.

Mr. Moss. Mr. President, today Senator Mansfield surpassed all longevity records for service as majority leader in the Senate.

I would say that he also surpasses all records for day-in, day-out, year-in, year-out patience, tolerance, discernment, wisdom, good judgment, rationality, and balance.

The durability of these qualities in his leadership has not only made these last 9 years and 165 days more endurable and rewarding to every member of the Senate, but they have been a bulwark upon which has been built much of the enormous legislative accomplishment of these years. The quiet strength of the majority leader has contributed much to the inner stability of the nation as well as to the inner stability of the Senate.

It has been more than leadership which he has given us, however, in the Senate. It has been a recognition — almost in the manner of a leader of a constitutional government — of the problems and differences of those of us who are members of this body, and the regions we represent. He has sensed in a special way that, dedicated as each of us is to the welfare of the country as a whole, we all remain close to the land and history from which we come. He understands the stresses and strains we each face. Without this understanding, without a recognition of these factors and a nod in their direction, the Senate could never have gotten on so well as it has with the nation's business.

There is another respect in which I feel Mike Mansfield has served both the Senate and his country especially well. He has been masterful in assessing the nation's ills and in speaking out with power and eloquence on them. He never blasts with rhetoric, but discusses an issue with calmness and candor.

He has made peace in Vietnam his first priority — and his statements on this, on crime, inflation, student discord and other issues of the day have all helped immensely in keeping the nation informed and in calming public opinion in times of tempest. His unflinching confidence in the democratic processes is one of America's great assets. . . .

Mr. Holland. Mr. President, from the moment I first met Mike Mansfield I have liked him and have been impressed with his gentleness, his kindness, his courtesy, his tolerance.

I happened to be at Mount Vernon at George Washington's Birthday observance, during the 80th Congress, when the customary tributes are laid at the tomb of the Father of Our Country. The Senator from Montana was then a member of the House of Representatives. I was a member of the Senate. We were both there to carry wreaths on behalf of patriotic groups in our respective states. There had been a heavy snowfall the night before, and I remember distinctly the first thing I saw him do was to help an ambassador from one of our South American countries, and his entourage, to find a spot where they could stand without being in deep snow, and to help them get with their floral offerings up to the tomb of George Washington.

From that time to this, I have noted always the fact that patience and tolerance and cooperation with others and gentle courtesy have been qualities that always showed in every act that I have seen Mike Mansfield perform.

It would be idle to say that I always agree with him, or he with me. He probably has been right in these disagreements more often than I. But I have noticed this wonderful attitude of tolerance and gentleness coupled, however, with a firmness which refused to yield when he thought that a certain course of action was right, whether that course of action was to keep us from meeting at night or on occasion to insist that we meet at night. Whatever he thought was right at the time, he was perfectly willing to stand by.

I noted a long time ago what a good family man he is. I had the honor of going to the statehood celebration at Hawaii. Mike and Mrs. Mansfield had been in Asia, and in the group with which I went was their daughter, Anne. I remember how eagerly she looked forward to the arrival of her mother and father, who joined us for the celebration of statehood; and I remember the quiet and gentle but unmistakable affection which prevailed among those three, and showed that here was a real family, after the most genuine American tradition. I have noted that always since.

Mr. President, something Mike Mansfield did the other day showed the measure of the man, I thought. I participated in the conference of Democratic Senators which arranged for him to procure, if he could, equal time from the National Broadcasting Company to speak on the economic problems of the country — somewhat in response to the speech which had been made a

249

couple of days before by the President of the United States. There may have been some in that group who thought Mike Mansfield would make a highly political speech, a speech full of blaming and criticism. I did not think so; and when I heard the speech, I realized that I had been right, because he carried into the speech the kindness and the courtesy and the tolerance which he always makes his hallmark. . . .

Mr. Jordan of North Carolina. Mr. President, I consider it a rare privilege to join today in saluting a majority leader, Mike Mansfield, because I know of no man more deserving of such a tribute. . . .

He has earned the respect and affection of all of us by his kindness, his understanding, and his ability to direct by gentle persuasion instead of demanding direction.

His example of dedication has been an inspiration throughout the years to those of us who have followed his leadership throughout his term, as well as to those who have come here in more recent times. I consider Mike Mansfield a true friend and adviser, and to me, at least, he is more than just the Democratic leader. I think he is a symbol of the Senate, and I am proud to salute him today in that role.

Mr. Pastore. Mr. President, to me it is not so much how long Mike Mansfield has been majority leader in the Senate as much as it matters to me what a great gentleman he is and what a great American he is.

The Senate of the United States of America is composed of 100 individuals. I know of no other body where individuality is in such evidence as in the Senate of the United States.

Mr. President, when you have a man who can bring divergent points of view together in such smooth fashion, there you find a good leader.

Mike Mansfield does it calmly. He does it temperately. He does it patiently. He does it very effectively. . . .

Mr. Case. Mr. President, I am happy to join with all my colleagues in expressing the esteem and affection we all hold for Mike Mansfield.

I, like many others here, have served with him for a quarter of a century and upward in the House and Senate. It has been one of the great privileges of my adult life to have had this association.

250

As a person, as a political leader, and as a Senator, Mike Mansfield has been everything that a person, a political leader, and a Senator should be.

It is because of people like Mike Mansfield that this institution has retained the strength, respect, and effectiveness it has. It is because of people like Mike Mansfield that this country has retained its greatness. It is because of people like Mike Mansfield that the human race has found coexistence tolerable.

Mr. Dominick. Mr. President, having observed some of the disagreements we have within our own party on the Republican side, and having admired our leadership and its ability to try to get us together on some kind of basis, and having also observed that the other side has even more members in disagreement than we have, I have been constantly delighted and amazed at the ability of Senator Mike Mansfield to absorb this tension and to maintain his calm, tact, and good humor for all of us in the Senate and almost at all times.

We have not always agreed. But at all times, whether we agreed or disagreed, he has been courteous, fair, full of good humor and continued friendly relationships, so far as people are concerned.

I am deeply indebted personally to Mike Mansfield for the fine support he gave to me throughout a period of five years in my efforts to try to revise our silver policy, which was headed in the wrong direction for so long. I shall always be grateful to him for that, and even more grateful for the sense of balance which he has given to the entire Senate.

Mr. Bennett. Mr. President, I am delighted that the distinguished Senator from Montana has had the privilege of serving in this body and in his position as majority leader longer than any other, which will place his name on the permanent records of this body. If any man deserves such a privilege, Mike Mansfield does.

I know that there have been times when his pattern of leadership has been criticized — that it was too kindly, too thoughtful, or too considerate. Some people have interpreted that as being weakness.

I have been the beneficiary of that kindness, thoughtfulness and consideration many, many times, even though I am on the other side of the aisle.

To me, these qualities are more significant characteristics of greatness than if he had been the kind that pounded the desk, hit people over the head, so to speak, and run roughshod over some of the wishes and needs of those of us who might not have been so important politically to him or to his party.

What I shall always remember about Mike Mansfield are his characteristic kindness, thoughtfulness, and consideration. . . .

Mr. Gurney. Mr. President, . . . my reflections would be those of a new Senator who has known Mike Mansfield only last year and this year to date, but I have always found him to be a most fair, a most considerate, and a most kindly man.

On the occasions I have had to talk to him, mainly concerning advice on Senate procedures when I was learning how this body operates, I have always found him willing to spare the time to advise me on what ought to be done and what ought not to be done.

Certainly his leadership is exemplified by fairness — and, I think, by example, a sort of light touch, a persuasive touch, rather than that of the sort of leader who drives one with the lash of a whip. Mike Mansfield is not that kind of man at all. Of course he is liked and respected by his colleagues on both sides of the aisle. And I think that in these troubled times the Senate is most fortunate in having Mike Mansfield as majority leader.

Mr. Inouye. Mr. President, I wish to pay tribute to a man who not only has served longer in the position of majority leader than any predecessor, but who while serving in that post has demonstrated unsurpassed leadership, patience, and understanding through difficult times in a most demanding role — our beloved Mike Mansfield.

Senator Mike Mansfield is a calm but firm leader, one who not only has demonstrated a desire to serve his colleagues on the Democratic side of the aisle, but also is known for his astute sense of fairness to those on the other side as well, and who has thereby gained their cooperation and respect. This is the mark of a true leader.

His quiet, reflective manner, his calm but firm demeanor, and his dedication to placing the national interest first and foremost over any personal or partisan preference make him a man admired and loved by his colleagues in the Senate as well as the overwhelming majority of the people of his own state of Montana and indeed of the nation.

Senator Mansfield has thoroughly demonstrated throughout his career an interest in the common good. In so doing he has also shown an independence which clearly designates him as no man's but his own. This may spring from the fact that Mike Mansfield is so clearly a self-made man, a Senator beholden to no one individual or interest.

He has demonstrated a tremendous capacity for hard work, and, although a busy man, he always has time to help an individual in need and to be considerate and courteous to all who seek his attention or counsel.

While it is not possible for any one man to express the desires or interest of 100 individual Senators, or even of the 56 Senators of our party, Mike Mansfield represents, and expresses in most literate fashion, the common will and consensus of his party in the Senate. We are all proud of you, Mr. Leader, and we appreciate and admire the leadership which you have provided us in making the U.S. Senate an institution of real substance and service to our people, our nation, and the cause of mankind. . . .

Mr. McGee. Mr. President, the record of longevity recently established by our majority leader is a measure of the high esteem in which the Senator from Montana is held. It speaks, of course, of the confidence members of his own party place in him, but the respect and admiration we in the majority party share for Mike Mansfield is, I know, shared also by those on the other side of the aisle who would prefer to see the Senator from Montana serving as the minority leader.

Mr. President, the legislative accomplishments of this body over the past nine, almost ten, years also stand as a measure of our majority leader. It has been a decade of most significant legislative accomplishment, marked by the enactment of measures of far-ranging and durable benefit to the United States and its people. Much of the credit for these accomplishments must go to the majority leader. His leadership has been of the persistent type, which wears well and long. Perhaps that is obvious because he has been retained in the post longer than any of his predecessors.

Senator Mansfield, as we in this chamber know, practically invented the low profile. One does not hear him claiming credit for his own achievements or see him flashing the outward signs of the power which vests in his office. As one who has had the honor to serve under his leadership, however, I wish to join my fellow Senators in paying tribute to his long and patient service, which has borne much good fruit. Finally, as a Senator from Wyoming, Montana's good neighbor to the south, I have a particular appreciation for Senator Mansfield's sound leadership and counsel. We in Wyoming are pleased to have the majority leader's office occupied by our wonderful friend and neighbor.

Mr. Harris. Mr. President, . . . Senator Mansfield has served a long time because he has served with exceptional distinction, served both the people of Montana and the Senate of the United States.

A man of fairness and firmness, conviction and compassion, Senator Mansfield leads the Senate because he is a leader of uncommon quality. . . .

Mr. Hollings. Mr. President, . . . Senator Mansfield is truly admired by all for his ability as majority leader. But more important than this, he has had the wisdom and fortitude to maintain the calm, deliberate debate within the Senate on issues which drive other, lesser men to distraction.

In recent months the patience of the Senators has been sorely tested. A man without the qualities of Senator Mansfield might not have been able to handle the task we now have before us and will have in the difficult days which are ahead.

Senator Mansfield has my deep and abiding respect, both as a Senator and as a gentleman. I am proud to call him majority leader.

Mr. Anderson. Mr. President, . . . one of the wisest of . . . philosophers, one to whom this and other republics owe so much, was the Baron de Montesquieu, who fully developed the principles that we know as the separation of powers and checks and balances.

Montesquieu believed, and wrote, that such principles would have to be institutionalized in order to preserve liberty because, he said, "every man invested with power is apt to abuse it."

Mr. President, I believe one of the finest tributes we can pay to our esteemed and distinguished majority leader, Mike Mansfield, is that he has been invested with great authority and power and has not abused it. He is universally regarded for his scrupulous

254

fairness, his honesty, his forthrightness, and, perhaps most of all, his forbearance, his steadfast refusal to abuse the power with which he has been invested.

Today it is my pleasure to join my colleagues in honoring Mike. Technically, we are paying tribute to him for having surpassed all records for length of service as majority leader. This is no small feat, and it certainly deserves tribute. The post of Senate majority leader is a demanding one. It requires both attention to minute, technical detail and a grasp of broad social and political issues. Senator Mansfield has performed both duties ably and diligently.

But we also are honoring Mike for the qualities which have enabled him to serve so long in such a demanding post without having incurred the enmity of even those who have differed with him. When we hear him described, we hear such words as "judicious," "fair," "accommodating," "helpful," "reasonable." Those adjectives are well chosen, Mr. President, when they are applied to our esteemed majority leader. . . .

Mr. Talmadge. Mr. President, . . . Senator Mansfield is an outstanding Senator who, regardless of party lines, has always endeavored to serve the best interests of his nation and state. As majority leader, his statesmanlike and gentlemanly conduct have earned him the respect and admiration of Senators on both sides of the aisle. He is a fair and generally quiet-spoken man, but, as we all know, he is firm in the courage of his convictions. This is to his credit as a man and as a Senator. He has indeed brought distinctive leadership to the important office of majority leader. . . .

Mr. McIntyre. Mr. President, there are many rewarding aspects of the task of representing one's fellow Americans in Congress. Not the least of these is the privilege of associating with others who bear this same responsibility.

Under the Constitution, all of us who serve in this body of Congress are equal. But having said that, let me hasten to recognize reality by pointing out that some are more equal than others. Then I must quickly add that there is one among us who is the most equal of all, and it is my most pleasant privilege to join with Senators to pay my respects today to the leader, to our friend — to my leader, to my friend — Mike Mansfield.

I, for one of many, am not at all surprised by the luminous longevity of his leadership. The only way he could not have reached this new milestone would have been for him to leave of his own volition. Thank goodness he has not.

I know that the people of his state will never keep him from this body. And I know that Senators on this side of the aisle will keep him as their leader as long as he wants to serve.

History will record what we have accomplished under Mike's leadership. It will record that he has kept us on an even keel during one of the most difficult eras in our history. And this, of course, is the real mark of a great leader: the ability to hold the keel steady when seas are rough, to keep the ship on course when the crosswinds blow, to reach the harbor through the treacherous reefs. We could not have asked for more, and Mike did not give us less.

Mike, our words today cannot begin to express the real admiration, the deep respect, and the great affection we feel for you.

Mr. Burdick. Mr. President, . . . citizens throughout the land are grateful to Mike for his many years of public service and as an advocate of justice for all our people. We in Congress are grateful for his warm friendship, his brilliant leadership, and his constant cooperation. Through our majority leader's leadership, some of the most important decisions ever made by this body were decided.

Truly this man from the "big sky country" of Montana is one man in public service who leads the humanitarian form of quality service to his fellow man.

Mr. Tydings. Mr. President, . . . few men reach that level of leadership where they can offer a significant contribution to the governing of our nation. Fewer men reach the highest level of leadership and remain in that position long enough to leave a lasting imprint on the course of national events. And fewer still are those who, having been given these awesome responsibilities, acquit themselves in such a manner as to be esteemed by their colleagues, by their nation, and by the students of government and history. One of these very few men is Senator Mansfield.

In nearly a decade as Senate majority leader, Senator Mansfield has made a great imprint upon the operation and policies of our government. In the complex and rugged combat over the course of national policy, the majority leader has often applied the key push or shove to guide us in a better direction.

Senator Mansfield does not lead by cracking heads together. He does not raise issues with loud cries of despair or elaborate promises of future bliss. His style of quiet reflection and discussion, of raising questions and indicating problems, of expertise that slowly pervades the thinking of those around him is so effective that it goes unnoticed by many outside the Senate. I can only say that I feel he has been a great Senate leader.

He has mastered the difficult balance between being leader of the Senate and of his party in the Senate, to the benefit of both. He is one of the moving forces in making our body into a more respected, more powerful, and more positive part of the Federal government. He has led a party with a great majority, so easily split into divisions, to become a responsible, cohesive unit that has contributed much in this decade.

Senator Mansfield has been a leader who has dipped into substantive areas, not being content to reign above the great issues of our day. As the most informed and expert Senate majority leader in the area of foreign affairs in our history, he has had a profound impact upon our policies. He is one of those few men who have reversed one of the most unfortunate ventures of our history and helped lead the renaissance of the Senate's power in foreign affairs. For this alone, Senator Mansfield must be called great.

Another example of the majority leader's skills as leader of the Senate and the nation was his decision to move ahead with the 18-year-old vote as part of the Voting Rights Act. This demonstrated a wise sensitivity to the trends in our nation and an acute reading of the legislative possibilities. This was Senator Mansfield at his best, a man of thoughtful and powerful action.

One of Senator Mansfield's great attributes is his disdain for the elaborate praise and formalities of high office. So I shall not go further. I am happy to note briefly my respect and admiration for a great Senate leader. We are fortunate that the man who has been the majority leader longest is also one of the best.

Mr. Boggs. Mr. President, . . . it has always been a great pleasure for me to be associated with Senator Mansfield in any endeavor. I remember warmly trips to Southeast Asia that a group of Senators made under Senator Mansfield's leadership in 1962 and 1965. His expertise in the field of foreign relations was most valuable to us, and, I believe, the reports which he was instrumental in writing were most excellent commentaries on the tragic conflict which still engulfs us.

In an adulthood that began prematurely at the age of fourteen, he has had many varying experiences — in the military, in industry, and in scholarly pursuits — that uniquely qualify him for his position.

It has been my experience that the distinguished majority leader has been absolutely fair and honest in his dealing with each of us, no matter the side of the aisle on which we sit. . . .

Mr. Ellender. Mr. President, . . . if we ponder upon the descriptions that have been used to characterize the "Mansfield leadership," we notice the many affirmative phrases dealing with his "fairness," his "impartiality," the fact that he "leans over backwards" to protect the rights of Senators, particularly those who may disagree with his own position on public policies. We can also notice what seems to be a consensus in the Senate, and one with which I wholeheartedly agree, that our majority leader has not been "heavy-handed," that he has not attempted to "force a decision" on the Senate and, as some have pointed out, that he is not prone to "arm-twisting tactics" in the conduct of the Senate business.

I do not think these descriptions can be argued with, and I think they are appreciated by all of us here on both sides of the aisle. I think there is something deeper involved, though, and I believe it is this function, as developed by Senator Mansfield, that is likely to stand as his most important contribution to the leadership role in the years ahead.

As I think back over the many issues that have divided this body over the last nine years — and they have been many, and the divisions have been deep and bitter on some occasions — I cannot escape the conclusion that the "light" guiding Senator Mansfield's attitude and actions has been a desire to see the Senate act as a mature legislative body in our democracy. He has been guided at all times, I believe, by a desire to see the Senate act responsibly and on its own on the public policy issues confronting us. I think this to be very important, and I think it will become more important in the years ahead as our government continues to expand. If the Senate is to recognize no master among the powerful outside forces — parties, Presidents, organized pressure groups — the Senate must master itself as an effective legislative body. As I read the record of these last nine years, this has been the overriding concern of the present majority leader.

I would hope that future scholars and historians of the Senate would give full attention to this feature of Senator Mansfield's leadership when this period of our history is analyzed. . . .

Mr. Magnuson. Mr. President, the distinguished majority leader of the Senate is a man to whom all types of tribute can be and have been paid. Yet the mark of a man deserving of tribute is how little really needs to be said of him in praise on special occasions.

It is not by virtue of what we say about him on a day like today that makes Senator Mansfield the truly great and historic leader that he is. Rather, it is in the smooth operation of the Senate and in the progressive legislative product of the Senate that Senator Mansfield is honored day after day, week after week, month after month, and year after year.

For nearly a decade now, Senator Mansfield has been our majority leader. Historians will note that his tenure was the longest in the long and colorful life of the Senate. But historians will note more than his endurance in a difficult and demanding post. They will note that, under his leadership, the Senate of which the majority leader is a beloved member passed the great landmark legislation that has reshaped, and will continue to reshape, the lives of millions of Americans. And historians will also note that the most significant and most far-reaching of these many important laws would not have been possible without the leadership, the intellect, and the compelling persuasiveness of this remarkable man. . . .

Mr. Muskie. Mr. President, modest, humble, fair, quiet, low-keyed, with simple tastes, unassuming, and without a single enemy — these are uncommon words to use in describing strong leadership. But with Mike Mansfield the definition of leadership must be expanded and rewritten. Indeed, what these phrases describe, at least in part, are the qualities of the man who, in my judgment, has led the Senate with greater effectiveness than in any other period in the entire history of this institution.

The Senator from Montana has been majority leader of the U.S. Senate longer than any other man. It is not surprising. When asked once how he would like to be recalled in history, he is reported to have replied, "When I am gone, I want to be forgotten." History would never honor that wish.

It is difficult to say now what single achievement will be most remembered about Mike Mansfield. It may be leading the fight to give 18-year-olds the vote. It could be a host of legislative monuments that occurred during the sixties — from Medicare for the elderly to civil rights for the racial minorities; from the Nuclear Test Ban Treaty to a breakthrough in Federal aid to education. It may be one that has not yet even been attained.

If I were to summarize his influence, it would be to say that Mike Mansfield has set the entire tone for this emerging decade. He has called us quietly and most effectively for a reappraisal — a reappraisal of our objectives, our policies, and our purposes — both at home and abroad.

At a time when it is not always popular to engage in politics, he has made me proud to be a politician. In an era when the Senate was at times relegated to a less than coequal status, he has led us in regaining the Senate's Constitutional role.

Stripping it all away, there is perhaps only a single word that is needed to describe the reason for his success. It is trust. It has been the immense faith generated by this kind and honest man from the West that has been his most valuable asset. With it he has gained the support of all his colleagues and associates. With it he has affected the very core of the U.S. Senate. With him I have developed more confidence in the direction of this republic.

I honor Mike Mansfield today. I do so as he would say it himself, without any ifs, ands or buts.

Mr. Cranston. Mr. President, on the Senate floor today, and off the floor on many occasions, I have heard Senators compare Mike Mansfield with other majority leaders under whom they have served.

I can make no such comparisons, for I have never served under any other leader. Nor do I wish to serve under any other leader, ever. I find it impossible to imagine a leader of greater grace and greatness, a leader more considerate, thoughtful, moral, wise, and effective than Mike Mansfield.

I am particularly appreciative, of course, for the guidance and the opportunities that Mike Mansfield, in his capacity as leader, offers to new Senators like myself.

Most of all, I respect Mike Mansfield not only as a leader of the majority, and hence of the whole Senate, but as a leader of the United States, and hence of the whole world.

Mr. Hansen. Mr. President, the quiet, scholarly, concise majority leader is indeed a most distinguished Senator. More than that, his fairness encourages each of us to bear greater regard for the interest of others.

His thoughtfulness, quietly displayed by his logic, prompts more reflection by each of us. His uncommon common sense is a stabilizing factor in even the worst of situations, although it has been characteristic of his attention to duty that such situations are seldom.

His abiding concern for fairness and his courtesy and thoughtfulness for his colleagues, regardless of party lines or differences of opinion, often belies a dedication to study and a toughness that may have had its beginnings during his days in the U.S. Marine Corps.

No one can ever question his integrity or loyalty to the Senate, his state, or his country. However, he always puts statesmanship and the national interest above strictly regional or partisan issues when he believes such interest transcends provincialism. And in spite of his gentle demeanor, he runs a tight ship and one on which we can all be more proud to serve.

Storms have raged within this body that have threatened, with the passions of the moment, to swamp the progress of legislation essential to this nation in many areas. The steady hand of the majority leader at the helm has led us to more reasonable solutions.

The leadership of the able Montanan has been instrumental in maintaining the traditional, reasoned deliberative approach of the Senate to critical and often emotional issues during years of some of the greatest unrest this nation has known. He has consistently exhibited a presence of wisdom that surpasses party lines and has often been quick to bring into perspective and help clarify the positions of Senators on each side of the aisle.

His understanding of the value of the two-party system which continues to make this nation the greatest on earth has prevented harsh divisions from forming on matters which a lesser man could have allowed to result in rigid and long-lasting lines of anger or discord.

Mr. President, the confidence of every American in the Congress is strengthened by the knowledge that men like the senior Senator from Montana are in service to this nation. . . .

Mr. Montoya. Mr. President, Mike Mansfield has occupied the post of majority leader longer than any other member of this body in its long-honored history. This chamber has seen many a Senator of significant stature. More than a few have left an imprint upon it that remains to this day.

The Senate became a part of them. In turn, they each left a part of themselves here in this chamber. It is because of such men that the Senate, as an institution, has evolved, grown, and had such an impact upon the history of our republic. Mike Mansfield is very much in the tradition of such towering figures.

A majority leader must be many things. Party leader. Statesman. Compromiser and peacemaker. A person whose mind and wit are able to cope with the myriad situations and human confrontations that occur on such a national stage as this. Mike Mansfield has been all of these and more.

He holds his position of eminence by dint of ability, knowledge of the body, and respect of his peers. The newest member of the Senate can unhesitatingly approach him on practically any matter, secure in the knowledge that Mike Mansfield will greet his request with sympathy, understanding, and awareness.

Practically every member of this body has come to him with the most involved problems confronting them. Each time some reasonable alternative or just compromise is offered. It would be easy indeed for a man in his position to act differently — negatively, patronizingly. This has not been known to happen.

Mike Mansfield has remained true to his heritage of toil, honesty, and courage. Surely the people of Montana are fortunate in having a man and Senator of such caliber representing them here. . . .

Mr. Pearson. Mr. President, . . . the senior Senator from Montana is well respected and loved on both sides of the aisle here in the Senate, both as an able public servant and as a fine, fair, God-fearing man who is a credit to his state and nation. . . .

Mr. Mondale. Mr. President, I wish to join my many colleagues who are today paying tribute to one of the most effective and admired leaders in the history of the U.S. Senate, the greatest deliberative body in the world.

Mike Mansfield has now been majority leader longer than any other Senator. In this capacity, he is known and will be remembered for his warmth, his leadership, and his unparalleled ability to provide effective leadership along with the utmost respect for the integrity of every member of this body.

I am proud to have served in the Senate for six years under the leadership of Mike Mansfield. He has done much for me through his wisdom, his leadership, and most of all his personal friendship. . . .

Mr. Stevens. Mr. President, I want to join the other members of this body in paying tribute to the majority leader. Although a freshman, and in this body by appointment, I am most pleased to be able to say that the senior Senator from Montana has accorded me every courtesy and has gone out of his way to ease the transition for our state from our previous membership in this body to the representation provided by Alaska's Senators now. Because of the untimely death of my predecessor and the election of my colleague, Alaska found itself with two freshmen Senators coming on the scene here within a matter of days. All the members of this body have been courteous and kind to both of us, but it is important for me to note that the majority leader has, in many ways, aided me in the performance of my duties for my state.

Of course, this action merely reflects his total qualities of fairness and the fact that he is a complete gentleman in every regard.

Mr. Proxmire. Mr. President, . . . as important as length of service is, the quality of that service is even more important. Senator Mansfield has excelled in both.

There are various ways to lead men. Some do it by the power and authority and domination over others which they exercise. On the whole, that is not the way to lead. It may get action. It may succeed at a given moment. But in the long run it will fail because free men resent these methods and smart under them even when they appear to accept them.

But Senator Mansfield leads the Senate by consent. It could be called the "Quaker Meeting" style of leadership. All feel free to express their views. All have a voice in policy. No one is forced to action against his will or against his better judgment. He is a master at leading the Senate to a judgment based on the free flow of opinion and debate. Under his leadership, the Senate really does "work its will."

Modest, self-effacing, but also determined and forthright, Senator Mansfield has made the Senate a pleasant place to be and to work. . . .

Mr. McGovern. Mr. President, Mike Mansfield is noted for his remarkable capacity to say important words with unusual brevity. Following his example, I simply wish to say that it has been one of the most satisfying experiences of my life to work under the leadership of Senator Mansfield since 1963. I treasure him as a friend, as a colleague, and as a wise and sensitive leader. . . .

Mr. Schweiker. Mr. President, . . . as a freshman Senator, I have been particularly appreciative of the majority leader's fairness, and his support and encouragement for greater participation in Senate business by new Senators. . . .

The majority leader has always put the interests of the nation, and the Congress, ahead of more parochial concerns, and in so doing has been a credit to his party, to every Senator, and to our great nation, and it is a pleasure to join my colleagues on both sides of the aisle in these words of praise today.

Mr. Nelson. Mr. President, . . . as majority leader of this body, Mike has certainly set a record which deserves to be recognized this afternoon. The measure of his achievement, however, has not been determined just by the unparalleled number of years and days in this position of leadership. Nor are we only calling attention to the list of important legislative innovations which Mike has steered through these halls in the last nine years and which are now part of the public law of the nation. Rather, we are giving recognition and public acknowledgment of our respect for a trusted colleague, an admired leader, and an exemplary man.

This is a political leader whose overriding concern for his country's welfare is such that he can tell members of his party at a recent campaign-fund-raising function, "In this year of national crisis, there is no partisanship. There is only national obligation."

This is a Senator in a position of great power who has chosen to employ reasoned dialogue and perseverance rather than force as the means to produce legislative action.

264

This is a gentleman whose sparse words are not rhetorical evasions, but statements of trust.

This is a man who views the Senate as a national legislative forum to produce agreement on the course of action for the country rather than a political arena in which to score ideological wins and losses.

I think that we and the country are extremely fortunate in having Mike Mansfield as our majority leader at this particular time of national uncertainty and bitter divisiveness. As a calm force for unified attention to the public welfare, he can direct cooperative political energy for the nation's benefit. In Mike's own words, this Congressional cooperation is given "without ifs, ands or buts. The republic deserves no less." And with Mike Mansfield's calm, steady voice in the chambers of the Senate, the Republic will continue to receive no less.

Mr. Mathias. Mr. President, in all the naval lore of Great Britain, no legend is more cherished than the story of Lord Nelson's constant consideration for his midshipmen and young officers. He gave them endless hours of his time and dedicated himself to helping them and promoting their professional education and training.

It has been my personal observation that great judges in both big and little courts are invariably interested in young members of the bar. . . .

But the task of perpetuating the best traditions of a noble profession is often left undone in the world of politics. Political life is often cruel, frequently bloodthirsty, and sometimes cannibalistic. It is also pressured and hurried, so that even the gentler and more considerate among us simply do not find time for such work. The center aisle is a possible partisan obstacle.

But as a member of the Senate who entered at the beginning of the present Congress, I want to testify that Senator Mansfield has always had the time, and the patience, and the interest to help a new member. To say that I am grateful is a gross understatement of the case.

I do not always agree with Senator Mansfield. At times our differences may be rooted in a divergence of opinion, and at times in a diversity of party loyalty. But however I may view his position on any one issue, I know that in his view of it he will be right with

265

himself and his conscience.

He has instilled in politics an air of nobility and purpose, and for this above all, the citizens of this republic should be glad that he is an American, a Senator, and a fellow citizen.

Mr. Brooke. Mr. President, I could not let this day pass without joining with my colleagues in a well-deserved tribute to our distinguished majority leader. . . .

No one knows better than he that his is not an easy task. Yet he has always carried out his duties with consummate skill, patience, integrity, and faith in his fellow men. It gives me great pleasure to salute our majority leader for his remarkable record, and to extend to him my personal gratitude for the many times that he has offered me his counsel and assistance.

Mr. Griffin. Mr. President, I am grateful for the opportunity to join in paying tribute to the distinguished majority leader, the Senator from Montana. By serving as majority leader longer than any other man in the Senate's history, he has confirmed what we all know.

He is a man of endurance. The majority leader is not only a man of endurance but he is relentless in pursuing a course which reflects credit on the Senate and serves the nation's interests best.

If one were to attempt to describe his manner and style in a phrase, I think we might say that his is "a quiet leadership." But his quiet leadership is most effective. It is an effective leadership because he is a good man who is thoughtful, considerate, patient, humble, and decent.

I salute him as a great leader and a great American.

Mr. Tower. Mr. President, . . . I know that all in this chamber will join with me in commending Senator Mansfield for the outstanding job which he has done. The patience and diplomacy which he has shown in guiding our discussions are particularly important in this very deliberative body. Beyond that, he is a fair-minded man and a man of his word. I offer my congratulations to the Senator on his past achievement and know that his future action will merit no less appreciation from his fellow Senators.

Mr. Cannon. Mr. President, . . . the dedication of Mike's outstanding talents to the manifold duties and responsibilities of his career as majority leader spans a decade of tremendous significance in the history of our country.

We have seen the greatest pieces of social legislation maneuvered through the Senate and the Congress under his guidance and leadership. He has contributed notably to America's social progress by his own spirit and intellect and energy.

As Senate majority leader he has been chosen for one of the most difficult assignments in Congress. Under circumstances that would try most men, Mike Mansfield's leadership qualities have been tested and found solid over and over again. . . .

Mr. Thurmond. Mr. President, . . . Senator Mansfield is not only a distinguished Senator but also an estimable gentleman who is held in high esteem by his colleagues on both sides of the aisle.

Though he and I frequently disagree on matters before the Senate, I have always found him to be courteous, considerate, and helpful as majority leader.

Mr. Kennedy. Mr. President, I ask unanimous consent to have printed in the Record tributes to the distinguished majority leader submitted by the Senator from Indiana, the Senator from Texas, and the Senator from New Jersey.

These Senators are necessarily absent from the Senate today but desired to participate in expressing their appreciation to the majority leader. (There being no objection, the tributes were ordered to be printed in the Record as follows.)

Mr. Bayh. Mr. President, . . . members of both sides of the aisle have long recognized Mike Mansfield as an able Senator, an outstanding leader, and a superb statesman. When Senator Mansfield ran for reelection in 1964, the late distinguished minority leader, Mr. Dirksen, informed his colleagues in the Senate that he was about to commit political heresy. Senator Dirksen said that, while he would be willing to go to the moon, he would not visit Montana to campaign for the Republicans because he would not and could not speak against Mansfield. Many other Republicans must have had the same attitude, because Mike won his 1964 reelection with 64.5 percent of the vote. . . .

During the almost three decades of his service as a legislator, few members of Congress have equaled the devotion to duty, absolute integrity, complete fairness, and parliamentary skill which he has displayed. He has led the Senate with patience, kindness and good humor. He has rendered invaluable service to both the nation as a whole and the people of his own state.

I am pleased to join other Senators in expressing my appreciation to Senator Mansfield for the many courtesies he has shown us through the years and to thank the "Big Sky Country" for sending to Washington one of its finest. . . .

Mr. Yarborough. Mr. President, . . .there are countless things that can be said about Senator Mansfield's excellent leadership, his ability, and his sense of statesmanship; however, as important as these things are, I think it also is important to point out that Senator Mansfield is a kind and considerate gentleman who has won the affection and respect of every member of this body.

It has been my pleasure to know and work with Senator Mansfield for over thirteen years. In the hard fights for progressive legislation, he has always been an eloquent and effective ally. As majority leader Senator Mansfield has always provided the forceful leadership that was needed to pass some of the most important social legislation in the history of this nation. Despite the difficulties and pressures imposed upon him as majority leader, Senator Mansfield has always treated every member of the Senate with the utmost courtesy and respect. Many times in the heat of a legislative battle, when tempers reached the boiling point and reason temporarily departed this chamber, it was Senator Mansfield's quick wit which was the "soft answer" that "turneth away wrath" and paved the way to a logical solution and reconciliation of differences. . . .

Mr. Williams. Mr. President, . . . I shall always be proud of the fact that I have worked with a man who has played so large a role in shaping the direction and greatness of our country. Few of us will ever forget his determined efforts to maintain and improve our VA hospitals, to bring enactment of the landmark Civil Rights Act of 1964, to establish a rational foreign policy and bring peace to the world, to insist that 1969 would be a year for meaningful tax reform, and, most recently, to invest our nation's youth with the right to vote.

I congratulate the distinguished majority leader who is a benefactor of his state, the nation, and the world.

Mr. Percy. Mr. President, . . . the Senator from Montana exemplifies the very best characteristics of the state he so ably represents — the individualism, openness, courage, and integrity so often associated with persons from the western states.

But he is no regional politician. He loves the West, but he is even more devoted to his country, to the solutions of the problems of all regions of this great nation, North, South, East, and West. Senator Mike Mansfield feels the needs of the inner city ghetto as deeply as those of the open prairies and lands. The range of his competence in legislative matters covers virtually the entire spectrum of issues that come before this chamber.

With his tenacity, his subject area knowledge and his parliamentary skill, the Senator from Montana can be a formidable adversary when he is on the other side of an issue, as all of us can testify. But whether Mike Mansfield is with you or against you on an issue, he always plays by the rules, and as a result the outcome invariably enhances, rather than diminishes, the esteem in which he is held. . . .

Mr. President, at this difficult time in our history, this body is particularly fortunate in having such a steady hand at its helm. I am confident that Mike Mansfield will continue to help steer us on a course toward a better and stronger America.

September 14, 1970:

On President Nixon's

"Call for Cooperation"

An impression one carries away from the more "intimate" Watergate journals is that most of Nixon's staff people were astonished to learn in August 1974 – when the troublesome tape of June 23, 1972, finally became public – that the Old Man had been systematically lying to them and to the American people ever since the Watergate bunglers had been caught in flagrante delicto. They seemed genuinely amazed, as though before then he had been universally, continuously and incontrovertibly admired for his rigorous candor. Mansfield, however, was not all that astonished. He was tolerant and ever disposed to focus on the good points of others, but, after so many years in Washington, he was

269

not naive.

Indeed, his eyes were allergic to wool pullovers, as he demonstrated in September 1970, in replying to another PR-begotten "Call for Cooperation," this one addressed by Nixon to the Senate. The Nixon trick of blaming the legislature for executive inaction (as well as legislative inaction) was somethng that Mansfield stoutly refused to countenance. But his refusal was firm, not truculent.

His refutation included many details on the work of the Senate in 1970, omitted here because the passage of time has somewhat obscured their eye-catching significance.

* * *

Mr. Mansfield. Mr. President, under the heading "A Call for Cooperation," the President last Friday transmitted a message to the Senate. With it he takes Congress to task for apparently failing to attend fully to what he defines as his legislative program. I have read through this message and I am somewhat puzzled. I am puzzled first of all because — at least as far as the Senate is concerned — just about every single item mentioned by the President has been, is now being, or will soon be considered and disposed of on the merits.

Indeed, the only explanation for such a message is that it has arrived on the eve of campaign time — not an unusual time, and not an unusual ploy. It has been a tactic employed by many Presidents. It is thus a message that should have been anticipated. But even if this is a document aimed at the Senate, it misses the mark by a wide margin. Whatever may be the reasons for criticizing the U.S. Senate, attention to the legislative items mentioned in this message is not one.

Many of these items were initiated right here in the Senate and only later were embraced by the administration. All or nearly all of them have been, or soon will be, considered. Some will no doubt be rejected as unfeasible or poorly conceived. Some will be changed drastically to do the job intended. And it is true that some, such as the National Institute for Education proposal, simply cannot be considered at all. Many reasons apply. In the case of this education measure, it is because the administration fired its

270

education chief on the eve of Senate hearings. No successor has been named, and therefore hearings would be futile with no administration spokesman.

What is apparent from this message is that it does not reflect the record, at least the record as far as the Senate is concerned. Speaking on behalf of the Senate, the only way to correct the record at this time would be to take the proposals cited, item by item, and recall the action taken by the Senate.

Under the caption, "Reforming the Institutions of the Past," for example, the message mentions the Tax Reform Act, the Economic Opportunity Act, and the Postal Reorganization Act. All of these measures were considered by the Senate. All passed the Senate. Each, as I recall, was initiated right here in Congress, and it was only later that the proposal was embraced by the administration. Most notable among them, perhaps, was the reform of our income tax laws. With this action Congress (and especially the Senate), acting on its own initiative, rewrote the tax laws to provide more equity and a greater distribution of the overall tax burden for the benefit of the lower- and middle-income groups.

Draft reform is then cited in the message. Of course, the reform of our draft was undertaken by Executive order with the institution of the lottery system. The President should be commended for that first step. But when his own proposal for a volunteer army was under consideration in the Senate as an amendment to the military authorization bill, the administration opposed it. It called for delay and urged rejection. I, along with many of my colleagues on this side of the aisle as well as on the other, supported the President on that occasion. Members of his own party in the Senate sought to defeat his volunteer proposal. Strangely missing in this reference to the military field were the cold-war GI bill benefits initiated by Congress; and, even more important, the whole attitude of Congress toward military expenditures. For example, it was Congress that cut so severely the administration's requests for military spending in order to provide more money for the poor, for environmental needs, for urban problems, and for education. . . .

Finally, I would only refer to the list of all measures passed by the Senate during this session of the Congress. I submitted that list for printing in the record on September 1. It shows that, as of that date, the Senate passed 535 measures this session; 200 of those have been signed into law. There have been five treaties ratified.

Mr. President, I ask unanimous consent that the list, updated, be printed in the *Record* at the conclusion of my remarks. . . .

Mr. President, we have cooperated and we will continue to cooperate with the President because we think the republic must come first, and must come first at all times.

March 29, 1971:

On distortions in the Nixon Doctrine

In the summer of 1969, President Nixon, on one of his invigorating foreign tours, announced what came to be known as the Nixon Doctrine. Its special feature was its emphasis on self-reliance for other countries, permitting a reduction in direct support from the United States. For Mansfield, the announcement was a welcome echo.

Like the announcement of the Family Assistance Plan, however, it had a pleasant ring to it but not much else, especially in Indochina. The reduction of American troops in Vietnam was accompanied by a vigorous expansion of the war, especially from the air. Nixon's 1968 campaign talk about a "secret plan to end the war" evidently had not been intended for the hapless people, including the women and children, of Vietnam, Cambodia and Laos.

In March 1971, some eighteen months after the announcement of the Doctrine and eleven months after the invasion of Cambodia, Mansfield delivered a lecture at Olivet College in Michigan. Its title pointedly summed up the words-and-deeds discrepancies of the preceding year and a half: "The Nixon Doctrine: Divergencies, Digressions, Dodges and Delays."

* * *

I have not come here to make a political speech. Spring is not the season for politics, unless you are a young man running for the Presidency. Or unless you are a President in your first term. I am no longer that young. I am in my fourth term in the Senate. I run for office only in Montana and I have only recently been reelected.

In any event, the subject of my remarks is not political. The Nixon Doctrine is not a partisan policy. It was not advanced by the President as a partisan thrust. It was not met in the Senate with a political parry. On the contrary, when the President issued this declaration on Asian policy eighteen months ago, support was immediately extended to him from the Senate. It came from Republicans and it came from Democrats.

What differences there are with regard to foreign relations derive from policies, not from politics, and they are shared by members of both parties. The Senate today is not an intensely partisan forum. As majority leader, I have no political axes to grind. My relationship with a Republican President has been correct and cordial. In matters of foreign policy, the relationship does not differ greatly from that which existed with his predecessor, a Democrat. . . . Three Presidents have known that I do not stand on partisan ground. They have also known where I stood on the issues. . . .

The Nixon Doctrine is one of those issues because it is a touchstone in our relations with Asia and the rest of the world. The Doctrine was set forth with the intent of bringing about an adjustment in U.S. policy in the western Pacific. Eighteen months later, there is concern with the follow-through. . . .

It seemed to me that the essence of the Nixon Doctrine was to be found in the President's frequent references to a new "lowprofile" policy. I agreed fully with that concept and so stated many times in Asia and at home. Moreover, the administration soon made clear that the new doctrine would apply not only in Asia but throughout the world. With that extension, too, I agreed completely. . . .

The Nixon Doctrine . . . promised to bring up to date the nation's international security affairs. It was most welcome in the Senate and in the nation. For a long time we had remained wedded to the needs of another era. We had continued to indulge ourselves with policies and practices born of another time. As a nation we had been so deeply concerned for two decades with threats from abroad that we had overlooked the erosion of the nation's inner security and well-being.

The Nixon Doctrine opened the shutters on these musty thought processes. In so doing, it revealed the possibility of adjustments of policy abroad which would also rebound to the benefit of the situation within the nation. Billions of dollars of taxes, not to speak of the creative skills and energy of young people, were involved in the excessive and increasingly isolated search for national security in Vietnam and elsewhere abroad. With the advent of the Nixon Doctrine, it seemed that some of these immense resources might begin to be channeled into urgent needs at home.

In my judgment, the President deserves great credit for having established this turning point. The Nixon Doctrine was an invitation to change — long overdue change — and, if I may use that overworked phrase, a change in priorities.

Then there was April 30, 1970, and the American military incursion into Cambodia. The event is recent. You remember it, and there is no point in a rerun. To make my position clear, let me say only that I opposed the incursion before it began; I was saddened by its beginning; I regard it, even now, with regret, although it is held in some quarters to have been a "successful operation."

At the time it seemed to me that the incursion thrust the war deep into what had been, for all practical purposes, the only nondependent nation in Indochina in which there existed a measure of stability self-achieved under a reasonably responsive civilian government. Most serious, the Cambodian incursion enlarged the battlefield. In so doing, it promised to prolong the U.S. involvement and open up a new source of U.S. casualties.

That position was not arrived at lightly. It is not reasserted lightly now. The Cambodian incursion was justified largely in terms of saving American lives. That is a consideration that has always weighed heavily with me and every other member of the Senate. It was apparent then, however, and it is apparent now that the termination of our involvement in the war in Vietnam and a prompt withdrawal would save far more American lives and return our POW's more quickly than an enlargement of the area of conflict. . . .

The prerequisite of a meaningful application of the Nixon Doctrine in Southeast Asia seems to me to be the termination of the U.S. military involvement — land, air and sea — in Indochina and military withdrawal from that region, lock, stock, and barrel. That termination is not yet visible. That withdrawal is not yet in sight.

It is not only with regard to Indochina that there are grounds for concern over what has happened to the Nixon Doctrine since April 1970. Digressions or delays appear to be developing elsewhere in Asia. It is many months later, but the details of the Okinawa settlement have yet to be completed by the executive branch. Difficulties with Japan have also arisen over trade questions and a short time ago were even allowed to reach a tempestuous stage. As I see it, U.S.-Japanese trade is of immense value to both countries even as a political relationship of mutual consideration and forebearance between the two countries is essential to the elaboration of the Nixon Doctrine in the western Pacific. It is disturbing, therefore, to find what appears to be the intrusion of petty bickering and personal pique into these vital ties.

Also of great importance to the Nixon Doctrine is the restoration of civility with the Chinese People's Republic. The President has shown a consistent initiative in this connection. Whether a satisfactory relationship can be achieved at this time is another matter. Certainly it is not a very promising prospect when the Indo-Chinese war has again been extended to within minutes' bombing range of the Chinese borders and, in the circumstances, the Chinese have reaffirmed publicly their complete support of the North Vietnamese. Moreover, U.S. policy has yet to come to grips with the vehement rejection of a "two-China" concept by both the government of the Republic of China and of the Chinese People's Republic. Both insist that Taiwan and mainland China are parts of one Chinese nation.

Elsewhere in the world, in Western Europe in particular, there seems also to have been a retrogression from the Nixon Doctrine. While the need for a cut in the consignment of U.S. forces to Europe is more and more recognized in the Senate, the reluctance of the executive branch remains as great under this administration as it was under its predecessor. It is reluctance, apparently, stimulated by the anxieties of the German and other European

275

governments who remain unwilling, nevertheless, to relieve this nation of any substantial part of the present one-sided burden of the costs of NATO defense. . . .

To bring these remarks to a close, I want to note again, as I did at the outset, my deep belief in the urgency of the adjustments of U.S. policy which are implicit in the Nixon Doctrine. I would be less than candid, however, if I did not express the concern which I have with the divergencies, digressions, dodges and delays which have been encountered in carrying out the doctrine. . . .

There is blame enough to spare for things done and not done. Where the finger points often depends on who is pointing, and I shall not point mine. The fundamental difficulty, as I see it, is that the President and the Congress function in a government grown immense. It is a government whose gears must grind in a complex synchronization if they are to grind at all. The machinery is not easily moved by the President alone and certainly not, alone, by the Congress. Yet it must be moved if there is to be a fulfillment of the promise of the Nixon Doctrine and a realistic adjustment of our policies in line with its implications. In my judgment, the primary need, the critical need, is an end to the involvement in Indochina: an end, period. In their separate Constitutional authority as necessary, and in cooperation where possible, the effort must be made by the President and the Congress to meet that need.

The republic deserves no less.

February 9, 1972:

On Senatorial irresponsibility

Despite his steady resistance to adverse criticism of the Senate from outsiders, Mansfield could at times be one of its sharpest critics on the floor. One day in February 1972, after a bill empowering the Equal Employment Opportunity Commission to take employers to Federal court for discrimination had been filibustered for some five weeks by the traditional whites-only cabal, Mansfield got out his barbs and his flaying knife and expressed his considered opinion in a schoolmasterly lecture. About a week later the filibuster was broken in a cloture vote, and the bill passed.

Mr. Mansfield. Mr. President, the vote showed 33 Senators for and 33 Senators against [a compromise amendment that would have ended the filibuster], with one pair. I am sure that the Senate knows enough about elementary arithmetic to know the difference between 100 and 67.

It is my understanding that the vote on the pending amendment will not occur until Tuesday next. That is six days away; another week wasted. I do not know what the Senate intends to do about facing up to its responsibility. I do not know how often they are going to count who is here and who is not here.

All I want to say is that you have a majority of the Senate here today and we are going to be in session all afternoon, whether we like it or not, because we are waiting to see what the House is going to do on the dock strike legislation which passed the Senate yesterday.

I do not intend to get down on my knees to this body because as a Senator from the state of Montana I am just as important as any other Senator in this body, just as important; but as majority leader I must concede that you have the joint leadership, including the minority leader, at your feet and at your disposal. We cannot force you if you do not want to face up to your responsibilities, but you are doing a distinct disservice to the Senate and to the people whom you have the honor to represent. May I say, as I said yesterday, that no one forced any of the 100 members of this body to become a Senator. We became Senators because we wanted to; we asked our people to vote for us and they sent us back here to represent them.

Sometimes I wonder just how much of a conscience this body has. Sometimes I wonder how they can delay, how they can postpone, how individual Senators can think of themselves foremost and the Senate secondarily.

We all happen to be lucky that we were elected to the Senate of the United States. There are thousands of people back home in our respective states who are smarter than we are, have more ability than we have, could do a better job than we do, but they have not had the breaks and the circumstances have not flexed to allow them to become members of this body.

We are given a pretty good salary. We receive a goodly number of fringe benefits. And all we are asked to do is to come in to look after the interests of the people of our states, to expedite legislation after appropriate debate.

And what do we do? We stall. We find excuses. Somebody is not here or somebody has to be there. We need our troops, or we might lose.

Well, this country and this Senate are supposed to run on a majority basis. The Senate is supposed to function when a quorum is present, and a quorum is present. What this Senate is degenerating into — and I use the words advisedly — is a three-day-a-week body. We are all becoming members of the Tuesday-through-Thursday club. And I think we are marking by our own actions here the apathy and the malaise which are affecting this republic today.

If we cannot attend to our duties, how can we expect the people of this nation to attend to theirs? What kind of an example do we furnish them? What sort of inspiration?

If this were an industry, we would pay a price for not being here, and if we did not produce we would be fired.

So I do not know what to do, frankly, because the power is not, and never has been, in the hands of the minority or the majority leaders. The power is in the hands of each Senator singly and the Senate collectively. And if you will not face up to your responsibilities, there is nothing — not a thing — that the leadership can do to force you.

So, as far as I am concerned, all I am interested in is getting the appropriations bills out of the way, and I would suggest to my colleagues, both those who are present and those who are absent, that we forget the rest of this business — authorizing legislation or continuing legislation needing new authorizations — and maybe in so doing we will be doing the country a favor. Maybe we will save a lot of money and a lot of strain. But, as far as I am concerned, I do not intend to lose any more sleep, as I have this past month, over the conduct of this body, which is supposed to be made up of mature people, people who can exercise sound and sober judgment, but instead includes people who are lacking, in my opinion, the attributes which should be the hallmark of this body and which should contribute to the morale and to the welfare of this republic.

May 11, 1972:

On U.S. policies

toward China and Indochina

Mansfield paid his fourth visit to China – his first visit to the People's Republic of China – in the spring of 1972. Between his third visit in the forties and this one, Chinese society had been turned upside down, with leaders of the formerly downtrodden masses now on top and the former local autocrats now on the bottom, or six feet under.

To Richard Nixon's everlasting credit, in February 1972 a President of the United States, defying a cult of hatred for the "godless Communism" that had reorganized Chinese society and governed it for the past two decades, had introduced a measure of polite communication between the American and Chinese governments with his visit to Peking. As for Mansfield, the Nixon visit naturally delighted him, since he had been urging some sort of ice-breaker for so many frustrating years.

On his return from China in May, the Senator reported at length to his colleagues from the Senate floor. His report, which sensibly contrasted the new China with the old China rather than with the present United States, was factual, rational, and very comprehensive. But, for all its considerable amount of detail (mostly omitted here), its strongest message was a simple one, to the effect that the road to a friendlier China would not be found in a devastated Indochina.

* * *

Mr. Mansfield. Mr. President, when the President returned from Peking last February, he transmitted an invitation from Premier Chou En-lai to the joint leadership of the Senate to visit the People's Republic of China. The invitation was accepted by Senator Scott and myself, and between April 15 and May 7 we undertook the journey.

On Monday last I gave to the President a written report on what I had observed, heard, and discussed in China, and conclusions which I had reached as a result, particularly with regard to Indochina. I have requested this time today to provide a general account of the journey to the Senate. . . .

Host for the visit was the People's Institute of Foreign Affairs, which is a quasi-official arm of the Chinese Foreign Ministry. I was deeply impressed both by the kindness and efficiency of the staff of the institute who accompanied us on the entire journey and by the warmth the of the reception we received everywhere in China. The hospitality shown to us by our hosts and the Chinese people was thoughtful and considerate. The friendliness was unmistakable.

I did not go to China with the expectation of becoming an instant expert on its government, its social structure, its economy, or its internal affairs. I went to see what I had seen a long time before as a private in the Marines in the early twenties and, twice again during and after World War II, as a representative of President Roosevelt and as a young member of the House of Representatives. After an absence of a quarter of a century, I went to compare the old China with the new and to explore current attitudes of the People's Republic toward the United States.

It is difficult today to look at China free of the distortions of national disparities, especially after two decades of separation. But the distortions can be tempered by perspective. It is possible, for example, to judge a bottle as half full or as half empty. If China is measured by some of our common yardsticks, whether they be highway mileage, the number of cars, television sets, kitchen gadgets, political parties, or newspaper editors, the bottle will be seen as half empty. If China is viewed in the light of its own past, the bottle is half full and rapidly filling.

Today's China is highly organized and self-disciplined. It is a hard-working, early-to-bed, early-to-rise society. The Chinese people are well fed, adequately clothed and, from all outward signs, contented with a government in which Mao Tse-tung is a revered teacher and whose major leaders are, for the most part, old revolutionaries.

There has not been a major flood, pestilence, or famine for many years. The cities are clean, orderly, and safe; the shops are well stocked with food, clothing, and other consumer items; policemen are evident only for controlling traffic and very few carry weapons. Soldiers are rarely seen. The housing is of a subsistence type but is now sufficient to end the spectacle of millions of the homeless and dispossessed who, in the past, walked the tracks and roads or anchored their sampans in the rivers of China and lived out their lives in a space little larger than a rowboat. Crime, begging, drug addiction, alcoholism, delinquency are conspicuous by their absence. Personal integrity is scrupulous. In Canton, for example, a display case for lost and found articles in the lobby of the People's Hotel contained, among other items, a half-empty package of cigarettes and a pencil.

The people appear to be well motivated and cooperative. Women and men work side by side for equal pay. There are no visible distinctions of rank in field, factory, armed services, or government offices. A casual sense of freedom pervades personal relationships with an air of easy egalitarianism. There is no kowtowing, not even to the highest officials.

A factory worker in Peking earns the equivalent of about U.S. $22 a month, and his wife works, making as much or more. That income is ample for a subsistence-plus existence because children are cared for free at a nursery or in public schools. Rent takes only about 5 percent of total income. Basic food prices are low and fixed. Medical care is free. Entertainment is cheap — admission to a movie is about 10 cents. Prices have been stable for years while wages have risen. . . .

Eighty percent of China's population is rural and is now largely organized into communes. The communes are in the nature of agro-towns and are a fundamental economic unit of the new China. They are also a new concept in social organization which acts to broaden and extend the virtues of interdependence of the old Chinese family system into a community of cooperation and group action by many families. . . .

Only a few years ago no modern medical care to speak of was available to the great preponderance of China's inhabitants. Now some kind of care is provided to every Chinese in need. In more remote regions it may be elementary, but it is available. There is no charge to workers in the cities but each family on the communes pays about 4 cents per month for medical services. . . .

In every aspect of society there is evidence of China being

rebuilt on the basis of Chairman Mao's dictum, "serve the people." The revolution has swept away much of the ineffectiveness of the past and enshrined a new concept of Chinese self-reliance. While the family remains as the basic unit of the social structure, it is no longer in-turned and indifferent. Members of a family are now, also, active participants in the life of the communes and factories, and they share a common pride in the achievements of Mao's revolution. In short, China has become a viable modern society, with an approach to social participation and responsibility which is rooted in the past, meets the needs of the present, and offers a soundly based hope for the future.

In the Chinese view, U.S. policy is seen as having pursued an unremitting hostility toward the People's Republic for at least two decades. That is how they regard the effort to wall off China by the trade quarantine for twenty years. That, too, is how they see the sending of troops north of the 38th parallel in Korea, the interposition of the Seventh Fleet between the mainland and Formosa, and the leadership of this nation in urging the United Nations to label China the aggressor in Korea. . . .

The United States and China have taken only the first steps to restore normal relations. In my judgment, the rapprochement actually began with the announcement of the Nixon Doctrine three years ago and the first draw-down of U.S. troops in Vietnam. The Chinese have been aware that the U.S. involvement was being reduced in Asia, even though it was accompanied, from time to time, by erratic military thrusts. Still, the troops were leaving, not coming into, Asia. This signal of a change in U.S. policy was unmistakable to the Chinese. It meant that the President was reducing the military presence of the United States in Asia.

A number of propitious developments in both nations also helped to lay the basis for rapprochement. In China the cultural revolution came to an end in a stronger, more united government, with a greater ability to handle its problems both at home and abroad. At the same time the people of this nation began to show a renewed interest in China. On October 25, 1971, the People's Republic of China was brought into the United Nations by a vote of 76 to 35. The world had begun to beat a path to China's door, and Peking was prepared to open it.

President Nixon's visit to China last February was a long overdue step in normalizing relations between the United States and China. I applauded this action at the time. I am more than ever persuaded, at the conclusion of this journey, that it was the right action.

Where the path which was opened by the President, and followed by the distinguished minority leader and myself, will now lead is not clear. If the idea of rapprochement does not sink in the mire of the escalating war in Indochina, the path can lead, in my judgment, to an improvement of relationships throughout Asia. . . .

How do the Chinese view the war in Vietnam? They see it as an attempt by the United States to dominate the political life of a region in which we have no business. Their memory of the tortured path of American involvement is long and sensitive. Readily recalled, for example, is John Foster Dulles' refusal to shake hands with Premier Chou En-lai at the Geneva Conference of 1954. So, too, is the disregard of the 1954 Geneva Accord by the United States.

The Chinese made clear their belief that the resumption of the bombing of the North would prolong rather than end the war. Strong exception was taken to the administration's contention that the action was justified because North Vietnamese armies had invaded the South. From their point of view, "the invasion of Vietnam began with the incident in 1964," the Tonkin Gulf incident; and United States actions in Laos and Cambodia, to them, also constituted invasion and aggression. . . .

In short, the Peking discussions painted a bleak picture of the prospects for peace on the basis of present policies of all concerned. Unless there are changes in the present course, therefore, visits to China will not alter the indefinite continuance of the bloodletting of American, Vietnamese, Cambodians, and Laotians, the destruction of the culture and environment of the Indochinese countries, the waste of tens of billions of dollars more of our resources, the sapping of the vitality of our government, the distortion of our political processes, and the further division and frustration of our people.

It seems to me high time to ask why we are using the most advanced machines of destruction in that primitive land. Are we doing so out of force of habit? Out of fear? Fear of what? The fact is that we are still engaged in a war which, to put the best face on it, was sanctioned by what has now become a discredited policy toward China. The President's visit to China had the symbolic effect of marking the end of that policy. If the old China policy is no longer valid, is not the present involvement in the Vietnam war which derived from that policy also invalid? How can conscience, in these circumstances, continue to ask sacrifices of the armed services?

If we feel deeply for the ordeal of the prisoners of war and the missing in action and for their families, we will no longer acquiesce in the distortion of the problem of their release. They are not going to be released by mining Haiphong Harbor, not by letter-writing campaigns to Hanoi, or by postage stamps issued in their honor. They are going to be released, if the air war leaves any of them alive to be released, only when U.S. air and naval operations cease. While we remain in the war, the promise is not for their release but for more missing in action, more prisoners of war, more casualties. . . .

Premier Chou En-lai closed our talks with these words: "Please convey to the American people the friendship and best respects of the Chinese people."

The joint leadership of the Senate responded in a similar fashion. In my judgment, only what transpires in Indochina blocks the way to a full fruition of these reciprocal sentiments. When they are fulfilled in reciprocal acts of respect and consideration, they will redound to the benefit of the people of the United States, the People's Republic of China, and the people of the rest of the world.

July 19, 1972:

On withdrawal from Indochina

By mid-1972, President Nixon had pulled out 90% of the American troops from Vietnam but had enlarged the war to cover all of Indochina. Vietnam had been bombed much more heavily than all of Europe and Japan in World War II. In the United States, the media bombarded American consciences with news reports and vivid pictures of the victims of this unparalleled American violence. Disenchantment with Nixon's ambiguous strategy was growing fast, though by no means fast enough to catapult a George McGovern into the White House.

In July, during a debate on the Foreign Assistance Act of 1972, in an exchange with Senator Tower of Texas, Mansfield expressed the feeling of millions of war-weary Americans in one of the most succinct statements ever made on the war.

* * *

Mr. Tower. The distinguished majority leader has indicated that he is prepared to give Mr. Kissinger and our other negotiators in Paris I suppose to the end of this week . . . pending some kind of conclusive results. Would the Senator explain what he envisions by conclusive results?

Mr. Mansfield. Well, the Senator is asking me a leading question which I cannot answer definitely, except on the basis of what I have thought personally down through the years would be a satisfactory, not conclusive necessarily, but a satisfactory result. I would like to see a cease-fire. I would like to see an agreement bring about the release as quickly as possible of the POW's and the recoverable MIA's, and I would like to see us withdraw, lock, stock and barrel once our POW's have been released and our recoverable MIA's set free, from all Indochina. I have never felt that we had any vital interests in that part of the world. I still feel that way. As a matter of fact, Indochina has been, not a comedy of errors, but a tragedy of errors for this nation, with 55,000 dead, with 305,000 casualties; with something on the order of $130 billion spent so far; with three times as many bombs being used, in tonnage, as was the case in all of the Second World War and Korea; with the tactics of defoliation and craterization of Indochina; with the difficulties it has caused us at home; with the difficulties it has caused us within the Army especially. All these factors, I think, should be taken into consideration, and if possible we should put Indochina behind us, wipe the slate clean, and start out to try to bind up some of the wounds and take care of some of our own concerns.

January 3, 1973:

On the strengthening

of checks and balances

After the electoral avalanche that buried George McGovern in November 1972, Congressional Democrats were happily surprised to discover that they were still in the majority in both houses. In the Senate they had even gained a couple of seats.

Although Mansfield obviously would have preferred to see McGovern in the White House, for more than merely partisan reasons, he was pleased by the split-ticket results, which he interpreted as popular support for an independent Congress. On the first working day of the new Congress – January 3, 1973 – he urged the Democratic Conference to assert the Senate's independence and not to allow the country to travel "the last mile down the road to government by Executive fiat." His voice was finally being heard, although another two years of Presidential imperialism and the turmoil of Watergate would be needed to provoke effective support for some energetic responses.

His statement to the Conference was a long one for him – some 5000 words – because he had to include considerable detail on plans for the coming session. One detailed comment, on Presidential campaigning, appears in this selection because it recommends "investigatory action" that was eventually to lead to the most serious Constitutional crisis in the history of the Presidency.

* * *

We meet today with a new majority. We meet with new responsibilities and a new mandate.

The recent election tells us something of what the people of the nation expect of the Senate. If there is one mandate to us above all others, it is to exercise our separate and distinct Constitutional role in the operation of the Federal government. The people have not chosen to be governed by one branch of government alone. They have not asked for government by a single party. Rather,

286

they have called for a reinforcement of the Constitution's checks and balances. This Democratic Conference must strive to provide that reinforcement. The people have asked of us an independent contribution to the nation's policies. To make that contribution is more than our prerogative, it is our obligation.

An independent Senate does not equate with an obstructionist Senate. Insofar as the leadership is concerned, the Senate will not be at loggerheads with the President personally, with his party, or with his administration. The Senate will give most respectful attention to the President's words, his program and his appointments. Every President deserves that courtesy. During the period in which you have entrusted me with the leadership, every President has had that courtesy.

With the election behind us, I most respectfully request every member of the Conference to examine his position and his conscience once again on the question of Vietnam. I do not know whether there is a legislative route to the end of this bloody travesty. I do know that the time is long since past when we can take shelter in a claim of legislative impotence. We cannot dismiss our own responsibility by deference to the President's. It is true that the President can still the guns of the nation in Vietnam and bring about the complete withdrawal of our forces by a stroke of the pen. It is equally true that Congress cannot do so. Nevertheless, Congress does have a responsibility. We are supplying the funds. We are supplying the men. So, until the war ends, the effort must be made and made again and again. The executive branch has failed to make peace by negotiation. It has failed to make peace by elaborating the war first into Cambodia, then into Laos and, this year with blockade and renewed bombing, into North Vietnam. The effort to salvage a shred of face from a senseless war has succeeded only in spreading devastation and clouding this nation's reputation.

It remains for the Congress to seek to bring about complete disinvolvement. We have no choice but to pursue this course. I urge every member of this caucus to act in concert with the Republican Senators, by resolution or any other legislative means, to close out the military involvement in Vietnam. If there is one area where Senate responsibility profoundly supersedes party responsibility, it is in ending the involvement in Vietnam.

In view of the tendency of this war to flare unexpectedly, the leadership now questions the desirability of the Congress ever again to be in *sine die* adjournment as we have been since October 18, 1972. In that Constitutional state the Congress cannot be reassembled on an urgent basis except by call of the President. It is the leadership's intention, therefore, to discuss this gap in Congressional continuity with the House leaders. It may well be desirable to provide, at all times, for recall of the Congress by the Congress itself. There is ample precedent for providing standby authority of this kind to the combined leaderships.

If Indochina continues to preoccupy us abroad, the Senate is confronted, similarly, with an overriding domestic issue. The issue is control of the expenditures of the Federal government. We must try to move to meet it, squarely, at the outset of the 93rd Congress.

In the closing days of the last session, the President asked of Congress unilateral authority to readjust downward expenditures approved by the Congress within an overall limit of $250 billion. The President's objectives were meritorious, but his concern at the imbalance of expenditures and revenues might better have been directed to the Federal budget, which is a tool not of the Congress but of the executive branch. It is there that the origins of the great Federal deficits of the past few years are to be found. The fact is that Congress has not increased but has reduced the administration's budget requests, overall, by $20.2 billion in the last four years.

As the Conference knows, the House did yield to the President's request for temporary authority to readjust downward, arbitrarily, Congressional appropriations. The Senate did not do so. The Senate did not do so for good and proper reasons. The power of the purse rests with Congress under the Constitution, and the usurpation or transfer of this fundamental power to the executive branch will take this nation a good part of the last mile down the road to government by executive fiat. That is not what the last election tells us to do. That is not what the Constitution requires us to do. . . .

This Congress must look, and look deeply, at where the nation's politics are headed. In my judgment, ways must be found to hold campaign expenditures within reasonable limits. Moreover, to insure open access to politics, I can think of no better application of public funds than, as necessary, to use them for the financing of elections so that public office will remain open to all, on an unfettered and impartial basis, for the better service of the nation. . . .

The Federal Election Campaign Contributions Act, which we enacted in the 92nd Congress and which was put into effect this past year, may also need refinement and modification to reduce undue paper-shuffling and other burdens without compromising the principle of full disclosure. There are also some specific matters relating to the past election which warrant investigatory attention. One is the so-called Watergate affair, which appears to have been nothing less than a callous attempt to subvert the political processes of the nation in blatant disregard of the law. Another is the circulation by mail of false accusations against our colleagues, Senator Muskie, Senator Jackson, and Senator Humphrey, during the Florida primary campaign with the clear intent, to say the least, of sowing political confusion.

Still another is the disconcerting news that dossiers on Congressional candidates have been kept by the FBI for the last 22 years. This practice has reportedly been stopped. It would be well for the appropriate committees to see to it that appointed employees in the agencies of this government are not placed again in the position of surreptitious meddling in the free operation of the electoral process. The FBI has, properly, sought to avoid that role in other situations. We must do whatever is necessary to see to it that neither the FBI, the military intelligence agencies, or any other appointive office of the government is turned by its temporary occupants into a secret intruder into the free operation of the system of representative government of the United States.

On November 17, 1972, I addressed letters to Chairman Eastland of the Judiciary Committee and Chairman Ervin of the Government Operations Committee. I requested that these two Chairmen get together and make a recommendation to the leadership on how to proceed to investigate these and related matters, to the end that the Senate's effort may be concentrated. I renew that request today. . . .

I will now close these remarks with a final reference to the last election. I suppose each of us interprets the national sentiment which is reflected in the outcome in terms of his own predilections. Certainly I have done so. Therefore "the state of the Senate," as seen from the viewpoint of the Democratic majority, might not necessarily dovetail with the mandate which the administration delineates from President Nixon's reelection or that which is seen by the Republican minority in Congress.

Nevertheless, it does seem that the election tells all of us — President, Democratic majority and Republican minority what the people do not want.

First. They do not want one-party or one-branch government during the next two years.

Second. They do not want us to turn back the clock on the national effort to improve the human climate and the physical environment in which the people of this nation must live.

Third. They do not want a rate of change which, whether too slow or too rapid, produces major internal chaos and disruption.

Fourth. Most of all, they do not want the President to persist nor the Congress to acquiesce in the indefinite continuance of the senseless bloodshed in Vietnam and, with it, accept the indefinite postponement of the return of the POW's and the recoverable MIA's.

These negatives point the way to the positive path which the Senate majority leadership intends to pursue during the next two years. We will not abandon the effort to end the U.S. involvement in Vietnam and to bring back the POW's and the recoverable MIA's, period. We will work to preserve and to enhance the faithfulness of this nation to its Constitutional principles and its highest ideals and, in so doing, we will not shut the door on essential hearings.

The leadership needs your cooperation, your understanding and your support. Ideas are welcomed, equally, from every member of this Conference, the oldest no less than the youngest, the most junior no less than the most senior. Together we are here, in the last analysis, with only one mandate: to serve the people of the several states and the nation. With your help, the leadership will strive to carry out that mandate in full.

April 30, 1973:

On getting Watergate

out in the open

April 30, 1973, was something of a high-fever day in the unfolding drama of Watergate. Early in the day the Nixon staff command post lost the invaluable services of Presidential Assistants Robert Haldeman and John Ehrlichman and of Counsel John Dean, and the Justice Department was decapitated, more or less, by the resignation of Attorney General Kleindienst. Two weeks earlier Press Secretary Ronald Ziegler had blandly declared all Presidential denials of White House complicity in Watergate to be retroactively "inoperative." By this time the Senate's select committee chaired by Senator Sam Ervin was in its third month of investigating such inoperations, among other things.

On the evening of April 30 Nixon formally confirmed the staff departures in a TV speech to the American people, praising Haldeman and Ehrlichman for their splendid public service and reasserting his own total ignorance and innocence of any chicanery. Nevertheless, he added, as "the top man in the organization," consecrated to noblesse oblige, he accepted responsibility for "people whose zeal exceeded their judgment and who may have done wrong in a cause they deeply believed to be right." The American flag, as usual, gleamed piously in his lapel.

In the Senate that afternoon Hugh Scott of Pennsylvania, the Republican minority leader who was to be so unscrupulously used by the White House, commended the President for his "firmness" and "determination" while ruefully deploring "this whole shabby, disgraceful episode." Mansfield, as majority leader, responded with restraint and sympathy but with a clear resolve not to let His Self-Anointed Majesty off the investigative hook.

* * *

Mr. Mansfield. Mr. President, I wish to commend the President of the United States for the action he has taken this morning. I know too little about the realities of the situation, but I am sure that the President had full access to all the facts finally and that, on the basis of those facts, he acted accordingly.

The Watergate affair and all its ramifications — and they extend far and wide and go back a long time, on the basis of the newspaper reports — is not a Republican tragedy but is, in essence, an American tragedy; because what it struck at were the roots of a democratic government, a Constitutional government, a government based on a two-party system.

The President, in acting as he did, displayed a greater loyalty to the American people, as he should, than to those around him.

It is a sad episode. The matter, of course, is not completed, because we still have the grand jury in operation, we still have the court of Judge Sirica in operation, and we still have the Ervin special committee in operation. So this is a start which will help to clear the air. But all the facts will have to be laid out; and out of this let us hope that all of us will learn a lesson as to how government should be operated — in the open — and all of us should become aware of the fact that the only loyalty we owe is to the people, because it is the people who are the government.

June 18, 1973:

On a hiatus in

the Watergate hearings

In May 1973 one of the most popular TV shows in history opened on Capitol Hill, scene of the similarly popular Army-McCarthy show twenty years earlier. The Ervin committee hearings were very respectable and deadly serious proceedings, but the roving, ubiquitous cameras lent them an unavoidable aura of show-biz spectacle.

They were still going strong in mid-June, and Mansfield was troubled that they would provide a highly incongruous backdrop for Soviet leader Brezhnev's official visit to Washington at that time. He therefore consulted the Republican leader, and together they addressed an urgent letter to Senator Ervin requesting a week's intermission. The request was granted, and Nixon and Brezhnev were thus able to hear themselves think during the summit conference, as well as to sign nine separate agreements. It seems to have been a week of statesmanship, all around.

* * *

U.S. Senate
June 18, 1973

Hon. Samuel J. Ervin
Chairman, Select Committee on Presidential
  Campaign Activities

Dear Mr. Chairman:

We have been discussing the fact that the hearings of the Select Committee on Presidential Campaign Activities and the official visit of Secretary General Leonid I. Brezhnev are both occurring during the same week.

After giving consideration to this duality of events, recognizing the importance of each, we have come to the conclusion that it is a part of our responsibility as the Joint Leaders of the United States Senate to request, most respectfully, that the Select Committee postpone its hearings until the conclusion of the state visit to this country by Secretary General Leonid Brezhnev.

It is not an easy decision for us to make because both the hearings and the visit are being conducted with the best interests of the country in mind, but it is our considered judgment that a delay of one week would not jeopardize the hearings and that one week might give President Nixon and Mr. Brezhnev the opportunity to reconcile differences, arrive at mutual agreements, and, in the field of foreign policy, be able to achieve results which would be beneficial not only to our two countries but, hopefully, to all mankind.

We would appreciate your consideration of this request and as early a response as possible.

Sincerely yours,

Mike Mansfield   *Hugh Scott*
Majority Leader   Republican Leader

October 30, 1973:

On continuing the Watergate investigations

As summer merged into fall in 1973, the Watergate compost heap was getting gamier every day. In October Donald Segretti testified about dirty tricks played on Democratic campaigners in 1972, reports began surfacing about $100,000 paid to Nixon pal Bebe Rebozo by Howard Hughes, the General Services Administration confessed to "mistakes" in furbishing King Richard's personal castles with gold from the public purse, and rumors were flying that His Majesty had ordered the royal attorney to thwart any antitrust action against ye International Telephone and Telegraph Company.

And then there was the Saturday Night Massacre. Special Prosecutor Archibald Cox, an uppity varlet with peculiar notions about popular sovereignty, had refused His Majesty's command to forego tapes which an appellate court had ordered to be surrendered to District Judge John Sirica. So Richard told his most recent attorney, Elliot Richardson, to get rid of the nettlesome Cox. Richardson refused and stalked out of the royal court. His deputy, William Ruckelshaus, also refused and was dismissed. Finally Solicitor General Richard Bork fired Cox, who went quietly.

Then came the firestorm of protest that eventually was to incinerate the Presidential throne. The Nixon courtiers, however, continued to use their old, now outmoded firefighting tactics — letting it be known, for instance, that the various Watergate investigations were endangering "national security" by jeopardizing U.S. negotiations in the Middle East. Indeed, they urged, the investigations were responsible for the outbreak of the war there and should be terminated at once for the good of the country.

Mansfield wasn't having any. In a late October statement to the Senate Democratic Conference, he made his position perfectly clear: there must be no shrinking from Bosworth Field.

* * *

Let me begin with a brief reference to the situation in the Middle East. The fourth war in a quarter of a century in that region has posed complex diplomatic questions for this nation. There ought to be, and there will be from the Senate, understanding and restraint as regards the Administration's handling of that situation. Speaking for myself, I have no hesitancy in expressing a high regard for the manner in which a lid has been kept on developments there.

In making that comment, I reject any inference that the effort of the Congress, the courts and the former Special Prosecutor to face up to Watergate and related matters in the workings of this government may have in any way, shaped or form precipitated the difficulties in the Middle East. This is the fourth Arab-Israeli war, not the first. These conflicts have occurred in both Democratic and Republican Administrations. They have occurred both in the presence and in the absence of Watergates. The fact is that, over the years, the outbreaks of war in the Middle East have shown a supreme indifference to the political situation inside this nation.

So I am hopeful that we will hear no more about how we must bury Watergate and all that it implies in other areas because of this or that crisis abroad. The conduct of foreign relations, whether in the Middle East or elsewhere, is always difficult. It is made more or less difficult not by the appearances at home but by the realities. We would do well, therefore, to avoid in the name of foreign policy a pretense of national well-being when the people are profoundly disturbed by what they see and hear in Washington. The pretense would fool no one but ourselves. It would serve no useful purpose abroad. It would serve only to dig deeper the mistrust and division at home. The need is not to beat the drums of self-deceit any louder in the name of foreign policy. The need is to restore the people's trust in government by restoring the government's integrity. Then, hopefully, the conduct of foreign policy may be eased. In the interim, it may be that senior officials of the Executive Branch are discommoded by a public cleansing of the nation's politics. Nevertheless, these officials will have to function within the parameters of a deep national concern over the state of the Federal government until there is no longer a need for that concern. I have every expectation that they will be able to deal effectively with events abroad so long as the situation at home is also confronted.

The primary responsibility of the Congress and the Presidency is to safeguard the people's right to a government — legislative, executive, judicial — that serves them with integrity and candor, with responsiveness and justice. If we do not act at home, in this city, to reaffirm that right when it has been jeopardized, what we do or do not do abroad will not much matter. Indeed, if we do not affirm and strengthen that right, in my judgment, whatever this administration or any other may think it is achieving in foreign relations will have little of lasting value in terms of the nation's well-being or world peace.

Against that backdrop, I would like to review events of the past ten days or so and their implications for the Senate and the Congress. In the first place, it seems to me that these events illuminate the essentiality of the Ervin Committee on the Watergate affair and the good sense of the Senate in establishing that Committee at the beginning of the year. A debt of gratitude is owed to the members of the Committee, Republicans and Democrats alike, for what they have already done in requiring a confrontation with the truth of Watergate and related matters. They proceeded in an orderly and impartial fashion and without any suggestion whatsoever of partisan politics. They moved deliberately but relentlessly to bring out the facts of illegality. They uncovered these facts in great numbers and in sordid detail. They laid them bare for the nation to see and for the Congress to act upon in order that what transpired in the name of a free election does not happen again.

So thorough and effective had been the work of the Ervin Committee in pursuit of its Senate mandate that, except for the affair of the tapes, it was possible to begin to think in terms of a final report and recommendations. That was before the Justice Department was torn asunder on direct orders of the White House on the night of October 20. Now it is no longer possible, in my judgment, to contemplate the shut-down of the Ervin Committee. On the contrary, I would hope and expect that the Senate would consider forthwith the extension of the Committee, with a mandate enlarged to include all the matters which were under consideration by the Special Prosecutor's office in the Justice Department at the time of the summary dismissal of Mr. Archibald Cox.

In so suggesting, I ask you to bear in mind that, as of now, if the Ervin Committee does not pursue these matters, who will? The executive branch? The courts? There are many proposals for action, but who is in a position, now, to act? As of now, the Ervin Committee is the only body in the Federal government that is duly constituted and equipped to continue an independent, impartial inquiry into the Watergate affair and related matters.

That will remain the case unless and until there is at least designated a new Special Prosecutor whose powers are as broad and whose integrity and courage are as great as that which surrounded Archibald Cox. I want to say for myself — and I think I am expressing the preponderant sentiment of the Senate in this connection — that Mr. Cox is an outstanding American who is to be commended for the distinguished service he performed in placing the law, as he sees it, above himself, above the Justice Department, and above any incumbent in any office of the Federal government.

I wish to commend, too, Mr. Elliot Richardson. He gave his word to the Senate, in connection with his confirmation as Attorney General. He gave his word, as an honorable man, that he would permit the Special Prosectuor full independence to deal judicially with the corrosive corruption which has been spread through the political processes of the nation. Mr. Richardson kept his word to the Senate, and when he was no longer permitted to keep his word, as an honorable man Mr. Richardson resigned from the office in which he had been confirmed by the Senate. So, too, did the Deputy Attorney General, Mr. Ruckelshaus. The administration and the government will suffer from the loss of the services of these men, but the nation has gained from their decency, courage, and integrity. . . .

I want to close by commending all the members of the Senate, Republicans and Democrats alike, for their steadfastness in these critical times. There has been manifested in the Senate, far beyond partisanship, a responsibility to the nation and a dedication to Constitutional principles and the stability of the republic which I find unmatched in my memory. This has been an incredibly troubled year in the life of the nation, an incredible month, incredible weeks and days. That the nation is coming through this period and, in my judgment, will emerge from it healthier and sounder in its political life has a great deal to do with the validity and vitality of its Constitutional structure. It has a great deal to do with the fact that we are a government not of one part but of three parts, and that, as the outset of this session, this Conference, the Senate and the Congress set out on a path of reminding the nation of that Constitutional fact. It has a great deal to do with the First Amendment, under which the press and other media are alive and well and doing their job with competence and persistnence. Finally, it has a lot to do with the capacity of the people of this nation — beset and beguiled, harried and harassed though they may be — still to express a thunderous indignation when their fundamental decency is outraged.

In the end, this government exists to serve those people. It is not the other way around. They deserve a government that can be trusted with their freedom, with their lives, and with their heritage. What has happened to cast a shadow on that unalienable right of the people of the United States must not be allowed to happen again.

April 2, 1974:

On foreign aid versus

helping the unfortunate

"Foreign aid" is a term with a charitable ring to it, but it has covered a multitude of sins. Mansfield refused to accept it as a euphemism for military and financial support of unsavory foreign regimes. In his last several years on Capitol Hill, therefore, he regularly voted against foreign aid bills. Yet he was never entirely comfortable in doing so, because so much was thus left undone.

He touched on this dilemma in April 1974 in a brief colloquy with Senator Edward Brooks of Massachusetts, who was proposing that the United States provide funds and technology to alleviate the ravages of "river blindness" in Africa, which affects some 30 million people.

Mr. Mansfield. Mr. President, will the Senator yield?

Mr. Brooke. I am very pleased to yield to the distinguished majority leader.

Mr. Mansfield. What the distinguished Senator from Massachusetts has just indicated is a most serious situation, and one to which our hearts go out.

May I say, while I no longer vote for foreign aid projects because they take in too much in the way of military assistance and economic assistance which is tied to military assistance and is operating all too often on a government-to-government basis, I would like to see something done to help people in this and similar categories because the real purpose of aid is to help people.

Thus I want to commend the distinguished Senator for calling this to the attention of the Senate. I do not believe it is a matter for private foundations alone to undertake. As long as the foreign aid program is a pipeline of 6, 7, 8, or 9 billion dollars, I see no reason why some of those funds cannot be diverted to help these people in these countries so that, in turn, the people who are citizens of these countries can be trained to carry on the work once it has gotten under way. I commend the distinguished Senator for calling this most difficult problem to the attention of the Senate, which cries out for assistance — and assistance now.

Mr. Brooke. I thank the distinguished majority leader for his contribution to this colloquy relative to river blindness. I know very well his strongly held beliefs regarding foreign aid. He has always fought for aid which would go directly to the relief of human suffering around the world. I quite concur that too much foreign aid has been used for military purposes. I am very much pleased to have him make the suggestions he has made on the floor of the Senate today. I hope that the Senate will adopt this resolution.

Mr. Mansfield. I would hope that in our AID programs we would return to the original Point Four concept of people to people — helping people so that they can help themselves, and get away from this widespread proliferation of our AID programs which has cost this country approximately $140 billion to date.

People to people — that is the answer.

April 8, 1974:

On impeachment trial

preparations in the Senate

Early in April 1974 an editorial appeared in The Wall Street Journal commenting on the epidemic of Watergate frenzy in Washington and deploring the tendency of some Capitol Hill denizens to quote odds publicly on impeachment or conviction, as though in competition with Jimmy the Greek. It was growing likely, the writer warned, that the President could not be given a fair trial in such an atmosphere: "The city seems so totally in the grip of Watergate fever that those elected representatives who will soon be sitting in solemn judgment of the President appear to have lost control of events, and are in danger of being swept along by an impeachment machine that could turn the proceedings into a lurid Roman circus."

Mansfield also was troubled by the Congressional excitement. He could understand it, for this was a drama that seemed headed for a humiliation of the arrogant, and some degree of eager antici-pation was inevitable, especially among the Congressional vic-tims of that arrogance. But this would be no excuse for injustice. As majority leader, of course, Mansfield had a special responsi-bility to make this clear not only to his fellow Democrats but also to Senate Republicans, some of whom still felt that the Watergate inquiries were nothing more than a liberal-Democrat vendetta against an outstanding Republican leader.

Asking that the editorial be reprinted in the Congressional Record, Mansfield urged his colleagues to weigh its words care-fully and behave accordingly. Yet at the same time he also urged that the Senate trial, if any, be televised. He was not about to have the Senate charged with conducting a Star Chamber proceeding.

His remarks, opening with an allusion to Nixon's complaint that one year of Watergate was enough, elicited a response from Republican leader Hugh Scott, which is included here.

* * *

Mr. Mansfield. Mr. President, one year of Watergate is too much; one day of Watergate is too much, but the issue will have to run its course. It would be my hope that the Senate Select Committee on Watergate and related matters would be able to complete its business by May 28 and, at that time, it would turn over the evidence accumulated and its recommendations to Special Prosecutor Leon Jaworski on the one hand, and the House Judiciary Committee on the other.

At the same time, I would hope it would make whatever legislative recommendations it feels necessary to the Senate for consideration. In my opinion, the Special Prosecutor and the courts are doing the job and doing it well. I note that Mr. Jaworski stated that it would take several years to clear the Watergate and related matters through the courts. The House Judiciary Committee is doing its job extremely well, and the lack of leaks out of that committee is a most encouraging sign. I would hope that the White House and the Committee would get together on the differences which are keeping them apart and arrive at a satisfactory accommodation so that the Judiciary Committee could get on with its hearings and make its judgment known to the House at the earliest possible date.

I have noted with some concern that polls of various kinds have been taken as to how the Judiciary Committee stands and even how individual Senators stand on this matter, before all the evidence is presented, either to the committee or to the Senate. There have also been editorials and commentaries on the issue of impeachment by the House and a trial by the Senate which, I think, anticipate the question. Some members of Congress have advocated resignation by the President. None in the Senate that I know of have suggested impeachment. My position on the question of resignation is well known: it is a question which will be decided by the President and the President alone. All this is being bruited about before the issue is directly presented, either to the House or to the Senate, in any Constitutional form.

The questions we should ask ourselves are as follows:

Are we being impartial in fact and appearance?

Are we aware of our responsibilities, potential and possibly real?

Are we shunting aside the basic principle of law which presumes the innocence of the accused until found guilty?

Are the media living up to their responsibilities in "telling it as it is" on the basis of corroboration, research and source material, or interpreting the news to support a point of view? Basically, I think, the press overall is doing an excellent job.

Are we exercising restraint and patience? In my view, by and large, the Senate is. Are we, all of us, too emotionally involved? In my judgment, we are involved, because one cannot follow the media reports, the court proceedings, and the Watergate hearings without being concerned.

Are too many of us saying, "The votes are there in the House of Representatives"? In my opinion, no one really knows; certainly I do not, and no one will really know until and unless a vote is taken in the House on the issue involved.

If and when the issue reaches the Senate — and no one can answer that question at this time — what should the procedures in the Senate be? Should the hearings be televised? Should new rules to fit the issue be adopted? I think serious consideration should be given to the televising of any proceedings which might occur in the Senate. Extraordinary historical significance does not alone justify television. More important, the American people should see the totality of evidence when and if it is presented to the Senate so that, when each Senator makes his final judgment of guilty or not guilty, the American people will be fully apprised of the basis for that judgment. I think this will be very important to assure the acceptance of the judgment of the Senate, if it should come to us, whatever it may be. However, this is a matter which will have to be decided if and when the issue comes to the Senate, and the decision will be made by the Senate as a whole, after giving full consideration to the views of all persons involved.

As far as procedures are concerned, it would be my intention to discuss this matter, if and when it comes before the Senate, with the Republican leader, the Senator from Pennsylvania, and to lay before him the proposition that there be a meeting of the full Senate in executive session to seek to make the proceedings as impartial and nonpartisan as possible.

As far as the Democratic leadership is concerned, it has at all times tried to work in accord with the President to the end that the

302

responsibilities of the executive and legislative branches under the Constitution would be carried out. It is well to keep in mind that while we are all transients insofar as the Presidency on the one hand and the Congress on the other are concerned, it is the institutions of the Presidency and the Congress which are permanent, continuing, and enduring. As long as a Senator holds his office, he has all the responsibilities that go with that office, and the same applies to a President. . . .

Mr. Hugh Scott. Mr. President, I will have more to say at a later time, because this suggestion has just been advanced by the distinguished majority leader. I will be glad, of course, to confer with him at any time on any matter that pertains to the Senate business if, as, and when there appears to be reason to believe that it will become Senate business.

I very much fear that the statement of the distinguished majority leader may not be brought to the attention of the American people with the full force of what he has said, because perhaps the news value, at first blush, is that he has suggested that the proceedings be televised. At this point I am not prepared to make any statement on that. But he has said a great many more important things than that, if we can get them brought to public notice.

For example, he has said that editorials and commentaries on the issue of impeachment by the House and also by the Senate anticipate the question. He has said something that both he and I have continually said, and I get the impression that we are simply talking into a high wind each time we say it. But he has said it again, and I repeat it: "Are we shunting aside the basic principle of law which presumes the innocence of the accused until found guilty?"

He has also cautioned against members of this body saying that the votes are there in the House of Representatives, and he has pointed out that he does not know — and he questions whether others know, unless and until a vote is taken in the House. I agree with that. Any estimate that I have heard from over there is subjectively expressed by the person who tells me. Some people say the votes are not there; some people say they are. . . .

The distinguished majority leader also says that the American people should see the totality of the evidence, when and if it is presented to the Senate.

I stress again, "when and if," so that this statement of the majority leader will not be treated as an assumption that the proceedings will occur before the Senate, but he has been most careful in his fairness, as he is always so far, to stress the "when and if."

He has said that, so far as the proceedings are concerned, if and when, he will discuss these matters with me, and of course an executive session would seem to be in order. . . .

Now we can head in one of two directions or pursue, as the Senate has tried to do generally, a middle course. The middle course, it seems to me, ought to steer us very much closer to one of the polarities than the other, and that one polarity would be a total and complete impartiality, an absence of any partisan fervor, and a full and dispassionate, as well as compassionate, approach to any problem that comes to us, if and when it does. . . .

On the other hand, it is impossible for humanity and human nature to be totally and completely dispassionate and impartial. I suggest that this is the time for us to consider that that is where our duty lies. . . .

Mr. Mansfield. Speaking as the majority leader, I want to assure you that, if and when the issue comes to the Senate, there will be as little partisanship as possible, and, as far as I am concerned, I would hope there would be none.

Furthermore, if and when the issue comes to the Senate, . . . then the Senate itself will also be on trial. I would point out further that while this Senate, if and when the issue comes to this body, renders a verdict, the final jury and the final judge will be out there among the people who elect us, because, after all, when we speak of the government of the United States, we speak of the people of this republic, and they are the final arbiters. They will watch us carefully, as they should.

May I say in passing that when an issue of this nature comes to the Senate and is to be televised, that would be subject to the approval of the Senate as a whole. I am expressing a personal opinion that there will be no circus, that there will be nothing in the way of hanky-panky, because I would expect and anticipate without question that every Senator would act with the greatest dignity and circumspection, and that there would be no hamming on the part of any member of this body, if it happens to turn out that the proceedings, if and when the question comes to this body, are televised.

Mr. Hugh Scott. There, justice must not only be done; justice must seem to have been done. *Fiat justitia* must be the guideline if and when this happens, and, finally, woe unto those who seek to act on other than the facts and evidence.

August 8, 1974:

On impeachment trial

procedures in the Senate

On July 24, 1974, the Supreme Court ruled unanimously that Nixon must surrender, "forthwith," the Watergate tapes and documents which he had been diffidently withholding from Special Prosecutor Leon Jaworski. In response his attorney, James St. Clair, reflecting his client's continuing diffidence, announced that the White House would begin the "time-consuming process" of reviewing, analyzing and indexing the tapes. Judge John Sirica, who had consumed three months waiting for them, impatiently informed St. Clair that the Supreme Court had ordered immediate surrender, not a leisurely review and analysis. St. Clair promised to get the first batch of tapes to him by July 30, although the distance between the White House and the courthouse was only about a mile.

Meanwhile the House Judiciary Committee, concluding a week of nationally televised hearings on July 30, recommended impeachment to the House of Representatives on three charges: obstruction of justice (by a vote of 27 to 11), abuses of power (28 to 10), and defiance of the committee's subpoenas (21 to 17). The House was expected to start proceedings in mid-August.

But back at the White House Nixon, in turning over the court-ordered tapes to his counsel, remarked that there might be a little legal problem with the tape of June 23, 1972, recorded only six days after the Watergate break-in. Indeed there was. It clearly revealed that the patron saint of law and order had been busily obstructing justice for more than two years. His horrified counsel *and staff, anxious now about their own reputations and possible complicity, among other things, insisted that he publicly release the tape. He did so on August 5, explaining that he had been guilty of an innocent oversight which might be interpreted as something else. The House would now surely impeach him, he added – his ten stalwart supporters on the committee soon announced that they all would vote for impeachment – but he hoped that the Senate would consider all the evidence "in perspective"; if they did so, he was confident of acquittal. On August 7 he assured his cabinet that he definitely would not resign. He was no quitter.*

On the morning of August 8, Mansfield spoke to the Democratic Conference, outlining the preparations being made for the possible Senate trial. His remarks are of considerable historical interest, although of course they were rendered irrelevant by the announcement, that evening, of irreversible abdication.

* * *

In this period of uncertainty, there is a responsibility to keep you informed of developments insofar as I am aware of them. By meeting with you from time to time, it would be my hope that a cohesive and orderly response will be possible to whatever eventualities may confront us in the days ahead. I will now proceed to lay before you such information as I am able to convey to you at this time.

First, let me say that I have been meeting frequently with the Republican Leader. Our perception of the President's situation and what may be required from the Senate in response thereto are substantially the same. The two of us have met with the party whips, Senator Byrd and Senator Griffin, for exchanges of views. Together the four of us introduced a resolution which was referred to the Rules Committee dealing with the adequacy of the existing rules and practices regarding impeachment trials. For the purposes of discussion, I also forwarded to the Committee a collation of views on possible changes in these rules. I am advised that consideration of the Leadership's resolution is proceeding deliberately in Senator Cannon's committee. That resolution, incidentally, provides for the committee to report its recommendations to the Senate by September 1, or sooner if circumstances require.

Senator Byrd and I also introduced a resolution which calls for suspension of the rule against broadcasting proceedings from the Senate chamber. It has the support of the Republican Leader. That resolution, too, is under active consideration in Senator Cannon's committee.

On Tuesday the Majority Policy Committee met to consider the responsibilities of the Senate in the light of the situation in the House. As you know, there was, first, the action of the Judiciary Committee on impeachment. Then came the decrease in the hours of floor debate which have been allotted to the question, from 55 to 25. The discussion which was prompted in your Policy Committee by the occurrences was sober in the extreme, with many ideas set forth, many questions raised, and many answered definitively.

This morning, just before the opening of this conference, the Leadership met with the Speaker and his House associates. Again, the discussion centered on impeachment. Events are now moving very rapidly in that direction in the House.

What is transpiring is beyond the personal experience of any of us. These are wrenching and difficult times for all involved. But the responsibility for us in the Senate is clear. We must be prepared to carry out our duties, . . . framed by Article I, Section 3 of the Constitution. . . .

Many Senators have already begun to define their roles in this context. There are differences — honest differences — as to what is at stake. By some it is said that guilt must be established beyond a reasonable doubt, that evidence must be shielded by self-incrimination privileges and so on. It is valid to raise these notions — all borrowed from the criminal law — for purposes of discussion. I expect, however, that each of us, in the end, will decide for ourself the criteria of judgment, even as the Senate as a whole will decide the questions of procedure. Speaking for myself, it seems to me that what must be kept in mind is the fact that the Senate does not determine criminal liability. At issue, rather, is the question of the handling of the Presidential trust. If the House so charges, then the Senate must decide whether that trust has been abridged, abused, breached or violated under the Constitution and laws of the United States.

Can we avoid facing this responsibility? Would not a Presidential resignation spare us the necessity? As I have said many times, the question of a Presidential resignation is solely one for the President. If he does reach that decision, then we will face a new situation. But, in my view, it would be an abuse for the Senate itself to stimulate resignation so as to avoid a judgment under the regular Constitutional procedures. I am not sure whose purposes would be served thereby.

Impeachment and trial is the only Constitutional method this nation provides to protect the Presidency. It is that ultimate safeguard — the protection of the Presidency, as important to our Constitutional structure as the Congress — which I would hope determines the manner by which the Senate proceeds in this matter.

If there is a standard on which to base an impeachment trial, most assuredly it must be that of fairness and fairness alone. But, above all, the kind of fairness that is called for is fairness to the people of this nation — to the people of today and of many tomorrows. . . .

As to the matter of television, I view its employment as essential if there is a trial. This caucus and the Senate concurring, I would expect ground rules for telecasting to be designed by the Joint Leadership in consultation with the Rules Committee. Our objective must be to safeguard fully the integrity and solemnity of the proceedings even as access to them is made available to the entire nation. We have had some dealings with the networks during the past few years, and I am confident that we shall be able to work out an appropriate arrangement. In that regard, I commend the networks' handling of the proceedings thus far in the House.

Senator Scott and I, together with Senator Griffin and Senator Byrd, have commended preliminary discussions to assure that, should the Senate approve telecasting, it will be employed with the greatest propriety. Other discussions under way within the Leadership and with the Senate's officers and pertinent staff include security precautions and the management of the galleries, provisions of accommodations on the floor, and the many other details which must be worked out meticulously in advance. Beyond this, it is anticipated that at an appropriate time the Chief Justice will be brought into preliminary discussions on fundamental matters which will arise in connection with the trial. All of these preliminaries, may I say, are essential to safeguard the ultimate fairness and propriety and the decorum of the proceedings. For similar reasons, I would hope that all of our decisions are arrived at with a minimum of dissension. So far, in that regard, the Senate and all Senators have acted in exemplary fashion, and I wish to commend, in particular, the other members of the Joint Leadership . . . and also Senator Cannon and the Rules Committee for their contributions to the common effort which is being made to cope with this most difficult situation. I am proud of the way the whole Senate has acted, with responsibility and restraint.

August 15-21, 1974:

Tributes to Mansfield on his

record term as a Senate leader

In June 1970 Mansfield surpassed the previous record of Kentucky's Alben Barkley for length of service as majority leader. On August 15, 1974, he surpassed the previous record of Arkansas' Joseph Robinson for service as a Senate leader. (Robinson served almost fourteen years, from 1923 to 1937, the first ten as minority leader.) As in 1970, the new record holder was subjected to an outpouring of tributes far surpassing the requirements of even Senatorial etiquette. This time the plaudits were scattered throughout five working days.

Some readers may think it a bit much to devote so much space to these tributes, and Senator Mansfield, who genuinely tried to escape the ecomiums, would be the first to say so, without wasting words. But the excerpts given here, which actually constitute only a minute sample, illustrate the universality of the respect for the man, as well as for the Senator and the majority leader, since the praise comes from the entire spectrum, from curmudgeon conservative to breathless liberal, from ancient fixture to greenest freshman. The reason for quoting from the tributes at such length

309

is neatly summed up in the remarks with which Senator Hart opened the second day (August 16). Mansfield's career, after all, offered a reassuring contrast to the reign of venal tyranny that had ended only six days before.

* * *

Mr. Hugh Scott. Mr. President, today marks a record pleasant to note, and a record of special meaning. In his capacity as majority leader, the distinguished Senator from Montana has served the nation, this body, and his colleagues — and the best causes and the good purposes for which he is so well known — for 13 years and 225 days. This is a longer period than any other majority or minority leader has ever served in the Senate, and we congratulate him for it.

As usual, when I started to speak, his mind was on service to his Montana constituency, some of whom are about to meet with him, and we will not keep him long.

I note this important anniversary in his life and our careers because when I came to these front desks, first as the whip and then as the minority leader, I did not come with what one might call unanimous approval. I was nervous and uncertain of my duties and how to conduct my responsibilities.

I am most indebted, and will always remain indebted, to my friend, the distinguished majority leader, for his wise counsel, his gentle words of caution and of advice, and his assurance to me in moments of pressure and times when the determination of the right thing to do weighed very heavily on me. . . .

Mr. Robert C. Byrd. Mr. President, a man who is clean inside and outside, who neither looks up to the rich nor down on the poor, who can lose without complaining and win without bragging, who is considerate of women and children and old people, who is too honest to cheat, too generous to lie, too sensible to loaf, who works for his share of the world's goods and lets others have theirs, is indeed an American gentleman.

Such an American gentleman is Mike Mansfield. . . .

As the Senate knows, its leaders do not enjoy an automatic and continuing incumbency. They are nominated and elected every two years by their party colleagues. Thus on seven separate occasions, in seven Congresses, the Senator from Montana has received an affirmative vote — may I add, a unanimous vote — of confidence from his peers for the leadership which he has given to his party and to the Senate.

That is the measure of the trust which has been reposed in him by his Democratic colleagues in the Senate. His decency, his patience, and his absolute fairness have also won for him a deep affection and a high esteem from Republicans no less than from Democrats.

Mike Mansfield is a dedicated Montanan, a superb Senator, and a great American whose contributions to his state and to the United States have been of surpassing significance. As a Senator, he has worked for Montana and spoken for himself. As majority leader, he has worked for this institution and spoken for all of us.

In short, he has zealously guarded his independence and the Constitutional position of the Senate. Notwithstanding, he has cooperated closely with Presidents of both parties in the higher interests of all the people of the United States. He has made notable contributions to the nation's foreign policy and international position and to the general effort to build a sane and peaceful world. He was a leader in bringing about an end to the war in Vietnam and played a significant part in the reopening of contact with the People's Republic of China. At least five Presidents have asked him to undertake missions overseas on behalf of the nation. Mike Mansfield is best described, as his friend from Vermont once categorized him, as "a valuable national asset." . . .

Mr. Eastland. . . . Senator Mansfield rates among the greatest of the majority leaders in the history of this body. If there is one word that I would always apply to Mike Mansfield, that word is fairness. While I may have in the past disagreed with Mike Mansfield on philosophical grounds, I have never questioned or doubted his absolute sincerity, honesty, and innate decency.

Under his leadership, the Democratic Party organizations — the policy committee, steering committee, and legislative review committee — have all been developed along strict geographic and philosophic lines. Every viewpoint, age group, and region is fairly represented, and democracy is demonstrated in its finest terms. Each section of America knows that while Mike Mansfield may not always vote with it, he will fight to protect the legitimate

311

interests of all areas in an impartial manner. . . .

Mr. Pastore. . . . Mike Mansfield is probably the most demonstrably fair human being I have ever known. His firm and continuous desire to render to each and every Senator his due, his efforts to be even-handed and impartial and unbiased are already legend among his colleagues. I have never seen him display animosity or a negative emotion toward anyone. He does not just talk about what it is right to do; he does it. He might be called truth in action. And how he remains calm and even-tempered through it all I will never know. . . .

Mr. Moss. . . . Only those who have known this good man can realize how we feel. I do not use the word "great" man because there are people who are great but are not necessarily good. But Mike Mansfield is a good man, a man who exemplifies and symbolizes in every way the American story. . . .

Mr. Metcalf. . . . In 1961 I was privileged as a freshman Senator to nominate Mike Mansfield for the office of Democratic leader. Since that time he has compiled an unparalleled inventory of achievements for the benefit of our nation. No man has held this position longer, it is true, but, more importantly, none has served with greater distinction than Mike Mansfield. I welcome the continued guidance of his firm yet gentle hand on our national legislative program.

Mr. Griffin. . . . We all welcome the opportunity the occasion affords us to tell Mike right to his face what we think of him — how much we like him, how much we respect him, and how much we admire him.

I suspect that all this fuss will make him a little uncomfortable, for he is a modest and unassuming person. But I am sure that he will just grin and bear it with that same degree of fortitude with which he faces up to the many problems he encounters daily as majority leader. . . .

Mr. Cotton. . . . Mike Mansfield is a gentleman in the truest sense of the word. He is a statesman. He is the type of man who brings honor rather than disrepute to the word "politician." He knows the all-important value of principles and the virtue of compromise without violating these principles. In sum, Mr. President, he has long been a leader through his daily thinking and actions, and it is this type of leadership that he has exercised so

312

effectively in the prestigious and powerful role he has now held for so long. . . .

Mr. Muskie. . . . Senator Mansfield can take a major part of the credit for the achievements of Congress over the years. His leadership is important because it is based on the personal respect and affection in which we all hold him. . . .

Mr. Kennedy. . . . For many of us in the Senate, myself included, we have known no other majority leader. For the past thirteen years he has been not only our leader but our valued friend and mentor, a rock of leadership and wisdom, performing with almost incredible skill the difficult job of guiding this chamber in its mission to serve the people of the nation.

To me, the Senator from Montana is a fine example of the Senate at its best. . . .

Mr. Thurmond. . . . Senator Mansfield has provided distinguished and competent leadership for this body. He has managed, with admirable skill, the time-consuming process of assuring that all of our legislative proposals receive their proper consideration and suitable disposition. He has fostered a spirit of friendliness and conciliation as we go about our business. It is a spirit which has made the Senate much more effective in carrying out its duties.

The distinguished Senator has consistently allowed all views to be heard on any legislation. An example of his true fairness can be seen in the accommodating manner with which he handles matters requiring extended debate. Senator Mansfield has made excellent use of the double-track system, thus avoiding the creation of a backlog of Senate business whenever a number of Senators wish to debate a piece of legislation on an extended basis. . . .

Mr. Stennis. . . . I have never heard the Senator from Montana utter a single self-serving statement, nor have I known him to cast a purely selfish vote. He looks after his state most effectively but always within the formula of what is best and sound for the nation. . . .

Mr. Helms. . . . The majority leader of the Senate bears many burdens not apparent to the people of this nation — nor, for that matter, to Senators. I have been a member of the Senate for just under twenty months, and every day I have been impressed with the constant good cheer and the unfailing spirit of helpfulness

313

and cooperation so manifest in the personality of Senator Mansfield.

He has never been too busy to counsel with me when I have needed him, and he has never failed to be helpful. He is a remarkable man, a splendid gentleman, and a true friend. I congratulate him on this latest achievement, and I thank him for being the fine, conscientious American that he is.

August 16, 1974

Mr. Hart. Mr. President, there is no word combination which can express the admiration and pride of this Senator from Michigan for the man from Montana whom we pause to honor.

Others have spoken correctly of his legislative skill, his patience, his integrity and decency. Indeed, these are the characteristics which brought him to the leadership. It was not ambition for place or position.

There is one easy way for me to explain for the record my feeling for Mike Mansfield. Repeatedly when one speaks with a student group, or a group of young people, the statement is made: "Well, maybe politics is important, but it tends to dirty one. No one can participate without compromising important principles." Repeatedly my answer is: "Not true. Senator Mansfield is proof positive that decency and moderation and accommodation can be maintained by one throughout a long and effective political life."

Now I can include in that answer the fact that such a man has served longer than any other man as the leader of his party in the Senate. . . .

Mr. Tunney. Mr. President, I join my colleagues today in paying tribute to the distinguished service of our esteemed majority leader. Senator Mansfield, through all the turbulence of recent years, has provided a steadiness of purpose and a strength of resolve that have brought the Senate back to its rightful balance within our Constitutional system.

His sense of commitment, his integrity serve as inspiration to all members of the Senate, and, of course, his unfailing fairness, the helping hand and counsel he gives incoming members further enrich the lives of all who serve here. He retains a calmness and sureness of judgment that assures a steady course of progressive legislation through the Senate.

314

Since coming to the Senate in 1953 and, conspicuously, since his election as majority leader in 1961, the senior Senator from Montana has, with quiet words and gentle suggestions, exercised leadership through a consensus of reason and mutual respect among all members of the Senate, regardless of their party. He has muted partisanship in favor of solid progress on the great issues before our nation.

Senator Mansfield may have served more years than others as majority leader, but it is not the longevity of his service that we honor today; it is his abiding commitment to the obligations and the opportunities of the Senate to serve all America. . . .

Mr. Fong. [Senator Mansfield] is the epitome of fairness, honesty, and honor. His word is his bond. He has done a great deal to restore and maintain dignity and decorum in the Senate. His manner is gentle, but we who serve with him know how very firm and strong he is beneath that gentle exterior . . . .

Mr. Javits. . . . With Mike Mansfield, partisanship is kept to a minimum, and the national interest is always put first. After dealing with him for many years, I can state that he is always willing to help any Senator as much as possible consistent with his responsibility as majority leader.

I also believe that Mike Mansfield has opened up the Senate and allowed all members, especially the junior members, to exercise their prerogatives to the fullest extent possible. This has allowed the Senate to function in a way it had not done in the past, when junior Senators were seen but not heard, and has allowed all members to participate to a greater extent in legislative business. . . .

Mr. Mondale. Mr. President, Harry Truman over fifteen years ago said, "Men make history, and not the other way around. Progress occurs when courageous, skillful leaders seize the opportunity to change things for the better." No description could better portray the career of our distinguished and beloved majority leader, the Senator from Montana. . . .

As a leader in bringing about our withdrawal from the long ordeal in Vietnam, as a leader in reopening our contacts with the People's Republic of China, and as one of the principal movers behind the enactment of meaningful campaign finance reform legislation, Senator Mansfield has shown time and again his capacity for leadership and his ability to persuade his colleagues on the rightness and wisdom of his cause. . . .

Mr. Symington. . . . All Americans can be proud of Mike Mansfield. He is a man of fairness and outstanding integrity. He has served not only the people of his state, but all Americans. He has served not only the Democratic majority in the Senate, but all Senators. It is a difficult job, and he has performed it with superb ability and fairness. . . .

I congratulate him not only on the length of his service but also on the quality, the dedication, and the courtesy of his leadership. It is a privilege to have had him over the years as a leader and as a friend.

Mr. Cannon. Mr. President, I have long valued my association and friendship with our distinguished majority leader. . . .

His leadership, concern, and spirit of cooperation and compromise have allowed this body to deliberate the crucial issues of America in an atmosphere of free exchange and honesty. He has emerged, after many harsh battles in this Senate during the last thirteen years, as the one man who provides the needed firmness and determination and at the same time the necessary open-mindedness and flexibility. He has deserved and gained respect on both sides of the aisle, and I am proud to pay homage to his unwavering service and dedication. . . .

Mr. Proxmire. [Senator Mansfield] is an extraordinary person. His is a rare combination of qualities: honesty, humility, erudition. He is persuasive, principled, patient. His attitude is positive, not negative. He has respect for his fellow man, regardless of station. He upholds justice without being self-righteous. He can condemn evil without condemning the evildoer. He fights for right without being unbending. He is fearless without instilling fear in others.

Mike Mansfield is a leader because he knows how to lead and because he is worthy of respect. . . .

Mr. Randolph. . . . This good man, this gentle man, has placed his imprint on some of the most significant social and economic laws ever produced. His resolute leadership has left its impact in so many areas of our national life and has helped shape the future of our people.

It is an extraordinary achievement to have enjoyed the trust and confidence of his colleagues on both sides of the aisle for so many years. On seven separate occasions, his Democratic peers have unanimously endorsed his leadership role. His calm and earnest demeanor, his simple honesty and his unswerving fairness have earned him the deep affection and high esteem that all of us feel for him. . . .

August 19, 1974

Mr. Hatfield. . . . I am reminded of the old adage, usually applied to kings of old, that a ruler can be either respected or loved, but not both, and it is better to be respected than loved. In my opinion, Mike Mansfield disproves this completely, for he is both. . . .

Mr. Magnuson. . . . I am pleased to call Mike Mansfield a close and personal friend. Under his leadership, the U.S. Senate has emerged in the public view as something much more than a debating forum. Senator Mansfield has presented to all of us a standard of fairness, integrity and moderation which has been the signal of true leadership. In the last 13 years and 258 days the U.S. Senate has moved toward real Democratic reform. Senator Mansfield is responsible for creating the environment and leading the changes. I am confident Senator Mansfield's position in American history is well preserved. . . .

August 20, 1974

Mr. Montoya. . . . As leader he has never sought power nor has he used his office to cause disadvantage to others. He has conducted his office out in the open, with honest concern for the integrity and image of this fine institution. He has done magnificently well in this regard. . . .

Mr. Bentsen. . . . Senators follow Mile Mansfield's leadership not because of fear of retribution or an anticipated favor or a quid pro quo, but because they know he has studied the issue well and his position reflects an honest commitment. He does not ask for support unless he feels the issue has major importance to the nation. . . .

His is the most difficult job in the Senate, yet he has provided the direction and guidance that has seen some of this country's finest and most honorable dreams become reality. . . .

And I take personal gratification in offering a note of thanks to him for all that he has done to assist those of us who are first-term Senators. I remember well, as one of the freshmen who took Senate seats in January 1971, the spirit with which Mike Mansfield agreed to assist the new class. Because of his leadership, the new Senators are quickly given an opportunity to participate and make meaningful contributions. He is my friend and colleague. He is a statesman of the highest caliber, always a gentleman. Mike Mansfield is a Senator's Senator. . . .

Mr. Hartke. . . . Mike Mansfield has served this Senate well, and he has served the American people well. He has given us the strength to perform our responsibilities, and he has always challenged us to do better. His leadership, fairness, and calm decisiveness are in the highest traditions of the Senate and will set a benchmark for decades to come. I am proud to join in saluting him today and look forward to many more years of his leadership.

Mr. Baker. Mr. President, during the past week the Senate has noted with pleasure and with pride the historic record of service established by the distinguished majority leader, Senator Mansfield. . . .

It is, I believe, no coincidence that this former professor has become a textbook model of an effective Senate leader. His approach to leadership and life has been hallmarked by rationality and respect for others. His fairness has been especially appreciated by those of us on the Republican side of the aisle. . . .

September 16, 1974:

On ownership of the Tapes

In September 1974 the question of who owned the treasuretrove of Presidential tapes and papers surfaced conspicuously. There were no precedents for the case of someone absconding with potential criminal evidence. Nixon, now pardoned for anything he did or might have done or even didn't do, insisted that these 42 million tapes, documents and other items, pertaining to government business and generated on government office

*machines, were his personal property. Mansfield thought other-
wise, and indeed thought further that, excepting portions
genuinely affecting national security, they should be made public
so that the people might eventually get some of the information
that had been denied them by the evasion of an impeachment and
trial. (The General Services Administration's concession of the
property was later overruled in court.)*

*On September 16 Mansfield took the Senate floor and reviewed
the situation.*

* * *

Mr. Mansfield. Mr. President, . . . Article IV, Section 3 of the
Constitution contains the following statement: "The Congress
shall have power to dispose of and make all needful rules and
regulations respecting the territory or other property belonging to
the United States; and nothing in this constitution shall be so
construed as to prejudice any claims of the United States, or of any
particular state."

[Five days ago,] on September 11, I introduced Senate Resolution 399, as follows: . . .

> *Whereas,* It is paramount to the national interest that the
> American public be made fully aware of all the facts con-
> nected with and related to Watergate matters and the fruits
> of all investigations conducted pursuant thereto; and
>
> *Whereas,* It is uncertain that there is now assured public
> access to all such facts as they are contained in papers,
> documents, memoranda, tapes and transcripts, Be It
> Therefore
>
> *Resolved,* That President Ford take all steps necessary to
> assure full public access to all facts connected with and
> related to Watergate matters and the fruits of all investiga-
> tions conducted pursuant thereto, and Be It Further
>
> *Resolved,* That except in cases clearly vital to the na-
> tional security interests of the United States, President
> Ford afford the American public full access to all such
> papers, documents, memoranda, tapes and transcripts
> originating at any time during the period January 20, 1969,

319

through August 9, 1974, at the earliest practicable time and in an adequate and effective manner.

This resolution speaks for itself. It calls upon President Ford to assure the American people that in the national interest they will be provided all the facts of Watergate and all the facts relating to matters connected therewith.

That the American people are entitled to these facts is unquestioned in my judgment; that they are not now assured of that opportunity is equally clear, however. . . .

In order to face up to what has become a custom based on precedents, but not on law, I have introduced Senate Resolution 399 along with a number of other Senators — I see that the distinguished Senator from New York (Mr. Javits), a cosponsor, is in the chamber — so that Congressional intent will be made clear that these papers are not private property but, in the last analysis, belong to the people.

Too many Presidents have stripped the White House of their official papers, some to preserve them in libraries, others to use them as a basis for books and interviews, and all of them being considered the private property of a President who was elected and who used public funds to be able to amass documents, papers, memoranda, tapes and transcripts, or whatever. I am today addressing a letter to the distinguished Chairman of the Committee on Government Operations, the Senator from North Carolina, Mr. Sam Ervin, and asking that he give consideration to S. 399 as expeditiously as possible to the end that these papers will not be stored away in a vault for three years under the joint ownership, so to speak — perhaps I should say under the joint supervision — of Mr. Arthur Sampson, Administrator of the General Services Administration, and Mr. Nixon or his designee, probably Mr. Ron Ziegler, after which time they would become the property of the former President to use as he saw fit.

Incidentally, there is a request before the Congress at this time for $100,000 to build a vault to store this accumulation of data in San Clemente, California. The place to store all this material is in the National Archives, where it can be made readily available — all of it except those parts dealing with national security — to the courts, to the Congress, and to the American people. . . .

320

November 20, 1974:

On wage- and price-control authority

In January 1971 President Nixon lifted all price controls with the intention, he solemnly averred, of reducing the annual inflation rate to 2.5%. By the fall of 1974, a year after the ungenerous boost from the OPEC oil cartel, inflation was running at about 14%. Yet, perhaps more alarmingly, the economy was showing symptoms of impending recession such as a shrinking production rate and rising unemployment.

President Ford's response to this unnerving situation was a threefold one: (1) Let's all wear WIN buttons, to Whip Inflation Now. (2) Let's all clean our plates at dinnertime. (3) Let us, the government, call a summit conference of economic experts, who can tell us what else to do.

The results were less than spectacularly successful. The button campaign produced a glut of unused lapel ornaments, thereby adding a bit to the inflation rate. The plate-cleaning campaign's effect was less visible than risible. As a result of the economic summit conference held in late September, Ford proposed a 5% income-tax increase in early October, urged Congress to get cracking on it in mid-November, and then, in January 1975, proposed an income-tax cut of $16 billion, including a tax rebate of $12 billion for 1974.

Amid the confusion Mansfield argued persistently for legislation restoring authority to the President to impose wage and price controls. (The previous standby authority had expired in April 1974.) In November 1974, for example, he took the floor to suggest this at least as a temporary measure, like a wet cloth on the forehead, to reduce the fever of inflation. His proposal succumbed to Ford's repeated statements that he would not use such authority, as well as to the growing alarm over the imminent recession – which eventually and painfully did slow down inflation somewhat. (The pain, of course, was felt mostly by the poor, whose influence is minimal in Republican economic policy.)

His analysis, however, was a perceptive one, worth noting for the record.

Mr. Mansfield. Mr. President, there is a good deal of talk going around about the economy, but that is all it is — talk. We note in this morning's paper that Chrysler is laying off something on the order of 44,000 workers. At the same time, Chrysler has increased its prices.

We see GM laying off workers, and we see Ford laying off workers. They, too, have raised their prices.

We see a situation developing which could, in my opinion, take us back to the terrible days of the depression of the thirties if we do not face up to our responsibilities. There are those of us who advocate wage, price, rent, profit, and other kinds of controls, and there are those of us who are opposed to them. But both of us are just talking unless we want to face up to the realities of today.

Volunteerism is not the answer. Wearing a button on one's lapel is not the answer. Cleaning one's plate is not the answer. Oil shortages alone are not the problem.

In my opinion, Mr. President, the basic reason for the recession in which we find ourselves today is twofold: Vietnam, a tragedy if there ever was one, and the turning off of the oil spigot just about a year ago. Vietnam, an unnecessary, brutal war which was not tied to the interests of the United States, cost this nation 55,000 American dead. Vietnam cost this nation 330,000 American wounded. Vietnam caused this nation to spend 140 billion American dollars, and before we are through, according to the "Statistical Abstract of the United States, 1973," issued by the Department of Commerce, Vietnam is going to cost us $352 billion, a cost that will extend into the latter part of the first half of the next century.

As to the other factor, petroleum, let us see what we are paying. In 1972, the cost of petroleum imports was about $4.7 billion. In 1973 the cost was about $8.3 billion. This year the cost is going to be in excess of $27 billion.

The inflation rate in August 1971 was 4.5 percent. Today the inflation is triple that figure. In fact, we have the same rhetoric against the strong remedy of controls from this Administration. But in the past 100 days unemployment has increased in America to 5½ million, or 6 percent of the total work force. It is expected to jump to 7 percent or more before the new Congress convenes in January. Automobile sales are down 38 percent from a year ago,

322

but the cost of cars has increased by $386 on the average. Assembly line layoffs are beginning to snowball. The cost of living keeps going up. Last month, on the eve of the election, wholesale prices increased at an annual rate of nearly 28 percent; wholesale prices for food increased by over 50 percent; the gross national product dropped 2.9 percent in the third quarter of this year. These statistics keep telling the story, but a sense of urgency seems to escape all but those in the grocery store lines.

A program of voluntary restraint — in effect since President Nixon's Phase II was abandoned — is inadequate to meet the economic crisis of the nation.

What is needed is a strong, fair, and total program to control the spiral of inflation. It is not satisfactory to blame it on an international oil conspiracy alone. Assessing blame does not provide a remedy. Getting our domestic house in order through a balanced program of energy conservation and economic restraint will do more to remedy the international recession than the rhetoric of countless international conferences.

The measure I introduce today should be considered as but one part of an overall program to meet the urgent needs of this nation. It will provide for the authority to exercise the appropriate control over our economy during this period of crisis. It is similar to the authority granted to President Nixon in 1970. It includes authority over wages, profits, rents, dividends, interest rates, and other economic transfers with a base period of April 30, 1974, the date the 1970 control authority expired.

A newly added feature will require the administration to submit to the Congress within 60 days after enactment a detailed plan on how this authority would be implemented if called upon by the President. This report will include specific descriptions of the manner in which such authority would be exercised and the organizational and administrative structures that would be undertaken. These reports would give Congress the ability to adjudge what measures are contemplated to assure that all sectors of the economy are to receive a comparable level of control; that all sections are to be treated fairly and equitably; and that comparable duties and sacrifices on individuals and organizations will be distributed throughout the economy.

I hope that the Committee on Housing, Banking, and Urban

Affairs . . . will give this matter its earliest consideration because, Mr. President, the bells are tolling, and we know for whom.

January 27, 1975:

On establishing a committee

to investigate government

intelligence activities

"I've been in politics a long time, and I don't shock very easily any more. I've been through the war, through Watergate – and, of all the things we went through, that episode affecting Martin Luther King was the most shocking, because it had all the elements of a dictatorship."

This was Senator Walter Mondale of Minnesota speaking during an interview with Martin Agronsky on the PBS "Evening Edition" program in late April 1976. Mondale was a member of the Senate Select Committee to Study Government Operations with Respect to Intelligence Activities, chaired by Senator Frank Church. Earlier that week the committee had issued its final report on the unlawful shenanigans of the CIA, the FBI, and other intelligence agencies since World War II; in the report, perhaps unfortunately, it had offered no less than 183 legislative proposals to improve the situation. Mondale was referring to J. Edgar Hoover's infamous vendetta against the indomitable King.

Some sixteen months earlier the Senate, at Mansfield's urging, had set up the committee to investigate and report on intelligence activities and to recommend legislation that would give Congress a reasonable amount of control over any Executive carelessness or megalomania supported by unquestioning obedience and/or delusions of national security. In January 1975, before announcing the names of the Senators chosen by the leadership to serve on the committee, he stressed the importance of the committee's charter to the survival of American democracy. Characteristically, he prefaced his remarks with a reassurance to Senator John

324

Stennis that the creation of the committee was not intended as a criticism.

* * *

Mr. Mansfield. Mr. President, I wish to state, before proceeding with the discussions and consideration of this resolution, that insofar as the majority leader is concerned, the Chairman of the Committee on Armed Services, our colleague from Mississippi, is owed a vote of thanks because throughout the years he has scrupulously endeavored, to the best of his ability and in line with his other responsibilities, to scrutinize all activities of intelligence agencies related to the defense community. He need not yield to any member of this body his stance as the preeminent "watchdog" of the Congress in performing this critical oversight function. I commend John Stennis. The Senate commends John Stennis for his assiduous and conscientious work in this endeavor.

Mr. President, now that the select committee has been approved by the Senate, the minority leader and I have directed a letter to the heads of agencies and departments of government most preeminently concerned with intelligence endeavors. The letter reads as follows:

> As you may be aware, the Senate is to conduct an investigation and study of government operations with respect to intelligence activities. The scope of the investigation is set out in S. Res. 21, a copy of which has been enclosed for your information.
>
> We are writing to request that you not destroy, remove from your possession or control, or otherwise dispose, or permit the disposal, of any records or documents which might have a bearing on the subjects under investigation, including but not limited to all records or documents pertaining in any way to the matters set out in Section 2 of S. Res. 21.

This letter is being directed to heads of nineteen separate governmental units. . . .

The task faced by the select committee which the Senate has

just established is to examine into the intelligence activities of the U.S. government. No more important responsibility to the people of the nation can be assumed by Senators than membership on this committee. What is asked of them, in the name of the Senate, is to probe fully and to assess completely, to understand thoroughly and to evaluate judiciously. To the extent that the intelligence agencies have acted correctly and within the law, that must be made known. If there have been abuses, they too must be set forth. There can be no whitewash in this inquiry, nor is there any room for a vendetta. In the end, the Senate must know what has transpired so that it may seek to close legal loopholes if there are any. In the end we must know so that, together with the House and the President, we may move to foreclose any demeaning of the basic premises of a free society.

What is at stake in the work of this committee is a resolution of doubts. What is at stake is a restoration of confidence in a large and costly and little known segment of the Federal government. The Senate must be satisfied that the intelligence community is doing the people's business as defined not by employees of a government agency, but the people's business as defined by the Constitution and the laws duly enacted thereunder. . . .

One aspect of the impending inquiry concerns covert activities. These activities have been acquiesced in, to say the least, by the Congress for a long time. No one should be surprised or appalled, therefore, to discover their existence a quarter of a century later. In recent years, however, the extent and necessity for them have come under question. Who sets the policy and why? What obtuse intrustions may there have been by these activities into the President's conduct of foreign affairs? What indifference, if any, to the laws passed by the Congress? What damage, if any, to the demeanor of the nation? What interference in the personal lives of Americans and by whose authority and under what guidelines? What public funds have been committed, and to what end? What proliferation of activities and how much overlap and duplication?

It used to be fashionable, Mr. President, for members of Congress to say that insofar as the intelligence agencies were concerned, the less they knew about such questions, the better. Well, in my judgment, it is about time that that attitude went out of fashion. It is time for the Senate to take the trouble and, yes, the risks of knowing more rather than less. We have a duty, individually and collectively, to know what legislation enacted by Congress and paid for by appropriations of the people's money has spawned in practice in the name of the United States. The Congress needs to recognize, to accept and to discharge with care its coequal responsibility with the Presidency in these matters.

The Senate has begun to address itself to these questions by approving the creation of this select committee. There is a need to understand not only the present intelligence requirements but also what systems or procedures for oversight and accountability may be required to keep them within bounds set by the Constitution, the President, and the elected representatives of the people in Congress. . . .

The select committee is equipped with a bipartisan membership. The Senators who will be selected for service on this committee are no different from the rest of us. They are not tied with a blue ribbon or a white or pink ribbon. There is no higher or lower order of patriotism in the Senate. There are no first- or second-class Senators. Those who will serve are men of competence, understanding, and decency. They will do the job which the circumstances and the Senate require of them.

The committee has been equipped with full authority to study, to hold hearings, and to investigate all activities, foreign and domestic, of the intelligence agencies of the Federal government. In pursuit of that mandate, I have every confidence that the committee will act with discretion, with restraint, and with a high sense of national responsibility. There is no cause or inclination to pursue this matter as a Roman circus or a TV spectacular. There is only the need to see to the sober discharge of very sober responsibilities.

How the committee proceeds is largely up to the members of the committee. They have the authority to make their rules and to define their procedures, and that would include the question of when to close or open the door to the use of television. As I have indicated, I would not anticipate any great requirements for the latter at this time. Most emphatically, I would express the hope, too, that committee staff would be selected with as much concern for discretion as for other qualifications. What comes to the public from this committee and when, ought to be solely — and I stress the word "solely" — determined by members of the committee.

The Senate is entrusting this committee with its deepest confidence. I know that trust is secure and that the results of the inquiry will reflect the highest credit on this institution. . . .

February 20, 1975:

On ending filibusters

The Senate, Mansfield always maintained, was the last hope — or refuge, from another viewpoint – of a dedicated minority. The Senate tradition of unlimited debate, he conceded, was customary rather than Constitutional, but the many Constitutional provisions for two-thirds votes, as well as the Bill of Rights, testified to this nation's inherent concern and respect for minority viewpoints. Although he himself had often enough been frustrated by minority obstructionism in the Senate – especially when the minority view being protected was the legitimacy of white oppression of blacks – he stoutly insisted that such obstacles offered the majority an opportunity for sober second thought, a chance to reconsider the wisdom of riding roughshod over the opinions of fellow human beings.

Just as his position was opposed to, and by, the doctrinaire, so he was not doctrinaire in his position. He certainly had no desire to return to the days before 1917, the year when Senate Rule 22 placed the first restriction on filibustering by permitting cloture to be invoked by two-thirds of the full Senate. Nor did he want to return to the days before 1959, when Rule 22 was amended to permit cloture by two-thirds of those present and voting. Indeed, he had long advocated further amending the rule to permit cloture by only three-fifths of those present and voting. But he flatly opposed permitting cloture by a simple majority vote. And he even more vigorously opposed any change in Rule 22 by a simple majority vote (proposed on the grounds that each Senate after a national election was a new body, without any binding precedents and therefore with the power to establish new rules by simple majority vote); this, he argued, would subvert the Senate's unique, continuing, essential tradition of consideration for minority views. Everyone, after all, holds some minority views and wants them weighed in the balance.

In the end the Senate agreed. And in the end the Senate also agreed, by the thinnest two-thirds vote possible (56-27), on a compromise measure permitting cloture by a three-fifths vote of the full membership. That final vote was taken on March 7, 1975. About two weeks earlier Mansfield had made his pitch for continuing the two-thirds requirement for amending Senate rules.

* * *

Mr. Mansfield. Mr. President, the motion before the Senate again raises the question that has confronted each Congress for nearly two decades. It is whether the Senate of the United States is a continuing body. One would suppose that the character of the Senate as a continuing entity has long been established; that two-thirds of its membership carries forward from one Congress to the next would appear to underscore that fact. Following each *sine die* adjournment the committees of the Senate continue to meet, seats are filled and, as has been highlighted in recent months, the Senate could even proceed with the trial of an impeachment originating in an earlier Congress. To say at the same time that somehow the Senate rules expire tests the most basic assumptions and procedures and responsibilities of this institution as prescribed by the Constitution.

That clearly was the view of the Senate in 1959 when Senate Resolution 5 was overwhelmingly adopted to amend Rule 22 so as to enable two-thirds of the Senate present and voting to close debate on any matter, including proposals for rules changes. That resolution also amended Rule 22 by adding this implicit language: "The rules of the Senate shall continue from one Congress to the next Congress unless they are changed as provided in these rules."

In spite of the history of the Senate as a continuing body with continuing rules, the issue of cloture by a majority is again before us and must again be resolved.

The Senate of the United States is unique among parliamentary bodies. Because of the tradition of unlimited debate in the Senate, even though that principle has been diminished by Rule 22, the rights of the minority have always been secure in this chamber. This is what gives the Senate of the United States a unique stature among parliamentary institutions.

What the motion before us seeks to do is to destroy — let me repeat, is to destroy — the very uniqueness of this body; to relegate it to the status of any other legislative body, and to diminish the Senate as an institution of this government.

The proposition now under discussion, to move to consideration of Senate Resolution 4, clearly envisions the invoking of cloture by a simple majority — let me repeat, by a simple majority — and I want the members to weigh that very, very carefully and to understand that, if this is agreed to, then one, two or three Senators who can be prevailed upon to change their minds, to loosen their consciences, can be the determining factor in a matter of moment that is important to this nation and the world. . . .

In the past I have favored proposals to change Rule 22 to require three-fifths of those present and voting, instead of the present two-thirds required, to invoke cloture. In all candor, however, I must say that with the passage of the landmark Civil Rights Act of 1964, I do not feel the sense of urgency for the change of Rule 22 that I once did. Even so, I still support the three-fifths concept embraced by Senate Resolution 4 because I think it would be an appropriate compromise between those who prefer the present rule and those who would prefer a simple majority rule.

I favor a three-fifths principle, too, because I believe it does not destroy the essential character of the institution of the Senate. But I will not, and I cannot, and I shall not go below three-fifths because I think of the inherent dangers in a proposal which is embarked upon imposing a majority rule in the case of a cloture, and I fear for the future of this unique institution and this republic if such a factor indeed becomes a fact.

A three-fifths rule, if adopted, would be an equitable way to balance the interests while, at the same time, preserving the principle of protecting the minority positions in this body, and that is extremely important, for that is one of the unique features of this institution.

That, too, I would hope would be kept in mind because, while I have been disconcerted, while I have not been pleased with filibusters that have been carried on, while I have had my embarrassing moments, I still believe that the rights of the minority must be protected. . . .

April 7, 1975:

On the disarray

in U.S. foreign policy

The first four months of 1975 brought the final chapter of the war in Vietnam. While President Thieu busied himself with trying to repress the irrepressible opposition in Saigon, Vietcong and North Vietnamese forces marched steadily toward that city, preceded by hordes of frantic refugees. And the U.S. Congress, finally fed up with Thieu and bolstered by the Cooper-Church amendment, refused to authorize the massive infusions of aid requested by a pipedreaming Ford Administration.

By early April the debacle was in its last stages. In Washington the situation was ripe for partisan recriminations, with a Republican President scoring the Democratic Congress for losing the war and Congress blaming the President for stringing it out. Instead, Ford showed restraint, and Mansfield reciprocated. On April 7 the majority leader asked that the end of U.S. involvement in Southeast Asia be viewed as an opportunity for a reassessment of all American foreign policy, which had not undergone a fundamental change, except perhaps for a new emphasis on "detente," for some thirty years. He deplored its current disarray but pointed out that it had become disarrayed under six Presidents and fifteen Congresses. For that very reason, he felt, it needed a thorough, all-embracing review, in an atmosphere of cooperation between Congress and the Executive.

* * *

Mr. Mansfield. Mr. President, . . .recent months have witnessed a breakdown in U.S. foreign policy in widely separated parts of the globe. At the present time our policy in Southeast Asia is in a state of disarray, and it might be said that we have no foreign policy at all, except to advocate more military and economic assistance.

In the eastern Mediterranean we have the situation on Cyprus involving Greece and Turkey, and, in the western part of that sea, an uncertain situation developing as it affects Portugal. In Latin America we have, over the years if not the decades, paid too little attention to that most important part of the world. At home we have 8.7 percent unemployment, or 8 million Americans out of work, inflation in the double figures, and a worsening farm situation, to mention just a few of our difficulties.

It is time that we base our foreign policy on the present rather than on the past, that we review and revise our defense arrangements all over the world, and that we do so in both areas on the basis of cooperation between the executive and legislative branches of government. We have paid a higher price — too high a price — for our participation in the Indochina tragedy, in men and money. The Cambodians, the Laotians, and the Vietnamese have likewise paid a terrible price in killed and wounded, in starvation and disease, and in an increasing number of refugees.

The results of a foreign policy inaugurated six Presidents ago and carried on down to the present are now at our doorstep. In our domestic policy, we have seen a bad economic situation become steadily more dangerous and more all-embracing as far as industry, agriculture, and the work force are concerned. The President and the Congress have approved a tax bill which will add enormously to the budget deficit, and we have passed a farm bill which will increase government costs.

We have become the world's chief supplier of arms, and it appears that we will sell to anyone, anywhere, anytime, who wants to buy our armaments, often at bargain-basement prices — and, in some cases, we have even given them away. We have helped to supply our opponents in Indochina with weapons to use against the governments in Saigon and Phnom Penh. This armament was not sold to the other side but was captured or acquired in various manners, as was the case of approximately $1 billion of military equipment left behind in the retreat to the south in Vietnam; and similar situations, though to a lesser degree, have occurred in Cambodia.

The President has indicated that there will be a reassessment of our foreign policy as it affects the Middle East. I would suggest, most respectfully, that this reassessment should be conducted on a worldwide basis. The time is long past due for such a reexamination of our foreign and defense policies to take place, because many of those policies go back to the end of the World War II and have long been subject to revision. We can no longer live in the past, but we must face up to the present and plan for the future. It is not a question of our credibility but our will to make necessary changes. It is a question of our judgment, and, in all too many parts of the world, that judgment has not been as sound as it should have been. Military interventions, except in the interests of our own security, should become a policy of the past and should be conducted only with proper consultation between the executive and legislative branches. The Nixon Doctrine was at least a step away from direct armed intervention and, in effect, a return to the Truman Doctrine. Developed further, it could perhaps provide a new and contemporaneous direction to foreign policy.

This is not the time for either the executive or the legislative branch to begin pointing the finger. If there is any blame to be attached, and there is a great deal, we must all share in it. None of us is guiltless. It is time for Congress and the President to work together in the area of foreign as well as domestic policy. The President, in his speech at San Diego last week, indicated that he was prepared to go more than halfway with in working with Congress, and I believe the Congress can and should do no less. This does not mean that there will not be differences between us, but it does mean that under the leadership of the President and with the cooperation of Congress we can and we will find a way out of the morass in which our country now finds itself. Cooperation will very likely not achieve much in the way of headlines, but those we can do without. Finger pointing will achieve headlines, temporarily, but the nation will suffer, and so will the executive and legislative branches. A few might like nothing better than to witness bitter recriminations between the executive and the legislative branches; the people, weighed down by the anxieties of these uncertain times, would like nothing less.

So let us start afresh. Let us recognize that there is enough blame to go around and that it affects all of us. Let us do what we can, together, to bring this country out of the economic morass and out of the quagmire which we helped to create in Indochina. The people cry out for leadership, and that leadership can come from the President assuming the initiative and the Congress working with him in tandem. The people expect no more; the people deserve no less.

April 30, 1975:

On cooperation between

the President and Congress in a crisis

On April 29, 1975, President Ford ordered a complete American evacuation from Vietnam, and on the following day 81 helicopters carried the last 395 Americans and almost 5000 Vietnamese from the surrounded city of Saigon to ships waiting for them offshore. A definition of "honorable" to cover the final American withdrawal has yet to be formulated.

Despite the Administration's persistent pleas for more money with which to prop up the government of President Thieu, who was then already decamping with his wife and ten tons of treasured bricabrac, Congress, feeling its newfound oats, flatly refused to contribute to the cause of further bloodshed, insisting instead on immediate and complete disentanglement. The Administration had no choice but to comply. Congress finally was rediscovering the power of the purse.

Since the Senate had been so adamant in this confrontation with the Executive, Mansfield hastened to defend its intransigence but at the same time to offer a pledge of cooperation. The American war in Indochina might be over, but the many problems it had created or worsened were not.

* * *

Mr. Mansfield. Mr. President, yesterday President Ford made the following statement: "This action closes a chapter in the American experience. I ask all Americans to close ranks, to avoid recrimination about the past, to look ahead to the many goals we share and to work together on the great tasks that remain to be accomplished."

A tragic episode in our history has now come to a close in Vietnam. There will be time enough to probe the wreckage of the policy of involvement. There will be time enough to draw new perceptions from the experience for future guidance.

For now, however, before these last impressions fade, it seems to me very necessary to underline one aspect of the matter. That is the immense difficulty, even at the end, to move the reluctant machinery of this government to the point where the last Americans could be removed in relative safety by the Marines. Even then, the cost was four more American lives, not to speak of the death and anguish of countless Vietnamese. In the end, it took the cooperation of the President and the Congress to bring about a termination. It came, finally, because Congress was unwilling to give the executive branch a blank check in providing the closeout funds. Congress insisted not only on the withdrawal of American personnel but on the speedup of that withdrawal as a precondition of further appropriations. Working with the Congress, moreover, the President moved the executive branch to proceed on that basis. So, together, the President and the Congress achieved the result. To be sure, it was late. To be sure, weeks were lost after the great collapse in the highlands. To be sure, there were last-minute human tragedies. But think what else might have been, had the procrastination been allowed to continue until an attack on Saigon was under way. Think what might have been, had a U.S. reinvolvement in the war taken place at that time.

So I wanted to take this moment to stress the importance of the closest collaboration between the President and the Congress. It was the decisive factor in this situation. He kept the Congress informed and consulted repeatedly. That is the only fashion in which this government can deal effectively with a critical confrontation abroad. In moments of crisis, at least, the President and the Congress cannot be adversaries; they must be allies who, together, must delineate the path to guide the nation's massive machinery of government in a fashion which serves the interests of the people and is acceptable to the people.

May 5, 1975:

On what's right in America

Early May 1975 was a very blue period for Americans generally. A twenty-year war had ended in a rout; some Americans were saddened by the loss of the war, others by the pursuit of it. The heavy stench of Watergate still hung in the political air, corroding Americans' confidence in representative government. The word "depression" was surfacing in economists' divinations for the first time in almost half a century.

It was time, Mansfield thought as he prepared a speech for a Washington dinner meeting, to include a few remarks on the upbeat. Nothing fatuously Pollyannish, of course, but at least a passing reference to a silver lining here and there.

* * *

It is not without some reticence that I choose to address you on the subject of Congressional leadership. As someone has recently pointed out, the trouble with being a political leader these days is that you cannot be sure whether people are following you or chasing you. Whether it is called a "message" or a "signal," some sort of shock has definitely been sent by the people to Washington. At a minimum, it causes a painful ringing in the ears. It can, in more serious cases, portend sudden political death. It is even rumored to be the only known cure for Potomac fever.

However that may be, it is obvious that the public impression of the Federal government at this time is not a happy one. An August 1974 public opinion poll showed the Congress at its highest point in history, at 48 percent, compared to 21 percent in December 1974. The Presidency has also had its ups and downs, as we all know. What our respective standings are now is open to question. . . .

Whatever the [people's] sense of frustration, I hasten to add that I do not think that the nation is at the end of the road. To the bumper sticker which commands, "America: Love It or Leave It," the response is simple: whatever the current irritants, who is leaving and who doesn't love it? . . .

Fourteen years ago I was elected the majority leader of the United States Senate. The mandate has been renewed by my colleagues at regular two-year intervals. Many have taken issue with that leadership over the years. It is a political fact of life that some individuals — Republicans, that is — would have preferred me to be the leader of a minority.

Notwithstanding my party role in the Senate, I can assure you that there exists a close working relationship with the leadership of the other party. To be sure, Senator Hugh Scott of Pennsylvania and I have our differences. Most of all, however, we share our problems in common. A Senate in continual partisan conflict is an ineffectual Senate. The Senates of the past few years have had their faults but, measured by any responsible yardstick, they have been effective. They have been active, innovative, careful, and cooperative, and they have been made up of Americans with a sense of decency, integrity, and fair play.

For the past two years in particular the legislative branch has been the principal rock of the republic and guardian of representative government. On the fundamental Constitutional questions, party labels have faded almost completely. On the many other issues — whether the energy crisis, taxes, appropriations, or whatever — there are differences between the parties and even within the parties in the Congress. There are also differences between the other branches and the Congress. It can be no other way. We are a government of separate branches; our politics remain lodged in two major parties. The juxtaposition of views from these various centers of political power are healthy and are essential under our system of government. . . .

In my judgment, the erosion of the system of checks and balances has been halted. It has not been easy. A President can make decisions as one person, and in a moment if he chooses to do so. In Congress, a majority of the 100 Senators and of the 435 House members not only have to agree on a goal but on what course to take to reach it. Then, if a Presidential veto stands in the way of

337

that course, we have to begin again and select a new one which will gain the adherence of two-thirds of the members.

If the country is not in the best of shape today, we might well ponder what the situation might have been if there had not been an independent Congress of dedicated members, Republicans and Democrats. The fact is that there has been a more constructive Congressional input into national leadership in the past two years than at any other time in many years. While it may be too early for this change to be felt or even to be widely perceived, it is, nevertheless, a change of great significance. . . .

Let me close by saying that there is a great deal that is right in this nation. We are a generous country, with a strong, decent, industrious, and compassionate people. There is ample intelligence and inventiveness and an immense experience and vitality in our midst. If today, working together, we will put these attributes to use for the benefit of all, there need be no fear for the nation's tomorrow.

This nation will withstand the adversity of the present. This nation will find again, in the months and years ahead, the essential political leadership in the Presidency and in the Congress. We will renew. We will endure. There is no other choice.

December 5, 1975:

On Senator Hugh Scott's

announcement of retirement

In December 1975 Senator Hugh Scott, the Senate Republican Leader since 1969, saddened and disillusioned by his painful experience with the Watergate jackals, announced that 1976 would be his last year in the Senate. Mansfield's brief remarks on the announcement illustrate the genuine esteem and affection that he could show a political adversary. Over the preceding seven years he and Scott had created a working partnership of competence and decency that did credit to their profession.

* * *

Mr. Mansfield. Mr. President, it was with great sadness, but with no surprise, that I read of the desire on the part of the distinguished Republican leader of the Senate not to be a candidate for reelection next year. Senator Scott did me the honor of informing me approximately two years ago that he would not be a candidate for reelection. He asked me to keep in confidence what he told me. Therefore I was not surprised.

However, not being surprised does not lessen my sense of sadness, because of all the Republican leaders alongside whom I have worked — there have been three — none has been more cooperative, more understanding, more of a partner than the distinguished Senator from Pennsylvania.

He has represented his party and the Senate well. He is a man of integrity, so far as my personal relationships with him are concerned, and I have nothing but admiration and respect for him.

I am sorry that he has decided not to be a candidate for reelection, because he has represented his state with distinction, with honor, and with a wide area of knowledge. He is a good man and has been an extraordinarily good Senator. He has represented his party extremely well in the Senate — and representing the Republicans in the Senate is not an easy job. I would say that my job on this side of the aisle has been far easier than his job on that side of the aisle.

I could not let this moment go, now that I have been released from the period of confidentiality, without expressing my personal admiration, affection, and respect for the distinguished Republican leader of the U.S. Senate.

March 4, 1976:

On his own retirement from the Senate;

tributes from colleagues

In mid-1974 Maureen and Mike Mansfield decided that it was time to go home. Confiding the decision to only a few close friends and associates, he withheld the formal announcement until March 4, 1976. The Senate chamber was very sparsely occupied at the time, and Mansfield had hoped to make the announcement and then leave immediately for a Democratic conference. His hope proved futile.

The tributes began at once and continued for some fifty minutes, when Mansfield excused himself on a plea of pressing business. They are severely abbreviated here.

* * *

Mr. Mansfield. Mr. President, in 1942 I was elected, for the first time, to serve in the 78th Congress as a Representative of the people of the western district of Montana — and, for an additional four consecutive terms, was reelected to the House.

In 1953 I entered the 83rd Congress after being elected as a Senator from Montana and sworn as a Senator of the United States — and, for three additional consecutive terms, was reelected to the Senate.

In 1957 the Senate elected me as majority whip and, in 1961, as majority leader.

The flow of responsibility has been continuous from 1943 onward.

These years in the Congress of the United States span a complete change in the membership of the Senate, except for the Senator from Mississippi (Mr. Eastland) and the Senator from Arkansas (Mr. McClellan), both of whom entered the Senate in the same year of my entry into the House.

These years encompass

one-sixth of the nation's history since independence,
the administrations of seven Presidents,
the assassination of a President and other extreme outrages against human decency,
able political leadership and seamy politics and chicanery,
the dawn of the nuclear age and men on the moon,
a great war and a prelude to two more wars and an uneasy peace, and
a dim perception of world order and an uncertain hope for international peace.

Through this and more, the Senate, together with the House,

has been the people's institution. In all this and more, I have believed and believe it still, that the Federal government will not atrophy and the people's liberties will be safe from tyranny if the Senate remains vigorous, independent, and vigilant. The Senate is stronger, more responsive, more alive, more innovative today than it was at the time of my entry so many years ago. As the 94th Congress — my 17th Congress — moves toward a close, I find myself in my 73rd year. I am in good health and of clear mind. My interest in the Senate remains deep, and I have not become indifferent to the nation's affairs.

Insofar as running for the Senate again is concerned, in a Constitutional sense, it is my judgment that only the people by their votes can deem a candidate too old for office. Or, to be sure, an incumbent may so deem himself. Either way, that is not a decisive factor in my own case.

My conclusion has been reached in this instance with my wife, Maureen Hayes Mansfield, who has been with me through all these years and whose sensitive counsel, deep understanding, and great love have been so much a part of whatever may be the sum of my contribution.

It seems to me that the time has come to perform a final public service to the nation, to the Senate, and to the people of Montana. A great public trust has been reposed in me in so many ways and for so many years. For whatever time remains to me I shall ever be grateful to the nation, to the Senate, and to my state for this confidence.

I ask now that this trust be shifted to other shoulders. In particular, I ask the people of Montana to tap a new source from within the state, a new source of dedication and leadership to send to the Senate in the 95th Congress.

There is a time to stay and a time to go. Thirty-four years is not a long time, but it is time enough.

I will not be a candidate for election to the Senate of the 95th Congress.

Mr. Hugh Scott. Mr. President, . . . it is not often that I go directly against the requests of the majority leader. He had expressed the hope to me that nothing would be said following his announcement. But this imposes too great an obligation on all of us who love him so dearly. . . .

I have never known a finer man. I have never known a man who is more distinguished by his complete fairness and his total integrity. He has in every instance put the interests of the country above any other consideration. He has never stooped to anything which would demean his conduct or lower the respect for the institutions of government. He is not only a kind man but a thoughtful man — his tribute to his dear wife is one more indication of that.

There will be, I am sure, other occasions to speak more at length. This is sad news for me and sad news for his colleagues and for the country. We believe that there is no such thing as an indispensable man. Nevertheless, we believe that there are some people whose services are so great that the very thought of the termination of those services is a recognition of a loss too vast to be smoothly or swiftly measured . . . .

Mr. Talmadge. . . . The job of majority leader is indeed a difficult one. We have 100 individuals in this body and sometimes their ideas, sometime their thoughts, sometimes their philosophies, sometimes their engagements are at a total variance with what the business in the U.S. Senate should be.

Mike has never diverted one iota from his sense of honor, duty, and dignity in carrying out his responsibilities in this exceedingly difficult task.

I know of no man in public life today more beloved and respected by his colleagues. . . .

Mr. Javits. . . . This is a very extraordinary man, Mr. President, and the country and the world should know it. . . .

I am deeply moved and touched by what he said about Maureen. This is one of the profoundest debts of his life, obviously, and he has given us the rare privilege of sharing it with us. . . .

Mr. Muskie. Mr. President,. . .because of Senator Mansfield's leadership, because of the contribution he has made to the shape and growth of this chamber, the Senate will be a greater place than it was when he assumed leadership a dozen years ago.

I enjoyed a couple of years under the leadership of Lyndon Johnson, and it was a different kind of leadership. It was hailed as strong leadership, as it was. But I think the Senate required a different kind of leadership thereafter, and Senator Mansfield has risen to the demands of the times. He recognized that the Senate can be great if it is possible for each Senator to rise to his or her own potential. So he has been willing to delegate responsibilities on the floor of the Senate. He has encouraged Senators to take initiative, to develop leadership, and to fight for their points of view, whether or not they agree with his, on the floor of the Senate.

Senator Mansfield has undertaken to drum home to us what we individually may not have always realized, that our individual performance and behavior are more important to the future of the Senate and its viability as a political institution. . . .

Mr. Tower. . . . This man has jealously guarded the rights of all in this body, regardless of party or philosophic disposition. He has been a real champion of the Senate but never an apologist for the Senate. He has had the capacity for analysis of this body and for criticism of it. I think this has caused us to repair to our consciences on many, many occasions.

Much could be said about what an even-handed and fair man he is, about his impeccable intellectual insight, his integrity, the fact that everyone who knows him values his word and trust. He has done much for us. . . .

Mr. Griffin. . . . Many of our great men have been humble men. Humility and greatness go together, and this humble man from Montana is one of the greatest men who have ever served in this body.

I particularly appreciate the fact that in his leadership in the Senate, while he has always been a good Democrat, he has been as nonpartisan a Democrat as he could possibly be. In fact, I think his title really has not been majority leader but leader of the Senate; and this, without question, has endeared him to those on this side of the aisle particularly. . . .

Mr. Kennedy. Mr. President, if the Senate could weep, it would weep today at the announcement of Mike Mansfield's retirement.

No one in this body personifies more nearly than Mike Mansfield the ideal of the Senate. Wisdom, integrity, compassion, fairness, humanity — these virtues are his daily life. He inspired all of us, Democrat and Republican, by his unequalled example. He could stretch this institution beyond its ordinary ability, as easily as he could shame it for failing to meet its responsibility. . . .

343

Mr. Humphrey. . . . . As majority leader, Senator Mansfield has consistently viewed his position as one requiring effective cooperation with the President in the discharge of his responsibility for the benefit of the nation. But he has also asserted the joint responsibility of the majority leader to serve and represent the majority party in the Senate — and this includes speaking out on behalf of the majority party's own concepts of our national priorities. From his leadership position, as well as in his capacity as a member of the Senate Appropriations Committee, he has fought to maintain the Constitutional responsibilities and powers of the purse that belong to the Congress, and he played a key role in the enactment of the Congressional Budget and Impoundment Control Act of 1974. His view of the real priorities of our nation is reflected in his consistent support of measures to expand educational opportunities and provide better health care for our people, to meet the needs of handicapped persons, and to help elderly people know a life of decency and dignity. He has helped to advance the frontiers of our national perception of the equal protection of the laws — for blacks, for Indians, and for youth who had been denied the right to vote.

Finally, Majority Leader Mike Mansfield has been a vital force for reform of government bureaucracy and in the functioning of Congress. The present democratic procedures in the Senate in designation of committee chairmen, in the nomination of Senators to committees, and in opening the doors of committee meetings are in large measure the result of Senator Mansfield's initiatives. Working long hours in the Senate chamber, he has continuously endeavored to see the work of the Senate carried through with dignity, with mutual respect among the members, and with attention to the constraints of time, so that each session of the Congress may reflect a responsible record of legislative accomplishment by the Senate. And, reflecting a deep concern over election campaign procedures, Senator Mansfield has been a strong proponent of campaign finance reform, and took a vital part in the enactment of the Federal Election Campaign Act of 1974.

I have been proud to serve in the Senate under the leadership of Senator Mike Mansfield. I know that all members join me in extending him our warm best wishes for the future. No tribute can be adequate to the greatness of this man. Therefore it must be the scope and strength of his accomplishments in service to his country that will remain his enduring testimonial. . . .

Mr. Cranston . . .If we are to strengthen the legislative branch to the coequal status which was conceived by our Founding Fathers, and do so in a way that all the people have an equal voice through their legislators' role in our nation's decision-making, then we must all understand and take inspiration from Mike Mansfield's decision to make our internal processes democratic, rather than to emulate the coercive, iron-fisted tactics of some of his predecessors. Mike taught us that every Senator should be free to vote his conscience, free to represent his state as he sees fit, free to dissent without fear of punishment, and free to seek to influence his fellow Senators on a totally equal basis. . . .

Mr. Mansfield. Mr. President, all I would like to say is thank you. I would like to be excused because I am afraid the Democrats in conference will finish their meal and get on to something else before they face up to the main business.

The Presiding Officer (Mr. Helms). Before the Senator leaves, if the Chair may bend the rules just a bit, the Chair would say that he wholeheartedly joins all the other Senators in their expressions of affection and respect for the Senator from Montana, who is and always has been one of nature's noblemen. The Senator from North Carolina is grateful for the opportunity to be associated with the distinguished majority leader in the Senate and sincerely regrets his decision to retire.

April 5, 1976:

On a lapse in decorum

As a gesture of good will during the U.S. bicentennial, the British offered the loan of an original copy of the Magna Carta, that declaration of independence from the divine right of kings, to go on display as part of the bicentennial celebration. To mark the transfer with what they considered appropriate ceremony, they invited a delegation of 25 members of Congress to come to London and formally accept the document.

345

The Senate accepted the invitation unanimously, but the House, more sensitive to election-year perils, decided to go on an extraordinary economy kick to impress the taxpayers back home. Sending 25 people would be too expensive, the Representatives decided; about half that number, or even a third, would be plenty. When their amendment was taken up in the Senate the debate, instead of being brief and routine as Mansfield evidently had expected, degenerated into a niggling squabble over Congressional junketing and expense-account padding. Finally John Pastore of Rhode Island, fed up with the posturing, urged that the Senate fish or cut bait and, in doing so, gave Mansfield an opening for the last of his ad hoc lectures on Senate dignity.

After his outburst the Senate reconsidered, later the House reconsidered, and eventually a full delegation of 25 traveled to London for the ceremony.

* * *

Mr. Pastore. . . . . I read of the Magna Carta the first day I went to school. I always thought it was the fundamental law that led to the dignity of man.

I do not know who invited whom, and I hope somebody will explain it to me here tonight. But, to me, this is a comedy. It is a comedy of errors.

If you want to go and get the Magna Carta, go over and get it.

I am not a candidate for the trip. I do not have the time. I really do not care for the air flight. But all of this comedy, all of this nonsense, I think is a disgrace. It *is* a disgrace.

Do you want the Magna Carta? Then do it the way the people over there asked you to do it, and if you do not want to do it, just tell them that you refuse the invitation. This is what you ought to do in a manly, courageous fashion. But all these gobbledygooks about junkets, and this and that — you ought to be ashamed of yourself.

Mr. Mansfield. Mr. President, I agree completely with the distinguished Senator from Rhode Island.

I do not know whether we are acting like barons or not. But I do know that we are making a ridiculous spectacle of ourselves. . . .

This is the 200th year of our independence, and here we are

making fools of ourselves. Do we have no appreciation of an offer extended in good faith by those whom we defeated to acquire our independence? Do we not have any sense of decency and dignity and decorum?

Talk about junkets. I have never made a trip overseas that I did not, on my return, file a report. Junkets. Almost every trip I have had has cost me money, not the government.

Here we have one plane going over, supposedly to take 25 members of the Congress of the United States. It costs just as much for 12 as it does for 25.

I hope we will get away from this immaturity. This body of mature people are supposedly capable of acting. I hope we will get down to the realities of the situation.

Two hundred years of independence is nothing to sneeze at. An invitation from the United Kingdom to look at the document which, along with the Bible, was the forerunner of the Constitution of the United States is nothing to sneeze at.

Have your fun. Cut down the funds. Make a mockery of these trips that we make overseas. Call us junketeers, if you will. But you are only making fools of yourselves, and, in doing that, you are making a fool out of this institition.

I hope that the Senate, now that it has had its moment of economy and jollity, will return to the business which it is supposed to do for the people of the United States who sent us here.

September 16, 1976:

The last day

September 16, 1976, was Mike Mansfield's last day in the Senate. He and Maureen were about to leave for a visit to the People's Republic of China, in response to an invitation that had not been affected by the death of Mao Tse-tung the week before, and they expected to return only after the 94th Congress had adjourned. His departure inevitably was accompanied by a great outpouring of tributes, which were to occupy 25 closely printed pages of the Congressional Record *for that day.*

As in the past, he was honored for the improvements he had introduced, the leadership he had provided, the example he had set. As the very few selections presented here suggest, this was a politician for whom authority meant responsibility and service, whose faith in himself was matched by his faith in others. He had brought great honor to the art of politics, and his fellow politicians accorded him great honor in return.

* * *

Mr. Muskie. Mr. President, . . . Mike Mansfield presided over a reform Senate. During his years, we have democratized many of our procedures, opened up our deliberations, and made accessible the inner workings.

And when the challenge came to reassert our role against the executive branch, he led the way.

But we will remember Mike Mansfield for more than legislative accomplishments.

During the agony of Watergate, when the raw abuse of power was defended by the allegation that everyone does it, Mike Mansfield provided through his character the rebuttal to that monumental lie.

The American people could see in him that morality, conscience, and decency could be practiced in high office . . . .

During his 15-year service as the majority leader — the longest tenure of any floor leader in the Senate's history — Mike has succeeded in developing this body into an effective element of the legislative branch. As the *New York Times* so aptly noted earlier this year, Mike had changed the Senate "into an assertive institution in which the voices of a new post-war generation of senators could be heard." His unique style of gentle persuasion but firm leadership has been successful in breaking countless legislative deadlocks and in guiding controversial and complicated measures through the Senate. Mike's able direction, coupled with a temperate attitude, has gained him the respect and deep affection of this body. . . .

Mr. Morgan. Mr. President, many of my constituents have been writing me letters which express their concern, their frustration, or their outright anger at hearing of misbehavior by their elected representatives in Washington. I have shared their disgust, and I respect their demand for action against any who have broken the law.

But, Mr. President, at the same time it worried me that the people could lose confidence in Congress as an institution. I know that the greatest number of my colleagues in the House and Senate are fine people, and work hard to serve our citizens well.

What could I tell people to reassure them about their Congress? What could I say that would be positive proof that honor was alive on Capitol Hill? Where was the most convincing argument I could find?

Mr. President, I believe I found the best evidence there is, and I have used it in letters and in speeches all during the scandals which have threatened to give everyone here a black eye. I asked the people this question: if honor is not admired in the U.S. Senate, if integrity is not valued, then why did we elect Mike Mansfield as majority leader? . . .

Mr. Hollings. . . . Mike Mansfield leaves the U.S. Senate a far better place than he found it. This is a more open, more public, and more representative body than ever before. It reflects more than we sometimes realize the image of the man who leads it, his openness, his tolerance, his civility. The Mansfield imprint is clearly upon this Senate, and we are just as clearly the better for it. . . .

Mr. President, no tribute to Mike Mansfield would be anywhere near complete without mention of his lovely wife, Maureen. Ever gracious, dedicated, and understanding, she has contributed much to the success of her husband and in her own right has been one of the most effective Senate wives in history. She, too, is responsible for the substance and good image of the Mansfield Senate. . . .

Mr. Stevenson. . . . Mike Mansfield is one of those rare leaders who lead not by main force, but by the quiet force of mind and character. In an institution that has been called the greatest deliberative body, he is the great deliberator. Soft of voice but strong of will, he leaves a gentle but indelible impression upon this institution.

Others have paid tribute to the depth and breadth of his intellect, to his steady and effective leadership against the war in

Indochina, to his unfailing good humor and his capacity for warm friendship. For my part, I shall remember all these things and more, including Senator Mansfield's role in the reform and modernization of the U.S. Senate. As a veteran member of the Senate and as its majority leader, he might have been expected to resist changes in the institution he knew and loved well; he might even have been forgiven for resisting such change.

But, to the contrary, Mike Mansfield has been an apostle of creative change in the Senate. Newer members pressing for improvements in the organization of the Senate and in the ways it conducts its business have found in Senator Mansfield a willing ally and a wise counselor. Their efforts and his leadership led to the creation of a new Committee on Committees, for which all our hopes are high. Whatever the Senate achieves in greater efficiency, fairness, and effectiveness will be due in large measure to the Senator from Montana. I am grateful to him. . . .

Mr. Mansfield. To paraphrase freely a great statesman, may I say, on behalf of Maureen and Mike Mansfield, never did two people owe so much to so many in this Senate, regardless of party, to the people of Montana, and to the nation as a whole.

It has long been obvious to me that the Senate is a place of eloquence, tolerance, and affection. These characteristics have been very evident in the remarks which have been made here today. Indeed, they have been present in oversupply. There has also been, I might add, a degree of benevolent exaggeration. Exaggerated or not, I am deeply grateful to all of you for the words which have been sent in my direction. Your kindness and generosity are not unusual. It is the way that I have been treated ever since my arrival in the Senate.

Your comments have touched off echoes deep in my personal feelings. In whatever lies ahead, I shall miss greatly the supportive warmth of the Senate's way. That is a gap which looms before me. If I were to dwell at length on the prospect, it would make me very sad. There is no need to do so. It is far better, in thanking you for your statements, to remind myself of what, together with Senate colleagues, has been faced and done during the last two dozen years.

In that span of time, much has come before the Senate in the way of national anxieties and hopes and needs and conflicts.

Much has flowed through the Senate and into the policies of the nation. In memory, only flashes of great issues emerge from these years. They are scattered eddies in the river of the Senate's affairs. When the issues were before us, however, they loomed large and as of profound and, often, passionate concern. Who would downgrade the Nuclear Test Ban Treaty, the first major achievement of the Kennedy administration in foreign affairs? What of Medicare and extensions of insured health care in the direction of national coverage? Other elaborations of the social security system? The great civil rights legislation achieved, after months of debate, in the aftermath of the assassination of President Kennedy?

The Indochina war which, first supported by the nation and then denounced by the nation, was finally brought to an end by the President under the persistent pressure of the Senate? What of the Senate's recent block of a similar misadventure in Angola? And what of the legislative efforts — some effective and many wanting but all reflective of the nation's finest sentiments — to come to grips with the nation's shame of widespread poverty in the midst of plenty?

Here in the Senate there were the first major responses in national policy to the Frankenstein's monster of environmental pollution. Here, too, was launched the drive to bring about the right to vote for 18-year-olds. Here, too, began the effort to reopen the door to relations with China.

And Watergate? And the investigation of the CIA and the FBI?

These headlines are the easily remembered moments of the last 24 years. They are but a fraction of actions deliberately taken and deliberately not taken by the Senate — a national park bill, the confirmation of a second lieutenant in the Army or a general, or the rejection of a Federal judge, or a bill to admit an immigrant to permanent residence. How many thousands, tens of thousands, of these actions in 24 years? Each has had its impact, however infinitesimal, on the shaping of the nation.

As certain events stand out in memory, so do the names of some of the colleagues who have come and gone from here — Taft of Ohio, Knowland of California, Vandenberg of Michigan, McCarthy of Wisconsin, George of Georgia and Russell of Georgia, Douglas of Illinois and Dirksen of Illinois, Aiken of Vermont, Murray of

Montana, Kefauver of Tennessee, Byrd of Virginia, Morse of Oregon, Kennedy of New York, Ervin of North Carolina, Hayden of Arizona, and Johnson of Texas. These and many more were my friends and colleagues of another time. They, too, were but a small part of those who shaped and were shaped by the Senate during these past 24 years. Of the Senators here when the Senator from Washington (Mr. Jackson) and the Senator from Missouri (Mr. Symington) and I were sworn in together on January 3, 1953, only seven remain.

In retrospect, it does not much matter whether or not the Senate is considered, legally, a continuing body. The lawyers of the Senate have argued that question since the beginning of the republic. What matters is that the institution goes on meeting its Constitutional responsibilities. In that respect the Senate has been continuous since the first session of the First Congress. So long as the Senate persists, I am confident that the liberties of the American people will be maintained and the government of the republic will remain receptive to their needs and aspirations.

So I do not leave this place in sadness. I leave as one who has lived as a part of it and loved it deeply. I leave personally fulfilled and contented to have been here, one Senator of the over 1700 men and women who have served their states and the republic in the Senate of the United States.

In closing, I want to thank Maureen Mansfield, my wife, who with infinite patience and understanding has sustained me through these years. I want to thank the members of the majority for choosing me as the leader of the majority and all the members of the Senate for accepting me and helping me in that capacity. I want to thank, in particular, the younger Senators, whose full and equal participation in every aspect of the Senate's endeavors has been of particular concern to me; it would be my hope that the window which has been opened in the Senate in that respect will never again be closed.

I want to thank the distinguished Republican leader, Mr. Hugh Scott, and his able assistant, Mr. Griffin, for a never-failing cooperation in the dignified and orderly operation of the Senate, a condition which could not possibly have been sustained without them. I want to thank the able majority whip, Senator Robert C. Byrd of West Virginia, who has given me outstanding support for many years and has served the majority and the Senate with great dedication.

As you are aware, I will be going shortly to the People's Republic of China in response to a long-standing invitation and in concert with the wishes of the President of the United States. I do not know, therefore, whether we shall meet again in the 94th Congress, or as this group, ever again. To you who are my friends — to all of you — I can only say thank you and good-bye.

(Prolonged applause. Senators rising.)

Selective Bibliography

Books, Major Studies and Reports

Baily, Stephen K. *The New Congress.* St. Martin's Press, 1966.

Clark, Joseph F. *The Senate Establishment.* Hill & Wang, 1963.

The Congressional Record, 1943-1976.

Douth, George. *Leaders in Profile, the United States Senate.* Sperr & Douth, Inc., 1972.

Evans, Rowland, and Robert Novak. *Lyndon B. Johnson, The Exercise of Power.* New American Library. 1966.

Evans, Rowland, and Robert Novak. *Nixon in the White House: The Frustration of Power.* Random House, 1971.

Green, Mark J., James M. Fallows and David R. Zwick. *Who Runs Congress?* (A Ralph Nader Congress Project.) Grossman Publishers, 1972.

Humphrey, Hubert. *The Education of a Public Man: My Life and Politics.* Doubleday, 1976.

Johnson, Ladybird. *A White House Diary.* Holt, 1970.

Keefe, William J., and Morris S. Ogul. *The American Legislative Process.* Prentice-Hall, 1973.

Orfield, Gary. *Congressional Power: Congress and Social Change.* Harcourt, 1975.

Riedel, Richard L. *Halls of the Mighty.* Robert B. Luce, 1969.

Rieselbach, Leroy N. *Congressional Politics.* McGraw-Hill, 1972.

Ripley, Randall B. *Congress: Process and Policy.* Norton, 1975.

Ripley, Randall B. *Majority Party Leadership in Congress.* Little, Brown, 1969.

Ripley, Randall B. *Power in the Senate.* St. Martin's Press, 1969.

Stewart, John G. "Two Strategies of Leadership : Johnson and Mansfield." In Nelson Polsby (ed.), *Congressional Behavior* (Random House, 1971), pp. 61-92.

Turner, Judy, and Robert Felmeth. *Mike Mansfield, Democratic Senator from Montana.* (A Ralph Nader Congress Project.) Grossman Publishers, 1972.

Journal Articles, News Items, Interviews, Etc.

"Bipartisanship: the Mansfield Version." *The Nation,* February 28, 1959, pp. 177-178.

Collins, Frederic W. "How to Be a Leader Without Leading." *New York Times Magazine,* July 30, 1961, pp. 9, 46, 50.

"Critical Look at Congress; Interview." *U.S. News and World Report,* December 1, 1969, pp. 25-27.

"Face the Nation." CBS-TV, March 28, 1976.

"Foreign Policy: Mansfield's Rebellion." *Newsweek,* May 24, 1971, pp. 18-19.

Glass, Andrew J. "Congressional Report: Mansfield reforms spark 'quiet revolution' in Senate." *National Journal,* March 6, 1971, pp. 499-512.

Glass, Andrew J. "The Democrats' 'Odd Duck.' " *The New Leader,* March 22, 1971, pp. 5-6.

Healy, Paul. "Mansfield of Montana." *The Saturday Evening Post,* October 1974, pp. 10, 12, 89.

" 'I Am What I Am': Mansfield Answers Critics." *U.S. News and World Report,* December 9, 1963, p. 20.

Kolodziej, Edward A. "The Senators: Recruitment, Style, and Norms." *Antioch Review,* Winter 1963-4, pp. 463-76.

Lindley, Ernest K. "Make No Mistake." *Newsweek,* February 23, 1959, p. 36.

" 'Lately, a Better Feeling' Between Congress and Nixon: Interview with Mike Mansfield, Senate Majority Leader." *U.S. News and World Report,* October 1, 1973, pp. 26-28.

MacNeil, Neil, on "Washington Week in Review" (PBS), March 5 and May 22, 1976.

"Majority Leader Mike Mansfield: There Is No Meanness in Him." *National Journal,* March 6, 1971, pp. 502-503.

"Mansfield: a Leader with a New Look." *U.S. News and World Report,* August 11, 1969, p. 16.

"Mansfield Steps Down." *Time,* March 15, 1976, p. 19.

"The Senate: A Crisis in Leadership." *Newsweek,* November 18, 1963, pp. 29-30.

"Senate Leadership: A 20th Century Innovation." *National Journal,* March 6, 1971, p. 511.

"Senator Mike Mansfield Tells Why Congress Is in the Doghouse." *U.S. News and World Report,* August 16, 1976, pp. 27-30.

"Two Key Senators Who Question LBJ's Policy on Vietnam." *U.S. News and World Report,* May 3, 1965, p. 17.

"A Watchdog at Last." *Time,* May 31, 1976, p. 20.

Weaver, Warren, Jr. *Both Your Houses: The Truth about Congress.* Praecer Press, 1972.

"When Is a Majority a Majority?" *Time,* March 20, 1964, pp. 22-26.

Index

360

361